Policing Paris

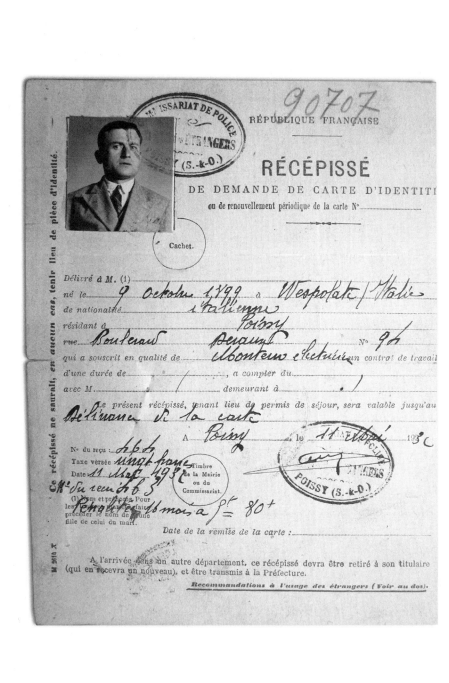

90707

RÉCÉPISSÉ

DE DEMANDE DE CARTE D'IDENTITÉ

ou de renouvellement périodique de la carte N° _____

Ce récépissé ne saurait, en aucun cas, tenir lieu de pièce d'identité.

COMMISSARIAT DE POLICE
ÉTRANGERS
(S.-&-O.)

Cachet.

Délivré à M. (1) _____

né le *9 octobre 1799* à *Wespolate / Italie*

de nationalité *italienne*

résidant à *Poissy*

rue *Boulerand Berain* N° *96*

qui a souscrit en qualité de *Monteur électricien* un contrat de travail

d'une durée de _____, à compter du _____

avec M. _____ demeurant à _____

Le présent récépissé, tenant lieu de permis de séjour, sera valable jusqu'au

Délivrance de la carte

À *Poissy* le *11 Avril* 193_

N° du reçu *666*

Taxe versée *vingt francs*

Date *11 Mai 193_*

N° du reçu *665*

Timbre
de la Mairie
ou du
Commissariat.

POISSY (S.-&-O.)

(1) Nom et prénoms. Pour
les femmes, faire
précéder le nom de jeune
fille de celui du mari.

Renouvelé 6 mois à f= 80+

Date de la remise de la carte : _____

À l'arrivée dans un autre département, ce récépissé devra être retiré à son titulaire
(qui en recevra un nouveau), et être transmis à la Préfecture.

Recommandations à l'usage des étrangers (Voir au dos).

Policing Paris

The Origins of Modern Immigration Control between the Wars

Clifford Rosenberg

Cornell University Press
Ithaca and London

frontispiece: Identification card courtesy of Archives Départementales des Yvelines (Versailles), 1 W 1146.

First published 2006 by Cornell University Press
First printing, Cornell Paperbacks, 2006
Printed in the United States of America

Library of Congress Cataloging-in-Publication Data

Rosenberg, Clifford D., 1969–
    Policing Paris : the origins of modern immigration control between the wars / Clifford Rosenberg.
        p. cm.
    Includes bibliographical references and index.
    ISBN-13: 978-0-8014-4427-2 (cloth : alk. paper)
    ISBN-10: 0-8014-4427-6 (cloth : alk. paper)
    ISBN-13: 978-0-8014-7315-9 (pbk. : alk. paper)
    ISBN-10: 0-8014-7315-2 (pbk. : alk. paper)
    1. Paris (France)—Emigration and immigration—
Government policy—History—20th century.   2. Police—
France—Paris—History—20th century.   3. Citizenship—
France—Paris—History—20th century.   4.
Immigrants—France—Paris—History—20th century.   5.
Aliens—France—Paris—History—20th century.   I. Title.
    JV7995.P37x R67 2006
    325.44'36109041—dc22
                        2006006040

Cornell University Press strives to use environmentally responsible suppliers and materials to the fullest extent possible in the publishing of its books. Such materials include vegetable-based, low-VOC inks and acid-free papers that are recycled, totally chlorine-free, or partly composed of nonwood fibers. For further information, visit our website at www.cornellpress.cornell.edu.

Cloth printing   10 9 8 7 6 5 4 3 2 1
Paperback printing   10 9 8 7 6 5 4 3 2 1

For Kim and Henry

Contents

List of Figures

List of Tables

Preface

More years ago than I would like to recall, I set out to write a social history of assimilation of immigrants in interwar Paris along the lines of Oscar Handlin's classic work on Boston or, in a different kind of setting, Eugen Weber's *Peasants into Frenchmen*.[1] In the late 1980s, Gérard Noiriel had begun to publish a series of path-breaking works taking his fellow French historians to task for their inability to think through their immigrant origins.[2] Unlike the Wars of Religion or the French Revolution, immigration, it seemed, offered the rare opportunity to write about a problem of manifest importance that had not already been worked over by generations of scholars. For weeks I searched for untapped riches in the archives, to no avail. In the midst of my search, however, France endured the greatest transport strike since the spring of 1968. It paralyzed Paris. I could not get anywhere.

Living near the Latin Quarter I made a virtue out of a necessity. Despite the warnings of my advisers and archivists on previous trips that the police archives held little of interest, I went to the massive bunker at the foot of the montagne Sainte-Geneviève. They were not entirely wrong. I found relatively little on the sociability of immigrant communities or their associational life. But after a period of weeks when I was one of the few scholars there, the director of the archives, Claude Charlot, took pity on me and sped up the notoriously cumbersome process for obtaining "dérogations," or authorization to see classified materials. Soon afterward, I stumbled

1. Oscar Handlin, *Boston's Immigrants, 1790–1865: A Study in Acculturation* (Cambridge: Harvard University Press, 1941); Eugen Weber, *Peasants into Frenchmen: The Modernization of Rural France, 1870–1914* (Stanford, : Stanford University Press, 1976).
2. Above all Gérard Noiriel, "Non-lieu de mémoire," chap. 1 in his *Le creuset français: Histoire de l'immigration, XIXe–XXe siècles* (Paris: Seuil, 1988), 14–67.

upon a Vichy report on the fate of archives I had to that point sought in vain. Reading that report, on Prefect of Police Roger Langeron's effort to keep his immigration archives out of enemy hands, immediately convinced me to change course, to concentrate my energies on the French response to immigration rather than the immigrant communities themselves.

The files were so important to France's control of its immigrant population and, by extension, its borders, I learned, that Langeron went to great lengths to hide them.[3] As German troops approached Paris in the spring of 1940, he frantically searched for a way to keep his papers secure. In a desperate move, he improvised, commandeering a pair of boats. Langeron wrote in his memoirs that there was so much material that it took a chain of inspectors at the Quai des Orfèvres forty-eight hours to fill the two boats, one of them exclusively with records on foreigners.[4] Finally, on Wednesday, 12 June 1940, two days before German troops entered Paris, a steamboat filled with immigration files chugged down the Seine toward the unoccupied zone.

After three days' journey, the boats encountered trouble at Bagneaux-sur-Loing (Seine-et-Marne). A boat transporting munitions had exploded at the lock there, igniting another boat carrying gasoline and blocking the canal. Unable to proceed, inspectors moored the boat carrying the immigration archives nearby and tried to hide its contents, but to no avail.[5] The Germans soon found the boat and had the files returned to the Prefecture in mid-July. After having spent a month in dank, musty conditions, partially submerged in water and slime, the files were a sodden mess; so the Germans

3. This account is based on the unpublished "Note sur le fonctionnement du Service Administratif des Étrangers de la Préfecture de Police depuis le 14 juin 1940, 1er jour de l'occupation jusqu'au 1er octobre 1940," 1 October 1940, in APP B/a 65ᴾ, dossier D-11; and the memoirs of the prefect of police, Roger Langeron, *Paris, juin 1940* (Paris: Flammarion, 1946); and those of the director of the political branch, the Renseignements généraux, Jacques Simon, "Comment furent sauvées les archives politiques de la Préfecture de Police," *Historia* 81 (August 1953): 155–60. Where the accounts conflict, I have preferred the manuscript report.

4. The other boat contained records of the Renseignements généraux (political police) and some material from the Police judiciaire. The RG files contained surveillance reports on political subversives and also had information on prominent politicians and public figures; as of 1925, the active branch of the immigration service, whose agents stopped people on the street to check their papers, was attached to the RG. The surviving manuscript account makes no mention of this second boat: "Note sur le fonctionnement . . ."

5. Langeron (*Paris, juin 1940*, 125–26) reported that the second boat, with the archives of the RG, was briefly delayed outside of Roanne, but that it continued on its way, successfully reaching its destination in Montauban along with the first boat, carrying the immigration archives. However, he also wrote (p. 58) that he had stocked one of the two boats with twenty-five kilos of dynamite (though he did not specify which one) and ordered his men to destroy their cargo rather than surrender it to the Germans. Perhaps those charges went off in the second boat, causing the blockage of river traffic? This is the account given, without attribution, by the journalist Frédéric Couderc in *Les RG sous l'Occupation: Quand la police française traquait les résistants* (Paris: Olivier Orban, 1992), 23–27; Couderc does not mention the immigration archives and suggests that the French returned the RG's archives to Paris of their own free will, after having fished them out of the river and dried them in a vacant factory.

ordered that all available French personnel dry the material that could be salvaged and copy the rest. Under German supervision, over one million files and three million cards were reorganized and returned to their shelves.

In the end, Langeron's efforts to hide his immigration archives turned out to be unnecessary. During the restoration and refiling of the archives, the occupation authorities realized the complexity and sheer volume of the material and gave up on the idea of using the information themselves. The Germans did confiscate some files, showing particular interest in letters requesting refugee status; but, according to the police report, "the German authorities agreed that each administrative bureau of the immigration service regain its archives and working papers."[6] Langeron's immigration service got back to work with virtually all of its records intact. It had stopped functioning for only two weeks.

Beyond their inherent drama, the documents Langeron sent off down the Seine immediately commanded my attention for the light they shed on Vichy's subsequent complicity in deporting Jews and tracking Resistance fighters. Historians had recently discovered that these files served as a model for the notorious *fichier*—or, more accurately, *fichiers—juif* used to prepare lists of Parisian Jews for the dozen dragnets ordered by the Germans and conducted largely by the Paris police between May 1941 and February 1944.[7] Of the 75,721 Jews deported from France, roughly 90 percent were arrested by French police forces.[8] Two decades' experience of monitoring the capital's foreign population shaped the treatment of Jews and others by the Vichy government in ways that remain misunderstood to this day, despite years of often bitter controversy.[9]

But, as I have pursued this story over the intervening years, I have become convinced that the primary interest of the material on those boats lies elsewhere, in the way bureaucratic controls altered the meaning of citizenship, protected access to rights, and enforced obligations for citizens and aliens alike. The detailed descriptions of the boats' contents testifies to a vast, sophisticated police bureaucracy that emerged sooner, and played a more important role in Parisians' day-to-day lives, than historians have realized.

In the aftermath of World War I, when France surpassed the United States as the world's leading immigrant-receiving nation, the Paris police

6. "Note sur le fonctionnement . . ."
7. Gilbert Badia, *Les barbelés de l'exil: Études sur l'émigration allemande et autrichienne, 1938–1940* (Grenoble: Presses universitaires de Grenoble, 1979), 94–95; Michael R. Marrus and Robert O. Paxton, *Vichy France and the Jews* (New York: Basic Books, 1981), 150, 243; and Couderc, *Les RG sous l'Occupation*, 23–27.
8. 2,564 Jews returned. Serge Klarsfeld, *Le calendrier de la persécution des juifs en France, 1940–1944* (Paris: Association les fils et filles des déportés juifs de France, 1993), 1091, 1125; and Jean-Marc Berlière and Laurent Chabrun, *Les policiers français sous l'Occupation: D'après les archives inédites de l'épuration* (Paris: Perrin, 2001), 247.
9. See the epilogue for a discussion of this controversy.

began to enforce long-standing laws governing foreigners' residence and mobility with a new intensity. To do so, they created the largest, most so-phisticated immigration service anywhere in the world, as the city emerged as a haven for refugees, exiles, some of whom were plotting against their home governments, and workers from all over. The police effort to keep track of constantly moving immigrant populations in Paris marks a funda-mental turning point in the broad transition from traditional, rural societies that tie people to the land with barriers to exit to modern, industrial, wel-fare states that keep people out with barriers to entry—with visas, pass-ports, identity cards, and the like.[10] France was the first country in the world to experience both massive foreign immigration and, at the same time, to create substantial assistance programs. Deciding who could receive benefits was more complicated there, especially in Paris, than anywhere else.

Before Vichy, the French police never intended to expel most of the mi-grants they caught. They sought above all to prevent political violence and to control the labor market. Compelled to keep their borders open and to recruit foreign workers, French officials built on controls established a gen-eration earlier. Beginning in Paris, they reorganized immigration services and sent agents to scour the city on an annual basis to verify declarations of residence, to stop people on the street to check their papers, and to conduct background checks on asylum seekers and whole communities. The police questioned anyone who looked out of place, or who kept what they consid-ered unsuitable company, routinely confiscating people's work and resi-dency papers when they refused to stay in line. A complex system of sus-pended sentences and stays of expulsion orders gave them powerful means to demand good behavior from migrants, who were desperate to hold on to their jobs and remain with their families.

Keeping lists of names was hardly unprecedented. Organized police forces have done so for as long as they have existed. Most earlier controls on movement, however, regulated movement *within* kingdoms and national territories, and they paid equal attention to foreigners and the "undeserv-ing" indigenous poor. As Paris emerged as a capital of refugees, revolution-aries, and governments-in-exile after World War I, the police there gave new meanings to cultural and legal categories, some of which had existed for centuries. Before their counterparts anywhere else, the Paris police radically improved their ability to intervene in the lives of foreign workers and colo-nial subjects. To distinguish entitled citizens from immigrant workers, local authorities in Paris began to send police officers around the city to verify declarations of residence and work permits. Without forcing many people

10. Aristide R. Zolberg, "International Migration Policies in a Changing World System," in *Human Migration: Patterns and Policies*, ed. William H. McNeill and Ruth S. Adams (Bloomington: Indiana University Press, 1978), 241–86; and John Torpey, *The Invention of the Passport: Surveillance, Citizenship, and the State* (Cambridge: Cambridge University Press, 2000).

to leave, the constant rounds of the political branch and its vast new card files made fluid populations "legible" in new ways.[11]

The legal categories of nationality and citizenship, which have existed for hundreds of years, increasingly determined whether families could remain together, whether people could keep their jobs, when they had them, or whether they had to flee. Since World War II, inequalities based on nationality and citizenship status have become pervasive, as countries around the world have increasingly found themselves compelled to provide substantial benefits to their own citizens and recruit foreigners to satisfy their labor needs. This is the story of the first police force in a major city to enforce systematically distinctions of citizenship and national origin.

So many people have helped me prepare this book that I fear I cannot thank them all. But I would like to single out three teachers whose influence has shaped the way I think about French history. I decided to become a historian in the spring of 1989, when Carl Weiner took me and a seminar of my Carleton classmates to Paris for an unforgettable semester, to celebrate the bicentennial of the Revolution. At Oxford, Robert Gildea challenged me to see the big picture, and then suffered through the results in our weekly tutorials. Philip Nord at Princeton University has supported this project from its inception, providing critical guidance without ever imposing his vision. I first became interested in the history of immigration in Phil's seminar on twentieth-century France, and his suggestions have prompted me to revise and above all to clarify my thinking throughout.

This book never would have been possible without the advice and assistance of dozens of librarians and archivists. Philippe Grand and Brigitte Lainé, both of the Archives de Paris, tracked down uncatalogued information and helped me find my way through their own and other collections. At the Prefecture of Police, the director, Claude Charlot, went out of his way to welcome me and facilitate access to classified material; MM. Ginhac and, especially, Lecudennec have gone beyond the call of duty over the years, answering my questions and locating material from the provisional classification. The entire staff at the old Bibliothèque nationale; the Archives nationales in Paris, Fontainebleau, and Aix-en-Provence; the Bibliothèque administrative de la ville de Paris; and departmental archives around Paris and in Carcassonne all offered invaluable assistance.

I owe a special debt of gratitude to Alice Conklin and Eric Jennings for our discussions and for wading through the entire manuscript several times. A number of other colleagues, friends, and family members have provided considerable help along the way. The book is vastly better for their comments even as its shortcomings remain my own. My thanks go out to Jean-

---

11. James C. Scott, *Seeing Like a State: How Certain Schemes to Improve the Human Condition Have Failed* (New Haven: Yale University Press, 1998), pt. 1.

Marc Berlière, Emmanuel Blanchard, Elisa Camiscioli, Herrick Chapman, Paul Cohen, the late William B. Cohen, Julia Clancy-Smith, Natalie Davis, Julia Franke, Nancy Green, Jennifer Heuer, Andreas Killen, Herman Lebovics, Mary Lewis, Arno Mayer, Mark Mazower, Gérard Noiriel, Robert Paxton, Gyan Prakash, Steven Remy, Rosalind Rosenberg, Philippe Rygiel, Martin Schain, Alexis Spire, Robert Tignor, Patrick Weil, and Ari Zolberg. The Davis Seminar at Princeton, as well as groups at the Université de Paris-I, New York University, the City University of New York Graduate Center, the New School, and the University of Toronto, afforded me the opportunity to present portions of this work at various stages of its evolution, and I thank the participants collectively for helping me to see the subject in new ways.

I would like to thank the French government for the exceptional generosity of its Bourse Chateaubriand, which supported my research. The Chateaubriand and additional funding from the Princeton University history department made it possible for me to stay in France for a second, and crucial, year of sustained archival research. A grant from the Research Foundation of the City University of New York supported subsequent trips to the archives, and a Rifkind Fellowship from the City College of New York provided a semester's leave to complete the revisions.

I cannot begin to express the thanks I owe my family both for sparking my interest in history and then supporting me patiently over the years it has taken to bring this work to fruition. My wife, Kim, has had to put up with my absentmindedness and preoccupation, and extended periods of emigration that dragged on far longer than I would have liked. Her love and support as well as her confidence in me made time spent on this project not merely endurable but extremely rewarding. Finally, I would like to express my deepest thanks to our son, Henry, both for his sense of humor and for providing a much needed sense of perspective. This book is dedicated to them.

I am grateful to the editors for permission to reprint portions of previously published material: "Une police de 'simple observation'? Le service actif des étrangers à Paris entre les deux guerres," *Genèses: Sciences sociales et histoire*, no. 54 (March 2004): 51–73; and "The Colonial Politics of Healthcare Provision in Interwar Paris," *French Historical Studies* 27, no. 3 (Summer 2004): 637–68.

Abbreviations

ADA	Archives Départementales de l'Aude, Carcassonne
ADHS	Archives Départementales des Hauts-de-Seine, Nanterre
ADSSD	Archives Départementales de la Seine Saint-Denis, Bobigny
ADY	Archives Départementales des Yvelines, the former Seine-et-Oise, Versailles
AN	Archives Nationales, Paris
AP	Archives de Paris, the former Archives Départementales de la Seine, Paris
APL	American Protective League
APP	Archives de la Préfecture de Police, Paris
BAVP	Bibliothèque administrative de la ville de Paris
BM	Bibliothèque Marxiste, Paris
CAC	Archives Nationales, Centre des archives contemporaines, Fontainebleau
CAOM	Archives Nationales, Centre des Archives d'Outre-Mer, Aix-en-Provence
CGT	Confédération général du travail
CGTU	Confédération général du travail unitaire
Cons. gén.	Conseil général de la Seine
Cons. mun.	Conseil municipal de Paris

FBI	Federal Bureau of Investigation
FLN	Front de libération national
HCM	Haut Comité Méditerranéen
INS	Immigration and Naturalization Service
JO	*Journal officiel de la République Française*
MAE	Ministère des Affaires Étrangères, Quai d'Orsay
MNA	Mouvement national algérien
OPHS	Office public d'hygiène sociale
OURS	Office universitaire de recherches socialistes
PCF	Parti Communiste Français
PM	Police Municipale
PP	Prefecture of Police, Paris
Proc-ver.	*Procès-verbaux*
Rap. et doc.	*Rapports et documents*
RG	Renseignements généraux, the political branch of the Prefecture of Police
SAINA	Service des affaires indigènes nord-africaines de Paris
SAS	Sections administratives spécialisées
SFIO	Section Française de l'Internationale Ouvrière (Socialist Party)
SLOTFOM	Service de Liaison entre les Originaires des Territoires d'Outre-Mer
SONACOTRA	Société nationale de construction de logements pour les travailleurs algériens en métropole
SRI	Secours rouge international

Policing Paris

Introduction

Immigration and the State

Although a linguistically based French cultural identity has existed since the Middle Ages, a French national identity emerged only in the middle decades of the eighteenth century and did not receive a stable legal basis until 1889. Until then, authorities drew distinctions between foreigners and French nationals only in a limited number of circumstances, with limited consequences. In the centuries before the Revolution, most foreign subjects wealthy enough to inherit or bequeath property required a letter of naturalization (*lettre de naturalité*) to do so.[1] From the time of the July Monarchy (1830–48) nationality was essential to vote and to hold some public offices, to receive a government pension, and to benefit from communal rights in some areas. For the unfortunate few who drew bad numbers in the annual draft lottery and were too poor to pay for a replacement—from ten thousand to sixty thousand men in the 1820s—French nationality also entailed lengthy military service.[2] Ordinary people, however, often had difficulty understanding the dis-

1. On the emergence of French as a national language, see Paul Cohen, "Courtly French, Learned Latin, and Peasant Patois: The Making of a National Language in Early Modern France" (PhD diss., Princeton University, 2001). On the origins of nationality as a legal and political category under the Old Regime, Peter Sahlins, *Unnaturally French: Foreign Citizens in the Old Regime and After* (Ithaca: Cornell University Press, 2004), and, in cultural terms, David Bell, *The Cult of the Nation in France: Inventing Nationalism, 1680–1800* (Cambridge: Harvard University Press, 2001). For nationality law since the Revolution, Patrick Weil, *Qu'est-ce qu'un français? Histoire de la nationalité française depuis la Révolution* (Paris: Grasset, 2002). For the term "nationality," Gérard Noiriel, "Socio-histoire d'un concept: Les usages du mot 'nationalité' au XIXe siècle," *Genèses: Sciences sociales et histoire*, no. 20 (September 1995): 4–23, and Weil, *Qu'est-ce qu'un français?* 398–99.
2. Bernard Schnapper, *Le remplacement militaire en France: Quelques aspects politiques, économiques et sociaux du recrutement au XIXe siècle* (Paris: Sevpen, 1968), 291, and Annie

tinction between the rights conferred by legal residence (*admission à domicile*) and nationality. Especially in border regions where upward of 50 percent of the population was foreign born in some cases, finding a job and a spouse, and having children, typically sufficed for acceptance into the local community.[3] But France increasingly encouraged massive foreign immigration in the second half of the nineteenth century to buttress chronic population shortages. From the 1890s, in order to offer social benefits exclusively to its own citizens, the Third Republic (1870–1940) began to mark national boundaries and identify foreigners much more intensively than any previous government. Especially after the dramatic growth of state power during World War I, nationality and citizenship status began to matter as never before—to get a job, move about, or simply to live where one pleased.

I

Before the late nineteenth century, however, government officials and police forces in France and across Europe worried relatively little about nationality. They were preoccupied above all with vagabonds and with what was often called a "floating population" of the desperately poor. From the emancipation of rural populations until World War I, immigration control on the Continent was part of a broad effort to combat vagrancy, banditry, disease, and disorder. Foreigners and the native-born poor were generally seen as part of a single "social problem." In the aftermath of the French Revolution, Napoleon imposed documentary controls on the territories he conquered. Especially in Central Europe, governments built on those measures by requiring people to obtain work papers, *livrets*, *Legitimationskarten*, visas, and various kinds of passports. As an abundant literature has shown, almost everyone had to carry papers to travel outside his or her home province. Traditional notions of the nineteenth century as a liberal era without state restrictions on mobility are no longer tenable.[4]

Crépin, *La conscription en débat ou le triple apprentissage de la Nation, de la Citoyenneté, de la République, 1798–1889* (Arras: Artois Presses Université, 1998), 35–67.

    3. Peter Sahlins, *Boundaries: The Making of France and Spain in the Pyrenees* (Berkeley: University of California Press, 1989), 212–37; Firmin Lentacker, *La frontière franco-belge: Étude géographique des effets d'une frontière internationale sur la vie des relations* (Lille: Université de Lille, 1974), 238–52, and Paul Leuilliot, *L'Alsace au début de XIXe siècle: Essais d'histoire politique, économique et religieux, 1815–1830*, 3 vols. (Paris: Sevpen, 1959), 2:12–17, 486–87.

    4. Jean François Dubost and Peter Sahlins, *Et si on faisait payer les étrangers? Louis XIV, les immigrés et quelques autres* (Paris: Flammarion, 1999); Daniel Roche, ed., *La ville promise: Mobilité et accueil à Paris, fin XVIIe–début XIXe siècle* (Paris: Fayard, 2000); Marie-Claude Blanc-Chaléard, Caroline Douki, Nicole Dyonet, and Vincent Milliot, eds., *Police et migrants: France, 1667–1939* (Rennes: Presses universitaires de Rennes, 2001); Andreas Fahrmeir, *Citizens and Aliens: Foreigners and the Law in Britain and the German States, 1789–1870* (New

Scholarly attempts to establish that there was a widespread concern with "foreigners" and "immigrants" before the late nineteenth century, however, often overlook how much the meaning of the terms has changed. The outsiders monitored by urban police forces were just as likely to come from the next village as a foreign state, indeed much more so before central governments took over poor relief from municipal governments. Although they recorded vast amounts of personal information, including nationality, the various systems of population registration that emerged in Napoleon's wake applied to everyone, citizens and foreigners alike.[5] The distinction between foreigner and citizen was further clouded by the continuing importance of local, hometown citizenship, the local *Gemeinde-* as opposed to national *Staatsangehörigkeit* in German-speaking Central Europe.[6] Many towns in France, too—Lille, Chartres, Toulouse, Dijon, and others besides—drafted legislation that considered anyone from beyond the city walls a "foreigner."[7] Throughout the nineteenth century, poor people faced restrictions and needed special permission to travel from one province to another, even within the administrative districts where they were born.[8] Wealthy foreigners willing to pay some additional taxes, on the other hand, had little cause for concern.

With the emergence of national welfare states in the late nineteenth century, the terms "foreigner" and "immigrant" became increasingly synonymous. Police concern gradually shifted from social class to nationality, as central governments began to invest significant sums in their own citizens. National states throughout Europe began to think differently about their populations, especially after the global economic downturn of the 1870s. With the emergence of statistical modes of thinking, they created special-

York: Berghahn, 2000); and John Torpey, *The Invention of the Passport: Surveillance, Citizenship, and the State* (Cambridge: Cambridge University Press, 2000).

5. United Nations, "Methodology and Evaluation of Population Registers and Similar Systems," *Studies in Methods*, series F, no. 15 (1969); Dorothy S. Thomas, "The Continuous Register System of Population Accounting," in *The Problems of a Changing Population* (Washington, D.C.: U.S. Government Printing Office, 1938), 276–97; and Fahrmeir, *Citizens and Aliens*, 102–4.

6. Mack Walker, *German Home Towns: Community, State, and General Estate, 1648–1817* (1971; Ithaca: Cornell University Press, 1998), 137–42, 336–53; Dieter Langewiesche, "'Staat' und 'Kommune': Zum Wandel der Staatsaufgaben in Deutschland im 19. Jahrhundert," *Historische Zeitschrift* 248 (1989): 621–35, esp. 626; Harald Wendelin, "Schub und Heimatrecht," in *Grenze und Staat: Paßwesen, Staatsbürgerschaft, Heimatrecht und Fremdengesetzgebung in der österreichischen Monarchie, 1750–1867*, ed. Waltraud Heindl and Edith Saurer (Vienna: Böhlau, 2000), esp. 195–230; and Fahrmeir, *Citizens and Aliens*, 169–74, 196–97.

7. Blanc-Chaléard et al., *Police et migrants*, 202–3, 209, 292; and Daniel Roche, *Humeurs vagabondes: De la circulation des hommes et de l'utilité des voyages* (Paris: Fayard, 2003), 380–83.

8. See, e.g., Andrea Geselle, "Domenica Saba Takes to the Road: Origins and Development of a Modern Passport System in Lombardy-Veneto," in *Documenting Individual Identity: The Development of State Practices in the Modern World*, ed. John Torpey and Jane Caplan (Princeton: Princeton University Press, 2001), 199.

ized bureaucracies to manage people, and increasingly intervened in their everyday lives.[9] Along with national token currencies, tariffs, compulsory public education, and mass conscript armies, new welfare programs led what Karl Polanyi famously called a "new crustacean type of nation" to replace the "easygoing nations of the past."[10] Desperately competing against one another, societies across Europe tried to stave off social unrest and to nurture potential soldiers by creating new privileges for their own citizens.

France, however, was the only country—indeed it was the first in the world—to create substantial assistance programs and, at the same time, to resort to massive foreign immigration to satisfy its labor needs. Unlike their British and German counterparts, nineteenth-century French peasants maintained an attachment to the land and resisted proletarianization by limiting their fertility—thus France's famously low birthrate—and by voting for sympathetic candidates. France's demographic and political "modernity," however, entailed a relative economic backwardness, compared to England and Germany. As Gérard Noiriel has argued, the political coalitions of the Third Republic depended on rural support, and industrialization was achieved only by importing massive numbers of foreigners to perform the jobs French peasants would not accept. Ultimately, peasants had little choice. If less completely than elsewhere in Europe, French farmers increasingly depended on industrial jobs after the 1873–95 worldwide depression in agricultural prices. As the economy deteriorated and organized labor emerged as a national political force at the turn of the twentieth century, politicians tried to win over and "attach" labor to the Republic by protecting French workers from foreign competition in the labor market and providing benefits to nationals that foreigners were denied.[11]

French workers, however, could receive preferential treatment only if they could be distinguished from foreigners. Before their counterparts in other countries, the French police developed systematic means to enforce

9. See esp. Ian Hacking, *The Taming of Chance* (Cambridge: Cambridge University Press, 1990); as well as Joshua Cole, *The Power of Large Numbers: Population, Politics, and Gender in Nineteenth-Century France* (Ithaca: Cornell University Press, 2000); Silvana Patriarca, *Numbers and Nationhood: Writing Statistics in Nineteenth-Century Italy* (Cambridge: Cambridge University Press, 1996); and Peter Holquist, "To Count, to Extract, and to Exterminate: Population Statistics and Population Politics in Late Imperial and Soviet Russia," in *A State of Nations: Empire and Nation-Making in the Age of Lenin and Stalin*, ed. Terry Martin and Ronald Grigor Suny (Oxford: Oxford University Press, 2001), 111–44.

10. Polanyi, *The Great Transformation: The Political and Economic Origins of Our Time* (Boston: Beacon Press, 1944), 122.

11. Noiriel, *Le creuset français*, esp. chaps. 2, 6; Noiriel, *La tyrannie du national: Le droit d'asile en Europe, 1793–1993* (Paris: Calmann-Lévy, 1991), 83–100, 155–80; and Noiriel, *Les origines républicaines de Vichy* (Paris: Hachette, 1999), chap. 2. See also Alain Cottereau, "The Distinctiveness of Working-Class Cultures in France, 1848–1900," in *Working-Class Formation: Nineteenth-Century Patterns in Europe and the United States*, ed. Ira Katznelson and Aristide R. Zolberg (Princeton: Princeton University Press, 1986), 111–54; and Gary Cross, *Immigrant Workers in Industrial France: The Making of a New Laboring Class* (Philadelphia: Temple University Press, 1983).

distinctions between citizens, nationals, and foreigners. They applied methods first developed to monitor criminal populations to a group that had done nothing wrong, experimenting with card files and other bureaucratic techniques to keep track of a constantly moving population.

II

My findings do not square with the past two generations of migration research. Since at least the 1960s, immigration specialists have dismissed the importance of nationality to immigrant communities and have portrayed those communities, by their very "otherness," as challenging the idea of the nation-state. Migration scholars have concentrated primarily on immigrants as workers, more recently on women workers, who opposed modern capitalism. They have focused on ethnic networks, diasporas, borderlands, and a variety of communities that cross national boundaries and ultimately erode them.[12] For a younger generation of specialists, nationality might have mattered in the past, but mass migration since World War II has undermined the nation-state as we know it, severing the essential connection between ethnic and political identities. Immigrants today, it is often said, are protected by a growing notion of human rights and international courts. They enjoy all the rights and privileges of citizenship, save the vote. Immigrants and immigrant communities thus offer an example of "postnational" forms of belonging.[13]

Whether in the guise of the "new social history" of the 1960s or more recent transnational scholarship, such arguments fail to account for the experience of other Europeans and North Africans in France between the world wars, or, since the wars, that of Muslims or Caribbean migrants in the United States or Moroccans and Turks throughout Europe, to mention only those groups. Neither the International Court of Justice at The Hague nor the United Nations has offered any tangible support to Muslims in the

12. The literature is now vast, inspired largely by Herbert Gutman's classic title essay in his *Work, Culture, and Society in Industrializing America* (New York: Knopf, 1966), 3–78, and by Frank Thistlethwaite, "Migrations from Europe Overseas in the Nineteenth and Twentieth Centuries," *A Century of European Migrations, 1830–1930*, ed. Rudolph J. Vecoli and Suzanne M. Sinke (Urbana: University of Illinois Press, 1991), 17–49. For syntheses, see John Bodnar, *The Transplanted: A History of Immigrants in Urban America* (Bloomington: Indiana University Press, 1987); Dirk Hoerder and Leslie Page Moch, eds., *European Migrants: Global and Local Perspectives* (Boston: Northeastern University Press, 1996); and Hoerder, *Cultures in Contact: World Migrations in the Second Millennium* (Durham, N.C.: Duke University Press, 2002).

13. This burgeoning literature includes Saskia Sassen, *The Global City: New York, London, Tokyo* (Princeton: Princeton University Press, 1991); Linda Basch, Nina Glick Schiller, and Christina Szanton Blanc, eds., *Nations Unbound: Transnational Projects and the Deterritorialized Nation-State* (New York: Gordon and Breach, 1993); and Yasemin Nuhoğlu Soysal, *Limits of Citizenship: Migrants and Postnational Membership in Europe* (Chicago: University of Chicago Press, 1989).

United States or in Europe. Their treatment is wholly at the discretion of the host governments, and of those governments' interpretations of their respective constitutions. As sociologists such as Rogers Brubaker and Christian Joppke have pointed out, for all their weaknesses, national states remain incredibly powerful mechanisms of social closure.[14]

My central goal in this book is to understand how that came to be the case. I have tried to add a political dimension to a migration literature that has often been wary of discussing nation-states at all for fear of reinforcing their power,[15] and historical depth to sociological studies, which assume that the guest-worker migration in Europe after World War II was historically unprecedented, a unique event that has now come to a close. I will explore how the meaning of crossing borders has changed, both for immigrants and host societies, by looking in detail at the crucial case of Paris. I have tried to show in particular how citizenship came to matter in people's everyday lives, as the barriers to exit that traditionally bound the poor to the land gave way to the barriers to entry familiar to us today.[16]

Understanding which groups the Paris police singled out, how they were treated, and what protections, if any, they enjoyed has required moving beyond the study of legal texts and parliamentary debate. Unlike the standard accounts of immigration policy,[17] which remain confined to these sources, I endeavor to examine in this book how legal and political texts were transformed by their application. Immigration, more than virtually any other policy area, was governed by administrative decrees and circulars, and only from a certain remove by judges or elected officials.[18]

III

Modern immigration controls emerged not in the face of mounting xenophobia in the 1930s, as is often assumed, but rather in the context of demo-

14. Brubaker, *Citizenship and Nationhood in France and Germany* (Cambridge: Harvard University Press, 1992); Joppke, *Immigration and the Nation–State: The United States, Germany, and Great Britain* (Oxford: Oxford University Press, 1999).

15. See the exchange between Gary Gerstle and Donna Gabaccia in *Journal of American History* 84, no. 2 (1997): esp. 574–75 and 580.

16. Aristide R. Zolberg, "International Migration Policies in a Changing World System," in *Human Migration: Patterns and Policies*, ed. William H. McNeill and Ruth S. Adams (Bloomington: Indiana University Press, 1978), 241–86; and Torpey, *Invention of the Passport*.

17. Jean-Charles Bonnet, *Les pouvoirs publics français et l'immigration dans l'entre-deux-guerres* (Lyon: Centre d'histoire économique et sociale de la région lyonnaise, n.d. [1976]); Patrick Weil, *La France et ses étrangers: L'aventure d'une politique de l'immigration, 1938–1991* (Paris: Calmann-Lévy, 1991); and Brubaker, *Citizenship and Nationhood in France and Germany*.

18. Alexis Spire, *Étrangers à la carte: L'administration de l'immigration en France, 1945–1975* (Paris: Grasset, 2005).

bilization after World War I, as part of the French government's effort to maintain public order while relinquishing wartime controls. I shall accordingly devote considerable attention to the critical period from the Armistice to the Bolshevization of the French Communist Party and the emergence of Algerian nationalism in Paris in the mid-1920s. I explore the alliances and compromises that made the new approach to immigration control possible and then chart its evolution.

The effort to track hundreds of thousands of people at a time grew out of bureaucratic fantasies of achieving total control over society that were given a new lease on life by the so-called national security state of World War I.[19] They bear a striking resemblance to what James Scott has called "high modernism," a sweeping vision of the benefits of technical and scientific progress applied to all fields of human activity—a means of simplifying a messy, complicated world in order to act upon it more effectively. But the Parisian immigration controls lacked an ideological dimension central to Scott's formulation and to others like it.[20] They set out to preserve and not to transform the social order. Nor were the new police measures imposed on a prostrate civil society by a monolithic state.

They were, rather, the product of negotiation. In the early 1920s, prominent national politicians, especially Camille Chautemps and Albert Sarraut, were so worried about immigrant criminality, foreign agitators, and Communists, that they were willing to make common cause with the avowed antirepublicans who controlled local government in the capital.[21] Paris had, by far, the country's most diverse immigrant community. The foreign-born population doubled over the course of the 1920s, reaching five hundred thousand by the onset of the Great Depression, and the city served as headquarters for scores of refugee groups plotting against their home governments. During the interwar years, Paris was the headquarters of colonial nationalisms from around the world—Nguyen Aï Quoc (the future Ho Chi Minh), Messali Hadj, Léopold Sédar Senghor, Aimé Césaire, and Deng Xiaoping all spent time there—and, after the Spanish Civil War, of antifascism

---

19. Michael Geyer, "The Militarization of Europe, 1914–1945," in *The Militarization of the Western World*, ed. John Gillis (New Brunswick, N.J.: Rutgers University Press, 1989), 65–102; and Peter Holquist, " 'Information Is the Alpha and Omega of Our Work': Bolshevik Surveillance in Its Pan-European Perspective," *Journal of Modern History* 69, no. 3 (September 1997): 415–50.

20. Scott, *Seeing Like a State: How Certain Schemes to Improve the Human Condition Have Failed* (New Haven: Yale University Press, 1998), chap. 3. The German historian Detlev J. K. Peukert writes of "classical modernism" in similar terms in *The Weimar Republic: The Crisis of Classical Modernity*, trans. Richard Deveson (New York: Hill and Wang, 1989), and "The Genesis of the 'Final Solution' from the Spirit of Science," in *Nazism and German Society, 1933–1945*, ed. David F. Crew (New York: Routledge, 1994), 274–99. See also Zygmunt Bauman, *Modernity and the Holocaust* (Ithaca: Cornell University Press, 1989), esp. 70–72 for his notion of the "gardening state."

21. On the Paris municipal council, Yvan Combeau, *Paris et les élections municipales sous la Troisième République: La scène capitale dans la vie politique française* (Paris: Harmattan, 1998).

in exile.[22] White Russians sought shelter from the Bolsheviks, many supporting themselves as taxi drivers, teachers, and itinerant workers. Italians arrived, first looking for work, then fleeing fascism. Spanish Republicans, eastern European Jews, colonial subjects, especially Algerian Muslims, people from all over came to Paris to find work and make a better life.

Chautemps, Sarraut, and their colleagues decided to work with local Paris politicians in part to avoid the famous inefficiencies of parliamentary politics, but also because the capital offered substantial means that even the national government lacked. While the minister of the interior named both the prefect and prefect of police who governed the capital—Paris was the only city in France under the Third Republic without an elected mayor[23]—the Paris Municipal Council drew up the city's budget. It paid roughly half of the prefect of police's budget and often granted significant discretionary funds for special projects, which it paid from its own coffers.[24] A Napoleonic creation at odds with republican legislation, the Prefecture of Police was enormously powerful. It employed more men that all of the other police forces in the country combined, excluding the gendarmerie, with nearly twelve thousand officers in the early 1920s.[25] At that time, a newly revitalized immigrant service employed more men and treated more matters than any other office in the prefecture.[26] A decade later, police chiefs came from around the world to study Parisian police methods, especially a massive card file listing every legal immigrant by nationality, profession, and by street of residence.[27]

In Part 1, I examine the immigration service in Paris responsible for foreign, mostly European, immigrants, which served as a model for other police forces in France and around the world. Among the first scholars to obtain access to police archives confiscated by the Nazis, then taken from them by the Soviets, and recently repatriated from Moscow,[28] I examine the ways in which the Paris police used immigration law to control marginal populations. Officers paid special attention to immigrant neighborhoods in an effort to scare illegal migrants into registering with authorities, and ar-

22. Georges Mauco, *Les étrangers en France: Leur rôle dans l'activité économique* (Paris: Armand Colin, 1932), chap. 9; and André Kaspi and Antoine Marès, *Le Paris des étrangers, 1919–1939* (Paris: Imprimerie nationale, 1992).

23. With the exception of Étienne Arago and Jules Ferry's brief tenures in 1870–71.

24. Maurice Félix, *Le régime administratif du département de la Seine et de la Ville de Paris*, 2 vols., 3rd. ed. (1922; Paris: Rousseau, 1946), esp. 1:29–30.

25. That number rose to twenty thousand by 1939. See Jean-Mark Berlière, *Le monde des polices en France, XIXe–XXe siècles* (Brussels: Complexe, 1996), 37.

26. Émile Massard, ". . . Création d'emplois au Service des étrangers," Cons. mun., *Proc.-ver.* (26 March 1926), 539.

27. Lucien Picard, "Les étrangers à Paris," *Police parisienne*, no. 5 (29 February 1936): 19.

28. Sophie Coeuré, Frédéric Monier, and Géraud Naud, "Le retour de Russie des archives françaises: Le cas du fonds de la Sûreté," *Vingtième siècle* 45 (January–March 1995): 133–39; and Dominique Deveaux, "Les archives de la direction de la sûreté rapatriées de Russie," *La gazette des archives*, no. 176 (1997): 78–86.

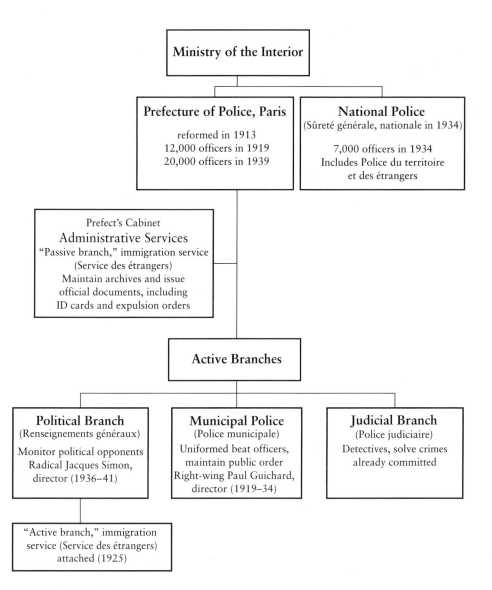

Figure 1. Police divisions.

Sources: Jean-Marc Berlière, *Le monde des polices en France: XIXe–XXe siècles* (Brussels: Complexe, 1996), 37; *Annuaire-almanach du commerce* (Paris: Société Didot-Bottin, 1918–19); "Note sur la réorganisation de l'Administration Centrale et des Services actifs de la Sûreté Générale devenue Sûreté Nationale," 1934, in Centre des Archives Contemporaines, Fontainebleau, 19940493, art. 123.

rested those whose papers were not in order. With the emergence of systematic immigration controls in the mid-1920s, crossing the border and finding work were no longer enough to establish a person in France. Stepped up enforcement of old laws gave the police enormous leverage over immigrants that they did not have over French citizens. The police now had the right to question anyone who looked out of place or kept the wrong company. Immigration control offered authorities a graduated series of measures from a stern warning to a renewable stay or suspended sentence to an immediate expulsion, which could be used for an infinite variety of offenses. If not actually deported, a substantial proportion of the capital's immigrants received an expulsion notice or knew someone who did.

A series of protections sheltered most migrants from abuse. The active branch of the immigration service was part of the elite political branch (Renseignements généraux or RG); officers enjoyed an increasingly well-defined career path between the wars and were acutely aware of the consequences of sparking a diplomatic crisis. Information gathered by those officers provided immigrants a legally recognized status. Work permits allowed them to live and work in peace, without fear of expulsion or harassment from local authorities. The commitment of governments of all ideological persuasions to provide asylum to the oppressed required authorities to conduct lengthy investigations to verify immigrants' claims, which gave many a chance to slip away. Moreover, a whole host of organizations from the League for the Rights of Man to the Socialist Party to Secours Rouge International often intervened on behalf of individual migrants.

The greatest distinction to emerge between the wars, ironically, was not between foreigners and French citizens, or between immigrant workers and political refugees, but rather between all of those groups and colonial subjects. Part 2 deals with a range of programs created exclusively for North African Muslims, most of them technically French nationals but not citizens—colonial subjects and protégés without the right to vote. Studying European and colonial migrants together draws attention to the interaction of common prejudices that most migrants have endured with the legal category of nationality and larger geopolitical concerns. Looking at North African immigration in comparative perspective highlights the crucial importance of citizenship, of the protection of an independent nation-state, and it helps show in concrete terms the difference between colonial racism and other forms of abuse.

Legally and politically, North Africans suffered a unique handicap. The constitution of the Third Republic was ratified by only the slimmest of margins in 1875, and that majority was obtained only by granting European settlers in Algeria considerable influence in the French parliament. As Patrick Weil has recently shown, they used their influence in 1889, in 1919, and again during the Popular Front to thwart metropolitan reform efforts that would have made French citizenship accessible to more than a tiny number of Muslims.[29] Without having to worry about sparking an international incident or repercussions at the ballot box, French authorities created what amounted to a parallel police force that commanded resources and resorted to methods unprecedented in peacetime. In the face of Algerian nationalism and Communist anti-imperialism, the coalition that overhauled the immigrant service that monitored foreign nationals in Paris expanded to include even the most progressive members of the Socialist Party. Ranging from Marius Moutet and Henri Sellier on the socialist left to the rabid anti-Semite Darquier de Pellepoix, who would later play a conspicuous role in Vichy, that coalition was broader than any other in French politics at the time, and it ran into no opposition in the international arena. The most important constraints that protected foreign, mostly European, migrants did not apply to North Africans.

These chapters stress the centrality of empire to local Parisian and French national politics. They reverse the common view of empire as a vast experimental terrain in which modes of seeing and disciplining subaltern groups emerged overseas before returning, fully formed, to the metropole.[30] Many organizers and agents of the Parisian North African services spent significant parts of their careers in the colonies, but they had to adapt their approach to law enforcement when they returned to the mainland. The left wing of what I have called the "colonial consensus" prevented authorities in Paris from acting the way their counterparts did overseas. Socialists shared widespread concerns that North African Muslims could never become fully French and grudgingly supported special surveillance measures, but they insisted that those measures serve the interests of the colonized. As a practical matter, they forced the Parisian services to provide social assistance on a scale unprecedented in the colonies, especially Algeria, where settlers jealously hoarded scarce resources;[31] they forced the former colonial officials who ran the programs to develop less violent but much more invasive means of stamping out dissent.

Popular and official opinion have considered successive waves of newcomers inherently dangerous and described them in broadly similar terms

29. Weil, *Qu'est-ce qu'un français?* 225–44.

30. The metaphor of colonies as "laboratories of modernity" has become pervasive in postcolonial scholarship. Among many others, Paul Rabinow, *French Modern: Norms and Forms of the Social Environment* (Cambridge: MIT Press, 1989); Gwendolyn Wright, *The Politics of Design in French Colonial Urbanism* (Chicago: University of Chicago Press, 1991). For arguments that "modern racism" emerged overseas, Ann Stoler, "Sexual Affronts and Racial Frontiers: European Identities and the Cultural Politics of Exclusion in Colonial Southeast Asia," in *Tensions of Empire: Colonial Cultures in a Bourgeois World,* ed. Frederick Cooper and Stoler (Berkeley: University of California Press, 1997), esp. 214; Neil MacMaster, *Colonial Migrants and Racism: Algerians in France, 1900–1962* (New York: St. Martin's, 1997); and Benjamin Stora, *Le transfert d'une mémoire: De l'"Algérie française" au racisme anti-arabe* (Paris: La Découverte, 1999).

31. On the settler dominance of the Algerian budget, Claude Collot, *Les institutions de l'Algérie durant la période coloniale, 1830–1962* (Algiers: Éditions du Cnrs, 1987), 207–35.

from at least the early nineteenth century. Rural migrants had terrible difficulty fitting into the Parisian working class during the July Monarchy. Their
supposedly heightened sexuality and frequent consorting with prostitutes
often struck fear into bourgeois observers.[32] At midcentury Belgian workers
frequently came to blows with their French counterparts in the north.[33]
Later on, French workers and elites derided Italians, too, as hypersexual
and prone to violence. Despite a shared Catholic culture, Italian and French
workers frequently came to blows in the late nineteenth century. The greatest "race" riot in French history took place in the summer of 1893, and it
targeted Italians.[34] Like the Irish in England and the United States, Italians
in France were often thought of as black when they first arrived.[35]

If these groups all endured harsh treatment, none of them lacked meaningful political representation while at the same time facing a broad political consensus that enabled a modern state to act decisively against them.
Combining strategic considerations and a traditional paternalism, as well as
a healthy dose of racial fear, organizers in Paris mobilized resources for
their own colonial subjects that remained unavailable for foreign nationals.
Segregating North African Muslims and subjecting them to an often coercive surveillance regime, republican authorities aggravated their already difficult circumstances in France. They began to transform an anti-"Arab"
prejudice that was broadly similar to the prejudices most other migrants encountered into something fundamentally worse.

IV

With its vast card files and agents scouring the city to monitor North
African Muslims and foreign migrants, modern immigration controls look
strikingly like the sort of abstract dystopia Michel Foucault imagined in
Discipline and Punish and in his lectures at the Collège de France before his
untimely death in 1984.[36] Recording people's comings and goings and
obliging them to obtain government permission to hold a job or change

32. Alain Corbin, *Les filles de noce: Misère sexuelle et prostitution, XIXe siècle* (Paris:
Flammarion, 1982), esp. pt. 1a and 275–78; and Louis Chevalier, *Classes laborieuses et classes
dangereuses à Paris pendant la première moitié du XIXe siècle* (1958; Paris: Hachette, 1978).

33. Lentacker, *La frontière franco-belge*, 241.

34. Pierre Milza, *Français et Italiens à la fin du XIXe siècle: Aux origines du rapproche-
ment franco-italien de 1900–1902*, 2 vols. (Rome: École française de Rome, 1981), 1:274–85;
and José Cubero, *Nationalistes et étrangers: Le massacre d'Aigues-Mortes* (Paris: Imago,
1996).

35. See esp. Matthew Frye Jacobson, *Whiteness of a Different Color: European Immigrants and the Alchemy of Race* (Cambridge: Harvard University Press, 1998).

36. Foucault, *Surveiller et punir: Naissance de la prison* (Paris: Gallimard, 1975); Foucault, *Sécurité, territoire, population: Cours au Collège de France, 1977–1978* (Paris: Seuil,
2004); and Foucault, *Naissance de la biopolitique: Cours au Collège de France, 1978–1979*
(Paris: Seuil, 2004).

apartments helped the French state pacify what it considered an unruly population at a time—immediately after World War I—when it found itself compelled to relinquish power in many other domains. The rights, privileges, and obligations established by these new controls would interest Foucault and his followers primarily in their capacity to forge new subjectivities. It may be, for example, that Algerian, Moroccan, and Tunisian Muslims began to consider themselves as North African only on arrival in Paris. They certainly recognized the opportunities presented by the institutions that received them. Moroccans and Tunisians frequently wondered why, as subjects of French protectorates, they endured all the same restrictions as foreigners without enjoying any of the benefits. At the same time, however, tensions between Algerian and Moroccan communities in Paris throughout the interwar period suggest that a North African identity was, at best, partial and bitterly contested. Whether from the Maghreb or elsewhere, immigrants often experienced identity checks as a wrenching violation. In his memoirs, Stefan Zweig wrote:

> We were constantly interrogated, registered, numbered, examined, stamped, and even today, I, the incorrigible survivor of a freer time and a citizen of the global republic I so often dreamed of, find each of those stamps printed in my passport a bitter stain, the searches a humiliation.[37]

Such humiliations no doubt led many migrants to seek protection from foreign nationalist organizations or the Communist Party, or simply to pack up and leave. But the very same police measures encouraged others to improve their accents, to fit in as best they could, sometimes to seek naturalization. There was a massive spike in naturalizations from 1938 to 1940, the greatest in all of French history, as the Third Republic cracked down on undocumented migrants and tried to force them to leave.[38] In her autobiographical novel *Adieu Volodia*, the actress Simone Signoret wrote of a pair of Polish Jews switching from Yiddish to French in Occupied Paris a few years later, so those around them would not mistake them for Germans.[39] During the war, Hannah Arendt recalled: "We were expelled from Germany because we were Jews. But having hardly crossed the French borderline, we were changed into "boches."" . . . During seven years we played the ridiculous role of trying to be Frenchmen—at least prospective citizens."[40] The very multiplicity of responses to coercive measures makes it difficult, if

---

37. Zweig, *Le monde d'hier* (1944; Paris: Belfond, 1982), 475, quoted by Spire, *Étrangers à la carte*, 51.

38. Weil, *Qu'est-ce qu'un français?* 156.

39. Signoret, *Adieu Volodia* (Paris: Fayard, 1985), 395.

40. Arendt, "We Refugees" (1943), quoted in Julia Franke, *Paris—eine neue Heimat: Jüdisches Emigranten aus Deutschland, 1933–1939* (Berlin: Dunker and Humblot, 2000), 279.

not impossible, to draw general conclusions about how they affected immigrants' views of themselves.

Moreover, the rights and obligations Foucault dismissed as so many forms of coercion played a vital role in structuring immigrants' opportunities and life chances. Labor economists and feminist scholars have long known that welfare states create social class and gender distinctions; social programs designed to address problems of social stratification also produce it.[41] The creation of new kinds of stratification and inequality, however, based on national origin and citizenship status has received much less attention.

Before World War II, modern immigration controls invested longstanding cultural and legal categories with new meanings. The distinction between foreigners and French nationals has existed on some level for hundreds of years, but it took on a whole new significance when the Paris police overhauled the immigration service in the early 1920s. In the latter years of the decade, and especially later, during the Depression, the police enforced labor laws that limited immigrants' ability to settle and work where they pleased. Starting in 1933, they stepped up scrutiny of asylum claims. What had to that point remained a theoretical distinction between political and labor migration increasingly took on material significance. Efforts to win over colonial migrants and to isolate them from Communist and nationalist revolutionaries created a profound new form of exclusion. It set apart people who had access to some sort of political representation or protected status from those who did not.

41. Gøsta Esping-Andersen, *The Three Worlds of Welfare Capitalism* (Princeton: Princeton University Press, 1990), chap. 3, "The Welfare State as a System of Stratification"; Linda Gordon, "The New Feminist Scholarship on the Welfare State," in *Women, the State, and Welfare,* ed. Gordon (Madison: University of Wisconsin Press, 1990), 9–35; and Carole Pateman, "The Patriarchal Welfare State," in *Democracy and The Welfare State*, ed. Amy Gutman (Princeton: Princeton University Press, 1988), 231–60.

Part I

Immigration and the Ambiguities of Political Policing

Chapter One

The Evolution of Immigration Control

Police forces have long fantasized about achieving total control of the societies they protect by accumulating vast stores of information. In his *Mémoire sur la réformation de la police de France* (1749), the police inspector and future *Encyclopédiste* Jacques-François Guillauté presented Louis XV with an elaborate file system that, he claimed, would allow authorities to know everything about everyone: their name, date of birth, origin, and status (*qualité*); the date of their arrival in Paris; where they were staying (not only the address but the stairway and room), with whom, and at what price; their profession, wages, and tax burden; and more besides. Writing of the lieutenant général de police: "He will come to know every inch of the city as well as his own house; he will know more about ordinary citizens than their own neighbors and the people who see them every day. . . . In their mass, copies of these certificates will provide him with an absolutely faithful image of the city."[1] To realize this vision, and manage the resulting mass of information, Guillauté devised a mechanical device he called a "serre papier," a giant wheel, thirty-six feet in circumference and three feet deep, divided in thirty-two main sections, each of which was subdivided into twenty more. Each of the giant devices would thus contain 640 sections, enough to house 25,600 sheets of paper. By his estimate, eleven or twelve men—each manipulating one of these giant apparatuses with his

---

1. Guillauté, *Mémoire sur la réformation de la police de France . . . , illustré de vingt-huit dessins de Gabriel de Saint-Aubin* (1749; Paris; Hermann, 1974), 47–48. On Guillauté, see Daniel Roche, *Le peuple de Paris: Essai sur la culture populaire au XVIIIe siècle* (1981; Paris: Fayard, 1998), 370; and Vincent Milliot, "La surveillance des migrants et des lieux d'accueil à Paris du XVIe siècle au années 1830," in Roche, ed., *La ville promise: Mobilité et accueil à Paris (fin XVIIe–début XIXe siècle)* (Paris: Fayard, 2000), 42–45.

feet, without leaving his desk—would be enough to run this fantastic system
and render the city transparent to the policeman's gaze.[2]

Guillauté's plan never materialized. Since the late Middle Ages, an overlapping series of religious, corporate, and, increasingly, royal institutions
made it possible for authorities in France to identify the king's subjects. Beginning in earnest in the early eighteenth century and continuing throughout the nineteenth, the Paris police refined their means of identifying mobile
populations, relying on written documents, especially passports and *livrets*.
Before the Third Republic, however, the immigrants authorities feared
came primarily from the French countryside. The police were preoccupied
above all with vagabonds and what was often called the "floating population" of desperately poor people. Despite considerable social dislocation,
which elites blamed on peasant migrants in the nineteenth century, police
efforts to control these migrants remained rather haphazard. As long as authorities worried about poor French workers, on whom they had a real if
uncertain grasp, the expense of abandoning their existing approach to identification ruled out a more systematic approach.

Other European countries collected more personal information from inhabitants than did France. The German-speaking states of the nineteenth
century, for example, kept great quantities of personal data on everyone. As
bureaucratic tools, however, the population registers they created were
quite inflexible. Organized alphabetically, and often bound in leather volumes, they provided detailed biographies of individuals and families, but
they yielded information on other groups only to those who made considerable effort. To compensate for the registers' limitations and to update
their criminal records, police departments in major cities in Germany and
across Europe developed new forms of identification and information-
retrieval systems in the last quarter of the century.[3] Even then, however,
they remained preoccupied with the so-called dangerous classes, with de-
viants and outcasts, wherever they came from.

2. Guillauté, *Mémoire sur la réformation de la police*, 40–68.
3. Miklos Vec, *Die Spur des Täters: Methoden der Identifikation in der Kriminalistik,
1879–1933* (Baden-Baden: Nomos, 2002); Peter Becker, *Verderbnis und Entartung: Eine
Geschichte der Kriminologie des 19. Jahrhunderts als Diskurs und Praxis* (Göttingen: Vandenhoeck and Ruprecht, 2002); Becker, "Vom 'Haltlosen' zur 'Bestie': Das polizeiliche Bild des
'Verbrechers' im 19. Jahrhundert," in *'Sicherheit' und 'Wohlfahrt': Polizei, Gesellschaft und
Herrschaft im 19. und 20. Jahrhundert*, ed. Alf Lüdke (Frankfurt-am-Main: Suhrkamp, 1992),
97–131, esp. 126–31; Ilsen About, "Naissance d'une science policière de l'identification en
Italie, 1902–1922," in the special issue "Police et identification: Enjeux, pratiques, techniques," ed. Pierre Piazza, *Les cahiers de la sécurité*, no. 56 (2005), 167–200; Martine
Kaluszynski, "Alphonse Bertillon et l'anthropométrie," in Philippe Vigier, ed., *Maintien de
l'ordre et polices en France au XIXe siècle* (Paris: Créaphis, 1987), 269–85; About, "Les fondations d'un système national d'identification policière en France, 1893–1914," *Genèses: Sciences sociales et histoire*, no. 54 (March 2004): 28–52; and Robert A. Nye, *Crime, Madness,
and Politics in Modern France: The Medical Concept of National Decline* (Princeton: Princeton University Press, 1984).

The Paris police began to shift their focus from social class and domestic criminals to national origins at least a decade before their counterparts anywhere else on the Continent. As French republican governments began negotiating with organized labor in the late nineteenth century, they began to offer benefits exclusively to French workers in an attempt to preserve social peace. Integrating the working class into the national community led authorities around the country to distinguish them from unentitled foreigners, who had begun to arrive in massive numbers.

Nowhere did this effort to track foreign nationals start sooner than in Paris, or take place on a comparable scale. As the national capital, Paris was simply too important to leave unprotected, and it had the most diverse immigrant community in the country; finding foreigners posed greater challenges there than anywhere else. Its local police and public health institutions, moreover, had long, distinguished histories, with established bureaucracies of their own. They offered resources matched by only a few other law-enforcement agencies in the world.[4] Finally, a revolution in local politics in the wake of the Dreyfus affair at the turn of the century installed a right-wing, nationalist majority at the Hôtel de Ville that was all too willing to abuse poor immigrants from other countries. Together with those Parisian leaders, centrist ministers of the interior took advantage of Paris's exceptional resources to develop new methods of immigration control directed at the foreign born.

I

A generation ago, immigration specialists overturned a vision of rural Europe, largely inspired by the classics of late-nineteenth-century social science, that portrayed peasant communities as an immobile, undifferentiated backward mass cut off from the outside world. The new social history of the 1960s and 1970s showed that rural folk were not "uprooted" when they left their fields for factory work and city life. People have always moved about, for all sorts of reasons. A premobile world has simply never existed.[5]

In the past decade, a growing body of work has shown that the effort to keep track of mobile populations also has a longer history than classical ac-

4. Raymond B. Fosdick, *European Police Systems* (New York: Century Co., 1915); and, for comparative purposes, Eric H. Monkkonen, *Police in Urban America, 1860–1920* (Cambridge: Cambridge University Press, 1981); Elise Tipton, *The Japanese Police State: The Tokkô in Interwar Japan* (Honolulu: University of Hawaii Press, 1990); and *Crime and Punishment in Latin America: Law and Society since Late Colonial Times*, ed. Ricardo Salvatore, Carlos Aguirre, and Gilbert Joseph (Durham, N.C.: Duke University Press, 2001).

5. For a good overview, see Leslie Page-Moch, *Moving Europeans: Migration in Western Europe since 1650* (Bloomington: Indiana University Press, 1992); and, specifically for France, Paul-André Rosental, *Les sentiers invisibles: Espace, familles et migrations dans la France du XIXe siècle* (Paris: Ehess, 1999).

counts allowed.[6] The transition from preliterate, visual modes of identification to standardized, written documents started much sooner, was less abrupt, and remains less complete, than the great treatises of Max Weber, Georg Simmel, and Ferdinand Tönnies would suggest.[7]

Concern with immigration control began well before Guillauté. Although official certificates of identity, such as letters of introduction, appear to have remained the privilege of a limited circle of ambassadors, merchants, and couriers in the fifteenth century, available to ordinary travelers only at great expense, such documents came to be demanded as a matter of course a century later.[8] In 1462, a royal decree in France required every furloughed soldier to carry a *cédule* issued by military authorities, which described him and justified his absence from his unit.[9] In Italy and territories north of the Alps, soldiers received similar *passaporti* or *Bassporten*. From the second half of the fifteenth century, the health passport—*billette de santé* or *bolleta di sanità*—played an increasingly important role as a compulsory identity document. Prison camps, poorhouses, corporate guilds, and hospitals all increasingly kept detailed records that enabled them to track down escapees and ferret out fraud. Measures initially taken during times of war or epidemic increasingly became common.[10]

In France demobilization after the reign of Louis XIV (1648–1715) and the last outbreak of the plague, in Marseille in 1720, marked a critical turning point. In cities across the country, growing mobility heightened efforts to track migrant populations. Whether in the person of military or tax officials, outsiders were increasingly brought in to take over responsibility for identification. By the end of the Regency, failure to carry a generally recog-

6. Much of this work in France has been done by scholars influenced by or working under Daniel Roche. See his recent *Humeurs vagabondes: De la circulation des hommes et de l'utilité des voyages* (Paris: Fayard, 2003) for a synthesis, esp. chap. 7.

7. On this point, see Vincent Milliot and Vincent Denis, "Police et identification dans la France des Lumières," *Genèses: Sciences sociales et histoire*, no. 54 (March 2004): 4–27, esp. 16. For the classic sociological works, see, e.g., Max Weber, *The City* (New York: Basic Books, 1958); Georg Simmel, "The Stranger," and esp. "The Metropolis and Mental Life," both in *The Sociology of Georg Simmel*, trans. Kurt Wolff (New York: Free Press, 1950), 402–8 and 409–24; and Ferdinand Tönnies, *Community and Society* (East Lansing: Michigan State University Press, 1957).

8. Daniel Nordman, "Sauf-conduits et passeports, en France, à la Renaissance," in *Voyager à la Renaissance*, ed. Jean Céard and Jean-Claude Margolin (Paris: Maisonneuve et Larose, 1987), 145–58.

9. Philippe Contamine, *Guerre, état et société à la fin du Moyen Age: Études sur les armées des rois de France, 1337–1494* (Paris: Mouton, 1972), 501.

10. Nicole Castan, *Justice et répression en Languedoc à l'époque des Lumières* (Paris: Flammarion, 1980), esp. 220; André Zysberg, *Vies et destins de 60,000 forçats sur les galères de France, 1680–1748* (Paris: Seuil, 1987), 45–48; Steven L. Kaplan, "Réflexions sur la police du monde du travail, 1700–1815," *Revue historique* 529 (January–March 1979): 17–77; and Valentin Groebner, "Describing the Person, Reading the Signs in Late Medieval and Renaissance Europe: Identity Papers, Vested Figures, and the Limits of Identification, 1400–1600," in *Documenting Individual Identity: The Development of State Practices in the Modern World*, ed. John Torpey and Jane Caplan (Cambridge: Cambridge University Press, 2000), 15–27, here esp. 16 and 20.

nized proof of identity could result in considerable penalties. Royal authorities began to push aside the Church and local elites in their bid to centralize identification of the king's subjects.[11] Whether they relied on military checkpoints, as in the walled towns of the north, or on the neighborhood watch committees, tax rolls, and rooming-house registers used elsewhere, urban authorities throughout France created a series of routine bureaucratic means of defining and protecting their privileged local communities against able-bodied beggars, the insane, and vagabonds from outside. Informal, local arrangements gradually gave way to standardized practices. To take a northern example, the two guard houses at the gate in Lille on the route to Paris used twice as much paper at the end of the eighteenth century as they did at the outset.[12]

State membership, however—what we would call nationality today—was among the less salient criteria urban officials used in determining who was "foreign" in the early modern period.[13] As Catherine Denys and a host of others have shown, a foreigner first and foremost was someone who resided outside the city walls: "Any individual coming from beyond a city's suburbs was legally a foreigner, whether he came from the neighboring countryside, a nearby town, or from farther afield."[14] Town fathers might recognize a shared cultural heritage with people from the same region, an "étranger du Pays," as an eighteenth-century magistrate in Valenciennes put it, apparently without noting any contradiction.[15] In important respects, that magistrate would likely have considered a Parisian migrant more alien than an Austrian subject from a nearby town.

When the Sun King died, Paris already had a considerable police bureaucracy responsible for monitoring the city's foreign population. Food riots and popular disturbances of all sorts posed obvious problems and attracted

11. Jean-Luc Laffont, "La police des étrangers à Toulouse sous l'Ancien Régime, in Blanc-Chaléard et al., eds., *Police et migrants:France, 1667–1939* (Rennes, Presses universitaires de Rennes, 2001), 289–313; and Vincent Denis, "Individu, identité et identification en France, 1715–1815" (thèse d'histoire, Université de Paris I, 2003).

12. Catherine Denys, *Police et sécurité au XVIIIe siècle dans les villes de la frontière franco-belge* (Paris: Harmattan, 2002), 341, for the example from Lille. More generally, see Philippe Guignet, *Le pouvoir dans la ville au XVIIIe siècle: Pratiques politiques, notabilité et éthique sociale de part et d'autre de la frontière franco-belge* (Paris: Ehess, 1990), 243–314; Michel Cassan, "Villes et cultures aux XVIe et XVIIe siècles," in *Société, culture, vie religieuse aux XVIe et XVIIe siècles*, actes du colloque 1995 de l'Association des historiens modernes (Paris: Publications de la Sorbonne, 1995), 27–44; Jean-Pierre Bardet, *Rouen aux XVIIe et XVIIIe siècles: Les mutations d'un espace social* (Paris: Sedes, 1983), 53–182; and Laffont, "La police des étrangers à Toulouse."

13. For the emergence of nationality, see Peter Sahlins, *Unnaturally French: Foreign Citizens in the Old Regime and After* (Ithaca: Cornell University Press, 2004).

14. Catherine Clémens-Denys, "Les transformations du contrôle des étrangers dans les villes de la frontière du Nord, 1667–1789," in *Polices et migrants*, 209.

15. Denys, *Police et sécurité au XVIIIe siècle*, 345. Cf. Hannelore Burger, "Paßwesen und Staatsbürgerschaft," in Heindl and Saurer, eds., *Grenze und Staat: Paßwesen, Staatsbürgerschaft, Heimatrecht, und Fremdengesetzgebung in der österreichischen Monarchie (1750–1867)* (Vienna: Böhlau, 2000), 79.

considerable attention from royal authorities, who increasingly took over responsibility for policing from the Parlement of Paris and local elites.[16] Longstanding regulations compelled Parisian rooming houses to keep registers of their guests. In 1708, a corps of forty police inspectors created the first specialized bureaucracy to monitor rooming houses in immigrant neighborhoods and make sure their registers were properly kept; they visited at night to make sure everything was in order.[17] The immigrants in question, it should be pointed out, were overwhelmingly French subjects, poor peasants from the countryside who came to find work in Paris.

In 1752 an inspector named Buhot was charged with the surveillance of foreign subjects, with special attention to be paid to ambassadors and ministers. Under the tenure of Lieutenant General of Police Gabriel de Sartine, tracking foreign subjects became something of a priority. A few years after Guillauté's book appeared, Denis Diderot wrote to Catherine the Great:

> When a foreigner arrives in the capital, they can tell you in less than twenty-four hours at the rue Neuve-Saint-Augustin [i.e., police headquarters] who he is, where he's from, where in town he's staying, where he's going, who he's in contact with, and who he's traveling with.[18]

The great philosophe clearly expressed the desire of police officials to regulate movement within the capital city but, in this case at least, had no grasp of the realities of everyday administration. As Jean-François Dubost has shown, eighteenth-century officials concentrated such lavish attention only on a tiny minority of foreign subjects. They paid special attention not to poor foreign workers and the indigent but rather to the social and economic elite. According to Dubost, nearly 95 percent of the police reports on foreign subjects dealt with nobles, who made up only a small minority of the capital's population of *non-régnicoles* (non-French).[19] Apart from periods of international tension—the War of the Austrian Succession (1740–48), the Seven Years' War (1756–63), the American Revolution (1776–83)—when they were on the lookout for foreign soldiers and spies, successive lieutenant generals worried much more about their own poor subjects.[20]

The Paris police worried most about the growing numbers of rural migrants from the French countryside struggling to make ends meet. They paid particular attention to those hovering just above the poverty line in

16. Paolo Piasenza, *Polizia e città: Stretegie d'ordine, conflitti e rivolte a Parigi tra sei e settecento* (Bologna: Il Mulino, 1990).
17. Milliot, "La surveillance des migrants," 28–29.
18. Quoted by Jean-François Dubost in "Les étrangers à Paris au siècle des Lumières," in *La ville promise*, 254.
19. Ibid., 258.
20. Milliot, "Migrants et 'étrangers' sous l'œil de la police: La surveillance des lieux d'accueil parisiens au Siècle des Lumières," in *Police et migrants*, 327.

rooming houses, which were not subject to any kind of guild regulations. Unwilling to follow every poor peasant migrant in the city, the police concentrated instead on the neighborhoods where they settled, notably the quartier Saint Denis, and the people who rented them rooms. Over the course of the eighteenth century, the new rooming-house service, the new police division devoted to keeping track of residents of rooming houses, made considerable gains. It used an increasingly elaborate system of registers and standardized forms to control both the capital's migrant population and, especially, those who served it. Checking the books and imposing fines for violations allowed royal agents to impose themselves on what had remained closed neighborhood and patronage networks, and to gain a measure of control over the population movements that had begun to take on massive proportions.[21]

II

Perhaps the most ambitious effort to keep track of mobile populations on the Continent in the precomputer era took place in the German-speaking territories of Central Europe. The French Revolution created obligatory, state-issued identity cards, and Napoleon imposed them on the territories he occupied. Unable to count on the support of local elites in territories they occupied, French authorities built a registration system from scratch to contend with newly emancipated rural populations. In Sweden, Denmark, the German states, and the Habsburg territories people had to register with local authorities every time they moved.[22] Anyone who traveled from one place to another had to notify authorities, in some places within twenty-four hours of arrival, and file an *Anmeldung*, or announcement of appearance.[23] This listed his or her name, business, date and place of birth, religion, former residence, and marital status. Employing new servants, the birth of a child, or a change of residence within the city limits, even a vacation, also required police notification. Similar requirements existed throughout the region. The great originality of the Central European systems was to create state-sanctioned, official lists that certified people's identity, instead of relying on newcomers' declarations, as the Paris police did up to that time. They recorded more personal information than had ever been kept in France.

21. Milliot, "La surveillance des migrants," 63–73.
22. United Nations, "Methodology and Evaluation of Population Registers and Similar Systems," *Studies in Methods*, ser. F, no. 15 (1969); Dorothy S. Thomas, "The Continuous Register System of Population Accounting," in *The Problems of a Changing Population* (Washington, D.C.: U.S. Government Printing Office, 1938), 276–97; and Andreas Fahrmeir, *Citizens and Aliens: Foreigners and the Law in Britain and the German States 1789–1870* (New York: Berghahn, 2000), 102–4.
23. Fosdick, *European Police Systems*, 351.

But the German systems, unlike the French, applied to everyone, nationals and foreigners alike. Many Central European cities, like Vienna, it is true, kept lists of foreigners separately.[24] As under the old regime in France, subjects or citizens of foreign states occupied a distinct legal status in nineteenth-century Central Europe, and poor foreigners were especially vulnerable. Authorities stopped them at the border or, on occasion, expelled them, usually following political upheaval or a particularly severe economic crisis.[25] State membership, however, was only one measure of "foreignness," and everyone needed documents to travel. Repressive measures threatened any potential public charge or political nuisance, no matter where they came from.[26] In Prussia, the ID Card and Aliens Police (Paß- und Fremdenpolizei) targeted all itinerants, vagrants, and wandering journeymen.[27] Before central states took over poor relief from municipalities, they remained just as worried about the poor peasant from the next village as the foreign worker from farther afield. According to Alf Lüdke, the "main victims of administrative hostility . . . were not 'criminals' or foreign, or revolutionary, 'emissaries,' but those considered 'fully able to work, but lacking the willingness to do so.' "[28] Few German states collected detailed information on resident aliens.[29]

For all the information they contained on individuals, population registries provided little information about ethno-religious minorities or professional groups. Registries that were organized alphabetically by name made it difficult to monitor segments of the population by any other criteria, even when authorities wanted to do so. They were simply too unwieldy to monitor subsets of the population. By the turn of the twentieth century, the Berlin registry housed records on some twelve million current and former residents. Names beginning with the letter *H* alone filled ten rooms; the letter *S* filled fifteen.[30] In the last quarter of the nineteenth century, a handful of major metropolitan police forces began to experiment with new

24. Wiener Stadt- und Landesarchiv, Konskriptionsamt/Volkszählung 1857, Konskriptionsbögen Wien-Leopoldstadt Haus Nr. 742 (1857), http://homepage.univie.ac.at/heinrich .berger/leo/quellen.html.
25. Cf. Sahlins, *Unnaturally French*, 189–97, and Fahrmeir, *Citizens and Aliens*, 187–93.
26. Fahrmeir, "Paßwesen und Staatsbildung im Deutschland des 19. Jahrhunderts," *Historische Zeitschrift* 271 (2000): 68–69; Fahrmeir, "Nineteenth-Century German Citizenships: A Reconsideration," *Historical Journal* 40 (1997): 734–36; Fahrmeir, *Citizens and Aliens*, 196–97; and Leo Lucassen, "A Many-Headed Monster: The Evolution of Passport Systems in the Netherlands and Germany in the Long Nineteenth Century," in *Documenting Individual Identity*, 54–55.
27. Alf Lüdke, *Police and State in Prussia*, trans. Pete Burgess (1982; Cambridge: Cambridge University Press, 1989), 77–89, and esp. 110.
28. Lüdke, *Police and State in Prussia*, 87. See also George Steinmetz, *Regulating the Social: The Welfare State and Local Politics in Imperial Germany* (Princeton: Princeton University Press, 1993), 113–18.
29. Fahrmeir, "Nineteenth-Century German Citizenships," 736 n. 87.
30. Fosdick, *European Police Systems*, 353.

archival techniques. They labeled increasing numbers of groups and behaviors as deviant and created a welter of smaller, specialized indexes and file systems to monitor potential threats to law and order.[31] Records of Sinta and Roma, for example, were kept separately, beginning with the creation of a "Gypsy information center" in 1899 in Bavaria.[32] In the 1930s, when the Nazis sought to isolate and identify German Jews, they created new card file systems rather than working through the existing population registries, which already recorded religion.[33]

Foreigners appear to have caused little concern at German police headquarters until just before World War II. With the advent of German unification in 1871, moving from town to town was less likely to entail crossing national boundaries; one of the region's most important migration systems, linking the East Prussian plains to the coalfields and factories of the Ruhr valley, was now within the national territory. In the early years of the Kaiserreich, German authorities worried less about the small number of foreign-born workers than about the millions of Poles, Danes, Sorbs, and Alsatians the new nation incorporated—often against their will—and who threatened to embroil the country in conflicts with its neighbors. As late as 1890, 99.8 percent of Polish speakers in Prussia had German citizenship.[34] Even after the creation of Bismarck's social welfare programs, the local *Länder* (or states) retained control over residence permits, access to bene-

31. For Berlin, Hermann Dennstedt and Willibald Von Wolffsburg, *Preussisches Polizei-Lexikon . . . Ein praktisches Hülfsbuch für Polizeibeamte und zur allgemeinen Belehrung für Jedermann*, 6 vols. (Berlin: W. Moeser, 1855–56), 1:774–82; for Hamburg, Gustav Roscher, *Großstadtpolizei: Eine praktisches Handbuch der deutschen Polizei* (Hamburg: O. Meissner, 1912), 71, 218–22; and, for the Ruhr, Ralph Jessen, "Polizei, Wohlfahrt und die Anfänge des modernen Sozialstaats in Preußen während des Kaisserreichs," *Geschichte und Gesellschaft* 20, no. 2 (1994): 157–80. See also Becker, *Verderbnis und Entartung*, 61–74, 189–93, 343–44; and Vec, *Die Spur des Täters*, 67–75.

32. Leo Lucassen, *Zigeuner: Die Geschichte eines polizeilichen Ordnungsbegriffes in Deutschland, 1700–1945* (Vienna: Böhlau, 1996), 175–88.

33. In large, cosmopolitan cities, such as Frankfurt am Main and Berlin, with the largest concentrations of Jews, the Gestapo generally coerced local Jewish organizations into providing updated information. For the most thorough study of these questions, see Jutta Wietog, *Volkszählungen unter dem Nationalsozialismus: Eine Dokumentation sur Bevölkerungsstatistik im Dritten Reich* (Berlin: Duncker and Humblot, 2001), esp. 68–80. For a greater stress on the central state's role in gathering information, see Saul Friedländer, *Nazi Germany and the Jews*, vol. 1, *The Years of Persecution, 1933–1939* (New York: HarperCollins, 1997), 194–203; Holger Berschel, *Bürokratie und Terror: Das Judenreferat der Gestapo Düsseldorf, 1935–1945* (Essen: Klartext, 2001), 171–204; Michael Wildt's introduction to *Die Judenpolitik des SD 1935 bis 1938: Eine Dokumentation* (Munich: R. Oldenbourg, 1995), 25–37; and Götz Aly and Karl Heinz Roth, *Die restlose Erfassung: Volkszählen, Identifizieren, Aussondern im Nationalsozialismus*, rev. ed. (1984; Frankfurt-am-Main: Fischer Taschenbuch, 2000), 67–105.

34. Dieter Gosewinkel, *Einbürgern und Ausschließen: Die Nationalisierung der Staatsangehörigkeit vom Deutschen Bund bis zur Budesrepublik Deutschland* (Göttingen: Vandenhoeck and Ruprecht, 2001), 178–218, here at 188. See also Torpey, *Invention of the Passport: Surveillance, Citizenship and the State* (Cambridge: Cambridge University Press, 2000), 71–92.

fits, and expulsion. Legal residence (*Wohnsitz*) rather than nationality governed access to benefits.[35] In the mid-1890s, under pressure from estate owners east of the Elbe, Prussian authorities allowed foreign Polish seasonal workers to arrive in considerable numbers at the great estates but forbade their traveling to the industrial regions of the Ruhr, where they might foment trouble with the Polish speakers there, German citizens who had already fled East Prussia. The new administrative measures, without legal foundation, forced all foreign Poles to register with the private Central Farm Bureau and to leave the territory for a fixed "closure period" every year.[36] Soon afterward, Prussian police forces extended control over industrial workers as well, and neighboring Länder gradually followed suit. The central state, however, only centralized control of the labor market and gave preference to its own nationals after World War I. By that time there were very few foreigners left in the country, and tracking nationality was a marginal concern.[37] The effort to create a single, unified national population registry, for example, undertaken in the late 1930s, applied only to ethnic Germans (*Volksgenossen*). Even in Hamburg, whose identification practices served as a model for the rulers of the Third Reich, whole neighborhoods escaped police control; authorities had to level an entire section of the port city to eliminate hiding places. As Götz Aly and Karl Heinz Roth have written, "Avoiding registration [before 1938] was considered a kind of national sport. . . . Only people who often traveled abroad bothered with identification papers. It simply was not common practice to carry identification within the borders of the Reich."[38]

In France, too, and especially Paris, efforts to track migrants by nationality remained an afterthought before World War I. Criminologists and police departments in France, like their counterparts elsewhere in Europe, looked primarily for new ways to identify "born criminals" and to contain

35. Steinmetz, *Regulating the Social*, 112–14; and Gosewinkel, *Einbürgern und Ausschließen*, 218–33, esp. 222.

36. Klaus Bade, "'Preußgänger' und 'Abwehrpolitik': Ausländerbeschäftigung, Ausländerpolitik und Ausländerkontrolle auf dem Arbeitsmarkt in Preußen vor dem Ersten Weltkrieg," *Archiv für Sozialgeschichte* 24 (1984): 91–162, esp. 111–30; and Knuth Dohse, *Ausländische Arbeiter und bürgerlicher Staat: Genese und Funktion von staatlicher Ausländerpolitik und Ausländerrecht. Vom Kaiserreich bis zur Bundesrepublik Deutschland* (Königstein: Anton Hain, 1981), 67–69.

37. Ulrich Herbert, *A History of Foreign Labor in Germany: Seasonal Workers/Forced Laborers/Guest Workers*, trans. William Templer (1986; Ann Arbor: University of Michigan Press, 1990), 34–37; Joachim Lehmann, "Ausländerbeschäftigung und Fremdarbeiterpolitik im faschistischen Deutschland," in Klaus Bade, ed., *Auswanderer, Wanderarbeiter, Gastarbeiter: Bevölkerung, Arbeitsmarkt und Wanderung in Deutschland seit der Mitte des 19. Jahrhunderts*, 2 vols. (Ostfildern: Scripta Mercaturae, 1984), 2:558–83.

38. Aly and Roth, *Die restlose Erfassung*, 132–33, quote on 160–61; and Lehmann, "Ausländerbeschäftigung und Fremdarbeiterpolitik," 566, who also stresses the porousness of controls on foreigners. For a different view, Ulrich Herbert, *Hitler's Foreign Workers: Enforced Foreign Labor in Germany under the Third Reich*, trans. William Templer (1985; Cambridge: Cambridge University Press, 1997), 411 n. 106.

strike activity. Having joined the Prefecture of Police as a clerk in 1879, Alphonse Bertillon developed an immensely influential method to identify repeat offenders, known as *bertillonage*, that soon became familiar to policemen across the Continent. He began from the observation that human bone structure is essentially fixed by age twenty and that individuals' skeletal measurements differ markedly from one another. Where physical anthropologists had previously searched for regular patterns within groups or races, Bertillon created a descriptive index based on stable measurements unique to each individual. To complement this approach, he devised the so-called *portrait parlé*, the spoken portrait, which listed marks or scars as well as distinctive features. In 1888 Prefect of Police Louis Lépine placed him in charge of the Prefecture's new Criminal Identification Department, where he organized new record-keeping systems for his anthropometric measurements, and later fingerprints and photographs of individuals and crime scenes. But he and his superiors remained preoccupied with the so-called undeserving poor, from wherever they came, for decades after the country had begun receiving massive numbers of foreign nationals in the second half of the nineteenth century.[39]

III

By the middle decades of the eighteenth century, the French capital emerged as a center of migration, both from within the kingdom and beyond, and massive numbers continued to arrive for over a hundred years.[40] Vast numbers of peasant migrants came to the capital from the French countryside over the course of the nineteenth century, with peaks during the July Monarchy and the Second Empire (1852–70). Despite riots and a devastating cholera epidemic, the Parisian population increased 10 percent between 1831 and 1836. In fifty years, from 1801 to 1851, the number of Parisians doubled. At midcentury, just over a third of the Parisian population had been born within the city limits.[41] During the second half of the century, the population of the Department of the Seine more than doubled, rising from almost 1.5 million to over 3.6 million, and the suburbs grew even faster.

39. See John Merriman, *Police Stories: Building the French State, 1815–1851* (Oxford: Oxford University Press, 2005), chap. 5, as well as the work of Kaluszynski, About, and Nye in note 3 above.

40. Roche, "Les migrants parisiens au XVIIIe siècle," *Cahiers d'histoire*, no. 3 (1979): 3–20; Roche, *Le peuple de Paris*, chap. 1; Bernard Marchand, *Paris, histoire d'une ville: XIXe–XXe siècle* (Paris: Seuil, 1993), chap. 1; Louis Chevalier, *La formation de la population parisienne* (Paris: Puf, 1950); and Alain Faure and Jean-Claude Farcy, *La mobilité d'une génération de français: Recherche sur les migrations et les déménagements vers et dans Paris à la fin du XIXe siècle* (Paris: Ined, 2003).

41. That proportion remained constant at least until the turn of the twentieth century. Chevalier, *La formation de la population parisienne*, 45–46.

The capital was far and away the nation's leading magnet of immigration throughout the century.[42]

Until the mid-nineteenth century, most immigrants came from the surrounding countryside, the plains of the Île-de-France, including the Brie, and the Valois, and from northern agricultural regions in crisis, especially Flanders and Picardy. In addition to the main reservoir in the north, small but important streams came from the Auvergne and Limousin regions.[43] Later on, as the rail network made travel easier, recruitment became increasingly national. Workers came from the Massif Central, especially the Creuse and the Loire, and, toward the end of the century, from Brittany as well. After the great urban planner Baron Georges-Eugène Haussmann cleared the center of Paris, new immigrants and native Parisians begrudgingly moved, first to peripheral neighborhoods and ultimately to the industrial suburbs.[44] They established residential patterns that have been followed by immigrants down to the present day.

Toward the end of the nineteenth century, after migration from the Auvergne and the Creuse had subsided and while the Bretons were still arriving en masse, French rural migrants were joined by foreigners. Italians came first, settling in eastern Paris and the northern suburbs during the early Third Republic and dominating the building trades. During the 1880s, eastern European Jews came to the Marais, working as peddlers, leather workers, seamstresses and tailors, and later as lawyers and doctors. Those groups continued to grow after World War I and were joined by Russian émigrés, Spaniards, Czechs, and Romanians, as well as North Africans, who were not strictly speaking foreigners.[45]

42. Ibid., 39–42, 145–48; and Jean Bastié, *La croissance de la banlieue parisienne* (Paris: Puf, 1964), 213–23.

43. Chevalier, *La formation de la population parisienne*; Philippe Ariès, "La population parisienne," in his *Histoire des populations françaises et de leurs attitudes devant la vie depuis le XVIIIe siècle* (1948; Paris: Seuil, 1971), 169–70; Alain Corbin, "Les paysans de Paris: Histoire des Limousins du bâtiment au XIXe siècle," *Ethnologie française* 10 (1980): 169–76; Françoise Raison-Jourde, *La colonie auvergnate de Paris au XIXe siècle* (Paris: Commission des travaux historiques de la Ville de Paris, 1976); and Gaillard, *Paris, la ville*, esp. 143–45.

44. Gaillard, *Paris, la ville*, 146–55; Gérard Jacquemet, *Belleville au XIXe siècle: Du faubourg à la ville* (Paris: Ehess, 1984), 101–2, 111–15, 222–26; and Bastié, *La croissance de la banlieue parisienne*, 213–23; but cf. Alain Faure, "Transfuges et colons: Le rôle des parisiens dans le peuplement des banlieues, 1880–1914," and Jean-Claude Farcy, "L'immigration provinciale en banlieue au début du XXe siècle," both in *Immigration, vie politique et populisme en banlieue parisienne, fin XIXe–XXe siècles*, ed. Jean-Paul Brunet (Paris: Harmattan, 1995), 29–48, 49–68; and Faure, ed., *Les premiers banlieusards: Aux origines des banlieues parisiennes, 1860–1940* (Paris: Créaphis, 1991).

45. Faure and Farcy, *La mobilité d'une génération de Français*; Laurent Couder, "Les immigrés italiens dans la région parisienne pendant les années 1920: Contribution à l'histoire du fait migratoire en France au XXe siècle" (thèse de doctorat, nouveau régime, Institut d'Études Politiques, 1987); Marie-Claude Blanc-Chaléard, *Les italiens dans l'est parisien des années 1880 aux années 1960: Une histoire d'intégration* (Rome: École française de Rome, 2000); Nancy L. Green, *The Pletzl of Paris: Jewish Immigrant Workers in the Belle Epoque* (New York: Holmes and Meier, 1986); *Le Paris des étrangers depuis un siècle*, ed. André Kaspi and Antoine Marès (Paris: Imprimerie nationale, 1989); Annie Benveniste, *Le Bosphore à la*

There had always been foreigners in Paris—during the nineteenth century they made up between 5 and 7 percent of the population. Before World War I, Paris had three times as many foreigners as the other great European capitals. In 1911, foreigners made up 6.8 percent of the Parisian population, compared to 3 percent in London, 2.6 percent in Berlin, and 2 percent in Vienna.[46] Between 1911 and 1926, however, their numbers doubled in absolute terms, and their character changed as well. Italian models, actors, and musicians; Swiss nannies; German craftsmen and bankers—they were not all as wealthy as Balzac's Baron de Nucingen, but only a minority were unskilled workers. That would soon change.

During the war, Germans, Austrians, Swiss, and, to a lesser extent, Belgians left France, either to fight under their own flags or to avoid being jailed for draft evasion or conscripted into the French army. After the armistice in the decade after the war ended, hundreds of thousands of Italians, eastern European Jews, Spaniards, Russians, Armenians, and Algerians came in search of jobs and a safe haven (see figure 2 and table 1). The composition of Paris's immigrant community was transformed, especially between 1923 and 1926; in 1923 the number of residency declarations received at the Prefecture of Police soared to sixty-seven thousand, almost thirty thousand more than the previous year.[47] By the mid-1920s over 10 percent of Paris's four million inhabitants, and about 20 percent of its manual laborers, were foreign born.[48] Over the course of the decade of the '20s, the capital's immigrant population more than doubled, and Paris remained a center of attraction even after the national immigration rate lowered, especially for Jewish refugees from Central Europe rejected by every other Western country.[49] Paris also attracted a significant number of foreign workers from the provinces whose contracts had expired, or who broke valid contracts, and who did not want to return "home."[50] At the peak of interwar immigration,

---

Roquette: *La communauté judéo-espagnole à Paris, 1914–1940* (Paris: Harmattan, 1989); and Chokry Ben Fredj, "Aux origines de l'émigration nord-africaine en France" (thèse d'histoire, Université de Paris VII, 1990).

46. Ariès, "La population parisienne," 185.

47. Cons. mun., *Rap. et doc.*, no. 153 (10 December 1923), 5, reports that 63,868 declarations were received from 1 January to 15 November 1923, about 28,000 more than the previous year.

48. "La main d'œuvre étrangère dans la région parisienne," 21 March 1925, APP B/a 67ᴾ, dossier 331.500–A, ouvriers étrangers en France—pièces de principe. Jean-Paul Brunet, "Une banlieue ouvrière: Saint-Denis, 1898–1939: Problèmes d'implantation du socialisme et du communisme," Thèse d'État (Lille: Service de reproduction des thèses, 1982), 3:792–806, provides demographic information for the entire Department of the Seine.

49. See esp. Pinelli, "Rapport au nom de la 2e Commission, sur le fonctionnement des services de la Préfecture de police au cours de l'année 1938," Cons. mun., *Rap. et doc.*, no. 39 (1939), 31.

50. Olivier Le Guillou, "Des émigrés russes ouvriers aux usines Renault de Boulogne-Billancourt en 1926: Étude de fichier de personnel" (Maîtrise, Université de Paris I, 1988), 95; APP D/b 341; Préfet de Police to Monsieur le Ministre de l'Intérieur (Direction de la Sûreté générale), 25 January 1921; APP D/b 336, dossier Étrangers; and APP D/a 745, dossier Etat-civil . . . extrait d'immatriculation. More generally, see Georges Mauco, "Le problème des étrangers en France," *Revue de Paris*, no. 18 (1935): 375–407.

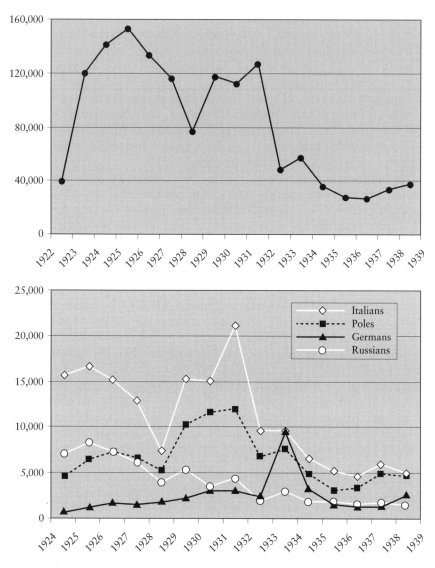

Figure 2a (top). Arrivals of foreign migrants to Paris, total.
Figure 2b (bottom). Arrivals of foreign migrants to Paris, by nationality.

Source: Cons. mun., *Rap. et doc.* Where results were provided in November or December (1924–31), I have projected annual totals. Many foreigners came to Paris on more than one occasion and are thus counted repeatedly in these figures. Although foreigners continued to arrive throughout the interwar years, their share of the population remained steady from 1926 to 1931 and declined thereafter. In 1921 foreigners made up 5.3 percent of inhabitants of Paris and its suburbs; that proportion rose to 9.3 percent in 1926 and remained there in 1931, declining to 8.2 percent in 1936. Jean-Paul Brunet, "Une banlieue ouvrière: Saint-Denis, 1890–1939: Problèmes d'implantation du socialisme et du communisme," Thèse d'État (1978; Lille: Service de Réproduction des Thèses, 1982), 3:793.

TABLE 1
Immigrants by nationality, Department of the Seine, 1921–26

	1926	Increase 1921–1926
Italians	101,800	95%
Belgians	50,200	0%
Russians	44,500	120%
Poles	36,300	145%
Spaniards	31,500	86%
Africans (mostly North Africans)	27,500	340%
Turks-Armenians	18,300	900%
Asians	13,600	91%
Czechs	6,600	245%
Other	102,800	—
Total	433,100	98%

Source: Census figures from Georges Mauco, *Les étrangers en France: Leur rôle dans l'activité économique* (Paris: Armand Colin, 1932), 285.
Note: Based on census figures, which undercount the immigration population.

in 1926, foreigners made up 10.2 percent of the *intra muros* population, and 9.3 percent of the Department of the Seine as a whole.[51] There were nearly three times as many foreigners in Paris as there were in all of Germany.[52]

As the foreign population changed, it became increasingly like the French peasant migrant population that preceded it. The new foreign migrants were also disproportionately single, young, working-class men. In cultural terms, a significant number of foreign migrants may actually have been closer to Parisian norms than some of their rural French counterparts. The Italian masons who came from Piedmont and the Val Nure to Nogent, for example, spoke dialects that were closer to the Parisian langue d'oïl than those of the Breton maids and cafe waiters who arrived at the same time. As the son of an Italian mason and a French peasant woman from Burgundy, François Cavanna, remembered in his classic account of growing up in the eastern suburbs: "Well, one thing that cracked him up, papa, was that rednecks who spoke French bumpkin patois could understand his *dialetto*, and he could understand their Limousin. *Ça, alors!*" To the young François, his father Luigi's dialect sounded just like his maternal grandfather Charvin's Movandiau. It sounded closer to the patois of the Nièvre, in fact, than to Dante's Italian.[53] While political considerations increasingly weighed on the migration decisions of Italians and Jews during the interwar years, many, if not most, foreign migrants like Cavanna's father performed the same jobs and settled in the same neighborhoods as the French peasants who came before them.[54]

51. Brunet, "Une banlieue ouvrière," 2:793.
52. Herbert, *History of Foreign Labor in Germany*, 121.
53. Cavanna, *Les ritals* (Paris: Belfond, 1978), 67–70, quote on 67.
54. Nancy L. Green, Laura Levine Frader, and Pierre Milza, "Paris: City of Light and Shadow," in *Distant Magnets: Expectations and Realities in the Immigrant Experience, 1840–1930*, ed. Dirk Hoerder and Horst Rössler (New York: Holmes and Meier, 1993), 34–51.

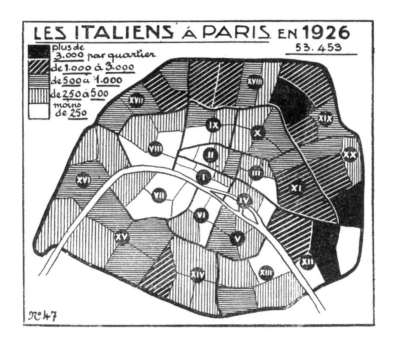

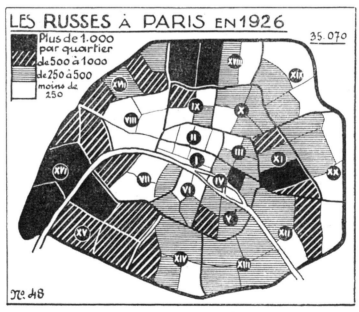

Figure 3. Geographic distribution of foreigners in Paris, 1926.

Source: Georges Mauco, *Les étrangers en France: Leur rôle dans l'activité économique* (Paris: Armand Colin, 1932), 288, 291, 294.

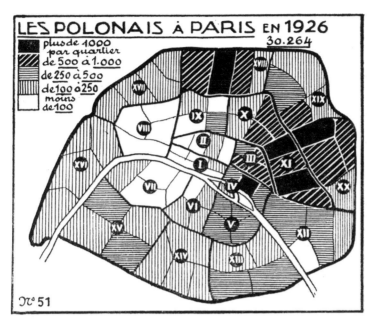

LES POLONAIS à PARIS EN 1926

30.264

- plus de 1000 par quartier
- de 500 à 1.000
- de 250 à 500
- de 100 à 250
- moins de 100

N° 51

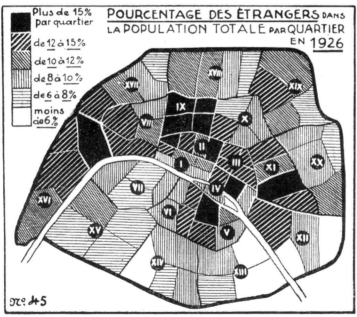

- Plus de 15% par quartier
- de 12 à 15%
- de 10 à 12%
- de 8 à 10%
- de 6 à 8%
- moins de 6%

POURCENTAGE DES ÉTRANGERS DANS LA POPULATION TOTALE PAR QUARTIER EN 1926

N° 45

Migration reached impressive levels in interwar Paris, causing concern for politicians and the public alike. But neither the scale nor the social dislocation of foreign immigration between the wars exceeded problems experienced during the nineteenth century. Overcrowding and disease posed far greater risks to the capital in the 1830s than they did a century later, and the social conflicts of the July Monarchy pitted indigenous elites against poor newcomers far more often. Louis Chevalier has been roundly criticized, and rightly so, for blaming the city's problems on peasant migrants.[55] It was not the migrants themselves but the awful conditions that awaited them in the city that posed problems. Jeanne Gaillard showed that peasant migrants were more active, younger, and taller than native-born Parisians and Alain Faure has confirmed that newcomers were no more likely to succumb to disease.[56] No one, however, can deny the strains placed on the city by the population explosion or the fears poor immigrants inspired in middle-class observers.

A generation of scholars has dismissed the "uprooting thesis" championed by Chevalier in France and Oscar Handlin in the United States, but they have overlooked the importance of elite anxieties, irrational as they may have been. The novels of Honoré de Balzac and Eugène Sue, in particular, are filled with bestial descriptions of the working poor, depicting them as lascivious, lazy, and biologically alien. The temporary rural migrants of the mid-nineteenth century had terrible difficulty fitting into the Parisian working class. Dr. Parent-Duchâtelet's famous *De la prostitution dans la ville de Paris* (1836) suggested a system of "seminal sewers" to protect the social body from these new arrivals.[57] For Balzac, like Parent-Duchâtelet, the Parisian poor posed a terrifying threat of violence and disease, and he could not imagine their ever becoming fully human.[58] Chevalier admirably expressed the view of nineteenth-century elites in his 1958 classic, *Laboring Classes, Dangerous Classes*, when he wrote of a "fundamental *biological difference* that made this people different in its very body, condemned by

55. Barrie Ratcliffe, "Classes Laborieuses et classes dangereuses à Paris pendant la première moitié du XIXe siècle? The Chevalier Thesis Reexamined," *French Historical Studies* 17, no. 2 (Fall 1991): 542–74.

56. Gaillard, *Paris, la ville*, 155–63; Jacquemet, *Belleville au XIXe siècle*, 249–53; and see also Jacquemet, "Aspects de la condition des milieux populaires dans un quartier de Paris entre les deux guerres mondiales," in *Villes et campagnes, XVe–XXe siècles* (Lyon: Presses universitaires, 1977), 325–56. Faure supports their conclusions in "Paris, 'gouffre de l'espèce humaine'?" *French Historical Studies* 27, no. 1 (Winter 2004): 49–86.

57. *De la prostitution dans la ville de Paris considérée sous le rapport de l'hygiène publique, de la morale et de l'administration* (1836; Paris: Seuil, 1981). On Parent-Duchâtelet, see Alain Corbin, *Les filles de noce: Misère sexuelle et prostitution, XIXe siècle* (Paris: Flammarion, 1982), esp. part 1a and 275–78; and Chevalier, *Classes laborieuses et classes dangereuses*.

58. See esp. the opening of *La fille aux yeux d'or* in vol. 5 of *La comédie humaine*, 12 vols., ed. Pierre-Georges Castex (Paris: Gallimard, 1976–81).

that body to every ugliness and vileness."[59] A substantial number of nineteenth-century bourgeois saw the working poor as biologically alien, a separate "nation," formed by a different breeding, fed by different food, ordered by different manners, and governed by different mores.[60] During the Commune of 1871, the forces of Louis-Adolphe Thiers massacred thousands of the overwhelmingly immigrant "barbarians."[61]

Even before foreign migrants started to arrive in massive numbers in the late nineteenth century, the means that local authorities used to identify marginal populations began to break down. As the nineteenth century progressed, the immigrant-sending reservoirs became more and more distant from the Paris basin. As this happened, verifying migrants' identities became increasingly difficult. Even native-born Parisians had a hard time proving their identity after the Communards burned the Hôtel de Ville, and with it millions of birth certificates. Politicians floated schemes to centralize all French citizens' birth, death, and marriage records (*état civil*). They provided family booklets (*livrets de famille*) free of charge, which certified vital information for entire households, allowing them to claim new welfare benefits and ensuring that they did not change their name to avoid the policeman.[62] If people needed written documents to prove their identity by the nineteenth century, the standard of proof remained unclear into the twentieth.[63]

In this context, foreigners posed an acute problem. Many came to France without birth certificates, and there was no practical means of verifying the information even if the immigrant did have one. Foreigners had a much harder time producing any of the other, less formal proofs of identity that French citizens still used, whether military discharge papers or notes from a hometown priest, mayor, or other notable. This was true throughout the country for decades after foreign immigration took on massive proportions.

French authorities took action in Paris first in part because of its importance as the nation's capital and the resources at its disposal but also because of a revolution that transformed the city's political landscape. Traditionally governed against the interests of its poor inhabitants, Paris politics shifted to the right at the turn of the twentieth century. Instead of seeking to

59. Chevalier, *Classes laborieuses*, 631, my emphasis.
60. Benjamin Disraeli, *Sybil, or the Two Nations* (1845; Ware, Herefordshire: Wordsworth, 1995), 58.
61. Of the 36,309 people who appeared before the conseils de guerre after the Commune, only 8,841 were born in the Department of the Seine; the 1872 census recorded 1,986,972 residents of the capital, 642,718 Parisians and 1,344,254 immigrants from the countryside and abroad. Marchand, *Paris: Histoire d'une ville*, 121.
62. Pierre Piazza, *Histoire de la carte nationale d'identité* (Paris: Odile Jacob, 2004), 77–78.
63. Cf. Denis, "Individu, identité et identification en France."

protect themselves from the capital city, national leaders found themselves besieged by demands from its local politicians to work together against a common enemy.

IV

For most of the nineteenth century, and indeed for hundreds of years before that, central authorities feared the capital city and especially its poor inhabitants. Royal and imperial forces always worried about local government as well as the unruly masses. Under the old regime, royal authorities never allowed Parisians to form a commune. The city's first mayor, Jean-Sylvain Bailly, proved singularly unable to control the people of Paris in 1789, and his successors fared no better. The role of the first Paris Commune in the outbreak and radicalization of the French Revolution made the Hôtel de Ville and the office of mayor potent symbols of revolution, and every subsequent regime over the course of the nineteenth century tried to minimize the importance of the city government. The Directory (1795–99) and the First Empire (1804–14) deprived the city of local representation, imposing a prefect to direct the city's affairs. In 1834, the July Monarchy formalized Paris's exceptional legal status, making it the only city governed by a prefect and a prefect of police instead of an elective mayor. While the Revolution of 1848 briefly revived the position of mayor, he remained firmly under the control of central authorities, and the position was abolished as soon as order was restored. Despite the best efforts of national leaders, the people of Paris imposed their political will on the nation repeatedly from 1789 to 1794, in 1830, and again in 1848, before the Commune was crushed in 1871.

After putting down the most violent urban rebellion of the century, the founders of the Third Republic, like their forebears, sought to keep the capital from deciding the nation's political fate. Although they allowed Parisians to elect a municipal council, they granted a disproportionate number of seats to wealthy, center-city districts at the expense of the working-class suburbs and deprived the city of an elective mayor. Instead, they named mayors for each of the city's twenty arrondissements. Central authorities required that voting be by quartier instead of the larger arrondissement to maintain a personal link between the representatives and their constituents, and they replaced voting by list with a simple majority to further limit the scope of party politics. The elected councilors named their own president, but his powers paled next to those of the prefect. The state's representative convened all four regular sessions of the municipal council, which lasted at least ten days and no longer than one month. Above all, he supervised its proceedings. Article 14 of the 14 April 1871 law governing the council enjoined the prefect to quash any deliberations

that strayed from municipal affairs, that had any hint of a political procla-
mation.[64]

This political reorganization, along with Haussmann's clearing of the
center city and the defeat of the Commune, put an end to the threat of left-
wing revolt within the city limits. The workers had either been killed or
forced beyond the fortifications into the suburbs, transforming the city's
balance of political power. That transformation ushered in a new breed of
local politician who was only too willing to resort to hard-line measures
and work with national leaders instead of fighting them. The revolution in
Parisian politics at the turn of the twentieth century played a critical role in
changing the focus of immigrant surveillance, a role far more important
than the changing nature of the immigrant communities themselves.

The political transformation of the capital was largely complete by the
turn of the twentieth century. Once a radical republican city with a venerable Jacobin tradition, Paris moved decisively to the right. The municipal
council and parliamentary delegation, for decades supported by a coalition
of workers, shopkeepers, and small businessmen, passed into the hands of
nationalists aligned with elements of the traditional Right in 1900; the new
right established itself definitively in 1909. They increasingly courted poor
and middle-class French voters, squeezed economically by the development
of heavy industry and large department stores, by demonizing foreigners, as
Maurice Barrès did in his 1893 election campaign for the Chamber.[65] In
1900 the council welcomed the Boer leader, Paul Kruger, to the Hôtel de
Ville to strike a symbolic blow in the name of small-owner values against
Anglo-Jewish finance.[66]

A number of anti-Dreyfusard leaders and militants won seats in the municipal council and remained there for decades, where they fulminated
against central authority and cracked down on foreign immigrants.[67] Among
those who pushed for tighter controls on foreigners before World War I were
Henri Galli, leader of the virulently anti-Semitic Ligue des patriotes after Paul

64. Félix, *Le régime administratif*, esp. 1:233–34, 2:651–53, 2:664–66, 2:786–87; Henri
Chrétien, *De l'organisation du Conseil municipal de Paris* (Paris: Giard et Brière, 1906); Hec-
tor Depasse, *Paris, son maire et sa police* (Paris: Flammarion, 1886); Alfred des Cilleuls, *L'administration parisienne sous la Troisième République* (Paris: Picard fils, 1910); Conseil municipal, *Attributions et pouvoirs du conseil municipal de Paris avant et après les décrets lois des 21
avril et 13 juin 1939 complétés par l'ordonnance du 13 avril 1945* (Paris: Imprimerie municipale, 1950); and Combeau, *Paris et les élections municipales*, 23–28, 65–70.
65. Barrès, *Contre les étrangers: Étude pour la protection des ouvriers français* (Paris:
Grande Imprimerie Parisienne, 1893).
66. Nord, *Paris Shopkeepers and the Politics of Resentment* (Princeton: Princeton University Press, 1986), 441.
67. Combeau, *Paris et les élections municipales*; D. R. Watson, "The Nationalist Movement
in Paris, 1900–1906," in *The Right in France, 1890–1919: Three Studies*, ed. David Shapiro
(London: Chatto and Windus, 1962), 49–84; Pierre Birnbaum, "Paris leur appartient: La mobilisation électorale nationaliste en 1902," in his *"La France aus français": Histoire des haines
nationalistes* (Paris: Seuil, 1993), 221–36; and Nord, *Paris Shopkeepers*, esp. chaps. 8 and 9.

Déroulède's exile; Louis Dausset, general secretary and head of the Paris offices of the more conservative Ligue de la patrie française; Joseph Denais, director of Édouard Drumont's former newspaper, *La libre parole*; and fellow travelers Émile Massard and Jean Le Corbeiller.[68] After the war, they were joined by Noël Pinelli, who had connections to the paramilitary veterans' organization, the Croix de Feu, as well as with his fellow Corsican, the notorious prefect of police Jean Chiappe. During the 1920s the council added leaders from a considerable number of veterans' leagues, including Pierre Taittinger of the Jeunesses patriotes, and Georges Lebecq, André Boulard, and Raymond Laurant of the Union des combattants. By the mid-1930s, all of the major right-wing leagues had leaders in the municipal council, and on 6 February 1934 they orchestrated the greatest street violence since the Commune.[69] A year later, the president of the Association des victimes du 6 février joined their ranks. Louis Darquier de Pellepoix, the vulgar anti-Semitic henchman later in charge of Vichy's Commissariat général aux questions juives from 1942 to 1944, got his start in politics at the Hôtel de Ville.[70]

Before World War I, the xenophobic, anti-Semitic municipal councilors were held in check by more moderate ministers of the interior, who feared that right-wing anti-Dreyfusards would prove no less troublesome than left-wing revolutionaries. After the war, however, and especially after the police disbanded the antiparliamentary right-wing leagues,[71] moderate politicians began to fear poor migrants and the Left once again. Fear of immigrants increased dramatically during the red scare of 1919–20. Having heeded calls to support the war effort, workers had put their own interests on hold whenever the enemy advanced. Inspired by the Russian Revolution, however, and frustrated by the failure of politicians to deliver improved working conditions and a higher standard of living, they took to the streets.[72]

68. For biographical information, see Ernest Gay, *Nos édiles* (Paris: Nouvelle Revue française illustrée, 1895); Watson, "Nationalist Movement in Paris," esp. 71–73; Nord, *Paris Shopkeepers*, 372–469; *Dictionnaire biographique français contemporain* , vol. 2 (Paris: Pharos, 1955); Henry Coston, *Dictionnaire de la politique française* (Paris: Librairie française, 1967); Nath. Imbert, *Dictionnaire national des contemporains*, vol. 3 (Paris: R. Lajeunesse, 1939); *Les archives biographiques contemporaines*, 2nd series (1906–17).

69. Combeau, *Paris et les élections municipales*, 366–71; and, more generally, Serge Berstein, *Le 6 février 1934* (Paris: Armand Colin, 1975), and Paul Jankowski, *Stavisky: A Confidence Man in the Republic of Virtue* (Ithaca: Cornell University Press, 2002).

70. On Pinelli, Marc-Olivier Baruch, *Servir l'État français: L'administration en France de 1940 à 1944* (Paris: Fayard, 1997), 387; and Jacques Nobécourt, *Le colonel de la Rocque, 1885–1946, ou les pièges du nationalisme chrétien* (Paris: Fayard, 1996), 254, 683. On Darquier, see Michael R. Marrus and Robert O. Paxton, *Vichy France and the Jews* (New York: Basic Books, 1981), chap. 7; and Laurant Joly, *Darquier de Pellepoix et l'antisémitisme français* (Paris: Berg International, 2002).

71. Jean-Marc Berlière, "La généalogie d'une double tradition policière," in *La France de l'Affaire Dreyfus*, ed. Pierre Birnbaum (Paris: Gallimard, 1994), 191–225, esp. 206.

72. Jean-Louis Robert, "Ouvriers et mouvement ouvrier parisiens pendant la Grande Guerre et l'immédiat après-guerre: Histoire et anthropologie" (Thèse d'État, Université de

Authorities put down the Parisian strikes with overwhelming force, but they remained terrified of armed insurrection and singled out foreigners as special threats to domestic security. In the spring of 1919 a brief but intense wave of unemployment in Paris brought renewed demands to protect the labor market and to disqualify foreigners from receiving assistance. The severity of the crisis was limited in Paris by France's two-stage demobilization and by the massive layoffs of women and foreigners. London and, especially, Berlin suffered much higher rates of unemployment in 1919. Nevertheless, the crisis did appear severe to Parisians; as in the 1880s and 1890s, foreigners were held responsible for the crisis.[73] After the bloody suppression of the revolutionary strikes, thousands of strikers were sacked and the ringleaders imprisoned. The leading trade union, the Confédération général du travail (CGT), hemorrhaged, losing roughly one million members. In 1921 it was left with six hundred thousand bitterly divided members split into rival Communist and Socialist confederations.[74] Labor did not recover until the Popular Front of 1936. Officials nevertheless continued to fear the insurrectionary threat posed by foreigners.

Their wartime experience gave bureaucrats and elected politicians the confidence that they could achieve a much greater degree of control over society than they had previously imagined.[75] Caught up in the postwar red scare, mainstream national officials—most notably the moderate Radical Party members Albert Sarraut and Camille Chautemps—worked out a marriage of convenience with the right-wing leaders at the Hôtel de Ville and worked with them to control immigration.[76] Interior Minister Sarraut himself named Chiappe prefect of police. Faced with Communist anti-imperialism and the emergence of colonial nationalist movements both in

Paris I, 1989); Annie Kriegel, *Aux origines du communisme français, 1914–1920: Contribution à l'histoire du mouvement ouvrier français*, 2 vols. (Paris: Mouton, 1964); Jean-Paul Brunet, "Une Banlieue ouvrière, 2:875–938; and Georges Lefranc, *Le mouvement syndicale sous la Troisième République* (Paris: Payot, 1967).

73. *Capital Cities at War: Paris, London, Berlin, 1914–1919*, ed. Jay Winter and Jean-Louis Robert (New York: Cambridge University Press, 1997), 198, 209–11; and Antoine Prost, *Les anciens combattants et la société française*, 3 vols. (Paris: Presses de la Fondation National de Sciences Politiques, 1977), vol. 1. Cf. "Question de M. Paris à M. le Préfet de la Seine sur les mesures que l'Administration compte prendre pour combattre le chômage," Cons. mun., *Proc.-ver.* (11 February 1921), 68–78, esp. interventions of M. Missoffe; and "Ordre du jour sur une proposition de M. Michel Missoffe tendant à réserver aux ouvriers en chômage, de nationalité française, les secours en nature accordés par la Ville," Cons. mun., *Proc.-ver.* (18 February 1921), 221–23.

74. See the work of Robert, Kriegel, Brunet, and Lefranc cited above, as well as Robert, *La scission syndicale de 1921: Essai de reconnaissance des formes* (Paris: Publications de la Sorbonne, 1980).

75. See chapter 2.

76. On the rightward drift of the Radical Party, Serge Berstein, *Histoire du Parti Radical*, esp. vol. 2, *Le temps des crises et des mutations, 1926–1939* (Paris: Presses de la Fondation nationale des sciences politiques, 1982).

the metropole and overseas, even prominent progressive figures such as Marius Moutet and Henry Sellier became willing to work with leaders of the Far Right. Over the course of the 1920s, they supported efforts to control the capital's colonial population.

Ostensibly barred from political debate and limited exclusively to deciding administrative matters, the municipal government promised national leaders a certain measure of secrecy. Reporters tended to ignore the Hôtel de Ville, and overwhelming conservative majorities reduced the risk of damaging protests. The capital also had substantial means that even national authorities lacked. With their considerable array of hospitals and social programs, the city's Assistance publique and the Departmental Health Office (OPHS) overshadowed the infant national Ministry of Public Health, which had just emerged from Rockefeller programs after the war.[77] Even more potent, the Paris police dwarfed the national Sûreté générale; the latter only created a special immigration unit in 1934, and, when it did, it was modeled on the one at the Prefecture in Paris. While the minister of the interior appointed the prefect and the prefect of police, the municipal council drew up and paid roughly half its budget, and it often granted significant discretionary funds for special projects, which it paid from its own coffers. The new, right-wing majority's dogged pursuit of strict controls on foreigners hastened changes in Paris that did not begin elsewhere for at least a dozen years.

V

The desire to render society transparent, to know everything about everyone, extends back at least as far as the European Enlightenment, if not earlier. Faced with the impossibility of realizing these ambitions, police forces have had to give priority to some categories of people or places to watch over. Even when the terms themselves remained constant—police forces have always worried about foreigners, aliens, outsiders, and marginal types—the meaning of the terms has changed considerably over time. Allegiance to a prince, state membership, entered into police calculations in France and elsewhere in Europe in the early modern period, but it did not consistently take priority until national states took over poor relief from

77. Lion Murard and Patrick Zylberman, *L'hygiène dans la République: La santé publique en France, ou l'utopie contrariée, 1870–1914* (Paris: Fayard, 1996); Murard and Zylberman, "L'autre guerre, 1914–1918: La Santé publique en France sous l'œil de l'Amérique," *Revue historique* 560 (October–December 1986): 367–97; Murard and Zylberman, "La mission Rockefeller en France et la création du Comité national de défense contre la tuberculose, 1917–1923," *Revue d'histoire moderne et contemporaine* 34 (April–June 1987): 257–81; and Brigitte Mazon, "La Fondation Rockefeller et les sciences sociales en France, 1925–1940," *Revue française de sociologie* 26 (1985): 311–42.

municipal governments and recruited foreign workers to satisfy their labor needs. The second German Reich (1871–1918) created extensive social programs, and its police forces monitored society with an unusually invasive series of registers, indexes, and card files. But apart from a brief period around the turn of the twentieth century, urban authorities there worried little about nationality or citizenship status before the general Reich Registration Order of 1938.

Foreign immigration emerged as a major issue throughout France in the last two decades of the nineteenth century, especially during the years between the World Wars. In some areas of the north and east foreigners made up a much greater share of the population than in Paris, making up more than 90 percent of the workforce in crucial sectors of the economy. The subprefect in Briey in Lorraine noted in 1909 that his district, recently among the most desolate in France, had turned into a "second Transvaal." Villerupt, a nearby town of ten thousand, had residents of twenty-one nationalities in 1928. But the very prevalence of unskilled, foreign workers eased the challenge faced by local police forces and gendarmes. Studies of marriage records show that intermarriage remained quite rare at least through the 1920s. In French centers of heavy industry, riven by hierarchy and segregation, distinguishing foreigners from the native-born posed relatively few problems. A handful of major employers controlled the labor market; they recruited immigrants from one or two foreign countries, and they often controlled the local housing market and assistance programs as well. The authoritarian owners of the iron mines and steel plants of Lorraine brooked no opposition. According to Gérard Noiriel, strikes in the region were rare and generally ended in failure. After an abortive strike at Leforest in the coalfields of the Nord in 1934, employers fired thousands of Polish workers, and they paid for trains to deport them. The Chambre des Houillères du Nord et du Pas-de-Calais (mine-owners' association) reported sending home 4,744 of the 5,000 to 6,000 men they fired that year on seventeen convoys. If not all of the 140,000 Poles who left the Department of the Nord from 1931 to 1936 did so under duress, over two-thirds of those who left in 1934 told interviewers they had been forced out.[78]

Matters were more complicated in Lyon. With its mixed industrial economy and relatively diverse immigrant population it more resembled Paris. As Mary Lewis has shown, however, the local police there showed little in-

---

78. For the centers of heavy industry in the north and east, Noiriel, *Longwy, immigrés et prolétaires, 1880–1980* (Paris: Puf, 1984), 165–212, 215–220 on marriage patterns; 243–45 and 262 on strike activity; and Janine Ponty, *Polonais méconnus: Histoire des travailleurs immigrés en France dans l'entre-deux-guerres* (Paris: Publications de la Sorbonne, 1990), 105–12, 287–318, 342–50; for marriage patterns, 352–65; for the expulsions, 309–16. More generally, see Philippe Rygiel, ed., *Le bon grain et l'ivraie: L'état-nation et les populations immigrées, fin XIXe–début XXe siècle. Sélection des migrants et régulation des stocks de populations étrangères* (Paris: Presses de L'École Normale Supérieure, 2004).

terest in immigration control before the Depression. Transformed by the war, Lyon grew at a fantastic rate in the 1920s. The city's population increased almost 9 percent, and the suburbs grew even faster: 74 percent in Saint-Fons, 234 percent in Vénissieux, 462 percent in Vaux-en-Velin. With little experience of foreign immigration and few resources at their disposal, local authorities struggled to keep up. Other problems vied for their attention before the economic downturn of the 1930s.[79]

The other leading urban center of immigration between the wars, Marseille, was less thoroughly policed than Lyon. Jean-Marc Berlière suggests that Marseille had one policeman for every 604 inhabitants at the turn of the twentieth century, compared to at least one for every 575 in Lyon and one for every 316 in Paris.[80] Successive ministers of the interior denied requests to increase manpower in Marseille, and a byzantine chain of command further hampered law enforcement there. Local authorities relied on a traditional targeting of particular areas in the city, especially around the old port, ignoring the rest, until the Sûreté générale created an immigration service on the Parisian model in the aftermath of the Paris riot of February 1934.[81]

Recognizing the Paris Prefecture's role in pioneering new forms of surveillance, historians have routinely called it a "laboratory of police modernity."[82] Since at least the first decade of the eighteenth century, Paris has been at the center of bureaucratic efforts to control immigration, because of its role as national capital and the strength of its local police force. After the Dreyfus affair, political constraints on police action there lifted, and foreign nationals emerged as a target of concern in ways they had not before. Right-wing municipal councilors, eager to curry favor with poor French workers and shopkeepers, urged more cautious national leaders to take action, to pay special attention to foreign migrants in ways that other cities would later emulate.

79. Mary D. Lewis, "Les pratiques d'expulsion dans le Rhône durant la crise," in *Le bon grain et l'ivraie*, 154. See also Michel Laferrère, *Lyon, ville industrielle: Essai d'une géographie urbaine des techniques et des entreprises* (Paris: Puf, 1960). For an intermediate case, more diverse than the north and east but less urban than Lyon, see Philippe Rygiel's work on the Cher, "Refoulements et renouvellement des cartes de 'travailleur étranger,' dans le Cher durant les années trente," in ibid.; and *Destins immigrés, Cher 1920–1980: Trajéctoires d'immigrés d'Europe* (Besançon: Annales littéraires de l'université de Franche-Comté, 2001).

80. Berlière, *Le monde des polices en France, XIXe–XXe siècles* (Brussels: Complexe, 1996), 28. Mary Lewis contends that Berlière has relied on inflated population statistics and that the disparity is thus even greater between Lyon and Marseille: "The Company of Strangers: Immigration and Citizenship in Interwar Lyon and Marseille" (PhD diss., New York University, 2000), 96 n. 35.

81. Cf. Lewis, "The Strangeness of Foreigners: Policing Migration and Nation in Interwar Marseille," *French Politics, Culture, and Society* 20, no. 3 (Fall 2002): 65–96, and Milliot, "La surveillance des migrants" (n. 1 above).

82. Milliot, "Migrants et 'étrangers' sous l'œil de la police" (n. 20 above), 331; About, "Les fondations d'un système d'identification policière en France," 29; and Berlière, *Le monde des polices*, 96.

In the early 1920s, Paris officials looked to the population registers of Belgium and Germany for models in the identification of immigrants. On his return from a trip to those countries, the leading municipal councilor Émile Massard expressed his wish that Paris might follow the lead of police departments elsewhere. He wrote to his colleagues:

> Let us hope that some day we might see our immigration service work as well as it does [in the registration offices] in Brussels, Berlin, or Hamburg. I recall that during my trip to study the functioning of their municipal governments, I found my own file at a police department four hours after arriving at my hotel. For the surveillance of foreigners, that must be some kind of a record!

A decade later, police officials from around the world would come to Paris to study the system Massard helped put in place.[83]

83. Émile Massard, "Rapport au nom de la 2e Commission, sur le fonctionnement du Service des étrangers à la Préfecture de police," Cons. mun., *Rap. et doc.*, no. 156 (1922), 3; and Picard, "Les étrangers à Paris," 22.

Chapter Two

The Watershed

World War I made the shortcomings of police surveillance painfully apparent. At the war's start, officials found themselves incapable of identifying many enemy nationals in their midst.[1] Nor were enemies the only problem. The Paris police also had no means of identifying draft-dodging males from allied powers. Paris experienced a series of anti-Semitic outbursts during the summer of 1915 when the wives and mothers of French soldiers singled out Russian Jews, protesting adamantly that potential soldiers were shirking their duty while French men were being slaughtered. The cry was taken up by a number of conservative municipal councilors who had been complaining for years about the presence of foreign Jews in central Paris. One of their number, Henri Galli, thundered: "While all our children are in the army spilling their blood on the battlefield, their very presence in Paris is scandalous, a provocation!"[2]

The minister of the interior, Louis Malvy, tried to keep the Parisian anti-Semites in check by calling on the moral authority of the great sociologist Émile Durkheim, whose son André had died on the Bulgarian front in 1915. Durkheim served as vice-president of the special commission Malvy formed to investigate the crisis. Durkheim presented a detailed report on the condition of Russian Jews in Paris that was sharply critical of the handling of the anti-Semitic outbursts and that pointed out that the municipal council had been trying to find ways of getting rid of Paris's Russian Jews since at least 1911. Russian Jews in France, he noted, had enlisted in impressive numbers

---

1. Lucien Picard, "Les étrangers à Paris," *Police parisienne*, no. 5 (29 February 1936): 20.
2. "Vœu relatif aux étrangers, résidant en France, en âge de servir et munis de permis de séjour," Cons. mun., *Proc.-ver.* (17 November 1915), 502–3.

initially, at a higher rate than Russians were enlisting at home, and all attempts to coerce more young men to fight had had regrettable consequences.
France's reputation suffered abroad when thousands of Russian Jews fled
from France, complaining of persecution. Those Jews stopped enlisting in
the French army, Durkheim explained, not from any lack of civic spirit but
because of the abominable treatment their peers had received in the army.[3]

To prevent similar incidents and to keep right-wing municipal councilors
from stirring up trouble, leading Radicals supported the municipal council's
demands for heightened police surveillance of immigrants. By working with
local government, moderate ministers of the interior thought they could
tame elements that had nearly brought down the republic during the Dreyfus affair while at the same protecting the capital against new threats. The
stunning success of the Bolshevik Revolution made improved police controls seem even more urgent. A foreign power now exerted a powerful influence over the French labor movement; many of the most devoted, experienced militants in France at this time were foreign born. The problem
became still worse with the collapse of revolutionary movements across
much of central and southern Europe—Italy above all. Thousands of Communists and other antifascist militants took refuge in France as Russian
émigrés continued to arrive. Even before the number of arrivals became
massive, the presence of foreign dissidents and political agitators inspired
Parisian authorities to pioneer new means of marking boundaries and enforcing distinctions of nationality.

While most other areas of heavy immigration in France continued to rely
on traditional police measures, as the Sûreté nationale did not create an immigration service until 1934, the Paris Prefecture of Police took action almost immediately after World War I.[4] Within a few years, the newly overhauled immigration service became the busiest branch of the Prefecture.

---

3. For the activity of the commission, APP B/a 896. Steven Lukes, *Émile Durkheim, His
Life and Work: A Historical and Critical Study* (London: Penguin, 1973), 554–59, has a brief
passage on the death of André Durkheim and a reference to the commission. Henry Maunoury, *Police de guerre, 1914–1919* (Paris: Éditions de la nouvelle revue critique, 1937),
34–35, provides an interesting account of the commission. Cf. Panikos Panayi, *The Enemy in
Our Midst: Germans in Britain during the First World War* (New York: Berg, 1991). For efforts to control foreigners in Paris during the war, see esp. APP B/a 67ᴾ, B/a 282ᴾ, and D/b 341,
as well as Arnaud Marsauche, "La 'Question des étrangers' à Paris, 1914–1918" (Maîtrise,
Université de Paris I, 1990). More generally, see Jean-Claude Farcy, *Les camps de concentration français de la première guerre mondiale, 1914–1920* (Paris: Anthropos, 1995); the relevant sections of Jean-Louis Robert's massive "Ouvriers et mouvement ouvrier parisiens pendant la Grande Guerre et l'immédiat après-guerre: Histoire et anthropologie" (Thèse d'État,
Université de Paris I, 1989); and Robert, "L'opposition générale à la main-d'œuvre immigrée,"
in *Prolétaires de tous les pays, unissez-vous? Les difficiles chemins de l'internationalisme,
1848–1956*, ed. Serge Wolikow and Michel Cordillot (Dijon: Publications de l'Université de
Bourgogne, 1993), 43–56.

4. Mary D. Lewis, "Les pratiques d'expulsion dans le Rhône durant la crise," in Philippe
Rygiel, ed., *Le bon grain et l'ivraie: L'état-nation et les populations immigrées, fin XIXe–début*

I

In France, as elsewhere, workers long hesitated to surrender their identity to the state. Steven Kaplan points out that skilled workers have always hated to register their identity. In the eighteenth century, they resented doing so as a "ritual humiliation, an act of subjection, a degradation that likened them to domestic servants."[5] Fingerprinting and photographing of criminals were initially opposed by the accused and their advocates in the nineteenth century on the grounds that they violated convicts' privacy. A report presented to the Chamber of Deputies in 1917 contended that the majority of French citizens rarely had dealings with government administrations above the local level and would view "an obligation to comply as an abusive constraint."[6] While ecclesiastical and, later, republican authorities recorded births for hundreds of years in what became registers of civil status, or *état civil*, those records contained only the most rudimentary information—name, date and place of birth, marital status—and they were scattered in city halls across the country.[7]

The promise of benefits, and fears that the undeserving might profit, gradually broke down popular resistance to identity controls. Workers increasingly registered to vote and to receive unemployment insurance, family allowances, and other welfare benefits over the course of the nineteenth century and into the twentieth. Throughout the tenure of the Third Republic, French citizens proved their identity with a welter of different documents, ranging from the optional identity cards produced by the Paris Prefecture of Police, copies of their *état civil*, and drivers' licenses, or the two letters post offices generally accepted as a proof of residence. But no uniform standard governed the forms of identification these programs accepted. As with the *état civil*, no central clearing house existed to organize the growing masses of records they produced. Before World War II, there were no checks to prevent someone from obtaining certified copies of a third party's papers, nor did any law punish those who did so. Forgeries abounded.[8]

XXe siècle. Sélection des migrants et régulation des stocks de populations étrangères (Paris: Presses de L'École Normale Supérieure, 2004), 152–63; Lewis, "The Strangeness of Foreigners: Policing Migration and Nation in Interwar Marseille," *French Politics, Culture, and Society* 20, no. 3 (Fall 2002): 65–96; Gérard Noiriel, *Longwy, immigrés et prolétaires, 1880–1980* (Paris: Puf, 1984), 177–212, 243–45; and Janine Ponty, *Polonais méconnus: Histoire des travailleurs immigrés en France dans l'entre-deux-guerres* (Paris: Publications de la Sorbonne, 1990), 105–12, 287–318, 342–50.

5. Kaplan, *La fin des corporations*, trans. Béatrice Vierne (Paris: Fayard, 2001), 299.

6. "Onzième Législature, session de 1917, annexe au procès-verbal de la séance du 24 Septembre 1917," report no. 3784, in APP D/b 336; and Noiriel, *La tyrannie du national: Le droit d'asile en Europe, 1793–1993* (Paris: Calmann-Lévy, 1991), 158, 165.

7. Gérard Noiriel, "L'identification des citoyens: Naissance de l'état civil républicain," *Genèses: Sciences sociales et histoire*, no. 13 (Fall 1993): 3–28.

8. Noiriel, "L'identification des citoyens"; Michel Offerlé, "L'électeur et ses papiers: Enquête sur les cartes et listes électorales, 1848–1939," *Genèses: Sciences sociales et histoire*, no. 13 (Fall 1993): 29–53; APP D/b 109, dossier cartes d'identité; and Pierre Piazza, *Histoire de la carte nationale d'identité* (Paris: Odile Jacob, 2004), 77–78, 257.

The police centralized and controlled information concerning foreigners much earlier than they did for French citizens. With the emergence of organized labor as a national political force in the early years of the Third Republic, politicians tried to win over French workers by protecting them from foreign competition in the labor market and by excluding foreign nationals from new social entitlement programs. But French workers could be provided preferential treatment only if they could be distinguished from foreigners. A pair of measures—an 1888 decree and an 1893 law—required all foreigners who came to live or work in France to prove their identity and register with authorities at the nearest city hall. The new measures sought to evade international treaties guaranteeing freedom of movement and to raise money by taxing migrants.[9] The 1888 decree required people seeking residence in France to prove their identity before they could register, for a fee, at the local city hall. Complaints surfaced immediately that the decree was ineffectual, especially in its main goal of protecting the labor market.[10] The 1893 law on the "protection of the national labor market" extended the decree by forcing all foreigners who sought work to comply; they could no longer evade the measure by failing to declare their residence.[11]

Prefects around the country bombarded the Sûreté générale with information about arrivals, departures, marriage, death, and divorce, details it often lacked for its own citizens,[12] but it took decades until the police bureaucracy was able to make use of the new information. As late as 1912, the immigration service in Paris employed only fourteen people full time.[13] A substantial proportion of foreigners—the police guessed about 70 percent[14]—simply ignored the new measures, and the information that did trickle in was dispersed among several police divisions.[15]

A pair of new measures enacted during World War I made large-scale

9. See the discussion in "Admission des Étrangers," n.d. [1 December 1918], MAE, Série C—Administrative 1908–1940, vol. 263.

10. Maurice Barrès, *Contre les étrangers: Étude pour la protection des ouvriers français* (Paris: Grande Imprimerie Parisienne, 1893).

11. For the definitive study of French nationality law, see Patrick Weil, *Qu'est-ce qu'un français? Histoire de la nationalité française depuis la Révolution* (Paris: Grasset, 2002). Although she makes no mention of immigration, Judith F. Stone, *The Search for Social Peace: Reform Legislation in France, 1891–1914* (Albany: State University of New Yor Press, 1985) provides an account of the late-nineteenth-century social legislation. See also Jean-Charles Bonnet, *Les pouvoirs publics français et l'immigration dans l'entre-deux-guerres* (Lyon: Centre d'histoire économique et sociale de la région lyonnaise, n.d. [1976]), 118–21; Piazza, *Histoire de la carte nationale d'identité*, 41–51; Gérard Noiriel, *Le creuset français: Histoire de l'immigration XIXe–XXe siècle* (Paris: Seuil, 1988), 81–89; and, esp., Noiriel, *La tyrannie du national: Le droit d'asile en Europe, 1793–1993* (Paris: Calmann-Lévy, 1991), 168–76.

12. Noiriel, *La tyrannie du national*, 169–70.

13. There had been as many as fifteen a decade earlier. APP D/b 302, dossier Étrangers . . . expulsions, clipping of the Cons. mun., *Rap. et doc.*, no. 125 (1913), 204–5.

14. Statistics of 17 April 1907 from the Direction générale des recherches, 2e Brigade, in APP B/a 67ᴾ, dossier 331.500–A, ouvriers étrangers en France.

15. APP D/b 302, dossier Étrangers . . . Expulsions, circular no. 9 from the prefect of police to Messieurs les Commissaires Divisionnaires et Commissaires de Police de Paris et des Com-

surveillance possible. The two decrees required foreigners to obtain and to carry identity cards with them at all times.[16] Thus armed, the ministries of labor and defense devoted tremendous energies during the war to managing immigrant populations, negotiating labor contracts and watching over foreign workers, especially in the state-run factories where they predominated.[17] At the end of the war, as the central state prepared to relinquish its wartime powers, the Paris prefect of police, Raux, consolidated all of his departments dealing with foreigners, passports, and naturalizations in one office under his direct supervision.[18] Even with these new measures, however, local authorities remained concerned about foreigners disrupting the peace, flooding the local labor market, and overwhelming local assistance programs. Local Paris politicians constantly demanded relief from burdens foreigners imposed.[19]

While the prefect of police routinely put on a brave face in public, he continued to fear unruly foreigners, especially after the massive postwar strikes. Despite the authorities' success in repressing any plausible revolutionary threat, and despite the relative absence of large-scale immigration until the mid-1920s, he continued to worry about foreign agents and terrorists fighting "their" battles on French soil, infecting French domestic politics and straining international relations.[20] The immigration service remained a skeletal operation. Record keeping was in a shambles and the repressive power of the dozen or so agents limited at best. In a series of let-

---

munes du Ressort, and the handful of pre-1914 annual reports of the immigration service in the same dossier. See also Picard, "Les étrangers à Paris," available but unclassified at the APP.

16. Decrees of 2 and 21 April 1917.

17. The history of immigration control during the war remains largely to be written. In the meantime, in addition to the works cited in note 3, Mireille Favre, "Un milieu porteur de modernisation: Travailleurs et tirailleurs vietnamiens en France pendant la première guerre mondiale" (thèse pour l'obtention du diplôme d'archiviste-paléographe, École nationale des chartes, 1986); Tyler Stovall, "Color-Blind France? Colonial Workers during the First World War," *Race & Class* 35, no. 2 (1993): 36–37; John Horne, "Immigrant Workers in France during World War I," *French Historical Studies* 14, no. 1 (Spring 1985): 59; Gary Cross, "Towards Social Peace and Prosperity: The Politics of Immigration in France during the Era of World War I," *French Historical Studies* 11 (Fall 1980): 610–32; and Jean Vidalenc, "La main-d'œuvre étrangère en France et la première guerre mondiale," *Francia* 2 (1974): 524–50.

18. Circular no. 9, the prefect of police [Raux] to Messieurs les Commissaires Divisionnaires et Commissaires de Police de Paris et des Communes du Ressort, 12 June 1918, APP D/b 302, dossier Étrangers . . . Expulsions. See also L. Achille, "Rapport au nom de la 2e Sous-Commission du Budget et du Contrôle, sur le budget des dépenses et des recettes de la Préfecture de Police pour l'exercice 1919," Cons. mun., *Rap. et doc.*, no. 95 (15 December 1918), 5–6.

19. See, e.g., "Ordre du jour sur une proposition de M. Michel Missoffe tendant à réserver aux ouvriers en chômage, de nationalité française, les secours en nature accordés par la Ville," Cons. mun., *Proc.-ver.* (18 February 1921), 221–23.

20. See the prefect of police's reply: "Question de M. Calmels à M. le Préfet de police sur les mesures qu'il compte prendre en vue de garantir la sécurité de la population de l'agglomération parisienne, de plus en plus menacée par l'audace croissante des malfaiteurs de toute nationalité," Cons. mun., *Proc.-ver.* (31 March 1920), 969–70.

ters to the minister of the interior, the prefect of police complained that he lacked the means or the authority to act.[21] He repeatedly pointed out the dire problems "created in Paris by many foreigners who have arrived in France without identity papers, without a passport, and without authorization." All his efforts to purge the capital of "undesirables," he reported, had failed.[22]

In the chaotic period after the Armistice, anxieties over foreigners remained at fever pitch as state power declined sharply. In a series of widely read first-hand accounts of working-class life in Paris, Dr. Louis Martin, better known under his pseudonym, Jacques Valdour, wrote of an invasion of foreign workers under the spell of the Soviets. Despite their modest, thrifty appearance, he wrote in 1921, the masses of foreign workers "nonetheless followed the revolutionary impulses of the CGT without having any idea where they lead. They would have been Radicals forty years ago; twenty years ago, they were Socialists, and today they have given themselves over to the Bolsheviks. They follow. It's a docile herd."[23] That same year, Michel Missoffe bombarded his colleagues in local government with complaints that foreigner workers stole French jobs and burdened welfare budgets. New unemployment benefits "far from stabilizing the situation, have attracted excessive numbers of foreign workers." At any cost, he insisted, the central government ought to "unclog Paris." Recruiting workers during France's national emergency made sense, he conceded, but it beggared the imagination that the government would encourage the immigration of over one hundred thousand foreign workers in 1920. "I will not dwell on the social dimension of this immigration," he went on, "[but] I would like to point out the financial burden it presents to Parisians. . . . Do I need to remind you that, in 1919, expenses in Paris and the Department of the Seine rose to 10 million francs?" Despite the newly signed bilateral treaties, which guaranteed most foreign migrants the same social benefits as French citizens, Missoffe concluded by proposing that the city bar foreigners from receiving any unemployment relief. The city, in his view, had not made any of those agreements and had not been consulted. It therefore ought to have no obligation to pay.[24]

Bolstered by these demands, the new right-wing majority at the Hôtel de Ville made controlling immigration a top priority. A former Bonapartist who passed into the camp of the authoritarian, populist General Boulanger

21. Letters of 10 and 26 February, 5 March, 14 May 1919, 28 February, 26 April, and 8 September 1920, 25 January, and 12 February 1921. APP D/b 336.
22. The prefect of police to the minister of the interior (Direction de la Sûreté générale), 25 January 1921, APP D/b 336, dossier Étrangers.
23. Valdour, *Ouvriers parisiens d'après-guerre: Observations vécues* (Paris: Arthur Rousseau; Lille: René Giard, 1921), 32.
24. Cons. mun., *Proc.-ver.* (11 February 1921), 69–73; Cons. mun., *Proc.-ver.* (14 February 1921), 101–42; and Cons. mun., *Proc.-ver.* (18 February 1921), 221–23.

before emerging as one of the most prominent nationalists in the municipal council, Émile Massard presided over the council's Second Commission, which set the budget of the Prefecture of Police.[25] He reported in early 1921 that the immigration service had been overburdened during the war, that it had survived only with the help of stopgap measures, and that it badly needed reform:

> Under the pressure of circumstances during the war and down to the present day, the immigration service has . . . been run by a haphazard group of auxiliaries, men and women. The time has come to give this Service a definitive organization.
>
> We need to know the precise number of foreigners living in or passing through Paris and their breakdown by nationality, their occupations and means of subsistence; in a word, we need to set up efficient immigration controls.[26]

That year he spearheaded an effort that completely renovated the service's space and radically increased its budget and manpower (see figure 4).

With Massard's help the Paris police adapted bureaucratic measures first developed for criminal populations to monitor the foreign born. Like a number of major metropolitan police forces on the Continent, the Paris Prefecture grew dramatically in the late nineteenth century.[27] Tough measures against recidivism in the 1880s had led police and justice department officials to work together to improve their ability to monitor repeat offenders.[28] One of the most important endeavors in this regard was Alphonse Bertillon's centralization of judicial records at the Prefecture and organizing them in a card system that could be broken down and used for police investigations. Along with these judicial records, Bertillon created a series of much smaller, interrelated card files, settling on a standard-sized "fiche Parisienne" to index everything from anthropometric measurements, photographs, and fingerprints to anarchists, prostitutes, and vagabonds. Most of these files, however, remained quite small, with no more than a few thou-

25. On Massard, see Combeau, *Paris et les élections municipales*, 346.

26. Émile Massard, "Rapport au nom de la 2e Commission, sur la réorganisation du service des étrangers à la Préfecture de police" Cons. mun., *Rap. et doc.*, no. 32 (7 March 1921; Paris: Imprimerie Municipale, 1922), 2–3.

27. Jean-Marc Berlière, "L'institution policière en France sous la IIIème République, 1870–1914" (Thèse d'État, Université de Bourgogne, 1991), 192–229 and 525–766.

28. Cf. Peter Becker, *Verderbnis und Entartung: Eine Geschichte der Kriminologie des 19. Jahrhunderts als Diskurs und Praxis* (Göttingen: Vandenhoeck and Ruprecht, 2002), 64–74, 282–88; Becker, "Vom 'Haltlosen' zur 'Bestie': Das polizeiliche Bild des 'Verbrechers' im 19. Jahrhundert," in *'Sicherheit' und 'Wolfahrt': Polizei, Gesellschaft und Herrschaft im 19. und 20. Jahrhundert*, ed. Alf Lüdtke (Frankfurt-am-Main: Suhrkamp, 1992), 97–131, esp. 126–31; and Ilsen About, "Naissance d'une science policière de l'identification en Italie, 1902–1922," in the special issue "Police et identification: Enjeux, pratiques, techniques," ed. Pierre Piazza, *Les cahiers de la sécurité*, no. 56 (2005): 167–200.

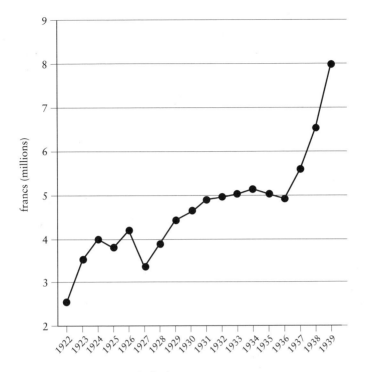

Figure 4. Immigration service budgets.

Source: Ville de Paris, *Budget de la Préfecture de Police* (Paris: Imprimerie Nouvelle, 1922–39), chaps. 3 and 4.

sand records. After the decree of 1888 required foreigners to declare their presence at the nearest city hall, Bertillon included their records as well, making them the first sizable group of legal residents to have their identities monitored. Bertillon initially grouped their files along with anarchists, nomads, and other suspect groups.[29] But by wartime, his system had become too cumbersome. The first anthropometric photo albums, for example, contained records on two thousand suspects; the first "gypsy book" published by the Bavarian Gypsy Information Center listed 3,350 names; the entire Italian national fingerprint archive contained just under thirty-three thousand records in 1911.[30]

The first priority for the Paris immigration service was to organize the

29. Ilsen About, "Les fondations d'un système national d'identification policière en France, 1893–1914," in the special issue "Vos Papiers!" *Genèses: Sciences sociales et histoire,* no. 54 (March 2004): 28–52, esp. 34.

30. Ibid., 42; Leo Lucassen, *Zigeuner: Die Geschichte eines polizeilichen Ordnungsbegriffes in Deutschland, 1700–1945* (Vienna: Böhlau, 1996), 181; and About, "Naissance d'une science policière de l'identification en Italie," 186.

considerable piles of material that had accumulated over the previous three decades. In addition to the perennial personnel shortages, the service's files were still impossible to use, despite those decades of experience. Files organized alphabetically by name, no matter how well kept, shed no light on the populations of the various immigrant communities. Massard wrote in his annual report on police activity: "Today, as in 1914, determining the precise number of foreigners of a given nationality living in the Department [of the Seine] would require going one by one through their declaration cards and then going house to house on an individual basis."[31]

Only by developing new archival techniques and recording even more information, the police claimed, could they keep track of the capital's foreigners. Instead of one unwieldy catalogue, they created several, by cross-referencing, and centralized over a million dossiers from various locations at the Prefecture by the end of 1921. Massard wrote that "before, one individual might have had a dossier in two, three or even four different services. Today, all of these dossiers—we had to move 1.2 million—have been grouped together and can easily be kept at our fingertips."[32] The newly devised system of cross-referenced card files allowed the Paris police to manage vast stores of information much more efficiently, maintaining parallel record systems and keeping them up to date. Every legal immigrant had a file, which in turn included references to dossiers in the central record hall (*casier central*) or elsewhere, perhaps to a naturalization request or a work permit, perhaps to a mention in the famous "Carnet B," the list of political enemies the government kept in case of a national emergency or war.[33] The Paris police organized their files not only alphabetically but also by nationality, profession, and by street, creating what amounted to a relational database to track hundreds of thousands of people at a time.

To house all of this information, and make it accessible, the immigration service ultimately took over a vast room, number 205, on the second floor, stairway F, at the Prefecture's headquarters on the boulevard du Palais. It was filled with desks and lined with shelves from floor to ceiling that were covered with specially built boxes overflowing with index cards of various colors. Massard noted:

> I have visited the premises and seen the attention to detail lavished on every decision: the dimension and color of the index cards and file folders, the wooden boxes that hold them, even the height of the chairs, custom built ac-

31. Massard, "Rapport au nom de la 2e Commission, sur la réorganisation du Service des étrangers à la Préfecture de police" Cons. mun., *Rap. et doc.*, no. 32 (7 March 1921; Paris: Imprimerie Municipale, 1922): 2–3.

32. Massard, "Rapport au nom de la 2e Commission, sur le fonctionnement du Service des étrangers à la Préfecture de police," Cons. mun., *Rap. et doc.*, no. 156 (21 December 1921; Paris: Imprimerie Municipale, 1922), 2–3.

33. Donald N. Baker, "The Surveillance of Subversion in Interwar France: The Carnet B in the Seine, 1922–1940," *French Historical Studies* 10 (1978): 486–516.

The central record hall of the Prefecture of Police, early 1920s. © Roger Viollet.

cording to the height of the employees, men and women; the arrangement of the work tables and shelves, everything has been taken into account and perfectly realized.[34]

Officials soon discovered that new catalogues and administrative advances were useless without thorough, current information to put in them, so they dispatched inspectors throughout the city to check the legal status of every immigrant they could find. In 1924, the prefect sent inspectors around the city, literally door to door, to verify the identity of every foreigner who had registered with the police. He bragged that by sending a "group of agents neighborhood by neighborhood, street by street, house by house" in early 1924, "the entire Paris region has been visited in depth; the job took about five months, but it enabled us to uncover a great number of foreigners who, whether by cunning or by carelessness, have failed to declare themselves."[35] The journal of the Paris police union, *Police parisienne*, reported that a group of fifty plainclothes officers, divided into eight divisions, took to the

34. Massard, "Rapport . . . sur le fonctionnement du Service des étrangers," Cons. mun., *Rap. et doc.*, no 156 (1922), 2.
35. The initial round of verifications was conducted by uniformed officers from the Municipal Police. "Communication de M. le Préfet de police sur le régime des étrangers," Cons. mun., *Proc.-ver.* (15 July 1925), 1596.

3 Inspecteurs des "Divisions-Etrangers"

Inspectors from the active branch of the immigration service, making their rounds. *Source: Police parisienne* 12 (December 1937). Collection Archives de la Préfecture de Police, Paris.

metro roughly once a year to renew the process. Street by street, house by house, each division made sure that "*all* of their clients" were duly noted and their papers in order.[36]

Demanding that citizens register their whereabouts with authorities remained an unthinkable intrusion. Sheer numbers ruled out such an effort in any event. Although Joseph Denais suggested in 1924 that his colleagues in the municipal council require all Parisians to carry cards, the proposal fell on deaf ears. Prefect of Police Alfred Morain agreed that registering all of the city's inhabitants would make his job easier, especially apprehending the "mobile" element of the population. Desirable as such a measure might be, he wrote, the technical difficulties involved were insurmountable. "My Prefecture would have to mount a vast and costly administrative reorganization. For the capital alone, approximately 3 million people would be concerned; granting people one year to comply, more than eight thousand cards a day would have to be prepared during the first year. A tremendous increase in personnel and space would be necessary."[37] Renewals and frequent changes of address, so common in Paris, meant that the expense was unlikely to be short term. Furthermore, local police stations would surely be overwhelmed with work, and thus they would have to hire more employees

36. The article complained that the officers were not allowed to take the bus. Jean Balensi, 'Divisions Étrangères': Cinquante hommes qui en contrôlent cinq cent mille," *Police parisienne*, no. 12 (December 1937), 18.

37. Morain, "Communication d'une lettre de M. le Préfet de police," Cons. mun., *Proc.-ver.* (4 June 1925), 782–83.

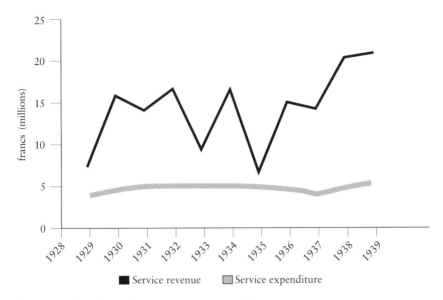

Figure 5. Immigration service revenue versus expenditures.

Source: Cons. mun., *Rap. et doc.* When the reports were submitted in November or December (1927–31), I have projected annual totals. Certain items, such as late fees, were not included every year; these figures, therefore, can be considered no more than orders of magnitude. Furthermore, passports for French nationals account for a small portion of total revenue.

as well. Finally, Morain reminded the councilors that identity cards had been available to Parisians since 1921; French nationals who wanted them for convenience in dealing with authorities were free to take advantage, and in three years almost one hundred thousand had done so. Only after World War II did French governments extend the identity card requirement to all citizens on a permanent basis.[38]

For the moment, the Paris police devoted all available resources to foreigners. Despite the considerable sums at its disposal, the revamped service struggled under the weight of new bureaucratic challenges. In addition to recording information, organizing it, and making sure it was current, the police had to overcome a tremendous array of mundane but unavoidable difficulties. They had to produce reams of forms, decide what information to include and in what order. They had to establish a procedure and a price for the renewal of identity cards, design them, and thwart counterfeiters. None of these problems was easily solved; some never were.

Even establishing the legal terms of residence proved difficult. The 1917 decree required every foreigner over fifteen, residing in France for more than two months, to pay ten francs and obtain an identity card at the Pre-

38. Piazza, *La carte nationale d'identité.*

fecture of Police. In 1924, after unknown thousands entered as tourists only to settle down, legislators reduced the two month grace period to two weeks, and foreigners were required to report all changes of address.[39] Not only would different cards be provided to subsequent arrivals, but authorities set out to replace all existing cards with a new model over the course of 1925 that would have to be renewed every three years—once the forms were printed. The prefect of police admitted late in 1924 that "at the present time, the new decree is not being applied because of material difficulties." The municipal councilor Albert Bérard explained: "We have no forms!"[40] For some of his colleagues, even two weeks was "superabundant." After all, "any foreigner can call himself a tourist."[41] Legislative authorities changed the law again before many of the cards could be renewed.[42] Foreigners once again had two months to present themselves, the price of doing so was raised, and the cards were valid for two instead of three years.[43]

In an attempt to collect more taxes from foreigners, by charging them at regular intervals to renew their papers, authorities created an administrative nightmare. Massard hoped that the effort to renew all foreigners' paperwork would be a one-time job, but it was not.[44] Because hundreds of thousands of new residency permits were delivered at the same time, all of which had to be renewed every two years, the problem never went away (see figure 5). Most of the foreigners who came to Paris between the wars had arrived by 1926, so the police had to renew the papers of almost every immigrant in the city every two years. Although the workload was eased somewhat in 1929, when renewals were staggered, it remained overwhelming.[45]

---

39. Decree of 25 October 1924. See Massard's annual report of police activity in 1924 in Cons. mun., *Rap. et doc.*, no. 157 (14 December 1924), 10.

40. "Question de M. Fernand-Laurant . . . ," Cons. mun., *Proc.-ver.* (21 November 1924), 181. See also Massard, "Rapport au nom de la 2e Commission, sur le fonctionnement des services de la Préfecture de police au cours de l'année 1924," Cons. mun., *Rap. et doc.*, no. 157 (14 December 1924), 10.

41. Fernand-Laurant, "Question de M. Fernand-Laurent à M. le Préfet de police sur les mesures prises par son Administration pour assurer l'exécution des délibérations du Conseil municipal en ce qui concerne le permis de séjour des étrangers à Paris," Cons. mun., *Proc-ver.* (21 November 1924), 174.

42. On the vicissitudes of the legislation on identity cards, see Bonnet, *Les pouvoirs publics*, 134, and Noiriel, *Le creuset français*, 90–91. By 1938, there would be twelve categories of identity cards. See Pinelli's report for that year in Cons. mun., *Rap. et doc.*, no. 39 (1939), 54.

43. For example, the two-month grace period for registering with authorities was shortened once again, in 1929, but tourists were exempted from the measure. Cons. mun., *Rap. et doc.*, no. 160 (1929), 15.

44. Cf. Massard's note on activity for 1924 with that for 1925: "Rapport au nom de la 2e Commission, sur le fonctionnement des services de la Préfecture de police au cours de l'année 1925," Cons. mun., *Rap. et doc.*, no. 159 (22 December 1925), 6–7.

45. In 1929, the cards became valid for a two-year period from the day of inscription, instead of 1 January of that year (Massard, in Cons. mun., *Rap. et doc.*, no. 160 [1929], 15). As

If it never fully resolved all of the challenges it faced, the immigration service was fully functional within the space of a few years of its overhaul. In 1923 Robert Leullier, the prefect of police, announced: "Created barely two years ago, the immigration service has become one of my most important services."[46] Three years later the service employed more officers and treated more matters than any other branch of the Prefecture.[47] Before the brief economic downturn of 1927, that is, the Paris police had transformed their ability to monitor foreign populations and verify individual identities; if not completely, they had largely succeeded in making Guillauté's dream a reality.[48] Police officers routinely stopped people on the street to check their papers and went door to door to verify declarations of residence, which kept their famous file system up to date.

Foreigners who failed to comply—at least, those who spoke imperfect French—sacrificed whatever social benefits they might have enjoyed. They faced limited job prospects, often heavy fines, and risked expulsion.[49] The law granted the prefect of police considerable latitude to issue or refuse identity papers. He could deny papers upon immigrants' arrival (*refus de séjour*); or, he could confiscate them whenever it suited him without explanation (*refoulement*), forcing people to flee the country or brave the consequences of illegality. *Refoulement* was an administrative formality that could not be appealed. However, it could not prevent foreigners from returning and requesting papers. Even more potent, the law of 3 December 1849 gave the minister of the interior and prefects of border departments the authority formally to expel, *manu militari*, any foreigner they thought posed a risk to public safety, with full legal sanctions. As the legal scholar Charles Ourgault put it, "The French system is quite liberal in theory, and often in fact. But it must be recognized that the government is not defense-

---

part of an effort to crack down on illegal immigration and protect the labor market, in 1931 the police set up additional registers of foreigners in each police station around the city and suburbs to monitor the comings and goings of foreigners more effectively and complete the information stored in the vast Casier central (Massard, report on 1931, Cons. mun., *Rap. et doc.*, no. 1 [1932], 22). Two years later, the Depression worsened and complaints about illegal immigration intensified, while thousands of German refugees arrived in Paris; in response, the police introduced new identity cards that were more difficult to counterfeit (Pinelli, report on 1933, Cons. mun., *Rap. et doc.*, no. 15 [1934], 30).

46. The prefect of police to the municipal council, 23 November 1923, in "Vœu tendant au renforcement des sanctions aux infractions aux arrêtés d'expulsion," *Bulletin municipal officiel de la ville de Paris* 42, no. 318 (25 November 1923): 4735.

47. Massard in Cons. mun., *Proc.-ver.* (26 March 1926), 539.

48. On Guillauté, see chapter 1 and Daniel Roche, *Le peuple de Paris: Essai sur la culture populaire au XVIIIe siècle* (1981; Paris: Fayard, 1998), 370.

49. For an example of foreigners who spoke good French evading these restrictions, see the letter from the Groupe des chambres syndicales du bâtiment et des industries diverses to the prefect of police, 8 March 1921, AN F[7] 13,651. The rate of clandestine immigration remains impossible to determine. The director of the RG in the late 1930s, Jacques Simon, put the number at around ten thousand (*La direction des Renseignements Généraux que j'ai connue* [Saint Brieuc, Les presses bretonnes, 1956], 11).

less: by not accepting, or by expelling, it can prevent foreigners from enjoying their rights."[50] The increasingly complex regulations governing foreigners gave the police a pretext to question people who looked out of place, and, indirectly, a means of limiting welfare expenses nominally protected by international treaties.[51]

II

Soon after the reorganization of the immigration services, in 1925, during the tenure of the center-left Cartel des Gauches, Prefect of Police Morain attached the active section of his immigration service to the political branch (RG) for reasons that remain obscure. The decision clearly violated one of the most hallowed principles of the Third Republic, that intelligence-gathering units should never play an active role in politics. A little more than a year earlier in the municipal council, the prefect of police went out of his way to deny any interest in immigrants' political views:

> Before I arrived [at the prefecture], my predecessor created a new service that, obviously, we desperately needed. It's a sort of central clearing house (*casier central*), where every foreigner has a card, so we can follow them, know where they work, know all about their past and any run-ins they may have had with the law.
>
> M. Besombes: . . . And their political opinions.
>
> Prefect of Police: Foreigners' political opinions have scarcely any importance, since they don't vote.
>
> M. Émile Faure: . . . But they influence elections.
>
> M. Fiancette: The prefect of police is much too liberal [in the classical, nineteenth-century sense of the term] to watch closely over foreigners' political opinions.
>
> Prefect of Police: M. Fiancette has expressed my sentiments much more eloquently than I could have done myself.[52]

Did something change in the interim? Was the prefect perhaps trying to mollify local Socialist councilors? Or was the decision a technical expedient? Was it simply a reversion to prewar practice, when the fourth brigade of the political service had been charged with searching immigrant rooming

---

50. Ourgault, *La surveillance des étrangers en France* (Toulouse: n.p., 1937), 13–14. For Ourgault, the problem was the politicians' too liberal interpretation of the law, not the law itself.

51. The bilateral treaties that guaranteed social protection to most foreign nationals only applied if their papers were in order. Local police officials, however, had the right to confiscate papers without approval from the Ministry of the Interior.

52. "Vœu tendant au renforcement des sanctions," 4734.

houses?[53] It is worth pausing over these questions, for France was the only country in the world to use its political branch to monitor everyday immigrants. While both London's Special Branch and the United States' Bureau of Investigation, run by the young J. Edgar Hoover, combined intelligence gathering and immigration control during World War I, both countries abandoned the practice after the Armistice.[54] Even the interwar dictatorships respected the distinction between political policing and civil population registration before the mid-1930s.[55]

One of the republican opposition's first demands under the Second Empire had been the abolition of the political branch of the Prefecture of Police, led by a certain Commissaire Lagrange. Jules Ferry and Léon Gambetta went so far as to demand the abolition of the post of prefect of police as well. They insisted that an open society had no need of a secret police to monitor public opinion; democracy could not be preserved by force without changing its nature. Only regimes that deprived people of free speech and elections, in their view, stood to gain by secret police measures. Although Lagrange was sacked, the post of prefect of police survived the regime change. The political branch survived too, but, as Jean-Marc Berlière has shown, only on condition that Fouché's notorious *police d'attaque* be officially replaced with a police of "pure observation."[56]

Historians have taken the politicians and policemen at their word, especially defense documents drawn up after World War II by Vichy officials to

53. Berlière, "L'institution policière en France," 738–39.

54. Bernard Porter, *The Origins of the Vigilant State: The London Metropolitan Police Special Branch before the First World War* (London: Weidenfeld and Nicolson, 1987), 168, for the aliens register; Porter, *Plots and Paranoia: A History of Political Espionage in Britain, 1790–1988* (London: Unwin Hyman, 1989), 137; John Agar, "Modern Horrors: British Identity and Identity Cards," in John Torpey and Jane Caplan, eds., *Documenting Individual Identity: The Development of State Practices in the Modern World* (Princeton: Princeton University Press, 2001), 101–20; and Nicholas Hiley, "Counter-Espionage and Security in Great Britain during the First World War," *English Historical Review* 101 (July 1986): 635–70. For the United States, Athan G. Theoharis and John Stuart Cox, *The Boss: J. Edgar Hoover and the Great American Inquisition* (Philadelphia: Temple University Press, 1988), 56–62, and Gary Gerstle, *American Crucible: Race and Nation in the Twentieth Century* (Princeton: Princeton University Press, 2001), 91–95, 113.

55. Carl Ipsen, *Dictating Demography: The Problem of Population in Fascist Italy* (Cambridge: Cambridge University Press, 1996), 40, 79–87, 100; Götz Aly and Karl Heinz Roth, *Die restlose Erfassung: Volkszählen, Identifizieren, Aussondern im Nationalsozialismus*, rev. ed. (1984; Frankfurt-am-Mein: Fischer Taschenbuch, 2000); Stephen Kotkin, *Magnetic Mountain: Stalinism as a Civilization* (Berkeley: University of California Press, 1995), 99–105, 166–67; Mervyn Matthews, *The Passport Society: Controlling Movement in Russia and the USSR* (Boulder, Colo.: Westview, 1993); Golfo Alexopoulos, *Stalin's Outcasts: Aliens, Citizens, and the Soviet State, 1926–1936* (Ithaca: Cornell University Press, 2003), 1–2, 160–62, 177–78, 183–84; Gijs Kessler, "The Passport System and State Control over Population Flows in the Soviet Union, 1932–1940," *Cahiers du monde russe* 42 (2001): 478–504; and David Shearer, "Elements Near and Alien: Passportization, Policing, and Identity in the Stalinist State, 1932–1952," *Journal of Modern History* 76, no. 4 (December 2004): 835–81.

56. Jean-Marc Berlière, *Le monde des polices en France, XIXe–XXe siècles* (Brussels: Complexe, 1996), 133–62.

defend themselves in purge proceedings.[57] They have insisted that, before Vichy, the RG respected the traditional distinction between action or repression, on the one hand, and information gathering on the other. Most historians have agreed that it marked a fundamental rupture with republican practice when the RG stopped people on the street to check their papers and resorted to what we would call racial profiling during the German Occupation. The spiral of police abuse that became pervasive under Vichy began when the Paris police created a special "repressive" unit in March 1940 that combed the streets, with the help of uniformed beat officers from the Municipal Police (PM), as part of a bitter fight against Communists. In this widely influential view, only occasional examples of provocation—when paid informants provoked responses they were supposed to be reporting on—compromised republican principles before then.[58]

Prefect of Police Morain made no mention of these concerns when he separated the active section of the immigration service from its "sedentary" administrative section, and attached the former to the RG on 1 January 1925. The municipal council's annual report on police activity noted only that the change had been made "in an effort to use all members of the active force for information-gathering and control operations, to use these agents as efficiently as possible and, if need be, to have them help regular uniformed officers on street duty (*Services de voie publique*)."[59] France had become, per capita, the leading country of immigration in the world during the interwar years. Politicians understandably looked to the police to distinguish militants and terrorists from ordinary immigrants, especially in Paris, where the foreign population doubled over the course of the 1920s, reaching five hundred thousand by the onset of the Depression.[60]

The decision may also have figured in one of the most bitter internecine struggles within the "grande maison." A vast society unto itself, the Prefecture of Police was made up of divisions, where jealousies and sometimes bitter rivalries, set one branch or category of personnel against another. As Berlière has pointed out, even prefects of police had to worry about subordinates gaining too much power, none more so than the head of the Municipal Police. For nearly sixty years in the nineteenth century, the director of

57. Above all, Émile Hennequin, "Notes établies par Monsieur Émile Hennequin en complément de la note générale," 1945, AN Z⁶ 447, folios 478–71 (in descending order in the carton).
58. Berlière and Laurent Chabrun, *Les policiers français sous l'Occupation, d'après les archives inédites de l'épuration* (Paris: Perrin, 2001), 254–55; Berlière and Franck Liaigre, *Le sang des communistes: Les bataillons de la jeunesse dans la lutte armée, automne 1941* (Paris: Fayard, 2004), 155; Denis Peschanski, "Dans la tourmente," in *La police française, 1930–1950: Entre bouleversements et permanences*, ed. Jean-Marc Berlière and Peschanski (Paris: La documentation française, 2000), 64; and Brunet, *Police de l'ombre*, chap. 9.
59. Émile Massard, "Rapport . . . sur le fonctionnement des services de la Préfecture de police au cours de l'année 1925," Cons. mun., *Rap. et doc.*, no. 159 (1925), 84.
60. Georges Mauco, *Les étrangers en France: Leur rôle dans l'activité économique* (Paris: Armand Colin, 1932), 284–312.

the PM controlled all of the Prefecture's active services, making the PM a veritable state within a state. Despite losing control of all plainclothes divisions in 1887, the director of the PM still commanded an army of *gardiens de paix* (uniformed beat officers) and played a crucial role in maintaining law and order in the capital, with thousands of men at his disposal.[61] Between the wars, the director of the Municipal Police, the "master of the street," Paul Guichard, was known for his extreme right-wing sympathies and his tenacity in defending the PM's prerogatives. During the 6 February 1934 riots, he had himself hospitalized for a mysterious case of appendicitis, apparently out of solidarity for his deposed boss, Jean Chiappe.[62] In the 1930s, a *gardien de la paix* under Guichard proudly described himself in print as "an expert on race." Another declared: "There are no individuals more morally depraved than the *métèques*.[63] For them, for this breed that inspires such disgust, regular punishment is not enough. . . . What they really need is corporal punishment, for *métèques* respond only to physical 'correction'—and it must be severe."[64]

Did Morain attach the active branch of the immigration service to the RG instead of the PM—as, logically, he should have—to keep it out of Guichard's hands? Did the longstanding conflict between the two branches, which would later fuel the intensification of police repression during the Occupation, play a role in 1925? The archives provide no answers. Morain's decision, as noted above, has left no trace. But the fantastic growth of the immigration service was already apparent. He must have known by then how important it would soon become.

Whether or not Morain considered internal police politics, he had ample reason for concern about the political threat immigrants posed. He made his decision in the midst of the Bolshevization of the French Communist Party (PCF). On 29 December 1920 the overwhelming majority of delegates at the French Socialist Party Congress at Tours had voted to accept Lenin and Zinoviev's twenty-one conditions for joining the Third International, thus splitting the French labor movement in two. The vote entailed a rejection of the French Left's time-honored traditions: by authorizing the creation of clandestine networks, ready to brave illegality; subjugating the press and unions to the party hierarchy; restructuring of party organizations along hierarchical, highly centralized, Leninist lines; replacing residential sections with factory cells; and promising blind obedience to the direc-

61. Berlière, *Le monde des polices en France*, 105–10.

62. André Benoist, *Les mystères de la police: Révélations par son ancien directeur* (Paris: Nouvelles éditions latines, 1934), 49–63, 72–74.

63. From the Greek *metoikos*, which designated aliens without citizenship or other rights in a Greek Polis, "métèque" was revived by the French nationalist Charles Maurras in 1894 and became a generic pejorative term for immigrants in France. See Eugen Weber, *The Hollow Years: France in the 1930s* (New York: Norton, 1994), 88.

64. Faralicq and Guillaume are both quoted by Jean-Marc Berlière, "La généalogie d'une double tradition policière," in *La France de l'Affaire Dreyfus*, ed. Pierre Birnbaum (Paris: Gallimard, 1994), 216.

Prefect of Police Jean Chiappe (left) with his wife and Director of the Municipal Police Paul Guichard at a soup kitchen, ca. 1933. © Keystone.

tives of the Comintern. Many of the leading supporters of adhesion argued at Tours that the Soviets would grant them latitude, respecting their knowledge of conditions on the ground in France. They were wrong.[65]

After two years of bitter factional struggle within the French Communist Party, and between Paris and Moscow, a new generation of leaders assumed control. By late 1923, the Central Committee was made up exclusively of men who had made the obligatory pilgrimage to Moscow. As Trotsky denounced overtures to the French Section of the Socialist International (SFIO), or the Socialist Party, and the center-left generally as a "Karensky moment"[66] in an impending revolution, the PCF embraced ever more extreme positions. In countless marches and flyer campaigns, they denounced the "formal liberties" of the press and the vote, defended by the bourgeois Republic, as tools of class oppression. They turned their backs on the patriotism of the war years and went out of their way to sabotage the army, urging soldiers occupying the Ruhr to fraternize with their German counterparts and to lay down their arms in the Moroccan Rif campaign to extinguish the Moroccan Berber republic.[67]

Paris, and especially its suburbs, played a pivotal role in the fortune and image of the party. On 11 May 1924 the party startled public opinion by taking 26 percent of the vote in legislative elections in the suburbs, with just over 24 percent in the neighboring Seine-et-Oise. Two days later the French representative to the Comintern, Paul Vaillant-Couturier, wrote an immensely influential article in *l'Humanité*, exulting that Paris was now encircled by a "red belt" of revolutionary proletarians. Six years after World War I ended, Vaillant-Couturier threatened republican leaders that the party could cut communication lines, disrupt transportation, and destroy industrial plants at will. That fall, on 24 November 1924, an estimated ten thousand marchers descended from the suburbs along with party leaders to celebrate the transfer of the remains of the great Socialist founder of *l'Humanité* and historian of the Revolution, Jean Jaurès, to the Pantheon. The next year, the père Lhande began his effort to evangelize the forsaken territory beyond the capital's old fortifications.[68] Édouard Blanc's *The Red Belt* (1927) warned that as many as three hundred thousand "Moscowteers," or fellow travelers, lived on the outskirts of Paris.[69] Valdour continued his se-

65. For the full text of the twenty-one conditions, and those who voted on Tours, Philippe Robrieux, *Histoire intérieure du parti communiste*, 4 vols. (Paris: Fayard, 1980–87), 1:555–66. More generally, see Annie Kriegel, *Aux origines du communisme français, 1914–1920: Contribution à l'histoire du mouvement ouvrier français*, 2 vols. (Paris: Mouton, 1964).

66. *l'Humanité*, 15 September 1923.

67. Robrieux, *Histoire intérieure*, vol. 1.

68. Pierre Lhande, *Le Christ dans la banlieue*, vol. 1, *Enquête sur la vie religieuse dans les milieux ouvriers de la banlieue de Paris*; vol. 2, *Le dieu qui bouge*; vol. 3, *La croix sur les fortifs* (Paris: Plon, 1927–31).

69. Blanc, *La ceinture rouge: Enquête sur la situation politique, morale et sociale de la banlieue de Paris* (Paris: Spes, 1927), 10.

ries of reports with *Workshops and Hovels in the Paris Suburbs* (1923), *The Outskirts* (1927), *In Moscow's Clutches* (1929), and *The Powers of Disorder Toward Revolution* (1935).[70] Estimates of the party's influence were wildly exaggerated in all of these studies. As Annie Fourcaut has pointed out, Blanc was off by orders of magnitude; in the mid-1920s, party membership dropped to roughly fifteen thousand. Subordination to Moscow, bitter factional struggles, and its extremism cost the PCF dearly. But as in so many other instances, anxieties over Communism ran highest as the party's influence hit bottom.[71]

Foreigners, moreover, played a critical role in the early history of the PCF. After losing the major part of its leadership in the split with the Socialist Party, the young PCF often depended upon experienced foreign militants as it struggled desperately to establish itself. The Comintern ordered each national party to create special, foreign-language sections. Even before receiving the official directive, in March 1923, the French Communist trade union (CGTU) opened a special office for immigrants in Paris at the union headquarters at number 33, rue de la Grange aux Belles, run by a Swiss man named Luigi Rainoni, who played an active role in socialist circles before the war. The first year witnessed a flurry of activity, with as many as five meetings a week and the creation of scores of foreign-language sections in different industries.[72] Two years later the PCF itself opened a foreign-language section, with subsections in a variety of languages, including Italian, Yiddish, Romanian, Hungarian, Czech, and Polish, among others. Party support for these groups should not be exaggerated. The French hierarchy constantly complained that the groups pursued their own agendas and purged them periodically. But the PCF could never mobilize enough interest from its often hostile French members to sustain revolutionary activity in Paris.[73] Julien Racamond, the CGTU leader in charge of immigrant affairs, had to stop his presentation at the 1925 annual party Congress at Lille when French militants got up and left the room as he was in the midst

70. Valdour, *Ateliers et taudis de la banlieue parisienne, observations vécues* (Paris: Spes, 1923); Valdour, *"Le Faubourg": Observations vécues* (Paris: Spes, 1925); Valdour, *Les puissances de désordre vers la révolution : Ouvriers de la Plaine Saint-Denis et d'Aubervilliers, Paris-Belleville . . .* (Paris: Nouvelles éditions latines, 1935).

71. Fourcaut, *Bobigny, banlieue rouge* (Paris: Les Éditions Ouvrières, 1986), 30.

72. The standard work on the subject, Stéphane Courtois, Denis Peschanski, and Adam Rayski, *Le sang de l'étranger: Les immigrés de la MOI dans la Résistance*, rev. ed. (Paris: Fayard, 1989), 16, places the opening of the CGTU's foreign-language section in May 1923. But the Bureau de la Main-d'œuvre Étrangère, "Rapport sur le travail accompli du 15 Mars au 15 Avril 1924," in the *Bulletin Officiel de l'Union des syndicats ouvriers du département de la Seine*, October 1924; an anonymous three-page note, dated February 1925, in AN F⁷ 13,456; and the untitled blue mimeograph, 26 August 1924, AN F⁷ 13,015 all place the opening on March 15.

73. The provinces were very different. Cf. Noiriel, *Longwy, immigrés et prolétaires*, chap. 6.

of explaining the importance of international solidarity.[74] Most of what the foreign-language sections accomplished they accomplished on their own.[75] As an internal party report noted:

> It's in the Paris region that the weakness of our work with foreign workers is felt, especially with respect to the unemployed. The regional foreign-language sections (about seventy-five) take care of their own business without contacting the party. As a practical matter, there are serious deviations in the struggle against unemployment, to which the Paris regional headquarters pays no mind.
>
> Thus our Jewish comrades have organized their own unemployed. In just a few days, they raised seventeen thousand francs and opened a restaurant for them to eat in, taking refuge in a narrow nationalism, resisting the common struggle on behalf of unemployed French workers.[76]

Indeed the strength of the foreign-language sections in the early years came precisely from the liberty they provided foreign militants to pursue their own ends. Whatever discord there may have been, foreign workers made up a powerful cadre of disciplined militants, many of them battle tested in their struggles against repressive regimes elsewhere. If they never numbered more than a few thousand before the revival of the party during the Popular Front (1936–38), foreign Communists had the power to embroil France in violent international disputes.

Nor were Communists the only political dissidents using Paris as a base to continue struggles that spilled beyond the borders of their homelands. Even before the Bolshevik Revolution, most of the thirty-five thousand Russian subjects in France lived in the capital. Lenin and Trotsky each spent time there. So, too, did members of Diaghilev's dance troop and scores of less famous workers, artists, and political opponents of the czarist regime. Jews fled pogroms, sought educational opportunity or simply the right to own a patch of land. While many Russian immigrants already in Paris welcomed the Russian Revolution, the vast majority of those who came in the exodus that followed in its wake did not. Whether they had taken up arms against the Red Army or fled famine during the civil war, most Russian émigrés between the wars harbored little sympathy for the Soviet Union. The Russian population more than doubled between 1921 and 1926 as Paris emerged as the world capital of the Russian diaspora. From monarchists to Mensheviks, with scores of groups in between, many organized to

74. *Compte rendu sténographique des débats du Congrès national ordinaire (3ème Congrès de la CGTU)* (Paris, 1925), 391–419.
75. For a revealing treatment of these issues, see the "Bulletin d'information mensuel de la Section Centrale de la M.O.E.," December 1929, BM B 50, no. 348; and "P.V. du Comité Central," 3 November 1925, BM B 11, no. 94.
76. "Projet de rapport sur la M.O.E.," 13 January 1932, BM B 69, no. 468.

help along the collapse of Communism.[77] Those groups, however, like the community as a whole, remained fragmented. The Paris police lumped them all together as "Whites." They monitored the Russian language press, kept track of the various political organizations, and recorded any incidents, as when Grand Duke Cyril's son marched through the forest of Saint-Germain with a band of extreme, right-wing Jeunesse Patriotes in December 1930.[78] But authorities generally welcomed the émigrés as defenders of order: "Many of them already speak French well, or learn it easily. They all came here planning to stay as long as the current regime in Russia remains unchanged. But they have the ability to adapt to our ways and our civilization that suggests that, if the event they long for does not come to pass, they will completely assimilate."[79] Although among the largest and most internally divided communities in interwar Paris, Russians did not preoccupy the police.

Except for North Africans, who began to arrive in significant numbers during World War I,[80] Italians scared the Paris police more than any other community in the mid-1920s. Unlike their Russian counterparts, Italians in Paris worried their home government enough to send spies and hit men after them. After the failed factory occupations of the revolutionary *biennio rosso* (red biennium) in Italy (1919–20), Mussolini's *squadristi* chased thousands of radicals into France, where they joined well-established communities of migrant workers. At first the more vulnerable rank-and-file militants predominated.[81] Already, in December 1919, the French ambassador to Italy, Camille Barrère, warned his minister of the interior:

> The way things are right now, we ought to be vigilant about people crossing our border and try to prevent known agitators from penetrating chez

77. Nina Berberova immortalized the Russian community in Paris in a number of works including *Billancourt Tales*, trans. Marian Schwartz (New York: New Directions, 2001), and "Salt of the Earth" in her *The Italics Are Mine*, trans. Philippe Radley (London: Chatto and Windus, 1991), 239–321. For secondary works, see Catherine Gousseff, "Immigrés russes en France, 1900–1950: Contribution à l'histoire politique et sociale des réfugiés" (thèse, nouveau régime, L'Ecole des Hautes Etudes en Sciences Sociales, 1996); Hélène Ménégaldo, *Les Russes à Paris, 1919–1939* (Paris: Autrement, 1998); Robert H. Johnson, *"New Mecca, New Babylon": Paris and the Russian Exiles, 1920–1945* (Montreal: McGill-Queen's University Press, 1988); and Marc Raeff, *Russia Abroad, 1919–1939* (Oxford: Oxford University Press, 1990).
78. Report of 1 October 1934, APP B/a 1710, dossier 7.023.H.
79. "La main d'œuvre étrangère dans la région parisienne," 21 March 1925, APP B/a 67ᵖ. See APP B/a 1709 for reports on various Russian associations.
80. See part 2.
81. Paolo Spriano, *L'occupazione delle fabbriche: Settembre 1920* (Turin: Einaudi, 1964); Giuseppe Maione, *Il biennio rosso: Autonomia e spontaneità operaia nel 1919–1920* (Bologna: Il Mulino, 1975); Aldo Garosci, *Storia dei fuorusciti* (Bari: G. Laterza, 1953); Simonetta Tombaccini, *Storia dei fuorusciti in Francia* (Milan: Mursia, 1988); Loris Orazio Castellani, "L'emigration communiste italienne en France, 1921–1928: Organisation et politique" (thèse de doctorat, nouveau régime, Institut d'Études Politiques, 1989); Laurent Couder, "Les immigrés italiens dans la région parisienne pendant les années vingt" (thèse de doctorat, nouveau régime, Institut d'Études Politiques, 1986).

nous. . . . It would be a good idea to follow the extremist press in Italy, *l'Avanti*, the other papers of the same type, [Fascist] Party publications, and to keep them from coming into France, Algeria, or Tunisia if they seem dangerous.[82]

A few weeks later, the French police drew up a list of Italian revolutionaries in France with 160 names on it; nearly half of them (44.8 percent) lived in Paris and its suburbs.[83] By the mid-1920s leaders from competing antifascist currents began to take the trip as well and began organizing the overthrow the Italian government.[84]

From 1923 to 1929, some sixty Italians were wounded and a dozen assassinated in factional struggles between fascists and antifascists in the French capital. In September 1923, antifascist gunmen shot dead a Tuscan mason named Gino Jeri and a carpenter named Silvio Lombardi at the café Madagascar. Both were prominent Italian fascists of the first hour. In response, the leading strongman of Mussolini's new Ceka del viminale,[85] the American-born Amerigo Dumini came to Paris to hunt down their assailants. He suspected radical militants and got himself a job working for *l'Humanité*. His cover did not last long. Waylaid on a rainy night by a pair of Communist toughs in the Bois de Boulogne, he shot his way out of trouble, killing both attackers. Wounded in the fracas, he limped out of the park, bleeding, to the house of one of the founders of the Paris *fascio*, Nicola Bonservizi. After being tended to by the fascio's doctor, Dumini snuck back to Italy, where he was thanked by Mussolini. Bonservizi was not so lucky. Several months later, in the most famous political assassination of the period, while eating dinner at a small Right Bank restaurant, he was shot at point-blank range by a young anarchist waiter named Ernesto Bonomini. He died from his wounds a little more than a month later.[86]

Mussolini progressively crushed any domestic opposition. A few months after Bonservizi's murder, in June 1924, Dumini and four other members of the Ceka kidnapped and killed the Socialist deputy Giacomo Matteotti in Rome, just as he was about bring to light proof of corruption at the highest reaches of the Italian government. In their crackdown, Mussolini, Count Costanzo Ciano, and Luigi Federzoni armed the *squadristi* with one hundred thousand new rifles. They dissolved branches of opposition parties, closed circles and clubs, even shut down taverns they suspected of serving as

---

82. Barrère letter to the minister of the interior, 15 December 1919, AN F⁷ 13,453.
83. AN F⁷ 13,068.
84. For overviews, Pierre Milza, "Le rouge et le noir," in his *Voyage en Ritalie* (Paris: Plon, 1993); and Tombaccini, *Storia dei fuorusciti*.
85. Mussolini was so impressed with the Russian secret police that he named his own after it. Franco Fucci, *Le polizie di Mussolini: La repressione dell'antifascismo nel "ventennio"* (Milan: Mursia, 1985), 14–15; and Mimmo Franzinelli, *I tentacoli dell'Ovra: Agenti, collaboratori e vittime della polizia politica fascista* (Turin: Bollati Boringhieri, 1999), 7.
86. Amerigo Dumini, *Diciasette colpi* (Milan: Longanesi, 1958), 26ff; Fucci, *Le polizie di Mussolini*, 15–17; and Milza, *Voyage en Ritalie*, 240–43.

meeting places of subversives. The measures amounted to a suppression of constitutional freedoms of assembly and association, backed by the frequent use of arbitrary arrest. In his memoirs Dumini excused his role in Matteotti's murder by putting forward a connection between the Socialist leader and Bonservizi's killer, Bonomini.[87] While historians have dismissed this claim as far-fetched—there is no evidence Matteotti had anything to do with his rival's murder—conflict between fascists and antifascists in Paris escalated radically as Mussolini secured his dictatorship at home.[88]

As Mimmo Franzinelli has recently shown, fascist Italy dramatically increased its political police capabilities in Paris at precisely this moment (1924–25). In addition to funding social assistance programs and events to promote Italian culture, Mussolini sent spies, double agents, and assassins like Dumini to Paris to pursue his enemies. Fascists also used Paris as a headquarters, in this case to launch counterespionage missions across the Continent. Under the direction of Carlo Sabbatini and a staff of forty, funded by a running account at the Bank of Italy, they sent double agents to infiltrate the Italian-language version of *l'Humanité* and other enemy organizations, taking advantage of internal rivalries within the antifascist camp. Franzinelli contends that scarcely any meetings took place without at least one double agent present, who sent reports to police headquarters in Rome.[89] According to the French police, fascist agents watched over the Italians in Paris and notified authorities back in Italy, who took revenge on family members of any migrants deemed unpatriotic.[90]

At the behest of the Comintern, the Italian Federation of the French Communist Party created paramilitary formations in response to the Matteotti affair. Called *centuries prolétariennes*, they began to hold maneuvers in the Paris suburbs in the fall of 1924.[91] Whatever stance Prefect of Police Morain took in public, minimizing his political concerns, secret police files carefully charted the fortunes of Italian Communists:

> The efforts of [Italian] Communists in France immediately succeeded. New members flocked to the party, and fifteen centuries were fully manned, organized, and given full military training in Paris. Each squad has sixteen to eighteen men; three squads make up a peloton; two pelotons make up a century; three centuries a battalion; three battalions a regiment.

---

87. Dumini, *Diciasette colpi*, 70.

88. On the Matteotti affair, see esp. Mauro Canali, *Il delitto Matteotti: Affarismo e politica nel primo governo Mussolini* (Bologna: Il Mulino, 1997); as well as Renzo De Felice, *Mussolini il fascista*, vol. 1, *La conquista del potere, 1921–1925* (Turin: Einaudi, 1966), chap. 7; Milza, *Mussolini* (Paris: Fayard, 1999), 333–55; and Adrian Lyttleton, *The Seizure of Power: Fascism in Italy, 1921–1929* (New York: Charles Scribner's, 1973), chap. 10.

89. Franzinelli, *I tentacoli dell'Ovra*, 125–36, 181–83, 203, 214–28.

90. Police report of 16 January 1930, APP B/a 278ᴾ, dossier 38.000–L-45.

91. Milza, *Voyage en Ritalie*, 231–32; and Castellani, "L'emigration communiste italienne," 239–338.

The [Communist controlled] Antifascist Workers' Committee has placed a general staff in control of the centuries, which itself has a Military Leadership, a sort of closed committee that makes all urgent decisions, and a Cheka. . . .

The general staff and leaders of the centuries meet often, either at the maison des Syndicats, 33, rue de la Grange aux Belles, or at the meeting place of the Communist groups, 4 bis, rue Pleyel, and 17, rue de Sambre-et-Meuse. It's up to the leaders of each century to watch over the military training and drilling of their men.

The same report went on to describe in detail the groups' first public exhibition, on September 28 in suburban Puteaux, where, as huge crowds cheered them on, hundreds of red-shirted militants marched behind banners with their division number and the names of Communist heroes emblazoned across them: Trotsky, Lenin, Spartacus: "The centuries marched silently, in matching step, down the middle of the street, while supporters, both French and foreign, milled about to either side. The latter cried out, 'Long live the Red Army!' "[92] In another file, the police captured party documents that confidently promised to recruit twenty thousand militants for the cause. Up to that point, the Communists exulted, the government's various crackdowns had only made them stronger. Prime Minister Raymond Poincaré's raids against their newspapers did nothing: "We started publishing *l'Ordine Nuouvo* with a run of 10,250; the Italian-language version of *l'Humanité* started with 11,000 and *la Riscossa* with 16,400. The result of the seizures: we published even more."[93]

According to Loris Castellani, the Italian authorities were not much impressed by the *centuries prolétariennes*. He cites a letter from the Italian Embassy in Paris to the Direzione Generale della Pubblica Sicurezza, which called the September 28 rally "picturesque," crediting the Communists with no more than three hundred red-shirted marchers.[94] Nor does Franzinelli, in the most thorough study of Italian counterespionage, make any mention of the episode. The French press also tried to brush it off.[95]

French authorities, however, took the rally rather more seriously. A few days later, the minister of the interior sent a letter to all of his prefects, asking them if they had any paramilitary formations in their departments.[96] The seventeen-page response from the Paris prefect of police remains one of

92. Anonymous, untitled report of February 1925, AN F[7] 13,456.

93. "Rapport moral de la Commission Exécutive Centrale des Groupes Italiens du Travail," n.d., AN F[7] 13,456. More generally, see "La main d'œuvre étrangère dans la région parisienne," 21 March 1925, APP B/a 67[p], dossier 331.500-A, ouvriers étrangers en France—pièces de principe.

94. Castellani, "L'émigration communiste italienne," 282.

95. See the brief articles in *Le figaro* and *Le temps* on 29 September. *L'humanité*, of course, was another matter.

96. Only a few did: the Aube; the Doubs; the Peugeot bicycle factory, in Audincourt; St. Étienne, in the Loire; and the arrondissement of Brieu in the Meurthe-et-Moselle. AN F[7] 13,455.

the crucial documents for understanding immigration to the capital in these years, and indeed most of what we know about the episode comes from the Paris police archives.[97] In October 1924 the French Ministry of the Interior began drawing up lists of Italian militants to expel. The minister, Camille Chautemps, went further. On October 25 he wrote to the prime minister asking for heightened powers: "The rules governing the residence of foreigners in France today are scattered in various texts. . . . Workers can enter France without our demanding any kind of guarantee from them." He went on: "Many undesirable types have taken advantage of that tolerance and slipped into our country. From now on, all workers will be subjected to background checks."[98] Italian antifascism, it appears, inspired a concerted effort to improve police control over immigration.

Those new controls immediately brought results. Within a few months, police disbanded the *centuries prolétariennes*.[99] Along with intense factional fighting within the Italian section of the PCF, between the rank and file who were loyal to Amadeo Bordiga (a founder of the Italian Communist Party and an opponent of Stalin) and the Stalinist leaders of the party hierarchy, the expulsion of leading militants between 1925 and 1927 decimated the party in France. The Paris police guessed that three thousand Italians left the party as a result of the factional fighting, leaving only four thousand; the total declined further in the years that followed until the revival of the Popular Front. Although historians have paid relatively little attention to Italian Communists in France,[100] their agitation at a critical, if brief, moment shaped the French approach to immigration control in important ways.

It was clear even before the Matteotti affair in 1924 that the political branch of the Paris police would have to create at least one special section to monitor foreign agitators. Entrusting that service with regular immigration control duties gave the RG added leverage over the immigrants they watched and avoided redundancy. Since the RG had to familiarize itself with Paris's foreign population, better that it should do so in a systematic manner.

III

The history of the interwar years mobilized by Vichy police officials in their self-defense at post–World War II purge trials needs to be qualified. The RG

---

97. For the response to Chautemps's circular, "La main d'œuvre étrangère dans la région parisienne," 21 March 1925, APP B/a 67ᴾ.

98. Chautemps's letter, in Bulletin du ministère de l'intérieur, October 1924, 287, quoted in Castellani, "L'émigration communiste italienne," 307–8.

99. Note de la Direction de la Sûreté générale, "Au sujet de la nouvelle tactique communiste," 6 February 1926, AN F⁷ 13,103.

100. Socialists, much more numerous in Paris, are better served in the literature. Castellani is the only historian to have devoted sustained attention to the Communists, and his major work remains unpublished.

may have respected the traditional distinction between information-gathering and repression in monitoring high-profile Communist militants, but the same cannot be said of its treatment of ordinary immigrants. The active branch of the immigration service paid special attention to immigrant neighborhoods in an effort to scare illegal aliens into registering with authorities, and it arrested those whose papers were not in order. Several months after attaching the active section of the immigrant service to his political branch, the prefect of police told the municipal council that the frequent raids on immigrant neighborhoods "are not only useful in themselves: the entire surrounding community, struck by this surveillance, will take care to get their paperwork in order with the police."[101] The annual reports on the RG's activity routinely mentioned "repressive actions," normally considered outside the purview of an information-gathering political unit. In its first full year, the active section of the immigration service:

> conducted a series of investigations both in Paris and the suburbs to identify the primary zones of foreign settlement and then combed those areas to weed out undesirable elements who refuse to respect the law and regulations concerning them. To this end, the service launched raids on ninety hotels and visited many of the "islands"[102] in the zone of fortifications [surrounding the city] where Spaniards and Italians live in conditions that enable them to avoid any kind of regular controls. In the course of these operations, 6,208 foreigners have been questioned and 437 citations handed out.[103]

In addition to taking over the annual rounds of verifications, checking foreigners' residency declarations, and filing tens of thousands of reports, the active branch delivered expulsion notices and conducted scores of raids on immigrant clubs and neighborhoods. They followed up on tips from neighbors and concierges,[104] from flower sellers,[105] from business owners,[106] or waiters who overheard customers swearing in particularly colorful language.[107] The service pursued more than two thousand anonymous denunciations in a single year: "So and so, a Pole, doesn't have the papers the law

101. "Communication de M. le Préfet de police sur le régime des étrangers," Cons. mun., Proc.-ver. (15 July 1925), 1596. The annual reports contain numerous references to searches and raids carried out to this end.

102. The allusion is to the "insalubrious islands" of disease monitored by city public health officials since 1894. See Henri Sellier and Henri Rousselle, L'office public d'hygiène sociale du département de la Seine et la lutte contre la tuberculose dans l'agglomération parisienne, report presented to the Cons. gén. (Paris: Ophs, n.d. [1920]), 37–38; and Yankel Fijalkow, La construction des îlots insalubres: Paris, 1850–1945 (Paris: Harmattan, 1998).

103. Massard, "Rapport . . . sur le fonctionnement des services de la Préfecture de police au cours de l'année 1925," Cons. mun., Rap. et doc., no. 1 (22 December 1925), 86.

104. ADY 1 W 1146.

105. Manuscript note, signed Patté, 8 November 1934, APP B/a 67ᴾ.

106. CAC 19940495 article 18.

107. CAC 19940488 article 20, dossier 1807.

requires," noted *Police parisienne*; "That one, a Yugoslav, doesn't have his worker's card."[108] Its responsibilities were so broad that already, before the war, it had to ask uniformed agents from the Municipal Police to help shoulder the burden.[109]

As economic conditions deteriorated, the police sought increasingly to protect French workers from foreign competition, and the role of the RG expanded. In addition to distinguishing political opponents from ordinary immigrants, the active section of the immigration service was charged with enforcing labor laws aimed at protecting French workers and limiting access to social services. With the economic downturn of 1926–27, the RG joined forces with labor inspectors; together, they enforced existing laws limiting the percentage of foreigners that could be employed in public-sector jobs by holding employers responsible.[110] Teams of officers checked all of the businesses in Paris and the suburbs for illegal workers.

An unsigned police report from early 1928 testified to a considerable growth in the immigration service's activity.[111] That year the active branch of the RG dedicated considerable energies to breaking a prostitution ring centered at the place Pigalle. Over the past few years, the report noted, Montparnasse and, especially, Montmartre had emerged as centers of prostitution, as the decline of the franc had attracted a large community of wealthy foreigners looking to explore the capital's red light districts.[112] Gambling, and organized crime by extension, it should be noted, entered into the RG's formal responsibilities; it's full title was Service for General Information *and Gaming*. At certain hours, drug dealers, pimps, and prostitutes of both sexes plied their trade in the open, working together with a network of Russian taxi drivers to provide them unsuspecting clients. The police began their investigation after some twenty-five thousand U.S. servicemen arrived in August 1927 and found themselves privileged targets of the criminal network. Along with the detectives of the Police Judiciaire and the uniformed officers from the Municipal Police, the active branch of the immigration service systematically stopped people in the street to check their papers, questioned them, and launched a repeated series of raids on nightclubs and brothels. They devoted particular attention to homosexual prostitutes. It was with this "category that the greatest results have been obtained. We can report that the measures we have taken—enforced closing

108. Jean Balensi, " 'Divisions étrangères': Cinquante hommes qui en contrôlent cinq cent mille," *Police parisienne*, no. 12 (December 1937): 18.

109. Ibid.

110. Massard, "Rapport au nom de la 2e Commission, sur le fonctionnement des services de la Préfecture de police au cours de l'année 1931," Cons. mun., *Rap. et doc.*, no. 1 (31 December 1931; published in 1932), 162–63.

111. The report of [10] January 1928, AN F⁷ 13,017, appears to be a copy from the Prefecture of Police.

112. Cf. Louis Chevalier, *Montmartre du plaisir et du crime* (Paris: R. Laffont, 1980) for a firsthand account of a "native" observer.

time at 2 a.m., prohibition of music, and repeated raids have taken a serious toll on male prostitution." The report continued, proudly:

> Some houses, with established reputations both in France and abroad, have been dealt a mortal blow, including: Le Roland's, 15, rue aux Ours; La Petite Chaumière, 2, rue Chevreuse and 127 bd. Montparnasse, which are now deserted.
>
> It's now quite common to hear professional male prostitutes complain that their business is much diminished lately, their clients more difficult to find.[113]

To bring the prostitution ring, especially its male component, under control, the police estimated that they stopped ten thousand foreigners on the street in the second quarter of 1927, "which allowed us to catch not only individuals who had violated immigration law but also people with counterfeit papers and those condemned in absentia for crimes and misdemeanors." Some 1,500 of those foreigners were taken to the immigration service offices on the boulevard du Palais, 109 sent to central lockup, and another 321 directly expelled.[114] As an unintended consequence of these raids, the service that delivered identity cards noticed a dramatic increase in activity over the course of the operation, "the fear of getting caught inspiring many foreigners to regularize their situation without delay."[115] Gradually the police came to appreciate the utility of immigration law for solving a wide variety of problems.

IV

Supported by the foreign-born taxpayers it monitored, the immigration service grew at an impressive rate. Having begun with an annual budget of 2.5 million francs, expenditures doubled within ten years. Municipal councilors insisted that foreigners pay for their own surveillance and complained that the state was taking more than its fair share of the proceeds.[116] One of the more outspoken members, René Fiquet, sounded a common theme when he complained in 1924 that "the Parisian taxpayer, the French taxpayer . . . is fed up with having always to pay for certain foreigners who, in France, have only rights."[117] Fiquet and his colleagues constantly complained about

113. Police report, [10] January 1928, AN F^7 13,017, pp. 5–6.
114. Ibid., 6.
115. Ibid.
116. The proceeds were divided between the central government and all departments and municipalities with immigrant populations; while Parisians paid for about half of the Prefecture's budget, they received a smaller share of the revenue it generated.
117. Fiquet in "Question de M. Fernand-Laurant à M. le Préfet de police sur les mesures prises par son Administration pour assurer l'exécution des délibérations du Conseil municipal en ce qui concerne le permis de séjour des étrangers à Paris," Cons. mun., Proc.-ver. (21 November 1924), 182.

wealthy British and American visitors and speculators who profited from the monetary crisis of the early 1920s, and every expenditure on foreigners elicited groans from conservative councilors.[118]

In fact, municipal authorities ended up reaping tremendous gains right away. Identity cards and passports brought tens of millions of francs into the public coffers every year. In 1926, the city government set up a special office, *la recette*, to determine how much money it received. The revenue produced by identity cards, passports, and visas varied substantially from year to year, depending primarily on when renewals were due. Somehow, even though immigration consistently exceeded expectations and bureaucracies had to improvise, the immigration service always managed to make money (see figure 5).

Local authorities devoted considerable energy to looking at one segment of the urban population. Having given up on the idea of making the city entirely transparent to the policeman's gaze, as the central state relinquished its wartime powers, they singled out foreign nationals. In an effort to contain immigrant criminality, protect the local labor market, and prevent France from being drawn into international conflict, especially with Italy, right-wing Paris municipal councils worked with mainstream republican ministers of the interior to create new forms of police control.

Fully functional by 1926, the Parisian immigration service soon became the envy of the world. *Police parisienne* reported during the Popular Front that the central record hall of the immigration service "constitutes a veritable gold mine of administrative and judicial information. It is unique in France, and representatives from most police forces around the world have come to study its organization."[119] Before the "strange defeat" to Nazi Germany in 1940, the central record hall of the Paris immigration service contained more than 1.6 million files and 2.6 million index cards.[120] Since the crisis over the Vichy-era *fichiers juif* broke in the early 1990s, the central record hall has become a *lieu de mémoire* in its own right, in Pierre Nora's sense, the symbol of a supposedly all-knowing administration. More than a half-century later, a former member of the administrative section of the immigration service recalled: "Bah, what a gold mine! Bon . . , people's whole lives were in there, their état civil, address, everything—everything, I tell 'ya, it had everything on everyone. It was all in there. The central record hall was *the* central record hall. I never noticed anything lost or missing. It worked quite well."[121]

118. On the crisis, Jean-Noël Jeanneney, *Leçon d'histoire pour une gauche au pouvoir: La faillite du Cartel, 1924–1926* (Paris: Seuil, 1977).

119. Picard, "Les étrangers à Paris," 22. Cf. D. Eleanor Westney, "The Emulation of Western Organizations in Meiji Japan: The Case of the Paris Prefecture of Police and the Keishi-chö," *Journal of Japanese Studies* 8, no. 2 (Summer 1982): 307–42.

120. Cons. mun., *Rap. et doc.*, no. 39 (1939), 46–47.

121. Quoted in Alexis Spire, *Étrangers à la carte: L'administration de l'immigration en France (1945–1975)* (Paris: Grasset, 2005), 146.

No city in the world paid closer attention to its immigrant population between the wars than Paris. With its annual door-to-door surveys and peri-
odic raids, the Prefecture of Police may never have enjoyed such thorough,
current information on the whereabouts of the foreign born as it did from
the mid-1920s until the end of World War II. Since the emergence of the European Union, France has had to share control of its borders with an ex-
panding list of countries, and the enormity of the task of monitoring contemporary population movements has compelled governments to rely once
again on private corporations to control the identity of their passengers.[122]
Despite constant technical improvements in the interim—from card files to
punch cards to the supercomputer used today—the French state has never
since taken on a greater a share of the burden of certifying immigrants'
identity.

122. In particular, transport companies. Didier Bigo, *Polices en réseaux: L'expérience eu-
ropéenne* (Paris: Fnsp, 1996).

Chapter Three

"Round Up the Usual Suspects"

Over the past fifteen years, an awareness of the French police authorities' role in the wartime deportation of Jews has fed images of an all-knowing state. Those images are at least somewhat misleading. Other governments recorded more information about a greater share of the population than the Paris Prefecture of Police ever did. At the same time, only a few of the foreigners the Paris police formally expelled between the wars ever left the country. Overlapping jurisdictions and administrative rivalry often hamstrung police measures. Effective action demanded a level of consensus that often proved difficult to achieve. Even the most ruthless interwar dictatorships had to contend with administrative rivalries, but in France the inevitable inefficiencies were compounded by a well-established tradition of due process.[1] The steadfast commitment of republican governments of all ideological persuasions to provide political asylum required lengthy inquiries. With their proclaimed respect for the Rights of Man France was open to powerful international scrutiny that antidemocratic regimes generally did not have to face.[2] Fear of sparking a diplomatic incident prevented Parisian authorities from taking full advantage of their coercive potential and gave foreign governments considerable power to protect their citizens on French soil.

Chapter title: Captain Louis Renaut (Claude Raines) in *Casablanca* (1942), dir. Michael Curtiz.

1. Thus, the opposite of what Ian Kershaw has called "working towards the Führer," *Hitler, 1889–1936: Hubris* (New York: W. W. Norton, 1999), chap. 13.

2. Dictatorships were not immune from such pressures. For example, repeated orders issued in Hitler's name prohibited a range of anti-Jewish actions before and during the 1936 Berlin Olympic Games. Saul Friedländer, *Nazi Germany and the Jews*, vol. 1, *The Years of Persecution, 1933–1939* (New York: HarperPerennial, 1997), 139, 180–81.

And yet the extension of nationality law to realms it had only vaguely governed brought with it new forms of inequality and exclusion. Especially in the 1930s, an ever-more-restrictive series of regulations limited foreigners' ability to find work and settle down. The police systematically wielded new measures to enforce conformity, creating what Robert Paxton has called "the dark underside of republican conceptions of citizenship and assimilation."[3]

Historians have tended to emphasize one side or the other. They stress, alternately, the extension of the rule of law and the protection of rights or the inevitable exclusions engendered by those legal categories.[4] My goal in this chapter is to show that both liberal protections and new forms of inequality must be considered together. The Paris police only forced a tiny minority to leave France before World War II, but they decisively shaped the terms on which foreigners could stay.

I

Legal measures bound the police as well as immigrants. The information agents gathered provided immigrants a legally recognized status. It enabled them to make important claims on the French state, which signed a series of treaties in the 1920s guaranteeing most legal foreign workers the same health and social benefits as French citizens.[5] Work permits allowed them to live and work in peace, without fear of expulsion or harassment from local authorities. Not least of the protections, ironically, was the Prefecture's decision to use its political branch, the RG, to track foreign migrants—a clear violation of republican principle.

The RG's professionalism moderated the severity of enforcement. Prospective recruits had to take classes at the Prefecture's police school for several months during their off-duty hours and work for years as uniformed beat officers before they could take the selective entrance exam. New men

3. Paxton, "Gérard Noiriel's Third Republic," *French Politics, Culture, and Society* 18, no. 2 (Summer 2000): 99.

4. See Patrick Weil, *Qu'est-ce qu'un français? Histoire de la nationalité française depuis la Révolution* (Paris: Grasset, 2002), for the first position. Gérard Noiriel, on the other hand, contends in *Les origines républicaines de Vichy* that the Republic's treatment of foreigners prepared the way for Vichy.

5. G. Bonvoisin and G. Maignan, *Allocations familiales et caisses de compensation* (Paris: Sirey, 1930), 45; Louis Stroh, *L'étranger et les assurances sociales* (Paris: Sirey, 1929); François Neuville, *Le statut juridique du travailleur étranger en France au regard des assurances sociales, de l'assistance et de prévoyance sociale* (Paris: Chauny et Quinsac, 1930); M. Barthélémy Raynaud, "Les étrangers et la législation française sur les allocations familiales," *Le journal de droit international* (May–June 1933), 590; Marcel Livian, *Le régime juridique des étrangers en France* (Paris: Librairie générale de droit et de jurisprudence, 1936), 119–22; and William Oualid, *L'aspect juridique de l'immigration ouvrière* (Paris: Alcan et Rivière, 1923), 19–29, 69–70.

_ Juifs polonais _

"Polish Jews" and "Russians" in a series of immigrant "types" by Gaston Hoffmann, in *Police parisienne* 12 (December 1937). Collection Archives de la Préfécture de Police, Paris.

Pages d'album de Gaston Hoffmann.
Types d'étrangers vivant à Paris.

Les Russes

Minister of the Interior Albert Sarraut gives a medal for dedication to several police officers on April 26, 1934. Prefect of Police Roger Langeron (left, wearing glasses) looks on. © Keystone.

learned the limits of acceptable behavior from senior officers during years of apprenticeship and assimilated a well-established professional culture. Time invested in reaching the rank of inspector reinforced those lessons. This provided powerful incentives to follow orders. The prospect of blowing a promotion, the fear of a humiliating demotion or a lost pension, alerted the active section of the Parisian immigration service to the risk of sparking an international incident. Officers constantly kept on their guard to avoid the intervention of foreign governments, which increasingly took an interest in the fate of their citizens on French soil.[6]

Xenophobia made significant inroads in other branches of the Prefecture, as throughout society, between the wars. In 1928 Minister of the Interior Albert Sarraut complained to a gathering of Paris policemen that masses of foreigners in Paris brought "their customs, their habits, their defects, and their vices, to the point that your job has become much more complex, and there truly are moments when I wonder by what sort of paradox the minis-

6. On the intervention of foreign governments on behalf of their nationals, see, e.g., APP D/a 742, D/a 744, and B/a 278ᵖ; AN F⁷ 13,455, and esp. F⁷ 13,652; ADY 1 W 1146 and 1147; MAE, Z—Europe, 1930–1940, vols. 206, 354, and 368; CAC 19940437, art. 234; CAC 19940457, art. 80; and CAC 19940500, art. 116.

ter of the interior is not called upon more often to step in and make excuses for your attitude and behavior."[7]

A decade later, the same gathering greeted Prefect of Police Roger Langeron with vigorous applause when he reported that the fourth section of the RG had conducted fifteen thousand investigations the previous trimester, which led them to deliver 140 expulsion notices.[8] The police union's own journal published a thirty-five-page essay celebrating Nazi Germany, its youth camps, the efficiency of its police, and the vitality of the SS. The same author, Madame R. Viellard, wrote about immigration to Paris in terms of an "invasion" of bloodthirsty "undesirables," in an article replete with anti-Semitic illustrations—part of a series that depicted foreign immigrants by types—and florid descriptions designed to shock. Her conclusion: "It is urgent that France put an end to its overly generous hospitality."[9]

Finally, the "sedentary," administrative branch of the immigration service—the desk unit that organized the card files and decided who could stay and whom to expel—was notorious among immigrants in the late 1930s for a professional culture of dismissive arrogance and condescension. Italians, Russians, Spaniards, eastern European Jews, people from all over had to wait for hours at their office and beg for indulgence. They all experienced the endless formalities and contradictory procedures of a system overwhelmed by the number of asylum claims, and many harbored bitter memories.[10] A preliminary review of the personnel files of that unit suggests that the generation of men who created the unit in the early 1920s, men who made their way up through the ranks at the Prefecture, began to give way in the mid-1930s to a group with more formal, legal training but less practical experience.[11]

What little evidence we have suggests that the active section of the Parisian immigration service was relatively free of the extreme xenophobia found elsewhere in the Prefecture. As we have seen, left-wing prefects of police took pains to use the RG as a counterweight to the PM throughout the interwar years. Their reports show an intimate familiarity with the capital's immigrant communities, and they often pointed out that the overwhelming majority of immigrants wanted nothing more than to work in peace.

7. ADA 12 J 36, "Discours de M. Albert Sarraut, Ministre de l'Intérieur," mimeographed speech to the Association de l'administration préfectorale, 2 July 1928, pp. 28, 30–31.

8. Préfecture de Police, Société Amicale et de Prévoyance, *Annuaire 1938*, vol. 55, in ADA 12 J 440.

9. Viellard, "Chez les étrangers à Paris," *Police parisienne*, no. 12 (December 1937): 19–53, esp. p. 25, 27–28, 34, 53. The earlier article appeared in *Police parisienne*, no. 7 (August 1937): 20–55.

10. Julia Franke, *Paris—eine neue Heimat? Jüdische Emigranten aus Deutschland, 1933–1939* (Berlin: Duncker and Humblot, 2000), 282.

11. APP, dossiers personnels de service.

In the aftermath of clashes between Italian fascists and antifascists at the time of the Matteotti affair, the Parisian RG provided a sober, well-informed overview of the capital's foreign immigrants. They noted that, despite the recent surge of immigration into the city, foreigners posed no threat to skilled French workers. Taking advantage of the RG's new ability to break the labor market down into its national components, the author informed the minister of the interior, Chautemps, that some industries would collapse and some neighborhoods would be depopulated without the new influx of immigrants. Jewish furriers from central Europe, for example, had no domestic competition and gave plenty of work both in their ateliers and to a fast-growing network of men and women working at home. The threat of unemployment was not a result of immigrant competition but of inflation and the instability of the exchange rate. Taking note of a growing apprehension in the popular press, the report took pains to point out that immigrant neighborhoods suffered no greater incidence of disease than the rest of the city. A careful examination of the statistics showed that "declarations of contagious diseases in the fourth, eleventh, fifteenth, and eighteenth arrondissements differ little from those with lesser significant foreign populations." While listing scores of different extremist groups, from Spanish anarchists to Russian royalists, the report emphasized that even the most dangerous of them—the Communists, in the author's estimation—did not pose a serious threat to public order. If foreigners tended to stay together and resisted assimilation, the vast majority of them, the report insisted, had no interest in politics.[12]

Perhaps the single most thorough surviving report on an immigrant community filed between the wars sought not to exclude foreigners but rather to facilitate their assimilation.[13] In late 1929 the ministry of foreign affairs at the Quai d'Orsay came upon a fascist propaganda tract that included a chapter surveying the composition of the Italian community in Paris and boasting of the consulate's successes in preventing its members from losing their cultural identity. The French foreign minister had the chapter translated and sent it to the minister of the interior who in turn forwarded it to the prefect of police, asking him to determine whether any Italian groups were breaking the law.

The minister of the interior feared that the fascist government was subverting French efforts to naturalize hard-working foreigners—to compensate for France's famously low birthrate[14]—and he directed the prefect to

12. Direction des Recherches, Service des Recherches Administratives et des Jeux, "La main d'œuvre étrangère dans la région parisienne," 21 March 1925, APP B/a 67ᴾ.

13. "Activité politique de la colonie italienne de la région parisienne au cours de l'année 1929," February 1930, APP B/a 1711, doss. 138.000–L-25.

14. A 1927 law made naturalization much easier for foreigners. See Weil, *Qu'est-ce qu'un français?* 76–81; Jean-Charles Bonnet, *Les pouvoirs publics français et l'immigration dans l'entre-deux-guerres* (Lyon: Centre d'histoire économique et sociale de la région lyonnaise, n.d. [1976]), 150–70; and Elisa Camiscioli, "Intermarriage, Independent Nationality, and the Indi-

investigate immigrant organizations and their leaders: "I would especially like to know," he wrote, "if these Italian associations are acting in strict accordance with our legislation and in particular our law of 1 July 1901," which required associations to abstain from politics.[15] The prefect of police replied a month later with a series of sixteen brief reports, apparently composed from material in his archives.[16] After a year of research in the field, the police produced a twenty-seven-page study examining the Italian consulate's claims.[17]

The police study revealed a broad range of underground publications and outlined the shifting alliances and changing fortunes of a number of different groups.[18] Authorities feared that in addition to disturbing the peace, militants would drag France into conflict with Italy. They complained that "the Italian press and public opinion represent Paris as 'the refuge and benevolent asylum of the enemies of order'; moreover, they claim that the attacks that sometimes trouble the fascists' serenity [in Italy] are, for the most part, hatched on our territory."[19] The most carefully examined group was the Italian Communist Party, which had set up a headquarters-in-exile in Paris: "As in previous years, the activity of Italian antifascists, and especially those active in the Communist Party, have been watched very closely."[20] Numerous penalties had been handed out to active militants, and the party still had yet to recover from a combination of police repression and internal factional fighting. The report proudly announced

vidual Rights of French Women: The Law of 10 August 1927," *French Politics, Culture, and Society* 17, nos. 3–4 (Summer–Fall 1999): 52–74.

15. Confidential letter from the minister of the interior to the prefect of police, 15 January 1929, APP B/a 1711, doss. 138.000–L-25, doc. no. 448.

16. The one to two page typed reports have no heading or signature but are dated February 1929, in APP B/a 1711, doss. 138.000–L-25. The reports provide the names, addresses, and registration numbers of all associations, as well as their stated purpose. Identity card numbers and brief biographies of leaders are provided as well. I have inferred the composition of these reports from a letter from the directeur-adjoint, chef du service des RG to the prefect of police, received by the Cabinet du Préfet on 20 February 1929 in the same dossier; it lists all of the organizations covered by the reports with the police dossier number of each written in pencil in the margin.

17. "Activité politique de la colonie italienne de la région parisienne au cours de l'année 1929," February 1930, APP B/a 1711, doss. 138.000–L-25. The dossier also contains an untitled, unsigned typed report of 21 February 1930, probably an appendix to "Activité politique de la colonie italienne." Although reports on the political activity of the Italian community appear to have been written fairly regularly, this is by far the most thorough.

18. It took police intelligence some time to become familiar with the nuances of left-wing politics. A 1915 report identified a certain "Vladimir Illitch" as a "volunteer enrolled in the Foreign Legion"! Jocelyne Masson-Fenner cited by Berlière, "A Republican Political Police? Political Policing in France Under the Third Republic," in *The Policing of Politics in the Twentieth Century*, ed. Mark Mazower (Oxford: Berghahn Books, 1997), 53 n. 46. Mistakes of this sort persisted throughout the interwar years but became increasingly rare as officers became familiar with radical politics.

19. Untitled, unsigned typed report of 21 February 1930, APP B/a 1711, doss. 138.000–L-25.

20. "Activité politique de la colonie italienne," 14.

that "thanks to the expulsion of ardent revolutionaries, dubious characters, and provocateurs, there have been no attacks to speak of in the Paris region in 1929."[21]

In addition to Communists, the police monitored fascist activity. The Italian government's efforts at "fascist penetration" were laid bare, from the use of undercover agents to the financing of social programs and propaganda campaigns. The report listed Italian schools and the programs funded by Mussolini's government, from the presents offered at the "fascist Christmas tree" celebrations to sending Italian women across the Alps to give birth and ensure their children would enjoy Italian nationality.[22] Officers had found that the history taught in Italian schools was "inexact" in previous years, when Corsica, Tunisia, and Savoy were all presented as belonging rightfully to Italy.[23] They had also complained that the fascist newspaper, *La nuova Italia*, was trying to slow the pace at which Italians were opting for French nationality.[24] By 1929, repeated protests from the Quai d'Orsay had given the French satisfaction. The paper stopped its propaganda campaign.

Although they tried to limit such propaganda when they encountered it, the immigration service at the Prefecture showed little concern for the effects of propaganda on ordinary Italian immigrants.[25] Like the report written five years earlier, this one glossed over the various shades of opinion of the vast majority of Italian immigrants in a single sentence:

> As for those established in France for many years, they have no interest in Italian domestic politics and are preoccupied solely with keeping the jobs they found during the labor shortage; the same goes for the shopkeepers who maintain a strict neutrality required for the success of their businesses.[26]

Most migrants, immigration specialists well knew, wanted nothing more than to settle down and live in peace. Sympathetic officials, from border guards to ministers, played often decisive roles in moderating the effect of

21. Ibid., 15.
22. Laurent Couder, "Les immigrés italiens dans la région parisienne pendant les années 1920: Contribution à l'histoire du fait migratoire en France au XXe siècle" (thèse de doctorat, nouveau régime, Institut d'Études Politiques, 1987); Loris Orazio Castellani, "L'émigration communiste italienne en France, 1921–1928: Organisation et politique" (thèse de doctorat, nouveau régime, Institut d'Études Politiques, 1989); Marie-Claude Blanc-Chaléard, *Les italiens dans l'est parisien des années 1880 aux années 1960: Une histoire d'intégration* (Rome: École française de Rome, 2000).
23. "Activité politique de la colonie italienne," 24.
24. Ibid., 25.
25. Those effects were not negligible. See Pierre Milza, "Le fascisme italien à Paris," *Revue d'histoire moderne et contemporaine* 30 (July–September 1983): 420–52.
26. "Activité politique de la colonie italienne," 1–2.

repressive measures.[27] In some cases, especially those concerning refugees, the police did not need external pressure to protect the disadvantaged. The American Jewish Joint Distribution Committee noted that "even if the police . . . saw some of these illegal entrants, they were so moved by their plight that they did not obey the orders of their superiors to send these people back, and brought them instead to the nearest Jewish refugee committee."[28] As Patrick Weil has shown, even at the height of the refugee crisis on the eve of World War II, elements within the Sûreté nationale defended the cause of Jewish refugees, recommending that entire communities of Jews be moved to France to bolster the economy. In a series of debates over the possibility of integrating migrants from central Europe, leaders of the Sûreté explained:

> In central Europe, especially in Thuringia and Bohemia, there are a great many small industries, called domestic industries (*Hausindustrien*) that produce games, jewelry, buttons . . . , thermometers. These articles are produced by artisans who work at home with their families and who deliver the product of their labor to a central bureau, which takes care of sales and export. The towns of Gablenz in the Sudetenland, Sonneberg and Ilmenau in Thuringia are the principal centers of these industries whose exports amount to millions of dollars every year.
>
> This work is carried out by Jews, almost exclusively in Gablenz and partially in Thuringia. A great many of those who have immigrated to France have the international connections necessary to export. The markets in England and America are, moreover, in the hands of their coreligionists. It would thus be easy to organize and, in certain underpopulated regions of France (the southwest for example), make industry and commerce prosper; all the vital elements exist already in this country.

The report went on, emphasizing the prosperity Huguenot immigrants brought to Prussia after the revocation of the Edict of Nantes three centuries earlier.[29] Later that year, after the Germans invaded Poland, the leaders of the Sûreté continued to urge agents to treat Poles with benevolence and to recommend that the government turn the war to its advantage by recruiting Jewish workers from central Europe for industries with labor shortages.[30] Vichy officials later complained of the Third Republic's director of the immigration service at the Sûreté M. Combes: "Assistant [*Chef adjoint*

27. Weil, "Politiques d'immigration de la France et des États-Unis à la veille de la Seconde Guerre mondiale," *Les cahiers de la Shoah*, special issue, ed. André Kaspi (1995): 70–72.

28. JDC report no. 658, 5 July 1939, quoted by Vicki Caron, *Uneasy Asylum: France and the Jewish Refugee Crisis, 1933–1942* (Stanford: Stanford University Press, 1999), 209.

29. AN F[60] 494, quoted by Weil in "Politiques d'immigration," 75–76.

30. AN F[7] 15,175, circular no. 408, 15 September 1939, and circular no. 416, 21 November 1939. My thanks to Patrick Weil for this reference.

du cabinet] to Blum in 1936, he has devoted himself with fanaticism, in all likelihood sincere, to the policies of the Popular Front, giving every possible privilege to the antifascists."[31]

A republican commitment to individual liberties survived throughout the interwar years because people—not least from within the administration—fought for them. As Weil, in particular, has emphasized, individuals ignored orders; they looked the other way.[32] Dealing with immigrants did not necessarily provoke a racist response. Even the notorious right-wing prefect of police, Jean Chiappe, went out of his way to give a second chance even to a handful of Communists on at least one occasion: "Nine of these foreigners, although extremist militants involved in spreading revolutionary propaganda, are for the most part heads of families, and I think it best to bring them in to my Prefecture to remind them to observe political neutrality or face extradition."[33]

II

Even when the police wanted to look closely at suspected troublemakers, administrative rivalries got in the way. Despite Paris's importance as a center of immigration and intrigue between the wars, and unlike his peers in frontier departments, the prefect of police was obliged to obtain the minister of the interior's assent to expel people. Raux, the prefect of police in 1921, pointed out the absurdity of this situation early on, in a letter to the minister of the interior:

> You must keep in mind that in 1849, when the law was written, rapid means of transport did not exist. Foreigners from neighboring countries could enter, but their penetration stopped there, in the border regions; that's why the prefects of departments on the border were given special powers.
>
> Since that time, however, conditions have completely changed; modern transport has spread widely, with all lines connected to Paris as the central hub. This particularity ought, by rights, to give the Department of the Seine the same rights as a border department.[34]

In practice, this made effective action quite difficult, because the Paris Prefecture and the Ministry of the Interior were forever at odds with one another.

---

31. "Note sur la Sûreté générale," n.d., AN 2AG 618, quoted by Marc-Olivier Baruch, *Servir l'État français: L'administration en France de 1940 à 1944* (Paris: Fayard, 1997), 378 fn.

32. Weil, "Politiques d'immigration," 66–67.

33. Mimeographed letter of 28 November 1933 from le Préfet de Police to le Ministre de l'Intérieur (Direction de la Sûreté générale, 2ème Bureau), APP B/a 65ᵖ, doss. 51343–10.

34. Raux to the minister of the interior, 25 January 1921, APP D/b 336, dossier Étrangers.

Long before the creation of the Prefecture of Police on 28 pluviôse an VIII (17 February 1800), Paris and the provinces were governed by different police administrations. By the late nineteenth century, the Prefecture of Police was responsible for the city and the Department of the Seine, while the Sûreté générale (later nationale) was responsible for the rest of the country. On a number of occasions, the last between 1874 and 1876, the Prefecture of Police was responsible for policing the entire country and the Sûreté générale was cast in a subordinate role, giving birth to a tradition of bad feeling between the two.[35] Modeled after the Prefecture of Police, the Sûreté never enjoyed the same resources and often lacked effective leadership. During World War I, and intermittently throughout the interwar period, partisans of each agency sought the abolition of the other as the only possible cure for what they considered an absurd division of responsibility.

The Third Republic's notorious ministerial instability extended to the director of the Sûreté, who was a political appointee usually without any police experience or enough time on the job to learn the ropes. Few lasted as long as two years. In fact, most hoped to be promoted to the safer waters of the Prefecture as soon as possible. According to André Benoist, a functionary who served in both administrations:

> The post of director of the Sûreté générale serves as a gateway to higher office. Normally held by second-tier prefects and sometimes, to the detriment of the government, by men not prepared for such delicate functions, it serves as a trampoline to the position of prefect of police or Conseiller d'État[36]—to a mid-level post in the Treasury Deparment (Trésorier Payeur général)—if his performance is unsatisfactory.[37]

By contrast, the Prefecture of Police was a stable, professionally run organization. Louis Lépine's tenure lasted eighteen years, Jean Chiappe's and Roger Langeron's lasted seven each. In his memoirs, Langeron noted that "during my stay at the Prefecture of Police, I must have seen twelve ministers of the interior come and go." Under such circumstances, it is little wonder that prefects had low regard for their colleagues. Langeron went on that "it was up to the prefects to adapt to the minister, but to obey only in part."[38]

---

35. Jean-Marc Berlière, "A Republican Political Police?" 51 n. 22, and Berlière, *Le monde des polices en France, XIXe–XXe siècles* (Brussels: Complexe, 1996), 92–113. For the most thorough account of the tensions between the Prefecture and the Sûreté during the early Third Republic, Berlière, "L'institution policière en France sous la IIIe République, 1875–1914" (Thèse d'État, Université de Bourgogne, 1991).

36. An advisor to the government and member of the highest administrative court in the land.

37. André Benoist, *Les mystères de la Police* (Paris: Nouvelle éditions latines, 1934), 36. See also Georges Carrot, *Histoire de la police française des origines à nos jours* (Paris: Tallandier, 1992), 129–34.

38. Roger Langeron, *Paris, juin 1940* (Paris: Flammarion, 1946), 10.

Petty personal rivalries often frustrated communication. Henry Maunoury, the chief of staff (*chef de cabinet*) at the Prefecture during World War I, claimed that it was routine for prefects of police to make a public showing of tearing up the secret files on incoming ministers, all the while keeping a copy for themselves; worse, he reported that files were only sent to the place Beauvau (the Ministry of the Interior) during his tenure at the minister's request.[39] In his short-lived newspaper, *Police et justice*, the Sûreté superintendent E. Bourgeois characterized the national police as a "two-headed monster," incapable of common action. "This terrible organization," he wrote, "creates stupid, funny incidents that we could laugh about if a lack of authority didn't lead to the most serious consequences."[40] As Bourgeois pointed out, the Prefecture was obliged to give up the trail of a criminal at the edge of the city and then turn over the investigation to the Sûreté—and vice versa. Despite the good intentions of some leaders, the rivalry between the two branches constantly got in the way. Benoist wrote that "each considered Paris and its suburbs a personal fiefdom [*chasse gardée*], destroying the collars and traps laid by the other."[41]

The most important internal constraint on police action was imposed by an unwavering commitment to provide political asylum to victims of repressive regimes. Governments of both the Right and Left considered the granting of political asylum central to the republican tradition, and they went to great trouble to verify candidates' claims. Throughout the interwar years, a significant pro-refugee lobby encouraged authorities to live up to their universalist principles. The size of the lobby shrank significantly during the Depression, but the Communist and especially the Socialist parties, the League for the Rights of Man and Citizen, the Catholic Left, and a handful of isolated conservatives campaigned doggedly for more liberal asylum laws.[42]

Although not required by law, ministers of the interior normally granted a stay, or "sursis," to immigrants and conducted at least one investigation before expelling them.[43] The police archives are filled with letters from the prefect of police to the place Beauvau complaining about the practical diffi-

39. Henry Maunoury, *Police de guerre, 1914–1919* (Paris: Éditions de la Nouvelle Revue Critique, 1937), both the quote and the anecdote are from 49.

40. E. Bourgeois, "La police," *Police et justice* 1 (June 1918): 2. On competing reform projects, see also Louis Andrieux, *Souvenirs d'un Préfet de Police*, 2 vols. (Paris: Rouff, 1885); Henri Chardon, *L'organisation de la police* (Paris: Bossard, 1917); Edmond Locard, *La police, ce qu'elle est, ce qu'elle devrait être* (Paris: Grasset, 1919); and Ernest Raynaud, "La Préfecture de Police," *Mercure de France* (June and August 1918). Despite a century of attacks, the Prefecture maintained its jurisdiction until 1971, when it was limited to Paris, *intra muros*.

41. Benoist, *Les mystères de la Police*, 42.

42. Caron, *Uneasy Asylum*, esp. 80–93.

43. For an explanation of the law, see Pascalis, "L'interdiction de séjour et le sursis," *Revue pénitentiaire* (1924); Xavier Barthelemy, *Des infractions aux arrêtés d'expulsion et d'interdiction de séjour* (Paris: Domat-Montchrestien, 1936); and Marcel Livian, "L'élimination des étrangers," chap. 15 of his *Le régime juridique des étrangers en France*.

culty of expelling "undesirables," of the endless formalities that gave criminals the chance to slip away. As a draft circular explains, the prefect would normally draw up a list of people "to expel who, for diverse reasons, seemed likely to disturb the public order and it is up to the minister of the interior to decide."[44] Expelling people appears to have been quite difficult if the minister and the prefect of police did not share the same priorities. Several warnings and repeated investigations were usually carried out before authorities would take action. According to the police, at least, it was extremely rare for someone to be expelled on the basis of only one report:

> For the most part, when we decide that a foreigner is an undesirable, a series of investigations are carried out over a period of months, several warnings are given, and it is only when the investigations turn up something decisive against him or when there is no hope of his reforming that expulsion is envisaged.[45]

Even then, the accused could request a stay from the minister of the interior, which often led to interminable series of "counter-investigations." A simple glance at the facts, the police protested, makes it plain that a "stay, which should only be granted in exceptional circumstances, has become the rule."[46]

In the midst of all these investigations and regulations, immigrants found a lot of room to maneuver. Their memoirs are filled with stories of evading the police. Léopold Trepper bragged that "for those who know what they're doing, legality in this country has always had vague limits that could easily be transgressed."[47] When a police officer menaced him, "It has been a month since your wife arrived and she has yet to regularize her situation," Trepper replied, whispering, "That's my mistress, not my wife! She'll be gone in forty-eight hours," which satisfied the officer, who left them alone.[48] Not as shrewd as Trepper, another Jewish militant, Moshé Zalçman, was caught and beaten by the police, and then expelled for his Communist sympathies. His guard, "a decent bugger," looked at him "with pity and said, 'You should have thought of three things: girls, wine, and the movies.'" Besides the beating he received, however, nothing prevented his return. No sooner had he arrived in Belgium than he turned around and

---

44. "Action de la Préfecture de Police à l'égard des Étrangers en infraction aux Règlements ou indésirables," n.d. [1929?], APP B/a 65ᴾ, doss. 51343–10.
45. Ibid.
46. Le Préfet de Police à M. le Ministre de l'Intérieur (Sûreté Nationale—Direction de la Police du Territoire, 7ème Bureau), 28 March 1939, APP B/a 65ᴾ. See also numerous items in APP D/b 336, dossier Étrangers; APP D/a 745, dossier État-civil . . . ; and APP D/a 746, dossier prolongations de séjour.
47. Trepper, *Le grand jeu: Mémoires du chef de l'Orchestre Rouge* (Paris: Albin Michel, 1975), 39.
48. Ibid., 42.

headed back to France. In the first town he came to he "got some chow, a shirt, and a beret. The next day I was in Paris."[49]

In addition to their own inefficiencies, French administrations had to contend with the interventions of foreign governments. Most European immigrants benefited from treaties that guaranteed them the same health and unemployment benefits as French workers.[50] Furthermore, the two most important countries of emigration, Italy and Poland, took special interest in the fate of their nationals. Their consulates often intervened on behalf of their citizens; they went to great lengths to provide assistance and tried as best they could to preserve their emigrants' culture of origin.[51] Not a few French politicians believed that such efforts compromised French sovereignty. In 1924, in a famous speech in the Chamber of Deputies, Bertrand Nogaro complained that

> the insufficiency of our efforts since the war has led certain countries of emigration to turn their consulates into veritable administrations on our territory. . . . French authority has been eliminated bit by bit from the control of immigration . . . , without our administration's disposing of the slightest means of action or information.[52]

Countries of emigration came to realize that their citizens were a source of political power and did not hesitate to bring their concerns to the attention of French authorities—so long as those citizens remained on good terms with the home government.[53]

The repressive effort also had to contend with civil rights groups. The head of the conservative Republican Federation, Louis Marin, spearheaded the parliamentary campaign to secure a chair at the Collège de France for Albert Einstein. The prorefugee lobby organized mass meetings to protest Nazism and helped formulate the Popular Front's refugee policy. Along with Jewish refugee organizations, it waged a spirited campaign to overturn

49. Moshé Zalçman, *La véridique histoire de Moshé, ouvrier juif et communiste au temps de Staline*, trans. Halina Edelstein (Paris: Club France Loisir, 1977), 58–59, which relates the author's brushes with the law; he was expelled from France twice and returned both times without problem.

50. Livian, *Le régime juridique des étrangers*; and Oualid, *L'aspect juridique de l'immigration ouvrière*.

51. MAE, Z—Europe (1918–1940), Italie, vol. 17, Ambassade et consulats italiens en France, 1918–1929; MAE Z—Europe (1918–1940, Italie, vols. 367–69, Italiens en France, 1930–1940; APP D/a 744; and numerous letters in AN F⁷ 13,652. For overviews, see Janine Ponty, *Polonais méconnus: Histoire des travailleurs immigrés en France dans l'entre-deux-guerres* (Paris: Publications de la Sorbonne, 1988); and Pierre Milza, *Voyage en Ritalie* (Paris: Plon, 1993).

52. Bertrand Nogaro, "Rapport fait au nom de la commission des finances chargé d'examiner le projet de loi portant fixation du budget général de l'exercice 1925 (ministère du travail, de l'hygiène, de l'assistance et de la prévoyance sociales)," Annexe no. 517, *Journal officiel, documents, Chambre, annexes, sessions ordinaires* (July–August 1924), pp. 1999, 2000.

53. See note 6.

the harsh, anti-immigrant decree-laws of 1938. If their major successes in that regard stemmed largely from military and economic exigencies that encouraged a more rational use of refugees in war preparations, these groups nonetheless helped temper the positions of less compassionate administrations.[54]

In a limited number of cases, when a consensus could be reached, repressive action against suspected troublemakers was swift and effective. Few issues united embattled French administrations more than anticommunism.[55] As the historian Ralph Schor has pointed out, it was Radicals Chautemps and Sarraut, politicians ostensibly of the Left, who were most active in this regard; the Right was content to follow their lead. French politicians and bureaucrats could not stand to see foreigners abuse their hospitality. In 1924, the police signaled "the growing numbers of foreign elements in Paris and the suburbs that fail to observe the political neutrality required of guests in a foreign country."[56] Countless official letters complain of foreigners "who are mixed up in political agitation and don't observe the proper attitude required of guests on our territory."[57] In the words of Albert Sarraut, "It is unacceptable, it is intolerable the abuses some foreigners commit with these freedoms"; he and his colleagues could not accept "public critiques of our institutions, of our regime or its leaders."[58] Above all, Sarraut and his colleagues insisted that foreigners who had come to France in search of opportunity not meddle in political conflicts that did not concern them. Foreigners were not allowed "to take an active part in internal [French] political discussions and provoke trouble or disorder."[59] That is, Communists were not allowed to take part in political discussion. Black-shirted fascists, by contrast, generally held rallies unmolested, even during the Popular Front.[60]

Ministers of the interior and prefects of police overcame their differences and administrative inertia to bring the full weight of French legislation to bear on immigrants. They routinely ignored their cosmopolitan tradition and found ways to act efficiently: "Essentially a repressive measure, expulsion occasionally takes on a slightly different form." Especially when used

54. Caron, *Uneasy Asylum*, esp. 80–93. See also Marcel Livian's papers, OURS 24 APO.
55. Jean-Jacques Becker and Serge Berstein, *Histoire de l'anticommunisme* (Paris: O. Orban, 1987).
56. "Au sujet de l'activité politique des italiens résidant en France," typed report of 15 October 1924, APP B/a 1711, doss. 138.000–L-25.
57. Letter of 28 November 1933 from the prefect of police the minister of the interior (Direction de la Sûreté générale, 2ème Bureau), APP B/a 65ᴾ, doss. 51.343–10.
58. Sarraut, circular of 26 October 1938, APP B/a 64ᴾ, doss. 51.343–5, circulaires de la Sûreté générale relatives aux étrangers (1924 à 1950).
59. From the minister of the interior, Salengro, S.N.6 [Sûreté Nationale, 6ème Bureau] to the governor general of Algeria, to the prefect of police, Paris, and to nation's prefects, 4 July 1936, APP D/a 745, dossier État-civil . . . extrait d'immatriculation, sous-dossier expulsés . . . extradés.
60. APP B/a 282ᴾ, doss. 138.000–C, "Affaires diverses concernant l'Italie, 1935–1939."

to prevent mass gatherings, "it can be considered a preventative measure. . . . In such cases, the procedure is obviously much faster and an expulsion can be proposed and executed within twenty-four hours."[61] In September 1927, the police began a massive crackdown on the PCF's foreign
language sections. Sixty militants were arrested in their homes early one
morning, of whom about twenty were Italians: leaders of the *sous-section
centrale*, of the press, of the labor movement, "that is to say the most capa-
ble militants, just because they were Communists."[62]

To foreign Communists, the French police were all too effective. They
lived in constant fear of their home government's intervention, especially if
they were German or Italian. Whereas French administrations feared an immigrant invasion, party members feared the police invasions of their cell
meetings and union organizations, scaring off sympathizers and crippling
their work. Police raids, Communists regularly complained, had no other
motive than expelling foreigners who dared to raise their voices. Participation in a rally, a meeting, or even a union gathering was enough to run afoul
of the law, and foreigners were regularly intimidated by agents. The threat
of expulsion was enough to keep many foreigners from expressing their
views. As the Communist union leader Julien Racamond put it:

> For French capitalists, the foreign worker is a beast of burden who should
> provide a maximum of work for a minimal cost, without complaints, without
> demands. He can't join the CGTU or, especially, the Communist Party. They
> vaunt his muscles but are sorry that he can speak and can't be locked up at
> night next to the tools and machines.[63]

Authorities granted immigrants all the civil liberties enjoyed by citizens, as
long as they did not voice opinions critical of the Republic or question its
benevolence. During the first serious crackdown, from 1 January 1927 until
28 February 1928, the Prefecture expelled 1,494 and repatriated 314.[64]

But many given expulsion notices managed to elude the police, or, like
Zalçman, returned to France. Only a fraction of deportation notices ever

61. "Action de la Préfecture de Police à l'égard des Étrangers en infraction aux Règlements
ou indésirables," n.d. [1929?], APP B/a 65ᴾ, doss. 51343–10.
62. "Rapport de la section centrale de la MOE, " p. 3, n.d. [November 1929], AN Fᐧ7 13,090.
See also the numerous reports in the archives of the Institut Marxiste-Léniniste, repatriated from
Moscow: among many others, "Rapport mensuel de la section centrale de la MOE," 26 December 1927, BM B 35, no. 250; BM B 68, no. 449; and the letter from the Secrétariat, presumably
to the leaders of the Section centrale de la MOE, 3 January 1930, BM B 60, no. 405.
63. Racamond, "La MOE: Défendons ses revendications," *La vie ouvrière*, 4 May 1929.
64. 3 March 1928, APP B/a 65ᴾ, doss. 51343–10. At the national level: 95,130 expulsions
were made between 1920 and 1933; from 1932 to 1934, the monthly average of repatriations
was 521. After the assassination of King Alexander of Yugoslavia, the monthly average rose to
1,000. Marcel Livian, *Le régime juridique des étrangers*, and *Le temps*, 11 October 1934, are
cited in Ralph Schor, *L'opinion française et les étrangers, 1919–1939* (Paris: Publications de la
Sorbonne, 1985), 281–82.

led to an immigrant's leaving the country. While 95,130 people were expelled from France from 1920 to 1933, 40,771 were found guilty of evading an expulsion order. In Paris, in 1935, the immigration service issued more than 2,000 *refus de séjours*, but it could only verify 223 departures; it issued over 1,400 expulsion orders, but arrested 720 for evading those orders.[65] (In Marseille, one foreigner was condemned twenty-nine times for this crime.)[66] After questioning 3,800 people on the street in 1937, the Parisian RG found that roughly one-third of foreigners who had received expulsion notices succeeded in getting those measures suspended.[67]

The police resorted to the administrative *refoulement* and *refus de séjour* much more often than formal expulsions.[68] It was much easier, if less effective, simply to confiscate identity papers than to go through the legal process required to expel someone. Expelling people prevented them from returning and renewing attempts to regularize their situation, but it took time and entailed review by the courts. While the types of measures used varied according to the priorities of the ruling coalition, one constant stands out. No matter what means the government employed, only a small percentage of those sent away seem to have left the country. These statistics, one might argue, show that the police did little with all the information they gathered.

III

The very real protections immigrants enjoyed under the Third Republic should not lead us to conclude, however, that the immigration service had no effect on their everyday lives. Republican administrations did not systematically oppose a public opinion hostile to foreigners so much as they reflected divisions within French society. Conflicts between different divisions of the police, and between the police and other branches of government, left foreigners increasingly vulnerable.

Beginning in the mid-1920s and in earnest with the economic downturn of 1926–27, the activity of the political branch expanded beyond the "Republican" limits of pure observation. Agents from the RG joined labor inspectors in their regular trips around the city and suburbs to make sure foreign workers had their papers in order. Those activities increased in the ensuing years, as labor legislation was tightened in 1933, and again in

---

65. Noël Pinelli, "Rapport au nom de la 2e Commission, sur le fonctionnement des services de la Préfecture de police au cours de l'année 1935," Cons. mun., *Rap. et doc.*, no. 98 (30 November 1936), 45, 254.

66. Mauco, "Le problème des étrangers en France," *Revue de Paris*, no. 18 (1935): 400.

67. Mimeographed report, 23 July 1937, APP B/a 65ᴾ.

68. See chapter 2.

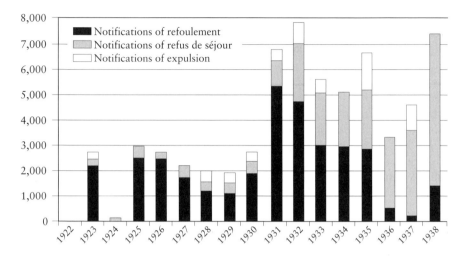

Figure 6. Types of deportation notice delivered.

Source: Cons. mun., *Rap. et doc.* No data for 1921–22.

1935,[69] and the police learned how useful immigration law could be in suppressing male prostitution, among other things.[70] If the political branch appears to have been relatively immune from prejudice, officers did not hesitate to resort to what we would call racial profiling. As the legal scholar Xavier Barthelemy noted in 1936: "Most of the time, an officer . . . will invite an individual who *looks suspicious* to 'display' his identity papers on a routine check of hotels and various public places." If the suspect seems foreign but cannot produce the proper papers, "he is taken down to the police station where an expulsion bulletin is drawn up."[71] The year after Barthelemy published his thesis, in the midst of the Popular Front, the political branch paid special attention to hotels that attracted foreign guests and stopped hundreds of thousands of immigrants on the street, some of them multiple times.[72]

The immigration service at the Prefecture did not hesitate to work with the antirepublican local authorities in Paris who controlled their funding. As we have seen, Prefect of Police Morain boasted to the right-wing councilors of using the service to intimidate ordinary immigrants into registering

69. Massard, "Rapport . . . sur le fonctionnement des services de la Préfecture de police au cours de l'année 1931," Cons. mun., *Rap. et doc.*, no. 1 (31 December 1931; published in 1932), 162–63; and Pinelli, "Rapport . . . sur le fonctionnement des services de la Préfecture de police au cours de l'année 1932," Cons. mun., *Rap. et doc.*, no. 14 (25 March 1933), 208–9. On the legislation, Bonnet, *Les pouvoirs publics*.

70. Police report, [10] January 1928, AN F[7] 13,017.

71. Barthelemy, *Des infractions*, 131–32, my emphasis.

72. Balensi, " 'Divisions étrangères,' " 18.

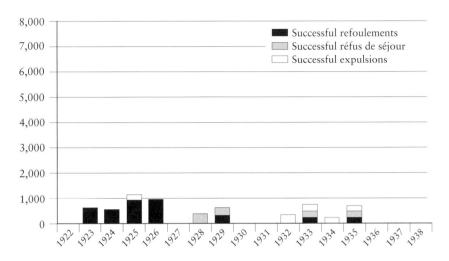

Figure 7. "Successful" deportations, by type.

Source: Cons. mun., *Rap. et doc.* No data for 1922, 1927, 1930–31, 1936–38.

at the nearest station house. While police chiefs issued balanced, moderate reports to mainstream Radical ministers of the interior, they often took a different line with local officials. When municipal councilor René Fiquet complained that "although the foreign population has barely reached one twentieth, in terms of criminality it was exactly one tenth in 1922,"[73] one of Morain's predecessors, Robert Leullier, replied: "Monsieur Fiquet has taken an example with only theoretical value." According to the prefect of police, immigrant criminality was even more threatening than the local politician supposed because the statistics only recorded the foreigners who got caught, leaving an uncertain number outside the grasp of the law: "precisely those whose identity papers are not in order, who move about Paris without authorization and who take pains to prevent us from uncovering their identity."[74]

The police regularly supplied bogus statistics that they knew would fuel municipal councilors' ranting about "invasion" and "degeneration." Twice in ten years, in 1921 and again in 1931, the Prefecture recorded arrests of foreigners at levels more than double their share of the population. Correcting for the age, sex, and social profile of the immigrant community would have sharply reduced the disparity: immigrants to Paris were disproportionately young, and hence unruly, unmarried, working-class men. Laws regulating identity cards did not apply to French nationals, and the police were

73. "Vœu tendant au renforcement des sanctions aux infractions aux arrêtés d'expulsion," *Bulletin municipal officiel de la ville de Paris,* supplément, compte rendu de la séance du vendredi 23 novembre 1923, vol. 42, no. 318 (25 November 1923): 4729.
74. The prefect of police to the municipal council, 23 November 1923, ibid., 4734–35.

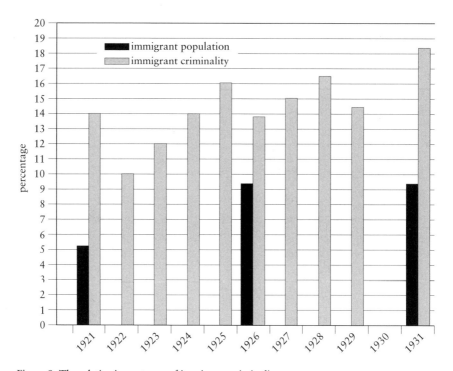

Figure 8. The relative importance of immigrant criminality.

Source: Annual reports on the Prefecture of Police in Cons. mun., *Rap. et doc.* (Paris, 1921–31). Quinquennial census figures from Jean-Paul Brunet, "Une banlieue ouvrière: Saint-Denis, 1890–1939: Problèmes d'implantation du socialisme et du communisme," Thèse d'État (1978; Lille: Service de Réproduction des Thèses, 1982), 3:793. No data for 1930.

extremely aggressive in searching out foreign offenders. They had a range of information about foreigners and their whereabouts that they lacked for French citizens.

The Paris police increasingly singled out foreign nationals quite simply because immigrants could not fight back. The central government routinely urged the pitiless suppression of the Republic's enemies. As minister of the interior, Albert Sarraut repeatedly told the Paris police to act boldly, that he would

> take full responsibility for your actions, I approve and thank you for them. . . . You can act boldly, for you have a leader, leaders, who are not in the habit of backing down when others question the behavior of their associates and subordinates. . . . I speak for all of your leaders who, well aware of their role, of their mission, will be constantly by your sides to defend you when you are right, and you will always be right, I am sure.[75]

75. ADA 12 J 36, "Discours de M. Albert Sarraut," 18, 28.

The problem for the Paris police was to avoid coming down too hard on opposition leaders who might soon be in power themselves. The Prefecture survived the Third Republic and its notorious political instability by obeying, but with a certain reserve. The evolution of the Carnet B in Paris, the list of subversives to be arrested in case of war, is quite revealing in this regard. It shows that 60 percent of those listed were French citizens in 1914; the proportion fell to 12 percent by 1936. Foreigners did not represent 10 percent of the Parisian population but made up nearly 90 percent of those listed in the Carnet B at that later date.[76] In part, this had to do with changing political threats. Obsessed with anarchists, pacifists, and revolutionary syndicalists at the turn of the century, authorities between the wars worried about Communists and fascists, many of whom were foreign. A growing xenophobia in the police surely played some role. But the police also singled out foreigners for less obvious reasons. Perhaps later purged during Vichy, the list drawn up in the spring of 1936 included no members of the right-wing leagues; it concentrated instead on second-rank French Communists, but not their leaders, and foreigners above all. As Donald Baker points out, the list was compiled during a period of great political uncertainty. Obliged to update their files with no way of knowing who would win the upcoming elections, the police included people on their lists who were unlikely to engage in a political backlash against them.[77] They were not so much a republican police force as a loyal police force serving a republic.

To understand how foreigners ended up in the Carnet B and other political files, and the consequences, we must leave the archives of the Prefecture, where personal files and expulsion records are almost entirely missing, perhaps lost on their trip down the Seine, perhaps burned in the Prefecture's furnace as the Germans approached. Those of the former Seine-et-Oise and, especially, the recently repatriated archives of the Sûreté help make up for that loss, with their copies of Parisian files, and a wealth of similar material. Established in 1934, the Sûreté's archives on potential political enemies focused predominantly on foreigners, and, modeled on the Prefecture of Police, they were organized in a similar manner. Using a single, enormous card file to keep track of all of their files on a given suspect, keeping it updated all the time, national authorities recorded not only the contents of those files and their location but who accessed them and when. The poor cousin of the Prefecture of Police, the Sûreté nationale quickly amassed vast amounts of information. Their archives grew so fast that within three years they had to buy a new building, in large measure to house them, and their central card file alone comprised some twenty thousand boxes that took up an entire floor.[78]

---

76. Donald N. Baker, "The Surveillance of Subversion in Interwar France: The Carnet B in the Seine, 1922–1940," *French Historical Studies* 10 (1978): 497.
77. Ibid.
78. CAC 19940500 art. 7, doss. 77.

It should be emphasized that the so-called Moscow files are not precisely analogous to those of the Parisian immigration service. Established to bring together all of their files in one place, the Sûreté archives contain information on French citizens, and the foreigners who figure in them often did so because they drew attention to themselves.[79] What stands out in these papers and others that survived the war is not the degree of control that police forces achieved but rather how little it took for immigrants to end up in political files, how fuzzy the distinction between immigration control and political policing turned out to be. A Polish citizen, Lucien Z., ran afoul of the law for straying too far to the left—on his bicycle! Without any other offenses on his record, Lucien was let off with a formal "stern warning" stamped in his file and told "at the first wrong turn, he would receive an expulsion notice."[80] A Russian émigré, Leon R., received a suspended sentence of four months in jail for petty theft and an expulsion notice in January 1923. He never left France, indeed, he was not allowed to leave the Paris region, and he had to write to the minister of the interior on special, taxed paper every four months to extend his stay. He did so assiduously for at least the next fourteen years.[81] Even the head chef of the Ministry of the Interior, expelled for a petty offense in 1919, had to keep requesting stays of his expulsion three times a year into the 1930s, despite his having married a Frenchwoman and never "having been the subject of unfavorable comments."[82] An Italian, Guiseppe G., got into trouble for swearing, refusing to place a light on his bicycle, and loitering in a café frequented by Communists. The local police commissioner in Essonne freely admitted that "no serious misconduct motivated my report," but he nevertheless proceeded to confiscate Guiseppe's papers and issued a refus de séjour.[83] Even without speaking out on political causes, a married couple made its way into one of the Prefecture's lists of political subversives because

> they received disreputable people in their home, accompanied by ladies of dubious morality, and we've been assured that their apartment is often the site of illicit rendez-vous. Moreover, their daily meetings with Samuel U., Else K., and other shady characters, their uncertain means of existence, and their ambiguous occupations make them suspect from both a national and a political point of view.[84]

79. On the creation of this archive, CAC 19940500, art. 7, dossiers 76–77.

80. Le Préfet du Doubs à M. le Ministre de l'Intérieur, Direction Générale de la Sûreté National, Direction de la Police du Territoire et des Étrangers, 6ème Bureau, letters of 26 December 1935 and 4 November 1936, CAC, 19940488 art. 20.

81. Le Préfet de Seine-et-Oise à Monsieur le Sous-Préfet de Corbeil, 13 July [1927?], ADY 1 W 1148–1149.

82. Le Commissaire de Police d'Enghien-les-Bains à M. Le Préfet du Département [Seine-et-Oise], Enghien, 5 July 1930, ADY 1 W 1148–1149.

83. Le Commissaire de Police d'Essonnes à Monsieur le Sous-Préfet de Corbeil, 20 December 1929, ADY 1 W 1146.

84. Mimeographed report, May 1938, APP B/a 65ᴾ, doss. 51343–10, Étrangers suspects, correspondance et rapports des RG.

Hanging out with an unseemly crowd, or attending a union meeting, frequently jeopardized immigrants' legal standing. The Paris police arrested Khil K., a Polish hatmaker, and drew up an expulsion notice because he attended a meeting of the radical Association ouvrière juive in 1920. Because Khil had never gotten into trouble before, they suspended his expulsion. For years thereafter, however, the police carefully monitored his mail, questioned his friends and associates, and spied on his comings and goings. They never found anything. The hatmaker constantly watched his step, afraid that his papers would be taken away. A decade later, even after the expulsion was formally commuted, the old blemish on his record continued to jeopardize his naturalization. Prefect of Police Langeron only began to reconsider as Khil's Polish-born son approached his eighteenth birthday, and thus became eligible for military service.[85] Magdalène R. arrived in Paris from Germany in 1933 with a passport properly stamped by the French consul in Cologne and an internship already arranged. When that contract expired she got special permission to stay on in France, until the police found out she was seeing a certain Siméon K., a member of the Bulgarian language section of the CGTU. They looked into her personal life and discovered that she "too is politically active and her sympathies lie with revolutionary extremists. She has, moreover, attracted attention to herself several times for voicing opinions hostile to France." When a warning and a refus de séjour failed to inspire her to steer clear of politics, the prefect of police sought her expulsion.[86] Once identified as a political risk, a foreigner endured all of the traditional methods of political policing. Agents went through their mail, questioned their friends and acquaintances, collected calling cards visitors left in their entryways, sometimes even tapped their phones.[87]

As the Depression worsened, life grew more difficult for everyone. The numbers of deportations began to rise dramatically in 1931, and the police began to deny papers to a significant number of newcomers (see figure 6). A spate of assassinations and terrorist attacks by foreigners led to redoubled surveillance efforts. The deranged Russian, Paul Gorguloff, gunned down President Paul Doumer in May 1932. Two years later it was the turn of King Alexander of Yugoslavia and of Louis Barthou, the French foreign minister, killed at the hands of Croatian nationalists. In the winter of 1934, the worst street fighting seen in Paris since the Commune was ignited in large measure by revelations of the financial scams and political blackmail of a naturalized Ukrainian Jew, Alexandre Stavisky.[88] Then there was a three-year lull, from 1934 to 1937, when no spectacular crimes were attrib-

---

85. CAC 19940457, art. 92, doss. 7878.

86. Le Préfet de Police à Monsieur le Président du Conseil, Ministre de l'Intérieur, 11 March 1936. CAC 19940472 art. 269.

87. CAC 19940499, art. 6, doss. 213 and 229.

88. Paul Jankowski, *Stavisky: A Confidence Man in the Republic of Virtue* (Ithaca: Cornell University Press, 2002), and Serge Berstein, *Le 6 février 1934* (Paris: Gallimard, 1975).

uted to foreigners in France. During 1937, however, at least fifteen gruesome attacks were recorded by fanatics of all ideological persuasions: abductions, arson, assassinations, and bombings filled the headlines. Especially after the assassinations of Doumer and King Alexander, surveillance intensified dramatically. The number of expulsions soared.[89]

On October 26, Minister of the Interior Paul Marchandeau warned all immigrants that they would be expelled if they committed even minor crimes or took part in any political activity. On November 6, he ordered the police to expel all foreigners whose papers were not in order. So many foreigners were dragged in to have their papers checked that the Service de la voie publique was given additional rooms to ease the clogging of the Prefecture's hallways.[90] In a letter of 23 November 1934, the prefect of police called the Sûreté's attention "to the particularly heavy workload that burdens the Inspectors of my service." Under normal circumstances, he wrote, inspectors worked overtime, often as late as three or four in the morning. But now, their workload was "heightened each time a foreign dignitary arrives, when the Sûreté nationale routinely sends us a list of approximately seven hundred suspects whose identification and surveillance must be taken care of right away."[91]

The Paris wedding of the Duke of Kent to Princess Marina of Greece in late 1934, following several spectacular assassinations and the street violence of 6 February, called for even more work. The prefect of police wrote that he was forced to use virtually all of his *inspecteurs généraux* as well as 150 inspectors from the Police judiciaire to carry out archival research on suspected foreign terrorists and conduct door-to-door searches: "Today alone, eight hundred searches have been carried out."[92] Even across the Atlantic, the *New York Times* ran stories on the raids.[93] In 1934 the police devoted thirty-four thousand man-days to surveillance and submitted forty-one thousand reports on foreign suspects.[94]

Authorities applied existing legislation more harshly to all immigrants, but certain groups suffered disproportionately. Persecuted by their own governments and without the help of any international organization, refugees

---

89. Schor, *L'opinion française*, 653–72.

90. Massard, "Rapport au nom de la 2e Commission, sur le fonctionnement des services de la Préfecture de police au cours de l'année 1934," Cons. mun., *Rap. et doc.*, no. 27 (15 November 1935), 221–22.

91. Prefect of police to the director general of the Sûreté générale, 23 November 1934, APP B/a 65ᴾ, doss. 51343–10, Étrangers suspects, correspondance et rapports des RG.

92. Prefect of police to the director general of the Sûreté générale, 23 [added by Directeur du Cabinet] November 1934, APP B/a 65ᴾ, doss. 51343–10.

93. "Paris Police Seize Hundreds in Café Raids in Drive to Rid City of Undesirable Aliens," *New York Times*, 27 November 1934, p. 46; and "Paris Raids Continue," *New York Times*, 27 November 1934, p. 10. Both cited by Caron, *Uneasy Asylum*, 398 nn. 11–12.

94. Massard, "Rapport sur le fonctionnement," Cons. mun., *Rap. et doc.*, no. 27 (15 November 1935), 224–25.

were particularly hard hit. Communists at least had the Secours rouge international.[95] In April 1933, the first refugees from Hitler's Germany were welcomed with open arms. The police asked only for a declaration that they were fleeing persecution. By August of that year, officers were instructed to turn away everyone whose papers were not in order, unless they could prove that they faced grave danger in Germany.[96] Refugees began calling the Prefecture the "Haus der Tränen," the house of tears. Already in November 1933, six had attempted suicide inside the Prefecture itself.[97]

In 1934–35, at the height of the Depression and the outset of the refugee crisis, the hard-line Bloc National governments of Pierre-Étienne Flandin and Pierre Laval unleashed what Vicki Caron has called a "veritable reign of terror" against the foreign population, and especially refugees.[98] As part of their anti-Depression campaign, the conservative governments targeted immigrant neighborhoods and took advantage of administrative refoulements to send migrants home, no matter how long they had lived in France or how deep their attachment to the country. The Popular Front changed tactics, granting amnesty to foreigners who had already taken up residence but refusing entry to any new migrants or refugees. Authorities eased the plight of those who had already managed to enter the country at the expense of those who followed, and eased the number of deportations. The respite proved short-lived.

Surveillance activity intensified sharply once more after Édouard Daladier came to power on 10 April 1938. Over the course of the 1930s, France welcomed more refugees than any other country in the world, per capita, even before more than 450,000 Spanish Republicans trudged over the border in the spring of 1939. By then French hospitality had given out. As conditions in central Europe worsened, the prospect of yet another great influx of refugees inspired renewed demands to close French borders. Implemented by then Minister of the Interior Albert Sarraut, the decree-laws of 1938 granted sweeping new powers to the police. While the new measures granted some new formal protections to refugees,[99] as a practical matter they made life much more difficult for them. Foreigners who lacked visas or identity cards, or those caught with false papers, were subject to fines of one hundred to one thousand francs and automatic prison sentences

95. The Secours rouge international, the Comintern's international aid agency, was created to help militants. As Trepper put it: "Un communiste sait qu'en France il pourra compter sur ses camarades du parti." *Le grand jeu*, 39.

96. Sommaire de la circulaire no. 222, in "Résumé des instructions ministérielles concernant les réfugiés d'Allemagne." Direction de l'administration de la police générale, sous-direction des étrangers et passeports, 27 November 1933, APP B/a 407, doss.13.112–1; circular from the minister of the interior, 2 August 1933, APP B/a 407, doss. 13.112–1.

97. Julia Franke, *Paris—eine neue Heimat?* 282; APP B/a 1814, doss. 241.155–1–A (November 1933).

98. Caron, *Uneasy Asylum*, chap. 3.

99. Weil, "Politiques d'immigration," 57.

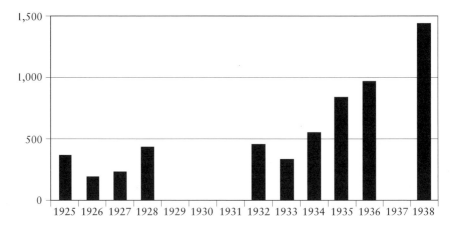

Figure 9. Expulsion orders received by foreigners in Paris.

Source: Cons. mun., Rap. et doc. No data for 1921–24, 1929–31, or 1937.

TABLE 2
Activity of the immigration service in 1937–38

Measure	1937	1938
foreigners arrested	363	2,100
refoulements/refus de séjour	3,577	8,813
proposed expulsions	1,089	1,512
expulsion notifications delivered	843	1,465
verifications of foreigners' declaration of residence	no data	688,992

Source: Cons. mun., Rap. et doc., no. 39 (1939): 69–70, 339.
Note: These figures do not include information from the Sûreté nationale, which would have made the totals higher.

of one month to one year. Anyone who helped illegal aliens enter the country or remain there was subject to the same sanctions. Failure to comply with an expulsion order now brought the prospect of a far stiffer sentence than in the past, and temporary extensions of residence permits were no longer provided. The new law authorized the police to deport people on their own initiative and provided them the funds to do so.[100]

The number of foreigners living in Paris rose from 370,701 in late 1936 to 438,688 in late 1938. The combination of massive arrivals and draconian new decree-laws sharply increased the severity of enforcement. The Pre-

100. For a thorough summary of the decree-laws with a commentary on their application in Paris, see Cons. mun., Rap. et doc., no. 39 (1939), 31–86. See also Caron, Uneasy Asylum, 174–75, and Schor, L'opinion française, 666–70.

Foreigners waiting in line to sort out their status at the offices of the Paris immigration service at the Prefecture of Police (May 31, 1938). © Keystone.

fecture took its stern new marching orders and faithfully carried them out. Officers not only cracked down on refugees but also trolled the city for foreigners working without proper authorization, for anyone whose papers did not comply with the decree-laws. The number of foreigners arrested increased nearly sixfold in one year, administrative refoulements more than doubled, and door-to-door searches continued unabated. In 1938 Parisian authorities collected 14.82 million francs from identity cards and 4.01 million francs in penalties.[101] On the night of 15–16 November 1938, a single officer from the RG questioned three hundred foreigners.[102]

IV

Foreigners attracted a considerable proportion of the RG's attention during the interwar years. If the annual reports are to be believed, foreigners never

101. Cons. mun., *Rap. et doc.*, no. 39 (1939), 62–63.
102. Principal chargé de la Section active des Étrangers au Directeur des RG, 16 November 1938 APP B/a 65ᵖ, doss. 51343–10.

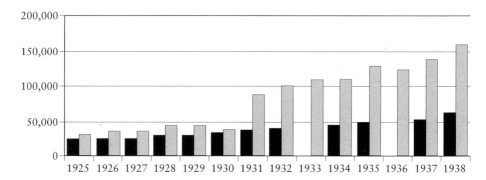

Figure 10. Renseignements généraux, immigration-related versus total reports.

Source: Cons. mun., *Rap. et doc.* Incomplete data in 1933 and 1936.

accounted for less than one-third of all RG reports and in 1930 made up an incredible 86 percent. Such figures are difficult to credit: Massard and Pinelli may have recorded only the total number of files that were passed from the Prefecture of Police to the Ministry of the Interior and other agencies, thus skewing the results. The total number of reports concerning foreigners is impressive nonetheless: three to six thousand reports filed every year.

Managing all the records they collected forced both the Sûreté and the Prefecture to experiment with new means of organizing and storing information. The scale of the effort, both in numbers of dossiers opened and agents involved, put immigration control at the forefront of an important growth in police power between the wars. No longer limited to specific neighborhoods or populations considered "at risk," the police set out to keep track of more people than ever before. They never realized Guillauté's dream of rendering the city completely transparent. The most complete records we have, those repatriated from Moscow, have more than a few references to people searched for in vain. Even when they got caught, most immigrants managed to avoid expulsion and stay in France. But immigration services did more than simply gather vast stores of information. Created in a bid to control the labor market and prevent political crime, the new immigrant service took advantage of its new powers to intervene in people's everyday lives.

The RG did more than observe population movements and track public opinion. As they had always done, the police questioned anyone who looked out of place or hung out with the wrong crowd. The need to police the boundary between entitled citizens and immigrant workers, moreover, increasingly led them to pay special attention to the foreign born. The police discovered in immigration control a powerful tool to control attitudes or behavior they considered deviant, especially with the tremendous growth of the unit during the Depression. Those controls gave the RG new leverage over foreigners that they did not enjoy for French citizens, ranging from a verbal caution or a formal "stern warning" stamped on their papers to a renewable stay, a suspended sentence, or an immediate expulsion that could be used for an infinite variety of offenses. With the emergence of systematic immigration controls in the mid-1920s, crossing the border and finding work were no longer enough to establish a person in France. François Cavanna spoke for many who increasingly worried about identity cards and work papers:

> Caught at a demonstration or a meeting, they take your work papers, the blue one, an' stick you with the green one. No setting foot on a worksite. Only permissible activity—tourism. Or they go all the way, label you a dangerous agitator, and expel your butt to the border.[103]

If the police forced relatively few people to flee, a substantial proportion of the capital's immigrants received an expulsion notice or knew someone who did. Over fifty thousand people received notices of expulsion or refoulement during the 1930s, out of a foreign population of 370,000 in 1936. Most families thus had at least one member or a close acquaintance who lost their papers and thus the right to stay.

In principle, all foreigners were equal before the law. As Rogers Brubaker has argued: "To be defined as a citizen is not to qualify as an insider for a particular instance or type of interaction; it is to be defined in a general, abstract, enduring, and context-independent way as a member of the state."[104] Writing the history of immigration and citizenship in these terms is relatively straightforward. Legal texts and administrative decrees reveal who is "in" and who is "out."[105] As a practical matter, however, context could make all the difference in the world. It mattered for everyone who sought naturalization, as authorities carefully scrutinized the company people kept and their political views. And it mattered in the daily lives of foreign citizens on French soil. To understand which laws were enforced,

103. François Cavanna, *Les ritals*, Livre de Poche (Paris: Belfond, 1978), 113.

104. Brubaker, *Citizenship and Nationality in France and Germany* (Cambridge: Harvard University Press, 1992), 29.

105. Giovanna Zincone, *Da sudditi a cittadini: Le vie dello stato e le vie della società civile* (Bologna: Il Mulino, 1992), 8–9. See also Mary Lewis, "The Company of Strangers: Immigration and Citizenship in Interwar Lyon and Marseille" (PhD diss., New York University, 2000), 15–16, and Alexis Spire, *Étrangers à la carte: L'administration de l'immigration en France (1945–1975)* (Paris: Grasset, 2005), 10–14.

when, and for which communities requires attention to local conditions. It requires attention to conflicts within the French administration, within immigrant communities, and between France and the rest of the world. To weigh the relative importance of the various different constraints that protected foreigners, we must now take a closer look at a community that did not enjoy those protections, at North African immigrants who were at once French and yet lacked the protections of citizenship.

Part II

Surveillance, Assistance, and Exclusion

Chapter Four

Race and Immigration

Little distinguished the initial reception of North Africans in France from that of preceding waves of immigrants. Neither the discrimination nor the violence they encountered set the first North Africans apart. Recruited as strikebreakers before World War I, North Africans, especially Algerians, played a crucial role in France's war effort both as soldiers and as civilian workers. As the war dragged on, however, colonial disturbances and the Republic's continuing reluctance to concede citizenship to Muslim Algerians began to change what had been an unexceptional prejudice against Algerians. Race played a role in metropolitan France's public policy for the first time during the war. Despite their universalist pretensions, French authorities declared North Africans too "ethnographically distinct"[1] after hostilities ended and did everything in their power to send every last colonial subject home. If racial fear drove their immigration policy, however, French politicians would simply have closed their southern border after the postwar expulsions. Unlike the United States, which enacted racially based national-origins quotas in the early 1920s, France abandoned the hope of closing the door to colonial migrants altogether.

Republican authorities did not see North African workers as essential for the economy. They dealt with the country's labor shortage instead primarily by recruiting unskilled workers from Italy, Poland, and other European nations, promising most of those foreigners the same social benefits as French citizens.[2] While as many as three million foreigners lived in the Hexagon, there

1. "La main-d'œuvre étrangère en France," *Bulletin du Ministère du travail et du prévoyance sociale* (January–February 1920): 20–21.

2. G. Bonvoisin and G. Maignan, *Allocations familiales et caisses de compensation* (Paris: Sirey, 1930), 45; Louis Stroh, *L'étranger et les assurances sociales* (Paris: Sirey, 1929); François

were never more than 160,000 North Africans on the mainland before World War II,[3] and successive governments maintained strict restrictions on entry. There were, however, political reasons for allowing at least some colonial migration. In the long run, politicians and leading colonial officials in Paris feared for the survival of their population-starved nation. In General Charles Mangin's famous words: "France does not end at the Mediterranean or even the Sahara; she extends down to the Congo; she constitutes an empire even more vast than Europe. . . . [I]n a half-century, she will have one hundred million inhabitants."[4] In other words: "France is a country of one hundred million inhabitants: forty million metropolitans, the rest natives and settlers in the colonies."[5] Forging this Greater France, mainstream politicians realized, entailed allowing at least some measure of colonial migration to the metropole, perhaps even making them fully French. Whatever misgivings they might have harbored, French officials considered Berber-speaking North Africans (Kabyles) the least physically and culturally alien elements in the empire.[6] As one of the leading experts on North Africa in the colonial administration, Octave Depont, explained: "If, in a half-century [Algeria] does not speak French and think in French, we shall have very nearly failed."[7] Despite many French officials' sympathy with

Neuville, *Le statut juridique du travailleur étranger en France au regard des assurances sociales, de l'assistance et de prévoyance sociale* (Paris: Chauny et Quinsac, 1930); M. Barthélémy Raynaud, "Les étrangers et la législation française sur les allocations familiales," *Le journal de droit international* (May–June 1933): 590; Marcel Livian, *Le régime juridique des étrangers en France* (Paris: Librairie générale de droit et de jurisprudence, 1936), 119–22; and William Oualid, *L'aspect juridique de l'immigration ouvrière* (Paris: Alcan et Rivière, 1923), 19–29, 69–70. According to Joanny Ray, from 1920 to 1931 many *caisses* (benefit offices) granted *allocations* to North African families, even if the women and children remained in the colonies; the level of the subsidies, however, remained below the normal levels for the métropole. The Parisian *caisse* stopped paying after the city's North African Services discovered numerous cases of fraud. Ray, *Les Marocains en France* (Paris: Institut des hautes études islamiques, 1938), 125.

   3. MacMaster, *Colonial Migrants and Racism: Algerians in France, 1900–1962* (New York: St. Martin's, 1997), 146–47, and Ray, *Les marocains en France.*

   4. Mangin, *La force noire* (Paris: Hachette, 1910), 355.

   5. Norbert Gomar, *L'émigration nord-africaine* (Paris: Presses modernes, 1931), 164.

   6. Clifford Rosenberg, "Albert Sarraut and Republican Racial Thought," *French Politics, Culture, and Society* 20, no. 3 (Fall 2002): 97–114.

   7. Depont had entered the Algerian civil administration in 1880, with the Prefecture of Constantine, and quickly moved on to a series of high-level posts. In a response to a reform campaign in Paris in 1911, the hard-line governor-general Charles Lutaud named him to supervise all of the colony's *communes mixtes*. In his official capacities and scholarly writings, Depont worried that Muslim populations would succumb to manipulation by religious leaders, especially in Pan-Islamic movements, and, later, to Communism. The quote is from Depont, *L'Algérie du centenaire: L'œuvre française de libération, de conquête morale et d'évolution sociale des indigènes; les Berbères en France; la représentation parlementaire des indigènes* (Paris: Sirey, 1928), 199. On Depont, see Charles-Robert Ageron, *Les algériens musulmans et la France, 1871–1919*, 2 vols. (Paris: Puf, 1968), esp. 2:619–21, and 2:1155–59; and Julia Clancy-Smith, "In the Eye of the Beholder: Sufi and Saint in North Africa and the Colonial Production of Knowledge, 1830–1900," *Africana Journal* 15 (1990): 246–49.

American restrictionists, they turned instead to the police to control workers they felt compelled to admit.

I

North Africans, primarily Algerian Kabyles, first came to work in mainland France more than a decade before World War I, even before the draconian travel restrictions of the *indigénat*, or "native code," were modified. Over the course of the 1870s, the settler delegation in Paris persuaded parliament to pass a series of exceptional laws, outside of French common law, to keep the peace in Algeria. The heart of the code was a series of thirty-three infractions that were not illegal under French common law but that were punishable in Algeria when committed by Muslims. In addition to traveling without a permit, offenses included speaking disrespectfully to or about a French official, defaming the Republic, or failing to answer an official's questions. Others included begging outside one's home commune, avoiding forced labor, refusing to fight forest fires or grasshoppers, and forgetting to declare a family birth or death. Enacted in the decade after massive uprisings in Kabylia, the *indigénat* constituted a humiliating regime of exception that survived largely intact until World War II.[8]

Berber-speaking Kabyles inhabited densely settled mountain regions, especially to the east of Algiers. They had a long tradition of migrating within Algeria and made up the overwhelming majority of Algerians in France until after the World War II. When the military gave way to civilian rule in Algeria with the advent of the Third Republic, Algerian Muslims were required to obtain a permit from authorities before leaving their *duwar*, the section of the commune in which they lived.[9] The French settler regime in Algeria limited internal migration in order to control vagrants, bandits, and Islamic agitators, as well as to guarantee a captive pool of low-wage laborers and to extort bribes. Restrictions on movement were eased somewhat over the following years and finally abolished in the face of mounting protests just before World War I.

At the turn of the century an emerging French-educated elite in Algeria and a coalition of liberal parliamentarians led a campaign for the assimilation of Algerians as French citizens with full rights. The hard-line governor-

8. See John Ruedy, *Modern Algeria: The Origins and Development of a Nation* (Bloomington: Indiana University Press, 1992), 89, for a concise overview; Isabelle Merle, "Retour sur le régime de l'indigénat: Genèse et contradictions des principes répressifs dans l'empire français," *French Politics, Culture, and Society* 20, no. 2 (Summer 2002): 77–97; and esp. François Marneur, *L'indigénat en Algérie* (Paris: Sirey, 1914).

9. The initial circular of 16 May 1874 was completed with another on 13 September 1882 that created sanctions for leaving one's commune of residence without having paid all applicable taxes or leaving without at least one of the following documents: a stamped passport or *livret ouvrier*, a *permis de voyage*, or a *carte de sûreté*. The new circular also punished all who failed to have their papers stamped in each commune visited during the trip.

general, Charles Lutaud, made a handful of concessions he considered trivial, as part of an effort to forestall more far-reaching changes. He published
a decree on 18 June 1913 exempting an extremely limited group of Muslims
from terms of the *indigénat* and abolished the travel permit required for
travel within Algeria and between Algeria and mainland France. Lutaud's
concessions, along with some others added by parliamentary liberals, were
voted into law the following year, on 15 July 1914.[10]
    A handful of Algerian immigrants made their way to France while re-
strictions were still in place. Arriving in the late 1880s and 1890s, they
worked primarily as servants, sailors, dockers, and itinerant salesmen. The
lifting of some restrictions on their movement in 1905 enabled Kabyle
drovers to travel with their flocks to Marseille and graze animals before selling them. Some settled in the port city and began taking jobs in local industry. The pace of migration increased dramatically in following years when
refineries began to recruit Algerians in a successful bid to break a strike of
immigrant Italian workers. Around 1910, the Michelin plant in Clermont-
Ferrand and the mines of the Pas-de-Calais began importing significant
numbers of Algerian workers, as did a number of Parisian industries. By
1912 Kabyles made up fully one quarter of all workers at the Say sugar re-
finery in southeastern Paris. Others worked in the chemical industry; in construction, helping to build the métro; for the railways; and for the Compagnie des omnibus. Itinerant salesman began to congregate in Montmartre
and around the place Maubert.[11] In 1914, the Parisian total had reached at
least 770, with over four hundred employed at the Say refineries.[12] The migration stream was well established.
    By 1911 the number of arrivals reached a sufficient level that M. Gérard,
the director of the Paris office of the governor-general of Algeria, reported
the need to organize and control the movement of "our natives."[13] The following year, the governor-general's office carried out the first of many surveys of North African immigration by asking all prefects in France to report

    10. Ageron, *Les algériens musulmans et la France*, 2:1093–1114, and Ageron, *Histoire de
l'Algérie contemporaine*, vol. 2., *De l'insurrection de 1871 au déclenchement de la guerre de
libération, 1954* (Paris: Puf, 1979), 250.
    11. Octave Depont, et al, *Les Kabyles en France: Rapport de la commission chargée
d'étudier les conditions du travail des indigènes algériens dans la métropole* (Beaugency: René
Barrillier, 1914); Ageron, *Les algériens musulmans et la France*, 2:854–58; R. Lopez and E.
Temime, *Migrance: Histoire des migrations à Marseille*, 2 vols. (Aix-en-Provence: Edisud,
1990), 2:152–55; MacMaster, *Colonial Migrants and Racism*, 52; and Gilbert Meynier, *L'Algérie révélée: La guerre de 1914–1918 et le premier quart du XXe siècle* (Geneva: Droz, 1981),
74.
    12. Depont, "Aperçus sur le recrutement de la main-d'œuvre indigène dans l'Afrique du
Nord." *Bulletin de la Société d'Économie sociale* (September–October 1925), 1, 7; Gomar,
L'émigration nord-africaine en France, 14; and Joseph Lugand, *L'immigration des ouvriers
étrangers et les enseignements de la guerre* (Paris: Librairies-imprimeries réunies, 1919),
20–22.
    13. Depont, *Les Kabyles en France*, 8.

the number, location, and occupation of Algerians under their jurisdiction. Each of the fifty-one responses mentioned at least a handful of itinerant hawkers or people passing through.[14] From the Hautes-Pyrénées to the Pas-de-Calais and Finistère, Algerians had covered most of the country, working in factories and selling trinkets and oriental rugs even before the conscription of the war. The 1912 survey guessed there were roughly four to five thousand Algerians in France. Within two years, historians estimate there were at least thirteen thousand; well-informed contemporaries put the figure as high as twenty to thirty thousand.[15]

The initial contact led to a handful of confrontations. Italian and Spanish workers in Marseille resented the use of Algerians as strikebreakers, and a number of fights broke out in 1909–10. In 1913, an ugly brawl at Fouquières-les-Lens in the Pas-de-Calais pitted Kabyles against Belgian miners upset at what they considered unfair competition. French workers at the Say refineries in Paris complained that Kabyle workers were injured so often—three times more often than their European counterparts—that they threatened to bankrupt the workers' mutual aid society.[16]

Tension between natives and newcomers was hardly new in France. The arrival in Paris of migrants from the Massif Central occasioned similar disturbances during the July Monarchy. In the 1840s and 1850s, French workers regularly attacked Belgians in the north for accepting low wages and dangerous working conditions.[17] A generation later, during the Great Depression of the late nineteenth century, Italians became prime targets of violence. At the time Algerians first began to arrive in France, French workers seem to have been more concerned with Italian immigration. Italian shops were periodically looted, workers intimidated and harassed and sometimes killed. Pitched battles broke out between French and Italian workers on numerous occasions, often involving thousands of people. During the notorious Aigues-Mortes massacre in the summer of 1893, the

14. While the report suggested that the failure of other prefects to reply indicated an absence of Algerians in their departments, it is clear from subsequent research that this is not the case. Depont, *Les Kabyles en France*, annex 1, p. 46; but cf. Geneviève Massard-Guilbaud, *Des algériens à Lyon: De la Grande Guerre au Front Populaire* (Paris: Harmattan, 1995), 45.

15. Depont, *Les Kabyles en France*, 8, for the 1912 report. Depont, "La main-d'œuvre indigène de l'Afrique du nord en France," *La réforme sociale: Bulletin de la Société d'économie sociale et des unions de la paix sociale*, new ser., vol. 3 (January–December 1923): 654–55, advances the figure of twenty thousand; Lieutenant-Colonel Lucien Weil in Bertrand Nogaro and Weil, *La main-d'œuvre étrangère et coloniale pendant la guerre* (Paris: Puf, 1926), 5, put the figure at thirty thousand. Recent historians have figured that the true number was lower: Meynier, *L'Algérie révélée*, 77, assumes that Depont's guess of twenty thousand accurately reflected the number of arrivals; correcting for returns, he estimates there were thirteen thousand Algerians in France before the war, and Neil MacMaster follows his lead in *Colonial Migrants and Racism*, appendix 1.

16. Depont, *Les Kabyles en France*, 29, 17–19, 25–26.

17. Firmin Lentacker, *La frontière franco-belge: Étude géographique des effets d'une frontière internationale sur la vie des relations* (Lille: Université de Lille, 1974), 241.

town's entire French male population, swollen with peasants in search of work from the surrounding hinterland, set out with rifles, pitchforks, truncheons, and shovel handles to hunt Italians. Official French sources record only eight deaths, but the violence dragged on for four days, from 16 to 19 August. The London *Times* put the figure closer to fifty dead and 150 wounded. The mayor had to call on all available gendarmes and get reinforcements from the cavalry and infantry stationed nearby to put an end to the violence.[18]

II

Not until World War I did colonial workers replace Italians as the prime targets of violence. Most Italians and Belgians left France during the war, replaced primarily by Spaniards and a substantial colonial and Chinese population. For the first time, massive numbers of non-European workers came to metropolitan France. Of the 662,000 "foreigners" recruited or conscripted to work in wartime France, nearly half came from the French colonies and China. Official sources registered 78,566 from Algeria alone; 48,995 from Indochina, especially Annam and Tonkin; 36,941 from China; 35,506 from Morocco; followed by 18,249 from Tunisia; and 4,546 from Madagascar.[19] Until 1915, workers came freely, mostly from Spain and Algeria. Late that year the government began to organize the recruitment, and increasingly the conscription, of colonial subjects to work in war factories. Beginning as an experimental trickle in 1915, the importation of colonial

18. José Cubero, *Nationalistes et étrangers: Le massacre d'Aigues-Mortes* (Paris: Imago, 1996); Michelle Perrot, "Les rapports entre ouvriers français et étrangers, 1871–1893," *Bulletin de la Société d'histoire moderne* 12th ser., no. 1 (1960): 4–9; Perrot, *Les ouvriers en grève, 1870–1900*, 2 vols. (Paris: Mouton, 1974); Anne-Marie Faidutti-Rudolph, *L'immigration italienne dans le sud-ouest de la France* (Gap: Louis-Jean, 1964), 1:164–79; Pierre Milza, *Voyage en Ritalie* (1993; Paris: Payot, 1995), 99–124; Milza, "Le racisme anti-italien en France: La tuerie d'Aigues-Mortes, 1893," *Histoire* 10 (March 1979); and Gérard Noiriel, *Le creuset français : Histoire de l'immigration, XIXe–XXe siècles* (Paris: Seuil, 1988), 258–62.

19. These figures are taken from Nogaro and Weil's semiofficial *La main-d'œuvre étrangère et coloniale pendant la guerre*, 25. See also Charles-Robert Ageron, "L'immigration maghrébine en France: Un survol historique," *Vingtième siècle* 7 (July–September 1985): 60, argues that all previous studies, including his own, had substantially overcounted; he suggested that ten thousand to fifteen thousand North African workers was a more realistic estimate. See also Mireille Favre, "Un milieu porteur de modernisation: Travailleurs et tirailleurs vietnamiens en France pendant la première guerre mondiale" (thèse pour l'obtention du diplôme d'archiviste-paléographe, École nationale des chartes, 1986); Tyler Stovall, "Color-Blind France? Colonial Workers during the First World War," *Race and Class* 35, no. 2 (1993): 36–37; John Horne, "Immigrant Workers in France during World War I," *French Historical Studies* 14, no. 1 (Spring 1985): 59; Gary Cross, "Towards Social Peace and Prosperity: The Politics of Immigration in France during the Era of World War I," *French Historical Studies* 11 (Fall 1980): 610–32; Jean Vidalenc, "La main-d'œuvre étrangère en France et la première guerre mondiale," *Francia* 2 (1974).

TABLE 3
Wartime immigrants by origin as a percentage of
the total immigrant population, compared with the
foreign population in 1911

National origin	1911	Increase 1914–18
Italians	38%	3%
Belgians	25%	5%
Spanish	9%	35%
North Africans	1%	20%
Indochinese	—	7%
Chinese	—	6%
Others	27%	24%

Source: John Horne, "Immigrant Workers in France
during World War One," *French Historical Studies* 14
(Spring 1985): 60.

laborers took on massive proportions by 1917 (see table 3). Many of the
conscripts brought that year were boys of no more than of twelve or thirteen.[20]

Enormous contingents of non-Europeans arrived after the French realized that war would drag on, in the wake of devastating military setbacks at
Verdun and at the Somme, in the face of a mutiny protesting governmental
efforts to "comb out" skilled French workers and send them to the front
(Mourier Law, August 1917), in the midst of organized labor's reawaken-
ing, and amid a more general crisis of confidence.[21] Foreigners of all origins
came into conflict with French workers at some point in the later stages of
the war, but the timing of their arrival and their segregation made non-
Europeans the most prominent scapegoats.[22]

Rumors swirled in Paris that North African workers were really soldiers
stationed in the capital to suppress any labor unrest, and the first skirmishes

20. Bernard, *L'Afrique du nord pendant la guerre*, 11, guesses that of the Algerian workers
during the war, thirty thousand came freely before October 1915 and another eighty-nine
thousand came later as contract workers—either as recruits or conscripts. See also Meynier,
L'Algérie révélée, 464.

21. Pierre Renouvin, "L'opinion publique et la guerre en 1917," *Revue d'histoire moderne
et contemporaine* (January–March 1968); Guy Pedroncini, *Les mutineries de 1917* (Paris: Puf,
1967); Leonard V. Smith, *Between Mutiny and Obedience: The Case of the French Fifth Infantry Division during World War I* (Princeton: Princeton University Press, 1994); Annie
Kriegel, *Aux origines du communisme français (1914–1920): Contribution à l'histoire du
mouvement ouvrier français*, 2 vols. (Paris: Mouton, 1964); Jean-Louis Robert, "Ouvriers et
mouvement ouvrier parisien pendant la Grande Guerre et l'immédiat après-guerre: Histoire et
anthropologie" (Thèse d'État, Université de Paris I, 1989); and Robert, "L'opposition générale
à la main-d'œuvre immigrée," in *Prolétaires de tous les pays, unissez-vous? Les difficiles
chemins de l'internationalisme (1848–1956)*, ed. Serge Wolikow and Michel Cordillot (Dijon:
Publications de l'Université de Bourgogne, 1993), 43–56.

22. The single most numerous foreign group, Spaniards, came as unregulated free workers,
and most of them had arrived before 1917.

broke out in May 1917. The military commander of North African workers in Paris reported fourteen assaults against his charges in May and June 1917, most of them isolated attacks by French soldiers or civilian citizens on North African street sweepers.[23] In late June, and again in August, a handful of serious uprisings took place. The most violent incident, a June 17 riot in the port city of Le Havre, led to a reported fifteen casualties.[24] Historians have suggested that the violent reception given colonial workers during the Great War differed in kind from that received by internal migrants and other Europeans during the nineteenth century. The introduction of "non-white,"[25] "third-world"[26] immigrants, in their view, introduced racial conflict to the European mainland for the first time.

The French routinely distinguished "exotic" non-European "indigènes," or "natives," from Europeans. Traveling expositions presenting colonial subjects in supposedly authentic surroundings to gawking crowds and heroic stories of colonial adventure had conditioned popular stereotypes of non-Europeans since the late nineteenth century. Government studies and surveys by industrialists regularly found colonial workers inferior to their French counterparts, reinforcing preconceptions of non-European inferiority.[27] In France, as in all other Western countries, there was a racial hierarchy with white clearly on top and black on the bottom, with red and yellow somewhere in between. The meaning of "blackness," however, has never been clear.

An ambient antiblack, anti-"oriental" racism pervaded the country, but every previous immigrant group, including peasants from the French countryside, had faced hostility with racial overtones as well. The pattern of violence against colonial workers during World War I was altogether similar to antimigrant violence throughout the nineteenth century, as was the initial official response. Popular and official opinion considered successive waves of foreigners inherently dangerous and described them in broadly similar terms from at least the time of the July Monarchy. To Balzac and his contemporaries, rural migrants might not have looked "black," but they were not exactly "white" either, and they were unlikely ever to become so.[28]

23. CAOM, DSM 5, cited by Tyler Stovall, "The Color Line behind the Lines: Racial Violence in France during the Great War," *American Historical Review* 103, no. 3 (June 1998): 753.
24. Stovall, "Color Line behind the Lines," 756.
25. Ibid., 737–69.
26. MacMaster, *Colonial Migrants and Racism*, 118.
27. William Schneider, *An Empire for the Masses: The French Popular Image of Africa, 1870–1900* (Westport, Conn.: Greenwood, 1982); and Thomas August, *The Selling of the Empire: British and French Imperialist Propaganda, 1890–1940* (Westport, Conn.: Greenwood, 1985). The industrial surveys themselves are highly contradictory and unreliable; moreover, when experienced teams of Algerians were tested, they sometimes outperformed Europeans. See Meynier, *L'Algérie révélée*, 465, 478–80.
28. See esp. the opening of *La fille aux yeux d'or* in vol. 5 of *La comédie humaine*, 12 vols., ed. Pierre-Georges Castex (Paris: Gallimard, 1976–81).

A shared Catholicism did not spare Belgian or Italian migrants a hostile reception. A common faith has often been held out as easing Italian integration in France, and in certain rural areas parish life did enable migrants to form bonds with the local community. But the ostentatious Christianity and superstition of Italian workers more often led to conflict in urban industrial areas where French workers labeled them "Christos." Italian dockers in Marseille hardly endeared themselves to their French comrades when they welcomed boats with cries of "Per Gesù e la madonna!" Like the ragpickers and masons from the Massif Central before them and North Africans and Portuguese after them, they were described as stinking, promiscuous degenerates with strange alimentary habits and a penchant for violence. They were not only rejected as strikebreakers and foreigners but also as "Kroumirs" and "Zulus." Like the Irish in England and the United States, Italians in France were often perceived to be "black" when they first arrived.[29] François Cavanna remembered suffering similar epithets in his youth. He mocked the pretensions of his northern-Italian neighbors in interwar Nogent-sur-Marne, in the Paris suburbs: "If only they realized, with their big fat heads, that for the French north and south don't matter—all "Ritals" are monkeys, darky kinky-haired mandolin players! Cheating tricksters, sly layabouts, jokers, and hotheads, who speak with their hands!" Italians for the French, like Neapolitans for northerners, were "a lower race, monkeys, shit. Everyone needs shit below him."[30]

North African migrants were initially received on much better terms than is often recognized. French workers were more curious about North Africans than hostile,[31] and the popular press and even French settlers in Algeria originally supported Kabyle emigration to the metropole. Senator Hughes Le Roux wrote in *Le matin* of a "good invasion."[32] In the north, the miners' "tchouk-tchouk" was closer to the Parisian "plouc," or bumpkin, than to subsequent epithets like "ratons" or "bougnouls." The ubiquitous "sidi," the Arabic word for "sir" that Algerian Muslims typically used to greet the French, had yet to take on the full range of its present derogatory connotations, and "bicot" had yet to cross the Mediterranean.[33]

29. Matthew Frye Jacobson, *Whiteness of a Different Color: European Immigrants and the Alchemy of Race* (Cambridge: Harvard University Press, 1998); Noel Ignatiev, *How the Irish Became White* (New York: Routledge, 1995); Richard Ned Lebow, *White Britain and Black Ireland: The Influence of Stereotype on Colonial Policy* (Philadelphia: Institute for the Study of Human Issues, 1976); Lynn Hollen Lees, *Exiles of Erin: Irish Migrants in Victorian London* (Ithaca: Cornell University Press, 1979); and Milza, *Voyage en Ritalie*.

30. Cavanna, *Les ritals* (Paris: Belfond, 1978), 65–66.

31. One Kabyle complained to the Depont commission of a flock of gawkers attracted to an Islamic burial—in Depont, *Les Kabyles en France*, 19.

32. Quoted by Meynier in *L'Algérie révélée*, 75.

33. Jules Roy, *The War in Algeria*, trans. Richard Howard (1960; New York: Grove Press, 1961), 15; and Meynier, *L'Algérie révélée*, 75–77.

Hostility toward colonial workers during World War I was not discernibly more racially charged than that toward any earlier wave of newcomers, and the idea that colonial workers were "racially distinct"[34] is difficult to sustain. Asians and black Africans, recruited and conscripted to help the war effort, differed more from the French population in terms of appearance, custom, and language than any previous migrants, but the case is not so clear with Algerian Kabyles, the single most numerous group. The first Algerian immigrants were more likely to speak French than were their European counterparts.[35] Some had extensive prior contact with French administrators and culture. Like Italians, the majority of the early Algerian immigrants came from a mountainous Mediterranean region, affected by the same economic and demographic crises. The leading French expert on Algerian immigration, Octave Depont, likened the migration of Kabyles to that of French peasants in "our alpine provinces, the Pyrénées and the Auvergne, where the same causes have for ages produced the same effects."[36] In a literal sense too, Algerians were closer to France than many European migrants. The trip from Algiers to Marseille took only twenty-six hours, shorter than the journey from many northern Italian centers of emigration, not to mention Salonika, Bratislava, or Warsaw.

Moreover, a venerable tradition of French ethnographic and historical writing dating back to the 1830s considered the overwhelming majority of Algerian immigrants "white." Inspired by what subsequent historians have called the "Kabyle myth," authorities long distinguished between the supposedly Caucasian Kabyles, descended from the original Berber inhabitants of Algeria, and the Arab invaders. Some nineteenth-century French writers suggested that the Kabyles descended from Roman Christians and bore merely superficial traces of Islam. Mgr. Lavigerie, archbishop of Algiers, supported measures "to bring back the Berbers to our [Christian] civilization that their forefathers shared."[37] Having twice rejected Abd al-Qadir's calls to insurrection, the mountain tribes of Kabylia were portrayed by colonial officials as fiercely independent and even protorepublican. The Kabyles, the French hoped, could be used to regenerate the Arabs and wean them from their obscurantist, feudal ways.[38] In the interwar years, French officials increasingly advocated a fusion of "healthy elements" with the

34. Stovall, "Color Line behind the Lines," 742.

35. Depont, Les Kabyles en France, 18.

36. Depont, "La main-d'œuvre indigène," 655.

37. Lavigerie is quoted by Ageron, Histoire de l'Algérie contemporaine, 2:12.

38. Ageron, Histoire de l'Algérie, 2:137–51; Ageron, Les algériens musulmans et la France, 1:267–92, 2:873–90; Ageron, "La France a-t-elle eu une politique Kabyle?" Revue historique 223–24 (April–June 1960): 311–52; Ageron, "La politique kabyle sous le Second Empire," Revue française d'histoire d'outre mer 52, no. 186 (1965): 67–105; Ageron, "Du Mythe kabyle aux politiques berbères," Mals de voir, Cahiers Jussieu 2 (1976): 331–48; and Patricia M. E. Lorcin, Imperial Identities: Stereotyping, Prejudice and Race in Colonial Algeria (London: I. B. Tauris, 1995).

"French race" to compensate for France's notoriously low birthrate. Some went so far as to advocate intermarriage.[39]

The racial discourse surrounding the Kabyle myth was never coherent. After years of studying Paris's Algerian population, the legal scholar Louis Milliot told an audience at the Sorbonne in 1931 that "most of them, by the way, are scarcely distinguishable from the mass of our workers," and then later called the Kabyle "eternally unruly, the most backward of Mediterraneans, the last of the white barbarians."[40] Claims that Algerians were white never went uncontested, but their prominence should give pause to a simple equation of colonial subjects and people of color. A clear black/white distinction did not exist.

III

Neither skin color, nor skull shape, hair type, nasal index, or any other racial measure influenced the treatment of North African Muslims by the Paris police as much as their colonial status did. From the conquest of Algeria until the end of the colonial period, Muslim immigrants endured a legal incapacity that left them particularly vulnerable.

When the Dey of Algiers capitulated to France on 5 July 1830, the French military delegation swore "to respect the freedom of religion of all [Algerian] inhabitants."[41] As a practical matter, Algerian Muslims and Jews were governed by distinct bodies of law, and neither enjoyed French nationality. With the annexation of Algeria in 1834, both were considered French subjects. But, according to Patrick Weil, they still did not have French nationality; no procedures allowed them to acquire it, even after the Constitution of 1848 declared Algeria part of France and divided it into three administrative departments.[42] To protect France's position in Algeria and contain what he saw as the European settlers' brutal exploitation of the native-born population, Napoleon III issued a pair of edicts (*sénatus-consultes*). The first, on 22 April 1863, protected tribal lands; the second, on 14

39. E.g., Gomar, *L'émigration nord-africaine*, 48–54. But cf. Elisa Camiscioli, "Producing Citizens, Reproducing the 'French Race': Immigration, Demography, and Pronatalism in Early Twentieth-Century France," *Gender and History* 13, no. 3 (November 2001): 593–621, for widespread concerns over intermarriage.

40. The public lecture was given on 11 December 1931 and later published as Milliot, "Les Kabyles à Paris," *Revue des études islamiques* 6 (1932): 162–75, quotes on 162, 173.

41. Quoted in Patrick Weil, *Qu'est-ce qu'un français? Histoire de la nationalité française depuis la Révolution* (Paris: Grasset, 2002), 225. On the conquest, Charles-André Julien, *Histoire de l'Algérie contemporain*, vol. 1, *La conquête et les débuts de la colonisation, 1827–1871* (Paris: Puf, 1964).

42. Weil, *Qu'est-ce qu'un français?* 225–27, and Emmanuelle Saada, "La 'question métis' dans les colonies françaises: Socio-histoire d'une catégorie juridique, Indochine et autres territoires de l'Empire français; années 1890–années 1950" (thèse, sciences sociales, L'Ecole des Hautes Etudes en Sciences Sociales, 2001), 1:336–42.

July 1865, explicitly granted Jews and Muslims French nationality. But the protections had little effect.

Algerian Muslims endured the burdens of nationality without any of the benefits of citizenship, which remained virtually impossible for them to acquire—much more difficult in fact than for foreign nationals. Successive French governments reserved the right to approve the "naturalization" of Algerian Muslims on a case-by-case basis, which they did with enormous reluctance. Muslims had to renounce their religion before a mayor or designated administrative official and embrace the French civil code. The local administration would investigate the applicant's morality and family background. The dossier was sent with the approval, or refusal, of the local prefect and the governor-general to the minister of justice in Paris, then to the Conseil d'État, before the president of the Republic would finally sign a formal decree. In fifty years, from 1865 to 1915, 2,396 Algerian Muslims acquired French citizenship. Until 1899 few were denied, but from that point on the number rose dramatically to a third, a half, even three-quarters of all requests.[43]

French jurists rejected even the applications of Muslim converts to Christianity, inserting an indisputably ethnic component into French nationality law.[44] Under the domination of the French military Arab Bureaus, Muslims could not vote or run for elected office. The one privilege of nationality they enjoyed, the protection of French consuls abroad, remained entirely theoretical because local rules prevented them from leaving.[45]

The collapse of the Second Empire in 1870 delivered control of Algeria to European settlers, thereby foreclosing the possibility that Muslims might receive full French citizenship. Hardly committed democrats, the settlers had chafed under military authority and sought to impose rule by the civil institutions they dominated already. In the wake of France's defeat at Sedan, the new republican government of national defense granted Algerian Jews' longstanding request for French citizenship with the Crémieux Decree of 24 October 1870. Algerian Jews had served for decades as intermediaries between French colonial officials and the Muslim populations. Granting them full citizenship helped metropolitan officials—desperate to reorganize the army and end the German military occupation—break the power of army officials still loyal to the Second Empire. It added thirty thousand devoted new supporters for the fledgling Republic to the ninety-five thousand European settlers in Algeria. There was no theoretical problem with granting French citizenship to Muslims as well, insofar as previous governments had bestowed

43. Weil, *Qu'est-ce qu'un français?* 234–37.

44. Laure Blévis, "Les avatars de la citoyenneté en Algérie coloniale ou les paradoxes d'une catégorisation," *Droit et société* 48 (2001): 557–80.

45. Julien, *Histoire de l'Algérie contemporain*; Annie Rey-Goldzeiguer, *Le royaume arabe: La politique algérienne de Napoléon III, 1861–1870* (Algiers: Société nationale d'édition et de diffusion, 1977); and Xavier Yacono, *Les bureaux arabes et l'évolution des genres de vie indigènes dans l'Ouest du Tell algérois (Dahra, Chélif, Ouarsenis, Sersou)* (Paris: Larose, 1953).

the privilege on members of the so-called Four Communes of Senegal and the five French towns in India.[46] In Paris, a growing number of liberal elites championed the Muslims' cause throughout the early years of the Third Republic. Their efforts, however, were doomed from the outset.

The fragile, young Republic depended on settler votes.[47] From its birth in defeat in the Franco-Prussian War until at least the constitutional crisis of 16 May 1877, if not the Dreyfus affair at the turn of the century, the Third Republic remained on shaky ground. Committed republicans were initially a distinct minority in parliament, 245 of the 645 elected in the wake of the Commune. The new regime's constitution was secured by only a single vote, 353 to 352, for the famous Wallon amendment in 1875.[48] In this context, Republican leaders awarded three seats (out of seventy-five) in the Senate and three more in the Chamber to Algerian settlers. After the suppression of a massive rebellion in Kabylia in 1871,[49] metropolitan officials turned to the European settlers both to shore up their own political position and to maintain the peace in Algeria. They consistently gave in to settler demands and reinforced Muslims' second-class status.[50]

When French nationality law was placed on a modern footing in 1889, Republican politicians worried above all about incorporating foreign nationals. They reintroduced the so-called *droit du sol* on the mainland—territorial, as opposed to blood-right citizenship—to incorporate a young generation of immigrants born in France who often opted to keep their nationality and thus avoid military service in their adopted country. To get this measure approved, they helped shore up the political control of European settlers in Algeria by making naturalization easy for foreigners but keeping barriers in place against Muslim subjects.[51]

IV

Colonial migrants were intrinsically no different from earlier migrants, but their position in French society changed dramatically in the context of total war. While Parisian workers and employers had long treated newcomers badly, no matter where they came from, the French government had never singled out a particular category of immigrants for differential treatment before the World War I.

The mobilization of French men created a pressing need for labor. Efforts

46. Weil, *Qu'est-ce qu'un français?* 235.
47. This point is generally lost in the literature, e.g., Ageron, *Les algériens musulmans et la France*, 1:397–446.
48. Jean-Marie Mayeur, *La vie politique sous la Troisième République, 1870–1940* (Paris: Seuil, 1984), 52–69.
49. Julien, *Histoire de l'Algérie contemporain*, 475–500.
50. See note 8 above.
51. Weil, *Qu'est-ce qu'un français?* 231–32.

to find workers within the country, especially women, proved insufficient. In early 1915, government and industry leaders began to look overseas. The effort to recruit and organize unprecedented numbers of workers from abroad led the government to control the labor market and intervene in people's lives as never before. When they did so, authorities took advantage of colonial subjects' political and legal disabilities, their lack of representation, to segregate them by ethnic origin and to subject them to ferocious discipline.

Latent prejudice and geopolitical concerns combined when the French government took control of the labor market in 1915. Albert Thomas's Ministry of Armaments, followed by the Ministry of Labor, distinguished between "foreign workers of the white race"[52] on the one hand, and Chinese and colonial workers on the other. French authorities could not afford to antagonize other European governments. Neutral Spain insisted that French recruiters stay off its soil; its workers, the vast majority of Europeans who worked in wartime France, came and went as they pleased. The French organized the movement of most other Europeans through diplomatic channels. Italians and Portuguese were recruited following rules set out in international accords, while French consuls in Salonika managed the emigration of Greeks. French officials might well have liked to separate Neapolitans from Venetians or Basques from Catalans, and they certainly would have liked to exert greater discipline over all workers, but foreign governments would not allow them to do so.

When France began to organize the movement of non-Europeans to the mainland, it relied on the military, and as the war wore on non-Europeans were increasingly subject to military control. The military office that oversaw colonial workers was divided into a number of sections, in the words of its director, "each one corresponding to a race of workers."[53] While the law guaranteed all workers equal pay for equal work, in practice Chinese and colonial workers were consistently underpaid, housed in deplorable conditions, and brutally disciplined for minor infractions.

French physical anthropologists and colonial administrators had long studied the various races of mankind and argued about their relative merits, but their findings had never been applied outside of the colonies.[54] Taking

52. Nogaro and Weil, *La main d'œuvre étrangère et coloniale pendant la guerre*, 43.
53. Weil, "L'administration des travailleurs coloniaux et chinois pendant la guerre," in Nogaro and Weil, *La main d'œuvre étrangère et coloniale pendant la guerre*, 19.
54. Joy Dorothy Harvey, "Races Specified, Evolution Transformed: The Social Context of Scientific Debates Originating in the Société d'anthropologie de Paris" (PhD diss., Harvard University, 1983); Claude Blanckaert, "La science de l'homme entre humanité et inhumanité," in Blanckaert, ed., *Des sciences contre l'homme* (Paris: Autrement, 1993); Alice L. Conklin, *A Mission to Civilize: The Republican Idea of Empire in France and West Africa, 1895–1930* (Stanford: Stanford University Press, 1997); William B. Cohen, *The French Encounter with Africans: White Response to Blacks, 1530–1880* (Bloomington: Indiana University Press, 1980); and Cohen, *Rulers of Empire: The French Colonial Service in Africa* (Stanford: Hoover Institute Press, 1971).

advantage of its expanded wartime powers, the government commissioned studies of racial aptitudes. These studies were no more than subjective, often contradictory, reports written by colonial officers or surveys filled out by businessmen. French officials used them, when they could, to organize the labor market. They also offered private employers the option of selecting the race of their workers on their forms. Further research would be required to determine how often rank prejudice sent Asians to jobs demanding manual dexterity and Africans to heavy labor, but it clearly occurred.[55] Racial categories determined the organization of government agencies and, at least to some degree, the labor market, but they remained quite unstable, even after the war.

While a handful of, mostly, Anglophone historians have studied racial conflict and discrimination during World War I, race played a more important role later, in the revolutionary spring of 1919. A series of debates at the Ministries of Labor, Foreign Affairs, and National Reconstruction led to a conscious effort to shape the ethnic composition of the labor market. Fearing unemployment and tensions between returning soldiers and the colonial subjects who had taken their place on the home front, authorities shared the settlers' fears about the presence of colonials in the metropole. They all worried that colonials might join revolutionary movements in Europe and foment their own in the colonies. Many sought to recruit Europeans to help rebuild and repopulate the nation and to exclude colonials on racist grounds. Bertrand Nogaro, an economist and law professor before the war who managed European labor during the hostilities, wrote:

> The Service de la Main-d'œuvre étrangère experienced notable success in adapting foreign elements, even with the limited resources at its disposal. As a general proposition, one can say that the son of any foreigner (of the white race), born or arrived young in France, will make a Frenchman similar in all respects to our own native sons.
>
> Thus it seems possible to remake the French population, that is to say to save it definitively, with a policy that would introduce chez nous a sufficient number of healthy and assimilable [i.e., white] foreigners.[56]

---

55. Mary Lewis, "Une théorie raciale des valeurs? Démobilisation des travailleurs immigrés et mobilisation des stéréotypes à la fin de la Grande Guerre," trans. Sandrine Bertaux, in *L'invention des populations: Biologie, idéologie et politique*, ed. Hervé Le Bras with Sandrine Bertaux (Paris: Odile Jacob, 2000). See also Nogaro and Weil, *La main d'œuvre étrangère et coloniale pendant la guerre*; Augustin Bernard, *L'Afrique du nord pendant la guerre* (Paris: Puf, 1926); Meynier, *L'Algérie révélée*; Favre, "Un milieu porteur de modernisation"; Marc Michel, *L'appel à l'Afrique: Contributions et réactions à l'effort de guerre en AOF, 1914–1919* (Paris: Publications de la Sorbonne, 1982); Laurent Dornel, "Les usages du racialisme: Le cas de la main-d'œuvre coloniale en France pendant la première guerre mondiale," *Genèses: Sciences sociales et histoire*, no. 20 (September 1995): 48–72; and Stovall, "Color-Blind France?"

56. Nogaro note of March 1919, MAE, C.P.C.—Série C. Administrative—1890–1940, vol. 347, folios 6–7.

Wary of colonial migrants, Nogaro and his colleagues pronounced them "too ethnographically distinct" from the native French population and voted to give priority to Europeans to rebuild the country after the war. In order, they recommended: Italians, Poles, Czechs, Portuguese, Spaniards, Greeks, Russians, Germans, Austro-Hungarians, and Bulgarians.[57] As the Palmer Raids turned politicians and public opinion against the deportation of foreign radicals in the United States,[58] the French Republic "deported" hundreds of thousands of its own nationals who had provided loyal service during the war.

Authorities decided to "repatriate" all colonial subjects after the war, despite the dubious legality of such an effort. Perhaps afraid of increased social tensions in the colony, officials in the Paris office of the Algerian government warned the Prefecture of Police that, as a French national, "an Algerian cannot be repatriated unless he has expressed a desire to return home beforehand." The law notwithstanding, virtually all colonial workers were sent home. In late May 1919, the minister of the interior disregarded that advice and decided that all North Africans without steady, permanent jobs would have to be repatriated. He instructed the prefect of police to "round up every individual you consider undesirable," without worrying about further authorization. In June the police combed Paris in search of unemployed North Africans and other colonial subjects, and later that month the cargo ship *Jabatoa* began a series of trips, ferrying one thousand North Africans at a time from Marseille to Algiers.[59]

Unable completely to expel the mainland's colonial population, French officials resorted to increasingly heavy-handed measures, hunting down anyone who looked out of place. In 1920, Parisian officers were ordered to drag in any suspicious looking foreigners, especially Chinese, to have their an-

57. The goal was to "give preference to European workers before colonial or exotic labor because of the potential for social or ethnic tensions that might result from the presence on French soil of groups that are too ethnologically distinct from the French population." "La main-d'œuvre étrangère en France," 20–21.

58. John Higham, *Strangers in the Land: Patterns of American Nativism*, 2nd ed. (1955; New Brunswick, N.J.: Rutgers University Press, 1988), chap. 8, esp. 210–12, 219–33; Higham, "The Politics of Immigration Restriction," in his *Send These to Me: Jews and Other Immigrants in Urban America* (New York: Atheneum, 1975), chap. 2; William Preston Jr., *Aliens and Dissenters: Federal Suppression of Radicals, 1903–1933* (Cambridge: Harvard University Press, 1963); Robert K. Murray, *Red Scare: A Study in National Hysteria, 1919–1920* (Minneapolis: University of Minnesota Press, 1955); and Mae M. Ngai, *Impossible Subjects: Illegal Aliens and the Making of Modern America* (Princeton: Princeton University Press, 2004), chaps. 1–2.

59. The prefect of police to the minister of the interior, 25 January 1921, APP D/b 336, dossier Étrangers, pp. 8–9. See also Le Ministère de l'Intérieur, Direction de la Sûreté Générale, Contrôle Général des services de Police Administrative, à Monsieur le Préfet de Police. doc. no. 2112, 30 May 1919, in APP B/a 67ᴾ, doss. 331.500–A; Le Préfet de Police (Direction de la Police Judiciaire) à M.M. les Commissaires Divisionnaires et Commissaires de Banlieue (marked "*Très Urgent*"), 4 June 1919, APP D/b 341, dossier travailleurs coloniaux et étrangers.

thropometric measurements taken—even if no crime had been committed.[60] By 1921, only two hundred of the wartime workers recruited from Algeria, Tunisia, and Morocco remained in the entire country;[61] and only about fourteen hundred Chinese and Indochinese workers were allowed to stay on, primarily to help rebuild the devastated areas in the northeast.[62] Over the next several years, the French government negotiated a series of bilateral treaties with Italy, Poland, Spain, Czechoslovakia, and other European countries, at least in part to ensure a predominantly European workforce.

<h2 style="text-align:center">V</h2>

The distinction, commonly made in the United States, between race and ethnicity depends on a clear black/white distinction that did not exist in early twentieth-century France. The racial status of North Africans remained ambiguous throughout the interwar years. For some, they could never be part of the white race. During the war "white" workers were regularly separated from Chinese and colonials on racial grounds. A semiofficial history of foreign labor in World War I continued to recognize the distinction eight years after the war ended.[63] Others, like the legal scholar Louis Milliot, described Algerians as "white" into the 1930s.[64] The suggestion, made by a number of Anglo-American historians, that violence and discrimination was "ethnic" when targeting French peasants or Italians but "racial" when aimed at North Africans ignores this ambiguity.[65] To argue that the racial identity of North Africans remained ambiguous throughout this period is not, however, to deny the existence of prejudice.

60. Le Commissaire Divisionnaire délégué dans les fonctions de Directeur de la Police Judiciaire, à MM les Commissaires de Police de la Ville de Paris et des communes du Ressort, 14 January 1920, in APP B/a 67ᴾ, doss. 331.500 main-d'œuvre étrangère pendant la guerre.

61. According to the Prefecture, one thousand North Africans remained, primarily by breaking their contracts. Préfecture de Police, Service des RG, Division du Cabinet, 1er Bureau, 21 February 1921, APP B/a 67ᴾ, doss. 331.500–A. According to a "minute" at the Quai d'Orsay, only eight Algerians were permitted to stay on as "travailleurs libres," not counting the 650 who remained at the Société de Gaz de Paris: Le Président du Conseil, Chargé de l'interim du Ministère des Affaires Étrangères à M le Ministre le l'Intérieur (Service des Affaires Algériennes), 24 December 1919, MAE, K—Afrique, sous-série Questions Générales, vol. 30.

62. Nogaro and Weil, *La main d'œuvre étrangère et coloniale pendant la guerre*, 28 n. 1. Gomar, *L'émigration nord-africaine en France*, 21.

63. Nogaro and Weil, *La main d'œuvre étrangère et coloniale pendant la guerre.*

64. See note 40

65. Stovall, "Color Line behind the Lines," 740, writes that "inter-ethnic violence has a long history in France," but that "[d]uring World War I, concepts of racial difference based on skin color became a significant factor in French working-class life for the first time." Here and in his more recent "National Identity and Shifting Imperial Frontiers: Whiteness and the Exclusion of Colonial Labor after World War I," *Representations* 84, no. 1 (November 2003): 52–72, Stovall equates non-Europeans with "people of color."

Desperate for workers during the war, France recruited and conscripted massive numbers of colonial workers after European labor became scarce. French authorities took advantage of their special wartime powers to segregate colonial workers from the civilian population, subject them to more stringent discipline and inferior pay, and often tried to allocate workers by their perceived racial aptitudes. North Africans were received on fairly good terms before World War I, at a time when French workers frequently came to blows with Italians, whom they often derided as "black." North Africans had been working in the metropole for years before tensions mounted during the war. After the armistice, French politicians decided to expel colonial subjects from the metropole for patently racist reasons. Fearing "ethnic incompatibility," as they put it, authorities deported as many colonials as they could.

Like France, the United States devoted considerable resources to the surveillance of foreigners and radicals during World War I. Woodrow Wilson invoked the 1798 Alien Enemies Act as soon as war was declared. Supernationalist secret volunteer societies, especially the American Protective League, acted as auxiliaries to the Justice Department and the Federal Bureau of Investigation. Established in March 1917, with the Justice Department's approval, the APL soon had more than twelve hundred separate units functioning throughout the country. With its help, the FBI continued to monitor foreigners after the armistice. The young J. Edgar Hoover compiled dossiers on more than two hundred thousand "suspects" and organizations, employing similar methods to France's postwar immigration service.[66] But after the Palmer Raids of January 1920, Congress turned against the extension of the wartime espionage and sedition acts. While political policing continued, the possibility of effective immigrant surveillance by the FBI disappeared.

In 1921 the United States replaced the police repression, Americanization campaigns, and deportations of the war years with a quota system that dramatically reduced the number of immigrants who could enter the country from southern and eastern Europe. Held in check since the 1880s, the restrictionist movement gained tremendous support during the war, with the growing influence of "100 percent Americanism" and the decline of Progressivism. American nativists of the "tribal twenties" pushed through a second, and more permanent, quota law in 1924, the Johnson-Reed Act, after leading industrialists gave up their opposition to restriction. By the 1920s, coal and steel had given way to electronics and chemicals, which depended on a stable, skilled workforce. With their profits increasing faster than wages, groups like the National Association of Man-

66. Athan G. Theoharis and John Stuart Cox, *The Boss: J. Edgar Hoover and the Great American Inquisition* (Philadelphia: Temple University Press, 1988), 56–62.

ufacturers and the United States Chambers of Commerce looked on pas-
sively, with little complaint, as politicians raised barriers against European
immigration.[67]

Many French nativists looked approvingly to the 1924 national-origins
quotas in the United States as a model for coping with massive immigration.
Even Socialists and Radicals envied the U.S. Bureau of Immigration and
Naturalization. Charles Lambert, the high commissioner of immigration
and naturalization, wrote in 1928 that "the example that it is indispensable
to recall, and in which we could truly find a model, is that of the United
States."[68] But the French Chamber of Deputies proved markedly less willing
than the U.S. Congress of the early 1920s to exclude migrants based on
their national origins. Once the revolutionary climate of 1919 passed, it became difficult for politicians to keep out the "ethnographically distinct."[69]
French business desperately needed the millions of Italians, Poles, and eastern European Jews the United States turned away, and put them to work in
the mines and steel plants of the industrial north and east, as well as in
Paris, Lyon, and Marseille.

At the same time, an influential minority of politicians and bureaucrats
reminded colleagues of colonials' wartime service and began to argue that
Algerians would prove even more useful to the nation than European immigrants because they were French. Unlike European foreigners, they argued,
Algerians would never form a national minority whose government could
challenge French sovereignty within the Hexagon and whose loyalty might
waver should war break out. For others, fear of continued unrest in the
colonies ruled out restrictive measures on the U.S. model. Racist restrictions
were thus a political impossibility in postwar France.

More than one-third of Muslim Algerian men between the ages of twenty
and forty were on the French mainland when the war ended,[70] and many of
them returned as soon as they could after being repatriated. The absence of
a formal quota system provided scant protection. After conducting its own
colonial Palmer Raids, the French Republic once again eschewed ethnic or
religious identification and looked instead to the police. Unable to bar entry
to colonial migrants, French authorities did everything in their power to pre-

---

67. Higham, *Strangers in the Land*, 316–18.
68. Lambert, *La France et les étrangers: Dépopulation, immigration, naturalisation* (Paris:
Delgrave, 1928), 96. Édouard Herriot, then minister of public education, praised U.S. methods
of organizing immigration in the book's preface. See also Albert Thomas's preface to Marcel
Paon, *L'immigration en France* (Paris: Payot, 1926); André Pairault, *L'immigration organisée
et l'emploi de la main d'œuvre étrangère en France* (Paris: Puf, 1926), 299–303; and Catherine
Collomp, "Regard sur les politiques de l'immigration: Le Marché du travail en France et aux
États-Unis, 1880–1930," *Annales, Histoire, Sciences Sociales* 51 (September–October 1996):
1107–35, for French misunderstandings of U.S. policy.
69. "La main-d'œuvre étrangère en France," 20–21.
70. Ageron, *Histoire de l'Algérie*, 2:262.

vent them from causing trouble in the metropole. The coalition of national leaders and local Parisian politicians that reorganized the immigration service at the Prefecture of Police also created a new surveillance network, exclusively for North Africans, that commanded exceptional resources in its bid to stamp out dissent.

Chapter Five

The Colonial Consensus

Most politicians looked on in dismay, but did nothing, as the North African population increased dramatically after World War I. A small minority of bureaucrats, politicians, and intellectuals supported coercive measures, but they could not realize their plans until moderates and liberals gave up their humanitarian scruples. A significant number of interwar French liberals supported hard-line tactics only if they furthered progressive aims. They would have agreed with John Stuart Mill that "despotism is a legitimate mode of government in dealing with barbarians, provided the end be their improvement and the means justified by actually effecting that end."[1] Progressives were loathe to rescind freedom of movement, granted to Muslim Algerians only in 1914—one of the few reforms they had been able to enact—and many feared that restrictions would lead to continued rebellion in Algeria. A combination of gratitude for the services colonials had performed and fear of continued unrest kept authorities from enacting restrictive measures on the American model. Although quotas remained impossible, the emergence of the French Communist Party's militant anti-imperialism and of Algerian nationalism in Paris persuaded even the most left-leaning Socialists to join their erstwhile enemies on the right in creating police networks with virtually unlimited powers.

Many historians have pointed to backroom deals as emblematic of French colonial policy and attributed abuses to the interference of powerful minority forces. In their view, the fragmented, dysfunctional nature of French parliamentary politics enabled a small elite of soldiers, settlers, businessmen, and bureaucrats to control Algerian affairs without having to con-

1. John Stuart Mill, *On Liberty* (1859; New York: Penguin, 1982), 69.

tend with the general will. Charles-Robert Ageron concluded his famous
study of the French "colonial party" by excusing the liberal Republic for
the excesses of its empire because "in its depths, France was not colonialist
in the nineteenth and twentieth centuries. . . . France was led by the colonial party which, alone, knew more-or-less what it had in mind for the Republic."[2] Neil MacMaster has been more inclined to blame metropolitan
conservatives, but he too points to entrenched "special interest groups"
whose demands were "implemented by administrative fiat. Nowhere were
these dangers greater than in the case of Algerian immigration. . . . The circuit of influence between the settlers, the *Gouvernement Général* [of Alge-
ria] and the Ministry of the Interior was tight and closed."[3] According to
this line of argument, the fate of some sixty million colonial subjects and
France's standing in the international community, as well as the expenditure
of many millions of francs, was decided without oversight by a small minority of retrograde zealots.

A great deal of decision making did go on behind closed doors, and neither empire nor migration figured prominently in parliamentary debates.
Apathy, however, can be construed as a form of approval. Both public opinion and representatives in parliament were well informed about efforts to
control colonial subjects in the metropole and the sums involved. Nothing
prevented challenges to government policy in the Chamber of Deputies.

If the control of North Africans in Paris was managed outside legislative
channels, it was hardly the work of an antidemocratic cabal. The men who
led the backroom meetings were no marginal figures, and the success of
their projects depended on the support of a wide variety of politicians from
across the ideological spectrum. By 1925, a consensus extending from the
most progressive figures in the Socialist Party on the left to members of
right-wing leagues had emerged regarding the management of North
African migration, a consensus broader than any other in French politics at
the time.

I

Passed in an effort to stave off more far-reaching reforms, the 1914 law
abolishing obligatory travel permits granted Algerians the right of free
movement to and from France. Departures from Algerian ports climbed
from 21,684 in 1920 to 71,028 in 1924.[4] The number of Algerians in Paris
increased 100-fold in less than two decades, rising from six hundred to at

2. Ageron, *France coloniale ou parti colonial?* (Paris: Puf, 1978), 297–98.
3. Neil MacMaster, *Colonial Migrants and Racism: Algerians in France, 1900–1962* (New
York: St. Martin's, 1997), 148–49, quote on 149.
4. Ibid., appendix, 223.

least sixty thousand between 1912 and 1928.[5] Well-informed politicians put the total as high as eighty thousand.[6] The capital soon outpaced Marseille as the leading center of migration in the country, providing a home for one-third of the Algerian population in France.[7]

The bright prospects of postwar Algeria soon turned when drought and famine descended on the countryside. The spring of 1920 was so dry that only a fraction of the wheat crop could be planted in what turned out to be the worst harvest in over a half century, with production more than 40 percent below average. Pastures withered and half of the grazing stock died of starvation, upward of three-quarters in some of the primarily Muslim *communes mixtes*. A deputy from Algiers reported that he had seen roads strewn with cadavers and that Arabs had resorted to eating inedible herbs and plants and even contaminated animal remains. Having just weathered the "Spanish flu" of 1918 and five years of war, Algeria suffered a typhus epidemic unleashed by the famine, which further devastated the colony. Although the harvest of 1921 proved bountiful, hard times returned in 1922–23. The Muslim population grew only 3.8 percent between 1911 and 1921, as opposed to 15.9 percent the previous decade.[8]

Algerians were attracted to France by a combination of organized industrial recruitment and, increasingly, word of mouth. Once a handful of pioneers found jobs with a particular company, they encouraged others in their village to follow them, establishing patterns of migration and employment that would last for the next fifty years. During the first two years of the war, when Algerians entered France freely, many settled in urban centers near their jobs. They formed close-knit enclaves—especially in Paris, Lyon, and Marseille—where recruits and conscripts later joined them to escape the crushing discipline of the military and work gangs, using forged identity papers to escape police de-

5. The chief of the North African Brigade, Adolphe Gérolami, guessed that only half of Algerians in France appeared on census returns; sixty thousand was his estimate of the true number of Algerians in Paris in 1928. See Louis Massignon, "Cartes de répartition des Kabyles dans la région parisienne," *Revue des études islamiques* 2 (1930): 167. The 1912 figure is from Depont, *Les Kabyles en France: Rapport de la Commission chargée d'étudier les conditions du travail des indigènes algériens dans la métropole* (Beaugency: René Barrillier, 1914), 24. Robert Sanson reported that there had been as many as sixty-five thousand, a figure apparently provided by the North African Brigade, in Sanson, "Les travailleurs nord-africains de la région parisienne," Institut National d'Études Démographiques, *Documents sur l'immigration*, travaux et documents 2 (1943; Paris: Puf, 1947), 170.

6. Godin, Cons. mun., *Proc.-ver.* (12 December 1932), 330. Although Godin was uniquely well informed, this figure is out of line with other reports, none of which cites a figure over sixty-five thousand.

7. Stéphane Sirot, "Les conditions de travail et les grèves des ouvriers à Paris de 1919 à 1935" (thèse de doctorat, nouveau régime, Université de Paris VII, 1994).

8. Jacques Berque, *Le Maghreb entre les deux guerres* (Paris: Seuil, 1962), esp. 97–98; Charles-Robert Ageron, *Histoire de l'Algérie contemporaine*, vol. 2, *De l'Insurrection de 1871 au déclenchement de la guerre de libération, 1954* (Paris: Puf, 1979), 294–95.

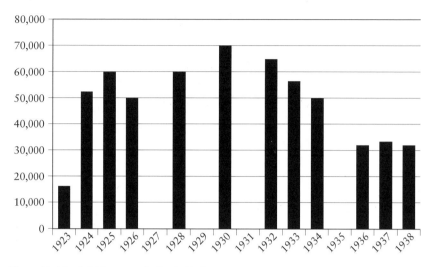

Figure 11. North African population in Paris.

Sources: Figures are provided by the North African Services at the Prefecture of Police:
1923:"Police et Assistance des travailleurs indigènes en France (Proposition de MM. Godin, Besombes et Posard [*sic*] au Conseil Municipal de Paris)," n.d. [1924], CAOM 9 H 113, cites a report conducted by the Algerian office in Paris on 11 October 1923 enumerating 8,360 *indigènes algériens* in Paris; 7,090 in the suburbs; and 16 in the hospital in Nanterre.
1924: Pierre Godin, "Proposition concernant la 'question kabyle' à Paris et confirmant une proposition antérieure de MM. Émile Massard, Besombes et Pierre Godin . . . ," Cons. mun., *Rap. et doc.*, no. 95 (31 July 1924), 1.
1925: Pierre Godin, "Fixation des attributions et de la situation du personnel de la section de surveillance et de protection des indigènes nord-africains," Cons. mun., *Proc.-ver.* (3 July 1925), 980.
1926: Cons. mun., *Proc.-ver.* (16 December 1926), 612.
1928: Louis Massignon, "Cartes de répartition des Kabyles," 167.
1930: Émile Massard, "Rapport au nom de la 2ème Commission, sur le fonctionnement des services de la Préfecture de police au cours de l'année 1930," Cons. mun., *Rap. et doc.*, no. 1 (30 December 1930; published in 1931): 158.
1932: Pierre Godin, "Note . . . sur le fonctionnement des services de surveillance, protection et assistance des indigènes nord-africains résidant ou de passage à Paris et dans le département de la Seine," Cons. mun., *Rap. et doc.*, no. 77 (1933), 18, quoting an unspecified report of 1932.
1933: Noël Pinelli, "Rapport au nom de la 2ème Commission, sur le fonctionnement des services de la Préfecture de police au cours de l'année 1933," Cons. mun., *Rap. et doc.*, no. 15 (31 January 1934), 229.
1934: Noël Pinelli, "Rapport au nom de la 2ème Commission, sur le fonctionnement des services de la Préfecture de police au cours de l'année 1934," Cons. mun., *Rap. et doc.*, no. 27 (15 November 1935), 240.
1936: Noël Pinelli, "Rapport au nom de la 2ème Commission, sur le fonctionnement des services de la Préfecture de police au cours de l'année 1936," Cons. mun., *Rap et doc.*, no. 83 (1 October 1937), 293.
1937: Noël Pinelli, "Rapport au nom de la 2ème Commission, sur le fonctionnement des services de la Préfecture de police au cours de l'année 1937," Cons. mun., *Rap. et doc.*, no. 71 (1 October 1938), 346.
1938: Conférence de coordination de l'Afrique du Nord, 27 January 1938, MAE, K—Afrique, 1918–1940, sous-série Questions Générales, vol. 80.

tection.[9] Before the war, several hundred Algerians lived near the café at 128, boulevard de la Gare, in Paris, where they socialized near their work at the Say refineries. By 1918, dense Algerian communities had formed in parts of the thirteenth, fifteenth, eighteenth, nineteenth, and twentieth arrondissements, as well as in the northern suburbs of Gennevilliers and Saint-Denis.[10]

Most were attracted to the industrial suburbs, working for automakers Citroën (Levallois, Clichy, St.-Ouen), Renault (Boulogne-Billancourt), and Hispano-Suiza (Courbevoie); metal-works like Bimétal (Alfortville) and Gnôme-et-Rhône (Colombes); a range of chemical plants, including Rippolin (Issy les Moulineaux), Air-Liquide and the Compagnie des Eaux (Gennevilliers), Fulmen and Goodrich (Colombes). By 1923, Renault employed fifteen hundred Algerians in its Billancourt factories,[11] and Citroën employed a reported seven thousand in its factories seven years later.[12]

More than any other immigrant group before them, the Algerian community was made up of unruly young men. Census figures do not even mention the presence of any Algerian women, while a 1926 report put their presence at 3 percent.[13] Algerian workers were almost exclusively working-age men, employed in the most unpleasant, poorly paid, and dangerous positions, and disdained not only by French workers but by other immigrants as well. They concentrated in automobile manufacturing, metallurgy, gas, chemicals, and maintenance (for example, most car washers were Algerian). Prefects and other local authorities never stopped complaining about these migrants, but only a tiny minority of politicians and administrators heeded their calls for several years.

II

Despite the return of so many colonial migrants, most surveillance organizations relinquished their power after the Armistice. The special branch of the Ministry of War devoted to controlling colonial subjects all but closed down, focusing primarily on a handful of demobilized black Africans and Madagascans. The army's special office in Les Invalides, created to help orient North Africans during hostilities, no longer had jurisdiction after the Armistice, and the North African section at the Ministry of the Interior ap-

9. On the early days of the Algerian community of Paris, see Mouloud Feraoun's novel *La terre et le sang* (Paris: Seuil, 1953).

10. MacMaster, *Colonial Migrants and Racism*, 63. See esp. Jacques Valdour's description of the thirteenth arrondissement, near the Say refineries, in *Ouvriers parisiens d'après-guerre: Observations vécues* (Paris and Lille, Arthur Rousseau and René Giard, 1921), esp. 74.

11. CAOM 9 H 113, "Rapport sur l'émigration des indigènes," 1923, pp. 15–17; MacMaster, *Colonial Migrants and Racism*, 79, 89.

12. Massignon, "Cartes de répartition des Kabyles," 166.

13. Georges Mauco, *Les étrangers en France: Leur rôle dans l'activité économique* (Paris: Armand Colin, 1932), 296.

pears to have been ineffectual, underfunded, and understaffed.[14] The only unit that continued to function was led by the Radical Albert Sarraut. One of the leading figures in the Radical Party between the wars, Albert Sarraut served as minister of colonies and minister of the interior on multiple occasions, and as prime minister once.[15] As resident-general of Indochina before World War I, he hoped to bring economic modernity to the colony without inciting labor unrest or demands for autonomy. His plan entailed sending small groups of Vietnamese workers to the metropole under close supervision for a brief period, and then bringing them back to the colony.[16] In October 1919, Sarraut convinced the minister of colonies, Henry Simon, not only to maintain the surveillance system they had created during the war but to develop it further.[17] With the help of retired officers from the Prefecture of Police, the service expanded its portfolio under Sarraut's direct supervision after he took over at the rue Oudinot in 1920.[18] In addition to soldiers, the service began to monitor all Indochinese subjects in the metropole. It opened files on every suspect individual, created a card index with their physical descriptions, and sent spies to follow them. After the war, Sarraut feared that colonial subjects would gain an apprenticeship in revolution in Paris and export it to their homelands.[19]

14. Benoit, "Rapport au Ministre," 12 December 1923, in CAOM, SLOTFOM, ser. I, cart. 4, doss. no. 2, "Contrôle et Assistance des Indigènes." See also Blaise Diagne report of 10 April 1922 in CAOM, SLOTFOM, ser. I, cart. 4, doss. "Rapports."

15. In addition to Mireille Favre, "Un milieu porteur de modernisation: Travailleurs et tirailleurs vietnamiens en France pendant la première guerre mondiale" (thèse pour l'obtention du diplôme d'archiviste-paléographe, École nationale des chartes, 1986), see Martin Thomas, "Albert Sarraut, French Colonial Development, and the Communist Threat, 1919–1930," *Journal of Modern History* 77, no. 4 (December 2005): 917–55; Philip Thomas Thornton, "Albert Sarraut, a Metropolitan in the Colonies: Indochina, 1911–1919" (PhD diss., University of Hawaii, 1980); Serge Berstein, *Histoire du Parti Radical*, 2 vols. (Paris: Presses de la Fondation Nationale des Sciences Politiques, 1980–1982); Peter Larmour, *The French Radical Party in the 1930s* (Stanford: Stanford University Press, 1964); Henri Lerner, *La dépêche, journal de la démocratie à l'histoire du radicalisme en France sous la Troisième République*, 2 vols. (Toulouse: Publications de l'Université de Toulouse–Le Mirail, 1978); and Jacques Gandouin, "Albert Sarraut, 1872–1962," *Administration* 116 (June 1982): 69–115.

16. CAOM, AOM 9 PA (fonds Sarraut), cart. 2, affaires politiques et indigènes, 1911–1914; Favre, "Un milieu porteur de modernisation," 1:295–99. See also Gilbert Meynier, *L'Algérie révélée: La guerre de 1914–1918 et le premier quart du XXe siècle* (Geneva: Droz, 1981), 75–77; Sarraut, *La mise en valeur des colonies françaises* (Paris: Payot, 1923); and Sarraut, *Grandeur et servitude coloniales* (Paris: Éditions du Sagittaire, 1931).

17. "Note d'ensemble concernant le Service de Renseignement Politiques créé au Ministère des Colonies, auprès du Contrôle Général des Troupes Indochinois," n.d. [1920?], CAOM, SLOTFOM, ser. I, cart. 11, folio 1; and Sarraut to the prefect of police, 19 June 1920, CAOM, SLOTFOM, ser. IX, cart. 3.

18. Sarraut to the prefect of police, 19 June 1920, in CAOM, SLOTFOM, ser. IX, cart. 3.

19. AD Aude 12 J 44, 162, and 172. See also Favre, "Un milieu porteur de modernisation," 1:5; David G. Marr, *Vietnamese Anticolonialism, 1885–1925* (Berkeley: University of California Press, 1971); William J. Duiker, *The Rise of Nationalism in Vietnam, 1900–1941* (Ithaca: Cornell University Press, 1976); and Scott McConnell, *Leftward Journey: The Education of Vietnamese Students in France, 1919–1939* (New Brunswick, N.J.: Rutgers University Press, 1989).

Sarraut and other leading policy-makers worried that colonial militants would transport European pathologies to homelands that were too "young" or "immature" to fight them off. Among the most feared "foreign" revolutionaries in Paris was a young photographic assistant, the "excessively sly"[20] Nguyen Aï Quoc, or Nguyen the Patriot, the future Ho Chi Minh. The Vietnamese representative at the Congress of Tours,[21] he participated actively in local cell meetings and worked closely with prominent French Communist leaders, contributing often to the party's daily, *l'Humanité*. One of the leaders of the Union intercoloniale, he also wrote for the Union's newspaper, *Le paria*.[22] A furious Sarraut complained to the prefect of police that even after several requests no one could determine the true identity of "this agitator with a genius for changing names and carefully hiding his true origins." He said he was from Annam, but was he really? Did he have the papers to prove it? How did he get to Europe in the first place, Sarraut wanted to know. Existing surveillance efforts had to be drastically augmented: "You must certainly find it unacceptable," he wrote to the police, "that by wandering around under a false name, Nguyen Aï Quoc meddles in our politics, belongs to political groups, and speaks during revolutionary meetings."[23] They kept him under almost constant surveillance but could not even discover his real name.[24]

Anticipating the approach later used for North Africans, Sarraut's service sought to monitor the small Vietnamese community and prevent it from falling prey to bad influences. As one administrator explained, it tried to inspire confidence in its charges, to provide assistance and help them navigate France's notoriously complex bureaucracy while policing them at the same time: "In all likelihood, once they realize that this service provides disinterested and effective support, they will respond less readily to the enemies of our colonization." Against the "revolutionary front," the new service countered with "a unified front of control and antirevolutionary propaganda."[25] Sarraut and his followers did not campaign to close the borders,

20. "Notes de Jean," 1–2 January 1920, CAOM SLOTFOM, ser. II, cart. 6, doss. Jean (1919–1920).

21. The French section of the Communist International broke away from the Socialist Party at this meeting in December 1920. See Annie Kriegel, *Aux origines du communisme français (1914–1920): Contribution à l'histoire du mouvement ouvrier français*, 2 vols. (Paris: Mouton, 1964), and *Le Congrès de Tours, 1920: Naissance du PCF* (Paris: Julliard, 1960).

22. Trang-Gaspard Thu, *Ho Chi Minh à Paris, 1917–1923* (Paris: Harmattan, 1992).

23. Minister of colonies to the prefect of police (Service des Renseignements généraux), no. 106 S.R., 17 August 1920, CAOM SLOTFOM, ser. I, cart. 11, doss. correspondance départ (1920).

24. "Déclarations de Jean," 3 November 1919, CAOM SLOTFOM, ser. II, cart. 6, doss. Jean (1919–1920). See also CAOM SLOTFOM, ser. I, carts. 3 and 11; and ser. III, cart. 40.

25. Benoit, "Rapport au Ministre," 12 December 1923, in CAOM, SLOTFOM, ser. I, cart. 4, doss. no. 2, "Contrôle et Assistance des Indigènes." See also Budin, "Rapport de M. Budin, Chef du 1er Bureau de la Direction des Affaires Politiques, sur sa mission à Marseille; propositions formulées en vue de la réorganisation du Service de Contrôle et d'Assistance des Indigènes," n.d. [October 1925] CAOM, SLOTFOM, ser. I, cart. 4, doss. no. 3, "Rapports."

in part because they feared doing so might lead to uprisings overseas but also because they thought allowing some workers to gain experience in the metropole would help develop the colonial economy and extend French influence into hinterlands it had yet to reach.

While the government had expressly expelled Chinese and colonial workers after the war and recruited Europeans to take their place, an influential minority of officials and intellectuals saw advantages in relying on colonial workers in the interwar years, especially Algerians.[26] As recent historians have stressed, authorities routinely referred to colonial subjects as ignorant children, prone to vice and unprepared for Western civilization. Some argued that North Africans were useless workers and dangerous as well, but they insisted, sometimes in the same breath, that they were no different from French peasants from the Midi or workers in Parisian factories.[27] They were frightened by the threats posed by exotic foreigners, and often expressed those fears in racist terms. But they also saw colonial migrants as a national resource and were unwilling entirely to exclude them.

A leading policymaker in the Ministry of the Interior, Octave Depont, feared miscegenation. He told an audience in 1922 that he had to warn fathers a few years earlier that their daughters had succumbed to the "aggressive flirting" of certain North African workers. Two such different civilizations and *mentalités*, he went on, could not be joined without significant preparation. But he concluded his presentation by reminding listeners of the sacrifices Algeria had made in sending one hundred thousand workers in France's hour of need. To forget the lessons of that experience would be willfully to ignore a tense international climate in which national resources could not be wasted.[28] Algerians had more than proved their worth as soldiers during the Great War, and, unlike foreign workers, the salaries they

26. A generous naturalization program combined with rigorous physical selection was central to a number of Radical proposals to change immigration policy, culminating in the famous reforms of 1927, which greatly eased restrictions on naturalization (Jean-Charles Bonnet, *Les pouvoirs publics français et l'immigration dans l'entre-deux-guerres* [Lyon: Centre d'histoire économique et sociale de la région lyonnaise, n.d. (1976)], 150–70, and Patrick Weil, *Qu'est-ce qu'un français? Histoire de la nationalité française depuis la Révolution* [Paris: Grasset, 2002], 76–78). The enormity of the task of closely regulating all immigrants, combined with the reluctance of business leaders to allow the government to restrict their supply of workers, limited the abuses suffered by most European immigrants, but once again North Africans were left fully exposed. See Charles Lambert, *La France et les étrangers: Dépopulation, immigration, naturalisation*, preface by Édouard Herriot (Paris: Delgrave, 1928); and Marcel Paon, *L'immigration en France*, preface by Albert Thomas (Paris: Payot, 1926), as well as the journals of such groups as Le Redressement français, Le Foyer français, and L'Amitié française.

27. Milliot, "Les Kabyles à Paris," *Revue des études islamiques* 6 (1932): 162–74.

28. Depont, "La main-d'œuvre indigène de l'Afrique du nord en France," *La réforme sociale: Bulletin de la Société d'économie sociale et des unions de la paix sociale*, n.s., vol. 3 (January–December 1923): 672–73.

sent home remained on French soil.[29] Algerian immigration could not be avoided and in any event provided interesting opportunities, as long as the immigrants were kept away from the bad influences of nationalists and Communist revolutionaries. In his view, the national interest justified much greater intervention into the lives of colonial migrants than those of foreigners, which in turn would benefit all involved.

In perhaps the most important expression of the value of Algerian immigration, the jurist Norbert Gomar wrote that "the indigenous Algerians constitute an interesting population source," and suggested that the French "set a long-term but generous and productive goal: the elevation and the assimilation of our Algerian populations. That can be our only policy."[30] For him, Algerian immigration was "more important than any other immigration, despite its numerical inferiority."[31] A country with France's low birthrate, he contended, could not afford to be too picky and had an obligation to take advantage of demographic resources wherever they could be found. Algerian migrants were, at least, French: "Is it not miraculous to see the men we lack running toward us from a French land, to see an insufficient birthrate increased without risking the emergence of national minorities?"[32] Incredible, perhaps, but true.

The process would take time and great care. Gomar and his contemporaries were obsessed with the notion of what they called "racial grafting," the idea that some infusions of new populations would "take" while others would be rejected.[33] Special measures would have to be implemented to ensure that only the most promising specimens made the trip. Neither Depont nor Gomar advocated free, unsupervised migration. Without state intervention, North

29. Depont et al., *Les Kabyles en France*, 34–35.

30. Norbert Gomar, *L'émigration nord-africaine en France* (Paris: Presses modernes, 1931), 53. See also Godin, "Note au sujet des services de surveillance, protection et assistance des indigènes Nord-Africains domiciliés ou de passage à Paris et dans le département de la Seine," Cons. mun., *Rap et doc.*, no. 67 (October 1930), p. 11; and Godin and Auguste Marie, "Proposition au nom du Groupe médical du Conseil municipal et du Conseil général, concernant le problème de l'immigration et la mise à l'étude d'un programme de création d'hôpitaux spéciaux pour étrangers," Cons. mun., *Rap et doc.*, no. 117 (15 December 1932), p. 3.

31. Gomar, *L'émigration nord-africaine*, 54.

32. Ibid., 48.

33. The classic text is René Martial, *Traité de l'immigration et de la greffe inter-raciale* (Paris: Larose, 1931). On Martial, see William H. Schneider, *Quality and Quantity: The Quest for Biological Regeneration in Twentieth-Century France* (New York: Cambridge University Press, 1990); and the numerous books and articles of Pierre-André Taguieff, esp. "Face à l'immigration: Mixophobie, xénophobie ou sélection. Un débat français dans l'entre-deux-guerres," *Vingtième siècle* 47 (July–September 1995): 103–31; Taguieff, "Théorie des races et biopolitique sélectionniste en France," *Sexe et race* 3 (1989): 12–60, and vol. 4 (1990): 3–33; and Taguieff, "Immigrés, métis, juifs: Les Raisons de l'inassimilabilité. Opinions et doctrines du Dr. Martial," in *Mélanges en l'honneur de Rita Thalmann* (Frankfurt: Peter Lang, 1994), 177–221. See also Claude Blanckaert, ed., *Des sciences contre l'homme* (Paris: Autrement, 1993).

Africans would be "completely torched"[34] (*brulé*) by Western civilization. Despite the risks, they, like Sarraut, thought that careful screening and constant surveillance would benefit both "races" and strengthen the empire.

Supporters of Sarraut's approach included such prominent intellectuals as Louis Massignon. The leading Arabist of his generation and a professor at the Collège de France, Massignon later participated in Paris's North African Service. He helped design the language courses the city offered. A Catholic mystic and specialist in the history of Islam, Massignon celebrated Arab civilization and thought that contact with France would benefit both civilizations.[35] The legal scholar Louis Milliot also contributed to the Parisian programs.

Despite the influence of its supporters, Sarraut's approach could not be applied to North Africans for several years. His surveillance outfit did an impressive job of keeping track of the small, highly politicized group of Vietnamese in the metropole and began to forge links between metropolitan and colonial police forces. An official report noted that "every letter from Indochina gives us invaluable information, in exchange for information collected by the Service de renseignements politiques de Paris."[36] The collaboration born in the early twenties lasted until the empire collapsed. By the end of the decade, authorities had files on a significant percentage of Vietnamese in France. But neither the handful of agents at Sarraut's disposal nor the even more embryonic services of the Ministry of the Interior in charge of Algerians were prepared for the number of North Africans who returned after the war.

A coercive regime of surveillance and assistance could not be applied to North Africans until progressive parliamentarians embraced it several years later. The "circuit of influence" between the settlers, authorities, and intellectuals might have been "tight and closed,"[37] but it was not powerful enough to act on its own.

III

Apart from convinced imperialists like Sarraut, Depont, and Gomar, few politicians were initially willing to support coercive measures. A significant number of humanitarians in the Chamber of Deputies believed that the le-

34. Depont, *L'Algérie du centenaire: L'œuvre française de libération, de conquête morale et d'évolution sociale des indigènes; les berbères en France; la représentation parlementaire des indigènes*, preface by Pierre Godin (Paris: Sirey, 1928), 131.

35. Christian Destremau and Jean Moncelon, *Louis Massignon* (Paris: Plon, 1994); *Louis Massignon et le dialogue des cultures*, ed. Daniel Massignon (Paris: Cerf, 1996); and Mary Louis Gude, *Louis Massignon: The Crucible of Compassion* (Notre Dame, Ind.: University of Notre Dame Press, 1996).

36. "Note d'ensemble concernant le Service de Renseignement Politiques créé au Ministère des Colonies, auprès du Contrôle Général des Troupes Indochinois," n.d. [1920?], CAOM, SLOTFOM, ser. I, cart. 11, folio 2.

37. MacMaster, *Colonial Migrants and Racism*, 148–49.

gitimacy of the French empire depended on reforming the legal status of colonial subjects. Before the war, the liberal deputy Albin Rozet, an iron-master from the Haute-Marne, led a campaign to improve Muslims' legal standing, offer better education, and in particular to curb the power of local settler authorities and the abuses of the notorious native code. After the war, the liberal cause was taken up by a young lawyer from Lyon, one of the leading members of the League For the Rights of Man, the Socialist deputy Marius Moutet. Having lobbied hard to reform the native code and having promised to reward Algerians for their loyal service during the war, Moutet and his fellow liberal parliamentarians were unwilling to take back one of the few reforms that had already been granted.

Largely overlooked at the time, as well as by subsequent historians,[38] the abolition of obligatory travel permits before World War I decisively limited French efforts to control Algerian immigration for more than a quarter century. At the turn of the century an emerging French-educated elite in Algeria and a coalition of liberal parliamentarians led a campaign for the assimilation of Algerians as French citizens with full rights.[39] Hard-line governor-general Lutaud granted a handful of concessions he considered trivial as part of an effort to forestall more far-reaching changes. He published a decree on 18 June 1913 exempting an extremely limited group of Muslims from the terms of the native code and abolished the travel permits required for travel within Algeria, and between Algeria and mainland France. Lutaud's concessions, along with some others added by parliamentary liberals, were voted into law the following year, on 15 July 1914.[40]

Despite a general wariness regarding colonial migration, no self-respecting republican could publicly advocate closing the border once social peace was restored. This was especially true for a staunch defender of human rights like Marius Moutet. As a young lawyer for the League for the Rights of Man, he won the admiration of the future Ho Chi Minh with his defense of Vietnamese nationalists in the early twenties.[41] He brought the plight of North Africans in the metropole to his colleagues' attention in November 1923. "They are completely abandoned, left entirely to themselves,"[42] he told the Chamber. "They are," he continued, "often the object of shameless exploitation by employers."[43] He warned

---

38. Meynier, *L'Algérie révélée: La guerre de 1914–1918 et le premier quart du xxe siècle* (Geneva: Droz, 1981), 49.

39. Ageron, *Les algériens musulmans et la France*, 2:1093–1114.

40. Ageron, *Histoire de l'Algérie contemporaine*, 2:250.

41. Jean Lacouture, *Léon Blum* (Paris: Seuil, 1977), 327, 353, 579–82.

42. Moutet in the *Journal officiel de la République Française, débats parlementaires*, no. 108, Chambre des Députés, session extraordinaire, compte rendu in extenso, 4ème séance, 21 November 1923, pp. 3626–27. See also Moutet, "La main-d'œuvre exotique—ce qu'on a fait, ce qu'on doit faire," *l'Humanité* (7 February 1916).

43. Ibid.

against "restrictions of liberty that are not absolutely necessary" and supported suggestions that the government take the initiative and create centers to assist them.[44] In a speech on "republican colonial policy," made soon after his appointment as the Popular Front's minister of colonies, Moutet professed France's commitment to a "colonial policy of liberation" and a "policy of humanism that would be loyal to freedom, justice, humanity" and to "the most beautiful traditions of liberalism and friendship between races."[45]

For all their talk of "liberation," however, few if any liberals could envision Algerian independence. They intended liberation in its particularly republican sense, freeing "natives" from their backward ways with the gift of French civilization.[46] Although he maintained close relations with a number of colonial nationalists like Ho Chi Minh and Messali Hadj, Moutet, like Jaurès before him, sought to rid empire of its nasty side while maintaining French influence.[47] He warned conservatives in the mid-1920s that "it would be wise to be more open-minded and negotiate, not to remain constantly and obstinately wedded to the status quo, and give natives the impression that you will only give them something by force."[48] He recommended assistance for colonials in the same terms conservatives used: "Without surveillance, without tutelage, without a moral guide . . . , they fall prey to all the temptations of the street." Like them, he worried about a lack of control and blamed the North African criminality on the government's inability to monitor the colonial population.[49]

Many liberals would have balked at Gomar and Depont's suggestion that Kabyles, much less Arabs, might ever be fully assimilated. Even the cosmopolitan Socialist leader and progressive intellectual Albert Thomas worried about ethnic incompatibility. "Given the experience of the past few years," he wrote in the preface of a 1926 monograph, "we must choose the races with the greatest affinity with ours: Italians, Belgians, Spaniards, Poles, etc.

44. Ibid. See also Moutet's introduction to Marcel Livian, *Le régime juridique des étrangers* (Paris: Librairie de Droit et de Jurisprudence, 1936), as well as Livian's memoirs, "Un vie, ma vie," in manuscript at the OURS, fonds Livian, 24 APO; and Livian, *Le Parti Socialiste et l'immigration: Le gouvernement Léon Blum, la main-d'œuvre immigrée et les réfugiés politiques, 1920–1940* (Paris: Anthropos, 1982).

45. Moutet, "Politique républicaine coloniale," n.d., CAOM PA28 1/1, quoted and trans. by Gary Wilder, "The History of Failure: Historicizing Popular Front Colonial Policy in French West Africa," in *French Colonial Empire and the Popular Front: Hope and Disillusion,* ed. Tony Chafer and Amanda Sackur (New York: St. Martin's, 1999), 33.

46. Robert Gildea, "The Soldiers of the Year II," in his *Past in French History* (London: Yale University Press, 1994), 134–53.

47. Federick Cooper, *Decolonization and African Society: The Labor Question in French and British Africa* (Cambridge: Cambridge University Press, 1996), chap. 3; Chafer and Sackur, eds., *French Colonial Empire and the Popular Front*; and William B. Cohen, "The Colonial Policy of the Popular Front," *French Historical Studies* 7 (1972): 368–93.

48. Moutet is quoted without attribution in Ageron, *Histoire de l'Algérie*, 2:307.

49. Moutet, in *Journal Officiel*, 21 November 1923, 3626.

The undesirables must be sent away."[50] Strict government control increasingly appealed even to progressive politicians. While liberal reformers never embraced racist quotas, they gave in to demands for heightened controls in the wake of a brutal crime that dominated newspaper headlines for days.

IV

The hesitation of progressive politicians ended in late 1923. At 4:30 p.m. on November 7, an unemployed, homeless man, a Kabyle from Algeria, entered a grocery store at number 43, rue Fondary in the fifteenth arrondissement. Khémili Mohamed Sulimane grabbed the grocer's wife, a thirty-year-old Parisian-born woman named Jeanne Billard, and dragged her out into the crowded street where he threw her to the ground. Brandishing an enormous kitchen knife he had stolen hours earlier, he kneeled over her, tore off her right cheek, and slit her throat, severing her left carotid artery. Covered in blood, he turned next to Louise Fougère, who was walking her eight-year-old grandson, Émile, home from school. Sulimane stabbed her. She collapsed, dying on the spot, and it took a quick-thinking neighbor to save little Émile by pulling him through her ground-floor window to safety. Then Sulimane ran across the street and slashed two more people: a young mother, who dropped to the ground, clutching her child, and a thirty-two-year-old shoemaker from Romania. Finally, while Sulimane stood menacing a group of schoolchildren, a construction worker entered the fracas and heaved a paving stone, distracting the madman until a pair of police officers arrived on bicycles and shot him. By the end of the sanguinary episode, two women had died and two more were taken to a nearby hospital for treatment. The Algerian was also taken to the hospital and treated for gunshot wounds to his hands and stomach.

The double murder dominated newspaper headlines and set off a series of popular disturbances.[51] Shortly after the murders, an unruly crowd tried

---

50. Thomas preface in Paon, *L'immigration en France*, 12. See also Elisa Camiscioli, "Producing Citizens, Reproducing the 'French Race': Immigration, Demography, and Pronatalism in Early Twentieth-Century France," *Gender and History* 13, no. 3 (November 2001): 593–621.

51. "Un algérien tue deux femmes et en blesse deux," *Le figaro*, 8 November 1923, D-1; "Deux femmes tuées, deux blessées par un arabe, rue Fondary," *Le petit parisien*, 8 November 1923, p. 1; "Drame épouvantable à Grenelle," *Le peuple*, 8 November 1923, p. 1; "Un arabe en délire tue une honorable commerçante et une passante, puis blesse deux personnes," *Le petit journal*, 8 November 1923, sec. 3, pp. 1, 3; "J'étais affolé . . . j'ai frappé . . . explique l'Arabe meurtrier de la rue Fondary," *Le petit parisien*, 9 November 1923, p. 1; "La tragédie de Grenelle," *Le petit journal*, 9 November 1923, p. 1; "Le crime de la rue Fondary," *L'action française*, 9 November 1923, B-2; "Le drame de la rue Fondary," *Le petit parisien*, 10 November 1923, p. 2; André Billy, "Paris le . . . criminalité exotique," *Le petit journal*, 13 November 1923, E-1.

to lynch an unsuspecting Algerian who happened upon them. Petitions cir-
culated demanding that "undesirable" elements be "expelled" from the
neighborhood.[52] Long articles recounted the lives of the young Billard
couple. Recently married and struggling to make ends meet, they had
moved into the diverse Grenelle neighborhood from the suburbs about a
year before. Camille Billard, the grocer husband, had taken a second job at
a nearby brasserie to earn extra money. Reporters tracked down witnesses
who claimed that Sulimane took advantage of Camille Billard's absence to
woo his wife, frequently stopping by the store to profess his love for her.
According to the newspapers, Jeanne Billard treated Sulimane generously,
sometimes giving him leftovers from her table, but she consistently rejected
his advances.

The theme of the invading, libidinous colonial subject laying waste to "la
douce France" could not be more stereotypical. The whole story sounds too
farfetched to be true.[53] The press undoubtedly garbled some of the details,
and vulgar prejudice distorted a number of articles. Prurient editors, however, cannot be blamed with dreaming up the entire episode, for much of
the story never became public. The precinct report includes the testimony of
a woman who told the police that she had been present in the Billards' store
a few days earlier when Sulimane entered and unleashed a torrent of pro-
fanity. Moreover, the building's concierge corroborated published reports
that Sulimane had been pursuing Mme. Billard for some six months, loitering in the street and hanging around the store. When the police asked Sulimane what could have motivated such a horrific crime, he replied, simply,
unrequited love.[54] One reporter quoted Sulimane as saying:

> My love for Mme. Billard completely changed my life. I could no longer work,
> eat, or sleep; my existence without her became impossible. I told her over and
> over again, but, each time, she burst out laughing and threw me out. Yesterday,
> I went again to beg her to come with me: she brutally rejected me. So I struck.[55]

Whatever the true nature of the killer's feelings for Jeanne Billard, news that
an Algerian man had murdered two French women and wounded two others in broad daylight outraged popular opinion and inspired a tremendous
response from authorities.

---

52. *Le petit parisien*, 9 November 1923, p. 1, and 10 November 1923, p. 2.

53. Ralph Schor does not mention the episode in his otherwise encyclopedic *L'opinion française et les étrangers, 1919–1939* (Paris: Publications de la Sorbonne, 1985). Neil Mac-Master has devoted a brief conference paper to the murder, "The Rue Fondary Murders of 1923 and the Origins of Anti-Arab Racism," in *Violence and Conflict in the Politics and Society of Modern France*, ed. Jan Windebank and Renate Günther (Lewiston, N.Y.: Edwin Mellen Press, 1995), 149–60.

54. APP, archives du commissariat de Grenelle, main courante, registre, 22 September 1923–30 January 1925, report no. 868, 7–8 November 1923.

55. *Le petit parisien*, 9 November 1923, p. 1.

The Fondary murders dominated newspaper headlines as the Moroccan rebel leader Abd el-Krim inflicted a series of stunning blows to the Spanish army in the Rif war, leading to a putsch and the rise of General Miguel Primo de Rivera's authoritarian regime in Spain. The French Communist Party (PCF) only became a mass party at the time of the Popular Front, but it exerted a powerful influence much earlier, especially on colonial matters. The newly formed party energetically supported Abd el-Krim's rebels, especially as it became clear that they would soon attack French positions. Against the "bankers' and capitalists' war," they demanded "the recognition of the independent Rif Republic." Soon after the rebel leader had demanded complete independence, on 10 September 1924, Jacques Doriot and Pierre Sémard wrote a telegram encouraging Abd el-Krim in the name of the French Communist Party, and Doriot toured the Hexagon in an effort to stir up hostility to the war.[56]

Communist protests outraged Socialists such as Moutet, making them increasingly willing to work with their erstwhile enemies on the right in supporting coercive measures.[57] That willingness only increased with the formal establishment in 1926 of Messali Hadj's Étoile Nord Africaine, an Algerian nationalist movement with close ties to the PCF;[58] nationalist uprisings in Indochina, leading up to the revolt at Yen Bey in 1930; the emergence of independence movements in Tunisia, Egypt, India, and elsewhere; and the advent of the Turkish Republic.[59]

Authorities feared that Communists and nationalist revolutionaries would exploit the freedoms of the metropole to prey on Paris's growing colonial proletariat, and then export revolution overseas. A later report explained: "Without Paris, Muslim agitation in the three North African territories could be easily contained."[60]

Shortly after the murders, in March 1924, the Radical minister of the interior, Camille Chautemps, created a special commission to prevent any sequels to the bloody episode, and especially to keep order in Paris. He called

56. Quotations from *L'humanité* in Raoul Girardet, *L'idée coloniale en France de 1871 à 1962* (Paris: La table ronde, 1972), 207. See also Jean-Paul Brunet, *Jacques Doriot: Du communisme au fascisme* (Paris: Balland, 1985), 54–60.

57. Girardet, *L'idée coloniale en France*, 213–14, 438–39.

58. Benjamin Stora, *Messali Hadj, 1889–1974: Pionnier du nationalisme algérien* (Paris: Harmattan, 1986), and Stora, "Histoire politique de l'immigration algérienne en France, 1922–1962" (thèse d'État, Université de Paris XII, 1991).

59. Pierre Brocheux and Daniel Hémery, *Indochine: La colonisation ambiguë* (Paris: La Découverte, 1995); Claude Liauzu, *Aux origines des tiers mondismes: Colonisés et anticolonialistes en France, 1919–1939* (Paris: Harmattan, 1982); Jamil Abun-Nasr, *A History of the Maghreb in the Islamic Period* (Cambridge: Cambridge University Press, 1987); Joel Beinin and Zachary Lockman, *Workers on the Nile: Nationalism, Communism, Islam, and the Egyptian Working Class, 1882–1954* (Princeton: Princeton University Press, 1987).

60. "Note sur la réorganisation de sûreté aux fins de surveillance de l'agitation musulmane en Afrique du nord," 11 May 1935, MAE, K—Afrique, sous-série questions générales, vol. 70, fol. 119.

together representatives from his own Department of Algerian Affairs as well as others from the Ministries of Colonies and Labor, and the Municipal Council of Paris to devise a strategy to restrict Algerian immigration and to provide assistance to those who, inevitably, would come anyway.[61]

Fearing that a complete ban on North African immigration would incite rebellion in the French colonies and drive immigrants into the arms of the Communist and nationalist opposition in the metropole, the Chautemps commission took advantage of France's colonial authority to impose a series of administrative hurdles that significantly limited freedoms guaranteed by existing legislation. The assembled officials, of various ideological orientations, voted unanimously to require all passengers traveling from Algeria to the metropole in third or fourth class to obtain a contract, approved by the Ministry of Labor; undergo a physical from a government doctor before departing, in order to rule out tuberculosis; and to prove their identity by presenting specially created identity cards with photographs.[62]

Ironically, the only opposition to restrictive measures came from a member of the commission concerned about poor settlers who stood to be affected along with colonial subjects. When dressed in European clothes, Algerians often passed as settlers, so one group could not be inconvenienced without also affecting the other. A colonial official admitted that "experience has shown that the distinction is not always easy to make, especially as many natives have begun to dress quite properly in Western clothes; the port police have serious difficulty doing their job as boats prepare to leave and they are faced with considerable crowds."[63]

The settler representative pointed out the patent illegality of restricting Algerian immigration or forcing immigrants to obtain any kind of papers in order to travel to the mainland. After the 1914 law abolishing obligatory travel permits, Algerians could not legally be forced to obtain travel documents except with the passage of a new law. Then he alluded to the bitter protests of Kabyle leaders in Algeria when they first heard of the new commission. Unconcerned about the fate of Algerian subjects, he argued that trying to restrict immigration from the colony would alienate poor settlers and, he implied, threaten French domination by inciting damaging protests by Kabyle elites. The convocation of the special commission alone had elicited a bitter petition campaign.

61. Minutes from the 10 April 1924 meeting of the "Commission instituée par arrêté du 24 mars 1924 en vue d'étudier et de réglementer la main d'œuvre nord africaine indigène dans la Métropole," in MAE K—Afrique 1918–1940, sous-série Questions Générales, vol. 31, Emploi de la main-d'œuvre indigène dans la métropole, folio 153–56.

62. A draft letter from Chautemps to the governor-general of Algeria, prefiguring the August 1924 circular, is included with the minutes of the commission's debate on 26 June 1924 in MAE K—Afrique 1918–1940, sous-série Questions Générales, vol. 31., fol. 164.

63. For the frequent difficulty Algerian authorities had in distinguishing between poor settlers and colonial subjects, see the undated letter [1924?] from Le Gouverneur Général de l'Algérie, Direction de la Sécurité Général, au Préfet de Constantine, CAOM 9 H 113.

The commission's president, the director of Algerian Affairs at the Sûreté, Duvernoy, deflected the question of legality. What is the risk, he asked, of pushing through a restrictive circular? We all agree on the need for immediate action. If the protests become too great, we can always submit a law to parliament later. As for the protests, Duvernoy assured his colleagues that Kabyle concerns would be assuaged with assurances of France's good intentions and the participation of such notable liberals as Marius Moutet, Christian Cherfils, and Lavenarde in their deliberations. Thus reassured, even the most progressive men present agreed that Algerian immigration had to be stopped in the interests of the immigrants themselves as well as the metropole. Without having to fear reprisals from any foreign government, the commission unanimously agreed on a series of restrictive measures, despite their conflicting with existing legislation.

The new measures had an immediate and dramatic impact on the Algerian community. The Chautemps circulars required Algerians to obtain identity cards to travel to the mainland. Unlike foreigners, they had to furnish a photograph as well. Access to a photographer was impossible for many, equivalent to a complete ban on movement. Local officials in Algeria increasingly opposed the departure of workers, as the price of labor rose, and they refused to grant the necessary paperwork, compelling many to borrow at usurious rates to pay the necessary bribes or the fees of the black marketeers who immediately stepped in to traffic in false papers. Some paid the extra money for first- or second-class tickets, thus avoiding the restrictions, while others stowed away and tried to make do without papers. Even regular workers home on vacation got stuck. Registered departures from Algeria collapsed in October of 1924: 7,640 left in September; only 331 made the trip a month later. Experienced migrants, however, soon learned how to cope with the new requirements, and illegal immigration soared. By 1926 the number of recorded departures from Algerian ports reached fifty thousand.[64]

V

It took the complicity of a wide range of public figures and agencies to keep immigration reform out of the public eye. Camille Chautemps was a leading figure in the centrist Radical Party and minister of the interior when he initiated repressive measures, and his special commission voted unanimously to support them. Whatever misgivings he may have had, Moutet never aired them in public or took decisive action behind the scenes.[65] He told his col-

64. MacMaster, Colonial Migrants and Racism, 147, 153.

65. Moutet does, in fact, appear to have had misgivings about the approach taken by Chautemps. He left it to his colleague Lavenarde to voice his misgivings in committee. Meeting of 27 October 1924, minutes in MAE K—Afrique 1918–1940, sous-série Questions Générales, vol. 31, Emploi de la main-d'œuvre indigène dans la métropole.

leagues on the commission not only that he agreed with imposing identity cards and preventing the sale of alcohol to North Africans but also that he supported the creation of a special bureau that would "allow the *penetration* of people who have not yet attained our level of civilization." He found the United States's racist quota system unacceptable, but he had no problem "with applying draconian measures" to keep colonials away from bad influences.[66]

For their most ambitious efforts to "penetrate" colonial immigrant communities, national figures like Chautemps and Moutet ultimately decided to work with the Paris Municipal Council, not the Chamber of Deputies. Immediately after the Fondary murders, three municipal councilors proposed the creation of a special bureau for the "surveillance and assistance" of North Africans in the capital. Besombes, a Socialist, spoke on behalf of the Grenelle neighborhood in the fifteenth arrondissement where the incident took place. Émile Massard, the former Bonapartist who passed into the camp of General Boulanger and then fought against Dreyfus in the ranks of the Ligue des Patriotes before emerging as one of the most prominent Nationalists in the municipal council, presided over the council's Second Commission, which set the budget of the Prefecture of Police.[67] Finally, Pierre Godin, a stridently right-wing *républicain de gauche*,[68] and former administrator of a *commune mixte* in the Algerian hinterland,[69] orchestrated the proposal and championed the new bureau.

Like Gomar and Depont, the three councilors argued that Algerian immigration could provide great assistance to the nation—if managed correctly. As Godin explained to the council: "The fatherland is much less an affair of blood and race than of education."[70] The sort of education Godin had in mind, however, differed strikingly from that offered to most French children in the metropole and stood at odds with his universalist rhetoric. He and his colleagues proposed creating a special organization under the direction of the prefect of police that would control and assist Algerians at the same time, taking advantage of the resources provided by a "young race" while minimizing any risk: "We must realize that the

66. Meeting of 10 April 1924, minutes in MAE K—Afrique 1918–1940, sous-série Questions Générales, vol. 31, Emploi de la main-d'œuvre indigène dans la métropole, quotes on folio 156. My emphasis.
67. On Massard, see Yvan Combeau, *Paris et les élections municipales: La scène capitale dans la vie politique française* (Paris: Harmattan, 1998), 346.
68. The Gauche républicaine began its political life on the left but took part in the broad rightward drift of republican parties at the time of the Dreyfus affair. See René Rémond, *Les droites en France*, rev. ed. (1954; Paris: Aubier, 1982), 190.
69. That is, he was the colony's man on the spot in an overwhelmingly "native" rural district.
70. Godin and M. Marie, "Proposition au nom du Groupe médical du Conseil municipal et du Conseil général, concernant le problème de l'immigration et la mise à l'étude d'un programme de création d'hôpitaux spéciaux pour étrangers," Cons. mun., *Rap et doc.*, no. 117 (15 December 1932): 3.

North African population is not only a very useful economic resource but it can become a political, indeed a national, resource as well, if we learn how to win it over and, discretely, to mold it [*l'encadrer*]."[71] Their petition began:

> A sensational crime—the assassination of two poor [French] women in the rue Fondary by an Algerian Kabyle—has recently drawn the attention of public opinion to the invasion of France by foreign or colonial elements, notably by North African emigrants. The public wonders if some precautions might not be in order to discipline, perhaps to limit this invasion, and, without losing sight of the national interest it serves, to reduce its risks to a minimum.[72]

While rejecting any suggestion of stopping North African immigration altogether as politically impossible, and undesirable in any event, they complained that no one even knew exactly how many North Africans lived in Paris. No statistics existed on the North African community, and no one had the capacity to produce them. After the abolition of travel permits, Algerians could come and go as they pleased. Authorities lacked any means to follow the peregrinations of the "wandering workers," who provided much needed assistance but who proved quite "worrisome" when they fell under the sway of corrupting influences, as they so often seemed to do.

According to the petition, and later confirmed by the prefect of police himself,[73] the Paris police were overwhelmed by a phenomenon they were unprepared to understand or to control. "What do the twenty to thirty thousand, perhaps forty thousand, Kabyles do who live scattered throughout the working-class neighborhoods of the city? They have no idea. They are not in a position to know."[74] Moreover, European police officers, they contended, could not appreciate the Kabyle mentality, so different from their own. They could not provide the firm, paternalistic guidance North Africans were used to in their village communities back home. Even when, by some chance, the police did stumble upon a North African criminal, they could not converse with him because of language barriers.

Whether as a result of Godin's tireless advocacy or the lobbying of colonial aid societies, the petition caught the eye of the Chautemps commission.

71. Godin, Besombes, and Massard, "Proposition tendant à créer à la Préfecture de police une section d'affaires indigènes nord-africaines qui s'occupera de la situation matérielle et morale et de la police des indigènes nord-africaines, résidant ou de passage à Paris," in Cons. mun., *Rap. et doc.*, no. 178 (20 December 1923).

72. Ibid., 1. See also the commentary of the Gouvernement Général of Algeria in "Police et Assistance des travailleurs indigènes en France (Proposition de MM. Godin, Besombes et Poisard [*sic*] au Conseil municipal de Paris)," n.d. [1924], CAOM 9 H 113; as well as the Laroque report, CAOM, 8 H 62, vol. 1, p. 62.

73. Morain is paraphrased by Godin in "Création d'une section d'affaires indigènes à la Préfecture de police," Cons. mun., *Proc.-ver.* (28 November 1924), 309.

74. Godin, Besombes, and Massard, "Proposition tendant à créer . . . une section d'affaires indigènes," 1.

On 24 October 1924, Chautemps chaired a special meeting with Massard, Besombes, and Godin; Prefect of Police Morain; Jean Chiappe, director of the Sûreté générale;[75] and a handful of others. Speaking with unusual candor, Chautemps explained:

> In fact, we want to weed out [*trier*] the bad ones, but we cannot give them the impression that we are treating them like foreigners, undesirable foreigners at that, and requiring passports for that reason. . . . We can demand passports under other pretexts but not to protect ourselves from them; we must appear to be protecting them.[76]

Chautemps and his colleagues worried that any measure that appeared to be aimed at excluding colonials would lead to dangerous protests. All of the men present agreed that the councilors' petition provided the most practical means to control North African immigration without provoking resistance, and, after a brief discussion, their colleagues in the commission unanimously agreed.

Nowhere was the alliance between moderate national politicians and right-wing Parisian municipal councilors more striking than in the surveillance of colonial subjects. Without the support of Chautemps and his commission, the North African Brigade at the Prefecture of Police could never have been created and might well have languished along with other pet projects in the council's archives. No police initiative could be undertaken without at least the tacit agreement of the minister of the interior, who had the power to replace the prefect and the prefect of police. Beyond mere existence, little could be accomplished without his intervention, both financially and politically. In fact, the municipal council agreed to consider creating a special Algerian service in December 1923, but it took no further action until Chautemps so instructed.

On a number of occasions, Chautemps and his successors at the place Beauvau went out of their way to help raise money for the operation and to obtain the cooperation of colonial authorities. The city of Paris paid all of the new brigade's expenses, but the money could only be raised by Chautemps's convincing parliament to add an additional thirty *centièmes*

---

75. Chiappe later developed the North African Brigade as a notoriously hard-line prefect of police, appointed by Albert Sarraut, with ties to antiparliamentary leagues. On Chiappe's tenure at the Prefecture, see Lucien Zimmer, *Un septennat policier* (Paris: Fayard, 1967).

76. Chautemps, AN F⁷ 13,412, quoted in Faithi Bentabet and Catherine Rodier, "L'immigration algérienne et l'hôpital franco-musulman dans la région parisienne entre les deux guerres, 1915–1947" (maîtrise, Université de Paris-I, 1980–1981), 40. I have been unable to locate the document in the AN. Norbert Gomar quotes a similar passage from the meeting in his *L'émigration nord-africaine en France*, 119–20. See also "Création d'une section d'affaires indigènes nord-africaines à Paris," *La correspondant d'Orient* (September 1924), in CAOM SLOTFOM, ser. IX, carts. 3–4.

de centime to the property taxes (*patente*) of Parisian businesses.[77] When his commission voted to create the new service, Chautemps wrote to the governor-general of Algeria that it would be "under my authority and control," to help ensure the cooperation of a colonial government initially hostile to the new project.[78] Writing about the creation of the brigade in the mid-1930s, Godin made a point of adding that Chautemps "took a personal interest [in the brigade] and intervened both directly and through his subordinates" in its organization and growth.[79] Albert Sarraut used all the weight of his office as minister of the interior to help raise money for the social assistance programs at the Prefecture. Writing to the governor-general of Algeria, he threatened that if the latter did not make a suitable contribution, he would simply take it out of their budget.[80]

Even this alliance was not enough to guarantee success. Having long criticized the inequity and brutality of French colonialism, prominent Socialists in the local government could have derailed surveillance efforts by sounding an alarm in the press. Parisian conservatives had the votes to deliver resources on their own, but they did not have the power to stifle dissent. Divisions within the Left prevented an effective challenge.[81] The more virulent the Communist protest, the more Socialists and progressive Radicals were willing to participate.

77. The law was passed, without debate, on 11 July 1926. The tax was raised to a full *centime* in 1927. Godin, "Note . . . sur le fonctionnement des services de surveillance, protection et assistance des indigènes nord-africains résidant ou de passage à Paris et dans le Département de la Seine," in Cons. mun., *Rap. et doc.*, no. 77 (1933), 29; and Godin, "Inscription au budget d'une subvention du Département de la Seine et création d'une imposition de 70 centièmes de centime aux trois contributions directes en vue de l'assistance aux indigènes Nord-africains dans la région parisienne," Cons. mun., *Proc.-ver.* (29 December 1927), 1066–67.

78. Chautemps to the Gouverneur Général de l'Algérie, 30 October 1924, 82/73 29 20H—Urgent, Intérieur à Gouveneur Général, Alg., Chiffré spécial, in CAOM 9 H 113. Algerian authorities initially had mixed feelings about the new service. A high official in the Gouvernement Général wrote in an unsigned note of March 1924 that "the Algerian administration considers this new creation to be exclusively in the interest of the metropole." Settlers feared that the new service would attract their workers, whom they desperately wanted to keep at artificially low wages, while colonial subjects feared for their freedom. "Police et Assistance des travailleurs indigènes en France (Proposition de MM. Godin, Besombes et Poisard [*sic*] au Conseil Municipal de Paris)," CAOM 9 H 113. See also Le Ministre des Colonies à Monsieur le Ministre de l'Intérieur, 9 October 1924, in CAOM SLOTFOM, ser. IX, carts. 3–4; the minister of colonies suggests that the CAI might fruitfully work with the new service and asks to be kept informed.

79. Pierre Godin, "Note . . . sur le fonctionnement," 7–8.

80. Minister of the interior (Sarraut) to the governor-general of Algeria, 6 October 1967, in Laroque papers, CAC, cart. 4, art. 14.

81. There was some initial ambivalence within the Chautemps commission about investing the prefect of police with responsibility for both the assistance and surveillance of North Africans. Two of the more progressive members, Lavenarde and Cherfils, expressed misgivings but ultimately went along with the unanimous vote to support the project. Meeting of 27 October 1924, minutes in MAE K—Afrique 1918–1940, sous-série Questions Générales, vol. 31, Emploi de la main-d'œuvre indigène dans la métropole.

Communist and Algerian nationalist groups began to organize protests soon after the city services began to function. The Communist municipal councilor, Camille Renault, lambasted the oversight committee of the city programs: It "could be very useful if it were actually controlled by civil authorities," but they chose a police superintendent to lead them. Renault went on:

> We think that if this committee were really interested in protection, it ought to include doctors and devoted citizens, whereas policemen make up the majority. What they wanted to do with this committee is above all to follow the North Africans who come to France and principally to Paris. They want to know what they do and where they go. It is a social program that has been deviated from its goal.[82]

According to police spies, a certain Yahiaoui, an editor of the North African newspaper *El Ouma*, complained that officers from the police brigade directed a "veritable terror" against North African workers and criticized the new Franco-Muslim Hospital in equally harsh terms.[83] Bourenane Mohand Ou Achour protested the creation of the hospital, claiming that the food and care of the sick "left something to be desired."[84] For all its anticolonial bluster, the Communist contingent spoke out only a handful of times on the floor of the Hôtel de Ville in the entire interwar period, and they were easily dismissed by the conservative majority and its liberal allies. When they spoke out, however, they hit the mark.[85]

82. Renault, "Création d'une imposition extraordinaire de trente centièmes de centime à la patente, en vue de la surveillance et de la protection des indigènes Nord-africaines dans le département de la Seine," Conseil Général de la Seine, *Proc.-ver.* (1 December 1926), 136.

83. Police report of a nationalist meeting held in the CGTU offices in the rue de la Grange aux Belles, 22 September 1936, APP B/a 56ᵖ, doss. 10.694–A, Glorieuse Étoile Nord Africaine, Correspondance générale. On the hospital, see chapter 7.

84. Le Directeur-Adjoint, Chef du Service des Affaires Indigènes Nord-Africaines à Le Directeur de l'Administration et de la Police Générales—1er Sous Direction—Service des Affaires de Sûreté Générale—1er Bureau, Préfecture de Police, 9 January 1936, APP B/a 56ᵖ, doss. 10.694–B, Glorieuse Etoile Nord Africaine, Rapports divers, comptes rendus de réunions, 1935 à . . . See also Georges Altman, "La sombre vie des travailleurs racolés dans l'Afrique du Nord . . . Avec les 'sidis,' dans les baraques et les caves de Gennevilliers," *l'Humanité*, 29 August 1926, p. 1, and the numerous complaints at political gatherings and Communist cell meetings, from police reports in CAOM 9 H 35; APP B/a 56ᵖ; and AN F⁷ 13,131.

85. "Ordre du jour sur une proposition de M. Camille Renault relative au projet de constitution d'une section des Affaires indigènes nord-africains à la Préfecture de police," Cons. mun., *Proc.-ver.* (1 December 1924), 416–18; Camille Renault, "Observations sur le procès-verbal," Cons. mun., *Proc.-ver.* (1 December 1924), 404–5; Renault, "Création d'une imposition extraordinaire de trente centièmes de centime à la patente, en vue de la surveillance et de la protection des indigènes Nord-africaines dans le département de la Seine," Conseil Général de la Seine, *Proc.-ver.* (1 December 1926), 135–37; Renault, "Observations sur le procès-verbal," Cons. mun., *Proc.-ver.* (9 December 1927), 345–46; and René Fodère, quoted by Ahmed Boukhelloua, *L'hôpital franco-musulman de Paris* (Algiers: S. Crescenzo, 1934), 31–32, 97.

One of the project's leaders, the Socialist Besombes, challenged Renault for suggesting that the police would control the new service:

> I was quite hurt by the words of Camille Renault. I do not want anyone to suppose that I, a Socialist, would associate myself in any manner with police measures.
> That is not what is at issue.
> We are asking that assistance be provided for North African natives, protection against the shameless exploitation of modern capitalism that so victimizes them. We are asking for social hygiene measures.[86]

Even the most progressive of interwar Socialists, Henri Sellier,[87] defended the new project against claims of police abuse, offering his own progressive credentials as a guarantee:

> Gentlemen, as secretary general of the Departmental Job Placement Office . . . , I would like to protest the imputation made recently from this tribune that an organization controlled by the Departmental Job Placement Office could have a coercive element [un caractère policier].[88]

A Communist for a brief time, Sellier was a follower of Édouard Vaillant, one of the few French Socialists to straddle the fence between the revolutionary wing of Jules Guèsde and the pragmatic republicanism of Jaurès. Close to his fellow Socialist Albert Thomas and the social reformers at the Musée Social, Sellier was resolutely pragmatic and saw incremental reform as the path to revolution. At the turn of the century, he worked in the new Ministry of Labor, implementing social legislation dealing with the length of the work day, hygiene, and physical safety in the work place. Elected mayor of suburban Suresnes in 1919, he played an active role in the General Council of the Seine (the suburban equivalent of the municipal council) throughout the interwar years. The capstone of his career came during the Popular Front, when he served as minister of public health in Léon Blum's

---

86. Besombes, "Ordre du jour sur une proposition de M. Camille Renault relative au projet de constitution d'une section des Affaires indigènes nord-africaines à la Préfecture de police," Cons. mun., Proc.-ver. (1 December 1924), 417.

87. La banlieue-oasis: Henri Sellier et les cités jardins, 1900–1940, ed. Katherine Burlen (Saint-Denis: Puv, 1987).

88. Sellier, "Création d'une imposition extraordinaire de trente centièmes de centime à la patente, en vue de la surveillance et de la protection des indigènes Nord-africaines dans le département de la Seine," Cons. mun., Proc.-ver. (1 December 1926), 136. For the importance of the patente in Sellier's agreeing to participate, see "Question de M. de Pressac à M. le Préfet de la Seine sur les terrains de jeu aménagés à Bobigny par le Stade français—Création sur ces terrains d'un hôpital franco-musulman et désignation de conseillers municipaux et généraux pour faire partie de la Commission de surveillance dudit hôpital," Conseil Général de la Seine, Proc.-ver. (9 July 1930), 511–12.

first government.[89] Sellier and his Socialist colleagues insisted that the new North African Services provided an opportunity to protect workers from exploitation by ruthless capitalists, and they resented any suggestion to the contrary.

Godin and his allies cemented the cooperation of municipal Socialists by paying for new agencies with taxes on business and by offering them token positions. Sellier went out of his way to mark his agreement with Godin largely because, "instead of entering the new expense in the regular budget and making all taxpayers pay, only one group will be singled out: industrialists." Socialists held employers responsible for the exploitation of colonial migrants and thought it fitting that business should have to pay to ease the suffering it had caused.[90] They retained a great faith in the power of state planning to improve people's lives. The proposed services created the illusion, at least, that Socialists would be allowed to make good on their promises. They had not yet begun to formulate a critique of empire.

The colonial consensus held firm until the Popular Front. Socialists, Radicals, and nationalists worked together to support the empire, which they all saw as crucial to France's standing as a great power. For a decade, the only voices of protest came from the Communist Party, colonial nationalists, and the odd renegade Socialist.

89. This sketch is drawn from Paul Rabinow, *French Modern: Norms and Forms of the Social Environment* (Cambridge: MIT Press, 1989), 263–66, and chap. 10. See also *La banlieue-oasis: Henri Sellier et les cités jardins.*
90. Sellier, "Question de M. de Pressac," 511–12.

Chapter Six

Open City or Police State?

Colonial subjects in general, and North Africans in particular, replaced Italians during World War I as prime scapegoats and targets of working-class hostility, but police controls eased after the Armistice. Grateful for their loyal service during the war and afraid of renewed popular disturbances in the Maghreb, metropolitan politicians initially respected the freedom of movement they had granted Algerians before the war. They rejected demands made by European settlers in Algeria that France keep its southern border closed. In the wake of the Fondary murders, however, uncontrolled arrivals and the first stirrings of a Communist-influenced, anticolonial nationalism inspired politicians from the left wing of the Socialist Party to join forces with the coalition that had recently overhauled the immigration service at the Prefecture of Police. The breadth of this support enabled Pierre Godin and his allies in the Paris Municipal Council to treat colonial migrants as they saw fit, without having to contend with an internal French opposition or intervention from a foreign power.

Socialists supported Godin's project reluctantly. Faced with open rebellion in Morocco and concerned that a lack of government supervision left colonial migrants vulnerable to abuse, they preferred to see North Africans in the hands of men like Godin than the popular Communist leader in the Chamber of Deputies, Jacques Doriot, and the Communist Party. After more than a decade of working with right-wing municipal councilors, Socialists tried, quietly, to improve the treatment of colonial migrants during the Popular Front. As with most Popular Front efforts at colonial reform, few concrete advances were made.[1] The Socialist government of Léon Blum

---

1. Frederick Cooper, *Decolonization and African Society: The Labor Question in French and British Africa* (Cambridge: Cambridge University Press, 1996), chap. 3; Tony Chafer and

did, however, produce a massive study documenting the extent of interwar abuses. In March 1937, Blum presided over a far-reaching debate on North African immigration at the interministerial Haut Comité Méditerranéen (High Commission on Mediterranean Affairs) that led to an investigation of their treatment throughout the country.[2] After four months interviewing businessmen, government officials, and immigrants, Pierre Laroque and François Ollive produced a massive report and a wide array of supporting documents that provide the only independent, nonpolice window into the activity of Paris's North African Services between the wars.[3] In neutral, bureaucratic terms, they show the absence of republican constraints that protected most migrants.

Having taken for themselves the right to represent North African Muslims, French officials displayed uncommon zeal in making sure Muslim migrants lived up to the standard of a "good native." For a store of images and ideals of the kind of individual they were trying to create, Godin and his allies drew from their colonial experience. Nowhere did a colonial vision dominate so clearly on the mainland as in the police brigade they created to protect the capital.

I

The driving force behind Paris's North African Services, Pierre Godin, spent a considerable amount of time overseas in North Africa. The child of schoolteachers in the Gironde, he followed in their footsteps before setting off to Algeria in 1896, where he entered the colonial administration as a clerk (*rédacteur*) for the Government General in Algiers. Four years later, still in Algiers, he was promoted to a supervisory role in the colonial police force.[4] From January 1905 to March 1909, he served as subprefect of the town of Médéa, on a plateau sixty-three miles southwest of the capital.

Amanda Sackur, eds., *French Colonial Empire and the Popular Front: Hope and Disillusion* (New York: St. Martin's, 1999); Julian Jackson, *The Popular Front in France: Defending Democracy, 1934–1938* (Cambridge: Cambridge University Press, 1988), 154–58; and William B. Cohen, "The Colonial Policy of the Popular Front," *French Historical Studies* 7 (1972): 368–93.

2. The committee, created by decree in February 1935, was one of a number of interwar attempts to coordinate policy for Algeria, Tunisia, and Morocco. For a detailed account of those efforts, "Le Haut Comité Méditerranéen et les organismes d'information musulmane," 15 January 1937, MAE, K—Afrique, 1918–1940, sous-série questions générales, vol. 79, fols. 6–47.

3. Copies of the report can be found in a number of locations, including CAOM 8 H 62. A significant run of supporting documentation can be found in the files of the Haute Comité Méditerranée in the MAE, and another one in the as yet uncataloged papers of Pierre Laroque at the CAC, cart. 4, art. 14.

4. Contrôleur général des services de police et de sécurité, in Algiers.

Pierre Godin, president of the Paris Municipal Council, 1926–27, and chief organizer of the city's North African Services. *Source: Nos édiles* (1934). Collection Bibliothèque Administrative de la Ville de Paris.

Godin thus spent most of his thirteen years in Algeria maintaining law and order.[5]

More than a generation after the Kabyle uprising of 1871–72, colonial authorities like Godin continued to fear insurrection, and they took advantage of a variety of legal and extralegal methods to impose their will. French colonizers routinely applied the law unequally overseas. Military and police forces enforced ordinary penal code provisions on vagabondage, lighting fires, carrying weapons, and cutting wood much more strictly for colonial subjects than for foreigners or French citizens, and even when jury trials took place, settlers dominated the proceedings. By 1881, Algerian settlers had prevailed upon metropolitan politicians to create a special "native code," the *indigénat*, outside of French common law.[6] In addition to limiting Muslims' freedom of movement, as we have seen, it placed strict controls on the sort of clothes they could wear, created special fines for Mus-

5. G. Rougeron, *Les administrateurs du département de l'Allier, An VIII-1950* (Montluçon: Grande imprimerie nouvelle, 1956), 110–11; and N. Imbert, ed., *Dictionnaire national des contemporains*, 3rd. ed., 3 vols. (1939), 3:313.

6. François Marneur, *L'indigénat en Algérie* (Paris: Sirey, 1914), and Charles-Robert Ageron, *Les algériens musulmans et la France, 1871–1919*, 2 vols. (Paris: Puf, 1968), 1:165–76.

lims who paid taxes late, and imposed severe penalties on those who failed
to provide information or showed disrespect even to off-duty public officials. Freedom of speech and assembly were further curtailed by a 26 August 1881 decree, which gave the governor-general free rein to intern anyone he pleased, without public debate or judicial review. According to the
legal scholar Claude Collot, the colonial state did so, quite arbitrarily,
roughly one hundred times a year from 1893 to 1900, not including illegal
internments pronounced by local officials. In 1900, the annual total rose
to 230, then to 360 in 1907—under the tenure of the supposedly *in-
digénophile*, Governor-General Charles Jonnart. Muslims routinely landed
in jail for making the pilgrimage to Mecca, for refusing to aid criminal investigations, even for being acquitted at trial for lack of evidence.[7]

Colonial officials resorted to such draconian measures in large part because they lacked the resources necessary for modern policing in most of the
colony. Although the military gave way to civilian rule with the advent of
the Third Republic, recruiting public servants posed enormous difficulties.
The predominantly European settlements (*communes de pleine exercice*) had
their own police forces and social services, but the same cannot be said of the
mountains of the Tell, the High Plateaux, and the Saharan Atlas where most
Muslims lived. There they were deprived of all but the most rudimentary services by the settler stranglehold on government.[8] The only civil police force
responsible for the entire colony, the Algerian Sûreté, reorganized in March
1908, had only eight inspectors and twenty-two agents. Surrounded by massive non-European populations, civil authorities in colonial hinterlands usually had no choice but to call on the military to curb disorder.[9]

The most serious challenge to colonial authority during Godin's Algerian tour of duty came not from the colonized, however, but from the European settler population. Political anti-Semitism emerged in the wake of
the Crémieux Decree of 1870, which naturalized native Algerian Jews.
By the late 1890s a powerful settler movement demanded independence
from the supposedly Jewish Republic, chafing in particular against reform
proposals that would have granted some limited autonomy to Muslims.
Two years after Godin's arrival in Algiers, in January 1898, thousands of
rioters took to the streets of the capital for five days, ransacked Jewish
shops, lit bonfires, killed two people, and injured one hundred.[10] Just a

7. Collot, *Les institutions de l'Algérie durant la période coloniale, 1830–1962* (Algiers: Cnrs, 1987), 191–92, and Ageron, *Les algériens musulmans et la France*, 2:657–59.

8. Collot, *Les institutions de l'Algérie*, 207–35.

9. Ageron, *Les algériens musulmans et la France*, 2:649 n. 3; and Martin Thomas, "Empire and Security in the Levant and French North Africa, 1919–1940" (paper presented to the annual conference of the Society for French Historical Studies, Toronto, 11–13 April 2002, p. 2).

10. David Prochaska, "History as Literature, Literature as History: Cagayous of Algiers," *American Historical Review* 101, no. 3 (June 1996): 694–98; Claude Martin, *Les israélites al-gériens de 1830 à 1902* (Paris: Herakles, 1936), 295–300; and Ageron, *Les algériens musul-mans et la France*, 1:595–96.

few years before Godin arrived in Médéa, local officials brutally crushed a minor revolt in the nearby town of Margueritte. Even moderate locals blamed the uprising on naive metropolitan politicians, ignorant of local conditions, whose misguided efforts at reform led only to anarchy and put their lives at risk. Many insisted that Arabs were incapable of assimilation. Metropolitan anti-Semites urged on the settlers. In the words of Edouard Drumont's *La libre parole*, the Arab "has but one master: force. So let's use force!"[11]

What sort of lessons did Godin draw from his time in the colonies? He clearly sympathized with settlers' complaints about metropolitan decision makers ignorant of conditions overseas. Back in Paris, he called attention to his colonial experience repeatedly throughout the interwar years. From his position in the municipal council, he went out of his way to recruit men who understood the "native mentality." In practice, that meant hiring retired colonial officials or soldiers who had served overseas; they inevitably brought their prejudices and means of dealing with "natives" to the metropole, and did not blanch at using force.

Unlike the active section of the immigrant service at the Prefecture of Police, a unit of the RG, the prestigious and professional political branch, the North African Brigade that Godin created was an irregular unit made up of colonial misfits with little hope of promotion. From the start, he had terrible difficulty in recruiting qualified men. Godin realized early on that he would have to provide attractive benefits to lure agents with appropriate skills and to avoid the "dead wood" (*fruits secs*) too often found in colonial administration, but his contacts failed him in this instance.[12] While his original plans called for twenty inspectors, an average of only twelve served in the first year; the total reached eighteen by December 1926, thirty-two in 1932, and thirty-seven in 1937.[13] Subsequent investigations revealed that the agents Godin was able to recruit failed to meet even minimum requirements.[14] A required test in Arabic or Kabyle diminished the pool of candidates, and the brigade's position within the civil service bureaucracy re-

11. Ageron, *Les algériens musulmans et la France*, 1:596–97, 1:607.

12. Godin, "Fixation des attributions et de la situation du personnel de la section de surveillance et de protection des indigènes nord-africains," Cons. mun., *Proc.-ver.* (3 July 1925), 980. On the colonial service, see William B. Cohen, *Rulers of Empire: The French Colonial Service in Africa* (Stanford: Hoover Institution Press, 1971).

13. "Question de M. Besombes à M. le Préfet de police sur les mesures qu'il compte prendre, d'accord avec la police indigène, pour assurer la sécurité des habitants de Grenelle à la suite du crime de la rue de Lourmel," Cons. mun., *Proc.-ver.* (16 December 1926), 615; Godin, "Fonctionnement du service de surveillance," 336; Godin, "Note . . . sur le fonctionnement des services de surveillance, protection et assistance des indigènes Nord-Africains," Cons. mun., *Rap. et doc.*, no. 77 (1933), 4–5; and "Les Nord-Africains en France," report no. 3, n.d. [1937], p. 292, in CAOM 8 H 62 (on p. 289, the report mentions eighty-three agents employed by the Prefecture of Police).

14. "Les nord-africains en France," report no. 3, n.d. [1937], p. 43, in CAOM 8 H 61.

mained vague until late 1932.[15] Although the foreign language requirement
might sound like a benevolent gesture on the part of local politicians, as a
practical matter it meant that officers would have to be colonial settlers and
soldiers. Two out of five officers were supposed to speak Arabic and
Kabyle, but this standard was not met.[16] A number of those who passed the
examinations nevertheless proved "incapable of providing the services we
expected," as the prefect of police diplomatically put it.[17] Godin later admitted that the brigade had been forced to resort to a hodge-podge of young
assistants, retired police officers, and "native" informants, none of whom
enjoyed the prospect of professional advancement.[18]

Inexperienced and often incompetent, the inspectors of the North
African Brigade soon earned a reputation for corruption and brutality. Al-
gerian nationalists, Communists, and even the mainstream press disparaged
Godin's men. A 1926 *l'Humanité* article complained about

> thirty provocateurs, native spies, speaking Arabic and Kabyle, scouring the
> [North African] colonies of Paris and the suburbs, terrorizing the immigrants,
> making them "sing" by introducing themselves as "police inspectors." . . .
> Several of these "chaouchs" [servants, in Arabic] are well-known pimps and
> blackmailers. Two just got nabbed in Gennevilliers for extortion![19]

Godin's own son, André, was the subject of a tawdry corruption scandal
shortly after his father named him head of the North African Services. A
group calling itself the French Berber Intellectuals and Naturalized Frenchmen of Paris accused him of pocketing vast sums of money and setting up
kept women with city funds.[20] Messali Hadj complained about "an important service handed over to an incompetent papa's boy."[21] Commenting

---

15. Godin, "Fonctionnement du service de surveillance, de protection et d'assistance des
indigènes Nord-africains de Paris," Cons. mun., *Proc.-ver.* (12 December 1932), 343–44; and
Godin, "Note . . . sur le fonctionnement," 119.

16. Haute Comité de l'Afrique du Nord, Aubaut report, March 1938, "Les nord-africains
en France," annex, p. 46, CAOM 3 Cab 36.

17. The prefect of police speaking before the municipal council, "Question de M. Besombes à M. le Préfet de police sur les mesures qu'il compte prendre, d'accord avec la police indigène, pour assurer la sécurité des habitants de Grenelle à la suite du crime de la rue de
Lourmel," Cons. mun., *Proc.-ver.* (16 December 1926), 615.

18. Godin, "Fonctionnement du service de surveillance," 341.

19. Georges Altman, "La sombre vie des travailleurs racolés dans l'Afrique du Nord . . .
Avec les 'sidis,' dans les baraques et les caves de Gennevilliers," *l'Humanité* (29 August 1969),
p. 1.

20. Les Intellectuels Berbères Français et naturalisés Français de Paris, "Lettre ouverte à
Monsieur André Godin, Directeur des Affaires Indigènes Nord Africaines," 18 September
1933, MAE, K—Afrique 1918–1940, sous-série Affaires Musulmanes, vol. 15.

21. "Réflexions de Messali Hadj au cours de converations, à bâtons rompus, par personne
interposée," typed note marked PB/B, 1 February 1934, MAE, K—Afrique 1918–1940, sous-
série Affaires Musulmanes.

obliquely on Godin junior's case, it appears, Laroque and Ollive dryly noted a pattern of corruption:

> On the eve of the 1932 elections, we hired a man who was arrested soon thereafter for breaking and entering; another went to prison for fraud; a third disappeared with the money from the social insurance fund, after winning over his boss and colleagues. Before that, high-ranking functionaries went so far as to show lapses of judgment [*indélicatesses*] that led to serious disciplinary action.[22]

Different from the notorious parallel institutions of Soviet Russia, Nazi Germany, or Fascist Italy, the North African Brigade remained under the direct control of the prefect of police.[23] The North African Brigade did not compete with other organizations that shared its jurisdiction, apart from the much weaker Sûreté générale. Like the Brigades spéciales, created by Roger Langeron and Jacques Simon at the Prefecture in March 1940 to hunt down Communists and, later, resistance fighters, the North African Brigade was at once part of the Paris police and yet outside its traditional command structure.[24] Its zeal came from elsewhere. Officers and spies had no fear of sparking a diplomatic incident—which had a powerful effect on the immigration service at the Prefecture—nor did they have to worry about blowing a promotion. Even Godin implied that the limited prospects of the brigade's agents increased their zeal and freed them from concerns over career advancement.[25]

II

With the support of leading Socialists in parliament and the municipal council, the North African Brigade began to function in the summer of

---

22. Laroque report, 3:290–91, CAOM 8 H 62.

23. On the importance of parallel institutions for authoritarian regimes, see, among others, Ernst Fraenkel's classic, *The Dual State* (Oxford: Oxford University Press, 1941); Hans Mommsen, *From Weimar to Auschwitz*, trans. Philip O'Connor (Princeton: Princeton University Press, 1991); Stephen Kotkin, *Magnetic Mountain: Stalinism as a Civilization* (Berkeley: University of California Press, 1995), esp. chap. 7; and Robert O. Paxton, *The Anatomy of Fascism* (New York: Knopf, 2004).

24. Unlike the North African Brigade, the BS did compete with a range of other police organizations. Berlière, *Le monde des polices en France, XIXe–XXe siècles*, 169–70, 180–81; Berlière and Denis Peschanski, "Police et policiers parisiens face à la lutte armée, 1941–1944," in *Pouvoirs et polices au XXe siècle: Europe, États-Unis, Japon*, ed. Berlière and Peschanski, eds. (Brussels: Complexe, 1997), 137–76; and Stéphane Courtois, Denis Peschanski, and Adam Rayski, *Le sang de l'étranger: Les immigrés de la MOI dans la Résistance*, rev. ed. (Paris: Fayard, 1989), chap. 9.

25. See note 18.

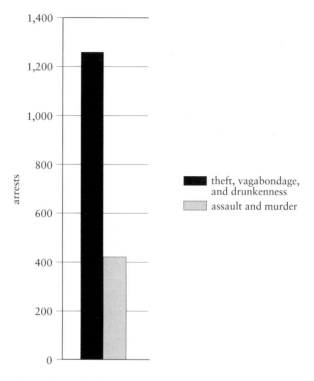

Figure 12. North Africans arrested in Paris, 1920–23, by offense.

Source: "État numérique établi par inculpation des indigènes algériens arrêtés depuis le 1er janvier 1920 dans le ressort de la Préfecture de Police,"
n.d. [1923?], CAOM 9 H 112, dossier "Sécurité."

1925, operating out of a converted school in a tiny street in the eastern section of the seventeenth arrondissement, at number 6, rue Lecomte. Like the
immigration service at the Prefecture, the brigade began by trying to identify its subjects, combing North African neighborhoods and staking out
their cafés. As with foreigners, the police required their "clients" to register
their identity and keep authorities informed of their whereabouts, and frequent dragnets made examples of those who failed to comply.

Without exception, contemporaries gave the police high marks for stopping crime. The Laroque report credited the police with lowering the crime
rate in the North African community. Even its fiercest critics, Communists
and Algerian nationalists, respected the force authorities brought to bear on
a community that was constantly in flux, in which people often lacked documentation and only rarely settled down.[26]

Upon closer inspection, however, it is not clear what influence police sur-

26. Laroque report, 3:292, CAOM 8 H 62.

veillance had on North African criminality. For North African migrants, unlike their European counterparts, the police left meticulous statistics. Even in the early 1920s, when the Fondary murders whipped public opinion into a frenzy, violent crime made up only a small percentage of North African arrests (see figure 11). From 1920 to 1923, roughly 2 percent of all arrests were for violent crimes. The police admitted that most of those cases involved the settling of scores between North Africans, not violence against French citizens. The overwhelming majority of North Africans were convicted for petty offenses. Violations of immigration rules, petty theft, public drunkenness, and vagabondage made up nearly 60 percent of arrests.[27]

North Africans in other parts of France often looked to the Paris services for help. Although most prefectures around France looked the other way when they came across undocumented immigrants from the colonies, a handful enforced the law energetically. The Paris office of the Moroccan Protectorate complained that none did so more energetically or capriciously than the Norman department of the Seine-Inférieure, on the coast of the British Channel. When a local police officer in Le Havre told Moulay B. in January 1938 that he would be summarily expelled (*refoulé*) at the expiration of his legal stay, or "sursis," the Moroccan promptly took off for Paris, to the rue Lecomte, with the hope of clearing up his problems. The Parisian North African Services promptly sent him back to Normandy, this time to Rouen, where officials told him that only the rue Lecomte could help him. All this travel cost Moulay some three hundred francs, in addition to a month and a half's wages. He finally straightened out his legal status, no thanks to the Paris branch of the North African Services.[28]

Ahmed L. worked for two years in the mid-1930s in Rouen. He took care of all the formalities to receive the identity card then required of all subjects of French protectorates. In late 1935, however, the local prefecture forgot to obtain one of the necessary elements, a certificate of moral probity from authorities in Morocco. Two years later, they took away his work papers while waiting for the requested paper to arrive. Even when the letter of recommendation arrived, they refused to tear up the refoulement notice they had sent him. The Moroccan took refuge in Paris and looked to the North African Services there for help, but in vain. They went the Norman authorities one better and expelled Ahmed on the spot. He lost seven months' wages and was nearly expelled, penniless, to Morocco before consular officials intervened.[29] Many others were not so lucky. They came from across France to avoid abusive treatment by local authorities, only to be

27. "État numérique établi par inculpation des indigènes algériens arrêtés depuis le 1er janvier 1920 dans le ressort de la Préfecture de Police," n.d. [1923?], CAOM 9H 112, doss. "Sécurité."
28. Several items in CAC, Laroque papers, art. 4, cart. 14.
29. "Note au sujet de l'attitude de certaines Préfectures et Municipalités vis-à-vis des travailleurs Marocains," 28 February 1938, CAC, Laroque papers, art. 4, cart. 14.

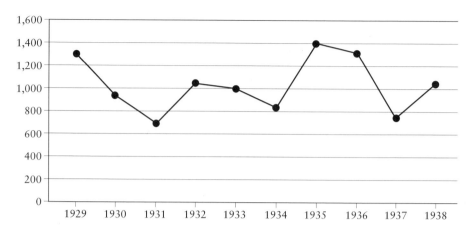

Figure 13. North Africans arrested in Paris, 1929–38.

Source: Cons. mun., *Rap. et doc.*

treated no better in Paris. Most of them appear to have taken refuge in the suburbs, especially in the nearby Seine-et-Oise. Many left Paris as well, as Albert Sarraut himself noted, precisely to get away from the Prefecture's North African Brigade.[30]

North Africans never posed a serious law-and-order threat, but the Paris police targeted them anyway. North Africans never made up more than 1.4 percent of the Parisian population, but never less than 2 percent of arrests in the surviving records. Whereas in two years during the 1920s European immigrants were arrested at a rate twice that of their share of the population, the percentage of North Africans arrested exceeded that level several times during the following decade. In 1935 North Africans were more than four times as likely to be arrested as members of the general population. More than 4 percent of the entire North African community was arrested the next year, and 12.5 percent was either arrested or deported in 1938. As striking as these figures are, a comparison of the police treatment of European and North African migrants can only be advanced with caution. Authorities recorded the criminality of European migrants from 1921 to 1931 but only began systematically to track North African arrests in 1929. Two years overlap, and the results are contradictory: North Africans were more likely to be arrested in 1929, Europeans in 1931. The surviving qualitative sources suggest that the isolation of North Africans and the zeal of the North African Brigade subjected them to more frequent arrest and harassment, but the surviving record does not permit a definitive answer.

30. Anonymous note, February 1927, p. 4, amid correspondence from Sarraut in CAC, Laroque papers, art. 4, cart. 14.

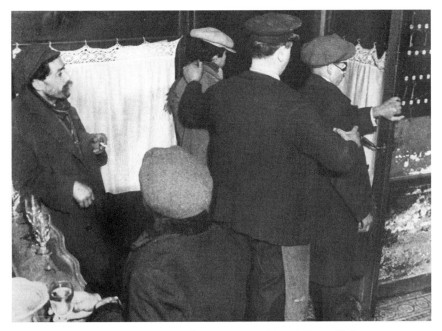

Police raid on a North African rooming house in Paris (1935). © Roger Viollet.

Unless more thorough records are discovered, the number and nature of deportations provide the most revealing comparison of the two groups' treatment. Unlike European immigrants, or Moroccans and Tunisians, Algerians could not be denied identity papers or have them confiscated, for the simple reason that they did not need them; in 1924 they were obliged to obtain special papers, but in principle they could not be denied in the same manner as foreigners. As French nationals they could not be expelled, which entailed sending people to another country. A 1914 law guaranteed them freedom of movement to and from Algeria, so authorities could only repatriate them "voluntarily." Many North African workers took advantage of the authorities' willingness to send them home when their contracts expired, but many others were forced to return against their will. During the boom years of 1920–23, the Prefecture of Police arrested 378 Algerians for begging or vagabondage, 16.5 percent of all Algerians arrested.[31]

Breathing the air as a poor North African was treated as a criminal offense, and most of those workers were sent home. Repatriation figures from those years have not survived, but the Algerian government saved form letters from the Paris police to administrators of *communes-mixtes*: "____,

31. "État numérique établi par inculpation des indigènes algériens."

born in the duwar of ____, son of ____, has been repatriated for: unemployment/sickness. Please see that he never receives papers allowing him to travel to France again."[32] The prefect of police often remarked that the unemployed must be sent away.

The difference between the deportation of Europeans and North Africans did not lie in the legal procedures used—Tunisians and Moroccans were, technically, foreigners too—but in the effectiveness of the various means that were used. North Africans lived in tightly knit neighborhoods, and especially by the mid-1930s the community was quite small, just over thirty thousand. The police reported that, in time, they were able to track down the perpetrators of every important crime. The municipal record does not include the number of North Africans who avoided deportation as part of the very detailed statistics on criminality and assistance. There is no mention of arrests for avoiding repatriation, so frequent for Europeans, in all likelihood because that number was negligible. Instead of a lengthy administrative or judicial process, the police could simply arrest colonial migrants for vagabondage and put them on a train to Marseille, where they would be forced onto a ferry crossing the Mediterranean.

No authority watched over agents at the Prefecture. The most thorough evidence comes from the Paris office of the Moroccan Protectorate. Apparently upset at the capriciousness of the capital's North African Services, it reported to Blum's investigators:

> Expulsions, refoulements, and repatriations are executed with no controls and, it appears, with no more than a single police inspector's report. Individual cases are not examined with sufficient care. Transport requisitions are sent to the Paris office of the Moroccan Protectorate, along with police reports [implausibly] claiming that the subjects in question have asked to be repatriated, while they have been doing the impossible to stay in France.[33]

A certain Inspector Guenancia wrote that Ali H. requested repatriation. When the colonial authorities in Paris interviewed him, however, Ali claimed never to have made any such request. He was six thousand francs in debt, having sold all his worldly possessions to make the trip to Paris. His wife and five children back home depended upon his support, and returning to them would condemn them all, he claimed, to die of starvation: "He begged us to let him stay in Paris, where he is confident of finding work soon if his immigration status is regularized."[34] Larbi B. worked for years in

32. CAOM 9 H 113.

33. Anon., in all likelihood from the Paris office of the Moroccan Protectorate, "Note au sujet des expulsions, refoulements et rapatriements pris à l'encontre de travailleurs Marocains par le Service des Affaires Nord-Africaines de Paris," n.d., p. 1, CAC, Laroque papers, art. 4, cart. 14.

34. Ibid., 1–2.

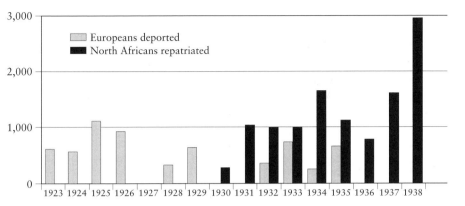

Figure 14. Successful "deportations," Europeans versus North Africans.

Source: Cons. mun., *Rap. et doc.* Incomplete data.

a metal-working shop in suburban Saint-Denis and made sure to keep his papers in order. In late 1936, he decided to take a few months off to see his family in Morocco, in Iguissel. When he tried to return, officials refused him passage in Casablanca; so he snuck into Algeria. But the police arrested him in Algiers before he could leave, and authorities there issued him an expulsion notice. He later made it back to Paris and resumed his job, but the Prefecture of Police went after him for evading his expulsion in Algiers. All this despite having his paperwork in order and an employer happy with his services. Nor was this case exceptional. The Sûreté has kept over thirty cartons of expulsion files exclusively on men named "Mohamed," most of whom were Moroccans and Tunisians expelled from Algeria in the 1930s, many in similar circumstances.[35]

If we assume that the number of North African repatriations listed in public records corresponds roughly to the number of European migrants who were successfully deported, and not merely asked to leave, the results are staggering. Authorities may have sent home more North Africans than Europeans in absolute terms, even though they never made up more than 14 percent of the city's "foreign" population, significantly less by the mid-1930s. While the police could not possibly keep track of every European who left, and some North Africans must have slipped from their grasp, the margin of error remains considerable. In 1933 and 1935, years with the most complete information on Europeans, the successful deportation rate was dramatically higher for North Africans even if we double the number of Europeans sent home and halve that of North Africans.

35. CAC 19940462, arts. 407–41.

Their dependent status left colonial subjects and protégés uniquely exposed to abuse and the whims of metropolitan officials. Officers from the North African Brigade routinely arrested them for petty offenses and successfully deported them far more often than foreign migrants. A constant fear of falling into the hands of the police figured prominently in their everyday lives, and many chose death rather than facing French authorities, as chapter 7 shows. While the consequences of surveillance on colonial migrants deserve further research, heavy-handed police measures clearly accentuated the high turnover of the colonial population and made even more difficult the prospects for migrants to settle down and become part of the Parisian community.

III

Other groups, to be sure, had received a violent reception. French peasant migrants, Belgians, and Italians often came in conflict with native-born Parisian workers in the latter half of the nineteenth century, and European migrants experienced considerable police surveillance between the world wars. A police unit paid special attention to the handful of Vietnamese who remained in the metropole after World War I and offered material assistance in an effort to keep them away from "bad influences." That service, however, operated on a meager budget, kept an eye on other groups as well, and never monitored more than a few thousand people at a time.[36] No previous immigrant community had lacked meaningful political representation while at the same time facing a broad political consensus that enabled a modern state to act so decisively against its members.

Agents for the Parisian services, however, could not ignore the law altogether. They could hardly call out the military, and they risked judicial sanctions if they resorted to house arrest and the other arbitrary measures that were so often used in the colonies. Above all, they had to worry about alienating the moderates who controlled the Ministry of the Interior and thus had the power to close down the operation.

In Paris, they did not need to resort exclusively to the sort of measures they had used overseas. For all that Godin drew on his colonial experiences, he had no patience for settler complaints that allowing immigration to the French mainland would result in labor shortages in North Africa. He believed that European settlers exploited Muslims so ruthlessly that they risked losing the empire altogether. Like Camille Chautemps, Albert Sarraut, and a number of influential members of the colonial administration in Paris, Godin believed that France's standing as a great power depended on

36. Philippe Dewitte relied almost exclusively on its archives for his thesis, *Les mouvements nègres en France, 1919–1939* (Paris: Harmattan, 1985).

holding on to the colonies. These men all agreed that this goal required forging closer ties to at least a significant minority of the non-European population and winning them over. To that end, Godin and his allies adapted colonial methods to metropolitan conditions. They took advantage of the vastly greater resources available in Paris to invest in social services, combining traditional police measures with expensive assistance programs.

Chapter Seven

Colonial Assistance and the Franco-Muslim Hospital

In retrospect, the most curious element of the French reception of North Africans was the government's willingness to invest massive sums in social programs for them. In some cases, they received care denied to French citizens.

Building hospitals and creating social welfare programs for anyone, French or foreign, was extremely difficult in the midst of the social tensions and economic dislocation of the interwar years. Paris offered no special services for the more than four hundred thousand Italians, Spaniards, and eastern European Jews, among others, who arrived there between the wars, and improvements to local hospitals never satisfied the increased demands placed on them. But for North Africans, a minority that represented at most 12 to 14 percent of the "foreign" population, authorities created subsidized housing, dispensaries, and a job placement center. Most strikingly, Parisian authorities built a new hospital at the nadir of the Great Depression that admitted only North African patients at a time when the city's crumbling, overcrowded hospitals regularly turned French citizens away.

Colonial officials often hoped modern medicine would help them govern more effectively overseas by winning over colonial populations and persuading them of the superiority of Western civilization. But, as with policing, they could not persuade European settlers to pay. No one did more to advance the idea of empire as a social laboratory than Marshal Hubert Lyautey. The famed resident-general of Morocco may well have quipped that a doctor was worth a battalion, but in the end he had to rely primarily on the military to keep the peace. Even after World War I, there were just over three doctors for every hundred thousand people in the protectorate, and those figures are skewed by the concentration of medical personnel in heavily European, urban areas on the coast. The vast majority of those doctors were themselves military men in Morocco, as were doctors elsewhere in the French empire, shifting from post to post without time to learn about a particular area or its inhabitants.[1] If forced vaccinations, fumigations, and quarantines began to introduce Western notions of sickness and health to colonial hinterlands, as a number of historians have suggested, they relied on brute force to do so.[2] In health care, as in prisons and police work, French colonial governments lacked the resources to experiment with anything resembling a comprehensive program for the identification, surveillance, and assistance of subject populations.[3] Not until the height of the Algerian War did French officials feel threatened enough to invest in significant social programs for non-Europeans in the colonies.[4]

Local government in Paris enjoyed resources colonial administrators could only dream about. Combining strategic considerations, well-founded reform arguments, and a traditional paternalism, as well as a healthy dose of racial fear, Pierre Godin and his allies took advantage of the financial and administrative wherewithal the capital afforded. Investing in social services and building a hospital enabled them to hold together a broad political coalition. With the hope of living up to their promises to make the empire more humane, and without having to worry about provoking a diplomatic crisis, moderates and Socialists agreed to a unique blend of surveillance and assistance to "civilize" their North African subjects and protégés and to ensure their loyalty.

The effort both to discipline and morally to justify the exploitation of colonial workers in France led to unprecedented forms of social control *and*

1. The percentage of civilian doctors increased after World War I, but they remained a distinct minority. Abdelmounim Aïssa, "La santé publique au Maroc à l'époque coloniale, 1907–1956" (thèse d'histoire, Université de Paris I, 1997), 202–4; Daniel Rivet, "Hygiénisme colonial et médicalisation de la société marocaine au temps du protectorat français, 1912–1956," in *Santé, médecine et société dans le monde arabe*, ed. Elisabeth Longuenesse (Paris: Harmattan, 1995), 105–28; Anne Marcovich, "French Colonial Medicine and Colonial Rule: Algeria and Indochina," in *Disease, Medicine, and Empire: Perspectives on Western Medicine and the Experience of European Expansion*, ed. Roy MacLeod and Milton Lewis (New York: Routledge, 1988), 103–17; Laurance Monnais-Rousselot, *Médecine et colonisation: L'aventure indochinoise, 1860–1939* (Paris: Éditions du Cnrs, 1999), 227–67; Richard Keller, "*Action Psychologique*: French Psychiatry in Colonial North Africa, 1900–1962" (PhD diss., Rutgers University, 2001); and Yvonne Turin, *Affrontements culturels dans l'Algérie coloniale: Écoles, médecines, religion, 1830–1880* (Paris: Maspero, 1971).

2. Esp. David Arnold, *Colonizing the Body: State Medicine and Epidemic Disease in Nineteenth-Century India* (Berkeley: University of California Press, 1993).

3. Peter Zinoman, *The Colonial Bastille: A History of Imprisonment in Vietnam, 1862–1940* (Berkeley: University of California Press, 2001).

4. Michel Déon, *L'armée d'Algérie et la pacification* (Paris: Plon, 1959); Philippe Tripier, *Autopsie de la guerre d'Algérie* (Paris: France-Empire, 1972), 174–76; and Grégor Mathias, *Les sections administratives spécialisées en Algérie: Entre idéal et réalité* (Paris: Harmattan, 1998).

exceptional forms of assistance. Nothing distinguished North Africans from other first-generation immigrants more than the assistance they received.

I

Soon after the North African Brigade was up and running at the Prefecture of Police, Pierre Godin and his colleagues began to create a series of social services for North Africans, nominally under the supervision of the prefect of the Seine. In the fall of 1925 the municipal council created a dispensary run by the Departmental Health Office at the rue Lecomte. It provided basic medical care and minor surgery, mainly for workplace accidents, as well as diagnosis and treatment of tuberculosis and venereal disease. Over the next few years a handful of other dispensaries that provided basic care opened around the city. One opened at the state-sponsored mosque in 1928,[5] and another on the rue Tiphanie in the fifteenth arrondissement in 1932.[6] Subsidized housing and a range of practical assistance was provided at the rue Lecomte office, which helped with job placement, paperwork,[7] settling disputes, and even letter writing for the illiterate.[8] The rue Lecomte offered translators and advisers to help North Africans with administrative problems, with the social security system, with unemployment benefits and workplace accident insurance claims, and the like. They explained the criteria for receiving family allowances and how to transfer funds to relatives in North Africa, as well as taking care of the endless documentation required for identity papers.

The city created subsidized housing. Two semiofficial hostels had been established, one in Marseille and another in Paris, in the wake of World War I. In July 1926, the municipal council sent a team to tour North African neighborhoods and decided to establish a special Housing Service (Service des foyers), with Octave Depont as its official inspector.[9] In the fall of 1927, a spartan eighty-bed facility opened on the premises of the rue Lecomte. A hostel with fifty beds opened the same year in Colombes, founded by a Mme. Lejars, the vice president of the Union des femmes

5. In the rue Geoffroy Saint Hilaire in the fifth arrondissement. See MAE, K—Afrique, 1918–1940, sous-série Affaires Musulmanes, vols. 11–14; and MAE, E—Asie, 1918–1929, sous-série Affaires Communes, vols. 44–45 and 98–100.

6. Neil MacMaster, *Colonial Migrants and Racism: Algerians in France, 1900–1962* (New York: St. Martin's, 1997), 166.

7. See, e.g., L'Administrateur Principal, Chef du Service des Affaires Indigènes Nord-Africaines à Monsieur le Ministre de l'Intérieur, Direction de la Sûreté Générale, 2ème Bureau, Contrôle Générale des Étrangers, in MAE, K—Afrique 1918–1940, sous-série Questions Générales, vol. 33, doc. 647. fol. 21.

8. Godin, "Note au sujet des services de surveillance, protection et assistance des indigènes Nord-Africains domiciliés ou de passage à Paris et dans le département de la Seine," Cons. mun., *Rap. et doc.*, no. 67 (25 October 1930).

9. MacMaster, *Colonial Migrants and Racism*, 165.

"An administration that serves as 'mother and father' for its charges." Drawing, A. Galland, in *Police parisienne* (1935). Collection Archives de la Préfecture de Police, Paris.

françaises, and ceded by her to the city. A new four-story building in the "Moorish style" opened in 1930 in the rue de l'Arbre Sec in Gennevilliers. It accommodated one hundred and had a large cafeteria, a prayer room, central heating, and showers and baths.[10] In December 1931 the municipal council accepted the prefect of the Seine's proposal to turn the management of the hostels over to a private company, the Régie des foyers ouvriers nord-africains. The city provided a loan of 17 million francs and sites for up to twenty foyers. Five ultimately were built between the wars, in suburbs with relatively high North African populations: Boulogne-Billancourt, Asnières, Saint-Ouen, Charenton, and Colombes.

The Depression hit North African workers especially hard. In the space of four months, from June through September 1932, the city provided 5,500 North Africans with social benefits (*assurances sociales*), and reported thirty thousand on their rolls.[11] In the mid-1930s, at least 150 North Africans sought help from the administrators at the rue Lecomte every day,

10. Joanny Ray, *Les marocains en France* (Paris: Institut des hautes études islamiques, 1938), 346, cited by MacMaster, *Colonial Migrants and Racism*, 165.
11. Pierre Godin, "Note sur les services nord-africains," Cons. mun., *Rap. et doc.*, no. 140 (1934), 2.

and well over half of the city's North Africans received welfare benefits.[12] As many as three hundred came to stamp their unemployment cards in the placement office every day. The dispensaries and X-ray center recorded twenty thousand visits in 1935 alone.[13]

The ease with which authorities created social programs for North African subjects contrasted markedly with their difficulty in improving local health-care facilities. Parisian hospitals had been decrepit and bursting at the seams since at least the turn of the twentieth century.[14] More than half of the city's twenty-seven hospitals were over fifty years old in 1925. Ten were built before Napoleon's defeat at Waterloo.[15] None had received more than makeshift repairs in at least a generation. The director of the Assistance publique lamented that "some of our hospitals are crumbling under the weight of years." A number of old hospitals were surrounded by temporary structures that were falling apart. The director went on:

> The barracks at Broussais, built as an emergency measure for cholera patients fifty years ago, are practically unusable today. An old military stronghold expanded with wooden barracks, Bichat can no longer receive patients from an area whose population is expanding every day.[16]

12. Of the fifty thousand North Africans in Paris, roughly thirty thousand were receiving assistance. Ibid.

13. See Pinelli's annual reports on the Prefecture of Police in Cons. mun., *Rap. et doc.*, for 1934 (no. 27, 1935) and 1935 (no. 98, 1936).

14. See Ambroise Rendu's intervention in "Budget de l'Assistance publique," Cons. mun., *Proc.-ver.* (28 December 1925), 836; this debate (pp. 821–54) provides an exceptionally rich description of hospital conditions in Paris. For more on the city's efforts to modernize its medical centers, see "Proposition de M. Paul Fleurot relative aux mesures à prendre pour éviter l'encombrement des hôpitaux," Cons. mun., *Proc.-ver.* (8 December 1913), 610; "Proposition de M. Tony Michaud relative à la construction de quatre hôpitaux nouveaux," Cons. mun., *Proc.-ver.* (19 June 1914), 604; Lemarchand and Varenne, "Proposition ayant pour objet de construire huit hôpitaux nouveaux sur l'emplacement des fortifications avec les ressources que procurerait la vente d'une partie des terrains sur lesquels sont édifiés de vieux hôpitaux à démolir . . ." Cons. mun., *Rap. et doc.*, no. 11 (1919); de Fontenay, "Rapport sur la politique hospitalière de la Ville de Paris," Cons. mun., *Rap. et doc.*, no. 22 (1921); "Proposition de M. Fernand Moriette relative à l'augmentation du nombre des hôpitaux et à l'extension des services de l'Assistance publique," Cons. mun., *Proc.-ver.* (27 June 1927), 1256–64; de Fontenay, "Programme de construction de nouveau hôpitaux dans la banlieue de Paris," Cons. mun., *Proc.-ver.* (28 March 1929), 423; Henri Sellier, "Approbation du programme de construction de nouveaux hôpitaux dans la banlieue de Paris," Cons. mun., *Proc.-ver.* (27 March 1929), 252–81; "Proposition de M. Gaston Pinot relative à l'agrandissement de divers sanatoriums," Cons. mun., *Proc.-ver.* (12 July 1929), 1285; de Fontenay, "Construction de deux hôpitaux, à Garches et à Rosny-sous-Bois," Cons. mun., *Proc.-ver.* (12 July 1929), 1316–1438; in addition to the annual debates over the budget of Assistance publique.

15. De Fontenay, "Renvoi à l'Administration d'une proposition de M. de Fontenay relative à l'élaboration d'un programme de grands travaux hospitaliers," Cons. mun., *Proc.-ver.* (6 July 1931), 797; and De Fontenay, "Proposition en vue de l'élaboration d'un programme de grands travaux hospitaliers . . . ," Cons. mun., *Rap. et doc.*, no. 43 (30 June 1931), 12.

16. "Budget de l'Assistance publique," Cons. mun., *Proc.-ver.* (28 December 1925), 847–48.

Outdated facilities could not bear the strain placed on them by increased use. According to Assistance publique, between 1910 and 1930 the number of patients increased by one hundred thousand[17] as hospital stays became increasingly common and tuberculosis continued to ravage the capital.[18] Urban renewal compounded matters. The demolition of the ring of fortifications around the city required the elimination of abutting hospitals with hundreds of existing beds, especially in the northern and eastern parts of the city that most needed them.[19]

Temporary beds filled hallways. Hospital rooms overflowed. Rooms built for twenty-four patients regularly housed twice that many.[20] A municipal councilor, de Fontenay, reminded his colleagues:

> We read, with a certain scorn for the past, that five patients slept in a single bed in seventeenth-century hospitals. I am quite concerned that our great-grandchildren will have the same scorn for us when they describe 1930, and yet we boast of being men of progress![21]

Authorities judged that having temporary beds comprise over 10 percent of the total paralyzed hospitals, making it impossible for doctors and nurses to move about. In the winter of 1925–26 there were two thousand patients sleeping on stretchers in Parisian hospitals, 31 to 32 percent of the beds in some cases.[22] On 20 December 1925, the city's hospitals were as full as they had been during the worst period of the preceding winter. The director of Assistance publique warned that, if admissions continued to increase, he would be unable to keep a roof over all of the patients. Conditions were so desperate that he drew up plans to construct tents in the courtyards of several hospitals, and others suggested commandeering army barracks to

17. I have been unable to determine what percentage this increase represented.

18. On hospitalization rates, see de Fontenay, "Proposition en vue de l'élaboration d'un programme de grands travaux . . . ," in Cons. mun., *Rap. et doc.*, no. 43 (30 June 1931), 24. On tuberculosis in Paris, Henri Sellier and Henri Rousselle, *L'office public d'hygiène sociale du département de la Seine et du lutte contre la tuberculose dans l'agglomération parisienne* (Paris: Ophs, n.d. [1920]); and Sellier, *La lutte contre la tuberculose dans la région parisienne, 1896–1927: Le rôle de l'Office public d'hygiène sociale*, 2 vols. (Paris: Ophs, 1928).

19. Henri Rousselle, "Budget de l'Assistance publique," Cons. mun., *Bulletin municipal officiel de la ville de Paris*, compte rendu of 28 December 1923, in vol. 42, no. 354 (31 December 1923): 5639–43. On the social conditions of the northern suburbs, see Jean-Paul Brunet, "Une banlieue ouvrière: Saint-Denis, 1890–1939: Problèmes d'implantation du socialisme et du communisme," Thèse d'État (1978; Lille: Service de Réproduction des Thèses, 1982); and Annie Fourcaut, *Bobigny, banlieue rouge* (Paris: Presses de la Fondation nationale des sciences politiques, 1986).

20. De Fontenay, "Proposition en vue de l'élaboration d'un programme de grands travaux . . . ," in Cons. mun., *Rap. et doc.*, no. 43 (30 June 1931), 26.

21. Ibid.

22. Jean Varenne and the director of Assistance publique in "Budget de l'Assistance publique," Cons. mun., *Proc.-ver.* (28 December 1925), 826, 843. Varenne does not specify which hospitals.

house the chronically ill.[23] Tuberculosis patients had to wait three or four months before finding a place in a sanatorium or suitable ward, taking up precious beds in city hospitals, often in intensive care units.[24] In the meantime, "only a few centimeters separate the beds, and the tubercular patients spit their bacilli on neighbors' sheets."[25] People spat everywhere, and the disinfection of patients' rooms often failed to kill the germs they left behind.[26] When the conservative budget director of the municipal council threatened to quash an emergency spending plan, one of his liberal colleagues reminded him that some old hospitals, Bichat and Broussais in particular, were in such bad condition that "at night . . . hospital employees have to keep rats from climbing into bed with the patients."[27]

Local politicians complained bitterly about having to spend millions of francs a year to care for immigrants when their own citizens were receiving such substandard care. In 1924 Assistance publique paid over 250,000 francs in assistance and roughly 12 million francs to hospitalize foreigners.[28] In 1926 foreigners cost the city some 15 million francs.[29] One does not have to look far to hear modern echoes in contemporary complaints.[30] Ambroise Rendu, a prominent philanthropist and president of the municipal council's Fifth Commission, which oversaw Assistance publique, offered a nativist's time-honored solution: "You have heard about the overcrowding of our hospitals. They certainly are, but if we didn't have all these foreigners, we wouldn't have to resort to temporary beds."[31] It did not mat-

23. "Budget de l'Assistance publique," Cons. mun., *Proc.-ver.* (28 December 1925), 843–44, 846. Although tuberculosis rates began to decline after the war, they remained high (see note 18). The director was not in favor of using army barracks. He pointed out that a number of the city's oldest hospitals—including Bichat, Andral, and le Bastion 29—were converted army barracks and that they did not function at all well.

24. "Budget de l'Assistance publique," Cons. mun., *Proc.-ver.* (28 December 1925), 844–45.

25. De Fontenay in "Budget de l'Assistance publique," Cons. mun., *Proc.-ver.* (28 December 1925), 826.

26. Sellier, *La lutte contre la tuberculose dans la région parisienne*, 1:19.

27. Jean Varenne in "Budget de l'Assistance publique," Cons. mun., *Proc.-ver.* (28 December 1925), 842. For public health during the early Third Republic, see Murard and Zylberman, *L'hygiène dans la République: La santé publique en France, ou l'utopie contrariée, 1870–1918* (Paris: Fayard, 1996).

28. Préfecture de Police, Direction des Recherches, Service des Recherches Administratives et des Jeux, "La main d'œuvre étrangère dans la région parisienne" (21 March 1925), APP B/a 67ᴾ, doss. 331.500–A.

29. Le directeur général de l'Administration général de l'Assistance publique, "Budget de l'Assistance publique," Cons. mun., *Proc.-ver.* (28 December 1925), 839, and Dr. Auguste Marie in *Le matin*, 7 January 1926.

30. "Immigrants = AIDS" and "One million unemployed, one million foreigners too many," Jean-Marie Le Pen. On Le Pen, see Nonna Mayer and Pascal Perrineau, eds., *Le Front National à découvert*, rev. ed. (Paris: Presses de la Fondation nationale de science politique, 1996), and Pierre-André Taguieff, *Face au racisme*, 2 vols. (Paris: La Découverte, 1991).

31. Rendu, "Budget de l'Assistance publique," Cons. mun., *Proc.-ver.* (28 December 1925), 839.

ter to Rendu and his like that the French were every bit as responsible for the overcrowding as immigrant workers. Foreigners made up over 10 percent of the *intra muros* population, and over 9 percent in the department as a whole, but only about 8 percent of the city's hospital patients in December 1925.[32] Foreigners were less likely than French citizens to seek hospital care.[33] Expelling immigrants would have freed up hospital beds but at the expense of a disproportionately young, working population, not to mention humanitarian concerns. Eminent doctors as well as scurrilous local politicians ignored the fact that foreigners were underrepresented in most area hospitals. They called attention instead to the dramatic exceptions, like Tenon,[34] or Saint-Louis, where foreigners made up 20 percent of the patients in the syphilis ward.[35] In one case, foreigners made up 37 percent of all patients.[36]

The medical community blamed foreigners not only for threatening their jobs and for filling Parisian hospitals but also for threatening the national health. Having played a critical role in establishing the liberal Third Republic,[37] the medical profession moved dramatically to the political right in the interwar period. Without question the most xenophobic of professional associations, the Confédération des Syndicats Médicaux, led a tireless campaign against foreign doctors and medical students.[38] Mainstream novelists, newspapers, and the popular press alike sounded the alarm against foreigners, and doctors were only too willing to lend their authority.

Critics focused on particular ailments that afflicted migrants more than the general population or for which immigrants were likely to need hospital care. In January 1926 the broad distribution *Le Matin* ran a series of twelve articles called "Paris, Hospital to the World," filled with purple prose backed by the authority of scientists and doctors. Later that year, *Le Matin*

---

32. The census figures, for 1926, are provided by Brunet, "Une banlieue ouvrière," 2:793. The percentage of foreigners in the entire Department of the Seine was slightly lower, 9.3 percent. On the percentage of foreigners in city hospitals, Le directeur général de l'Administration général de l'Assistance publique, "Budget de l'Assistance publique," Cons. mun., *Proc.-ver.* (28 December 1925), 839.

33. See the figures given in the annual debates over the budget of Assistance publique.

34. Dr. Prosper-Émile Weil, "Les malades étrangers à l'hôpital Tenon: Statistiques portant sur six mois," *Bulletin de l'Académie de médecine* 44, no. 36 (10 November 1925): 991.

35. Dr. Jeanselme, "Rapport de la commission sur les malades étrangers dans les hôpitaux," *Bulletin de l'Académie de médecine* 45, no. 3 (19 January 1926).

36. Bernard in the debate following the "Rapport de la commission sur les malades étrangers dans les hôpitaux," ibid., 65.

37. Jack Ellis, *The Physician-Legislators of France: Medicine and Politics in the Early Third Republic, 1870–1914* (Cambridge: Cambridge University Press, 1990).

38. Vicki Caron, "The Anti-Semitic Revival in France in the 1930s: The Socioeconomic Dimension Reconsidered," *Journal of Modern History* 70, no. 1 (March 1998): 24–73, esp. 41—56, and Julie Fette, "Xenophobia and Exclusion in the Professions in Interwar France" (PhD diss., New York University, 2001).

warned that "an admirable assortment of germs" threatened the capital.[39] In a report on "undesirable" immigrants, Dr. Auguste Marie, the director of the Sainte-Anne Asylum in Paris, reported that 15 percent of the mental patients his service examined each year were foreign born.[40] Isolated outbreaks of the plague in 1923 and smallpox in 1925–26 also attracted considerable attention.[41] Ralph Schor has suggested that Parisian doctors, eager to benefit from widespread anxieties over France's low birthrate and supposed racial degeneration, lent their reputations to the miserabilist descriptions in the hope of scaring authorities into granting resources for public hygiene reforms.[42]

Whatever their motivations, doctors almost universally failed to report that most of the immigrants in local hospitals contracted their diseases, especially tuberculosis and syphilis, after they arrived in France. If foreigners were more likely to suffer from tuberculosis, as was generally believed, it had far more to do with conditions in France than in their homelands.[43] In the comfortable obscurity of a medical journal, a leading specialist in venereology, Dr. Jeanselme, reported that 83 percent of the syphilis patients in his clinic had contracted the disease in France. He quickly pointed out that, in his opinion, "it matters little whether these foreigners contracted syphilis here or in their country; the crucial point is that these germ-carriers are nomads and thus active agents of dissemination."[44] A later study, conducted at the Franco-Muslim Hospital, concluded that 98 percent of the patients were infected in France.[45]

39. *Le matin*, quoted in Ralph Schor, *L'opinion française et les étrangers, 1919–1939* (Paris: Publications de la Sorbonne, 1985), 419.

40. Marie, "A propos des indésirables," *Bulletin de la Société de médecine de Paris* 3 (1926): 107.

41. Schor, *L'opinion française et les étrangers*, 415–25, esp. 417.

42. Ibid., 419.

43. Gérard Jacquemet pointed out in his studies of Belleville that native Parisians were more likely to succumb to the disease than newcomers. See his "Les maladies populaires à Paris à la fin du XIXe siècle," *Recherches* 29 (1977): 349–64; Jacquemet, "Aspects de la condition des milieux populaires dans un quartier de Paris entre les deux guerres mondiales," in *Villes et campagnes, XVe–XXe siècles, troisième rencontre franco-suisse* (Lyon: Presses universitaires, 1977), 325–56; and Alain Faure, "Paris, 'gouffre de l'espèce humaine'?" *French Historical Studies* 27, no. 1 (Winter 2004): 49–86.

44. Jeanselme participating in the debate following Pr. Léon Bernard, "Rapport de la commission sur les malades étrangers dans les hôpitaux," *Bulletin de l'Académie de médecine* 45 (19 January 1926): 70.

45. Robert Sanson, "Les travailleurs nord-africains de la région parisienne," Institut National d'Études Démographiques, *Documents sur l'immigration*, travaux et documents 2 (1943; Paris: Puf, 1947), 183–84. The figures are from 1936 to 1943. Sanson also cites an unpublished study by an social worker for Secours national, Mlle. Moisonnier, who conducted a thorough study of the venereal diseases of North Africans treated at the three Parisian dispensaries. She wrote that, contrary to legend, very few had tertiary syphilis, or the most advanced stage. Most had contracted the disease recently, since their arrival. Of the roughly twenty thousand North Africans examined, 10 percent had venereal diseases.

The medical community managed to obtain quota laws excluding foreign doctors from practicing in France,[46] but they proved unable to exclude foreign patients. A law dating from the Second Republic (7 August 1851) obliged French hospitals to admit patients regardless of their nationality or their ability to pay. A number of countries signed treaties with France, agreeing to pay for their nationals' care. Those treaties required that foreigners receive the same treatment the French received but guaranteed reimbursement only if the patient remained in hospital for forty-five days, sixty for Poles.[47] Few foreigners remained hospitalized for such extended periods, preventing the state from collecting money to repay local authorities, much to the latter's consternation. Local authorities, bound by international treaties they had not negotiated, were stuck with the expense.[48] The municipal councilor responsible for the city's public health budget insisted that "the Seine must make it known [to parliament] that Parisians refuse to be the eternal dupes of policies they had no part in enacting."[49]

Hospital conditions did improve. Beaujon, Broussais, and a handful of the city's oldest hospitals were either rebuilt or thoroughly renovated. The Marmottan Foundation hospital opened in the heart of Paris. Treatment centers in the nearby Departments of the Oise and the Seine-et-Oise opened for tuberculosis patients. A new hospital for chronic patients opened in the town of Garches, in the Marne, in 1938. By the end of that year the city had created roughly eleven thousand new beds, but overcrowding remained a serious problem.[50] Temporary beds continued to clutter hallways, and public health officials complained about the burden of treating foreigners throughout the interwar period.[51]

Problems remained most acute in the northern suburbs, where the population was growing fastest, but political infighting between local politicians and their center-city rivals slowed hospital construction to an almost complete standstill. Suburban politicians protested the management of Assistance publique hospitals, controlled exclusively by *intra muros* politicians, and insisted that they receive some measure of control. They complained that city hospitals failed to verify the residence of their patients; since the

---

46. Schor, *L'opinion française et les étrangers*, 607–11.

47. By 1938, treaties had been signed with Italy, Poland, Belgium, Luxembourg, Austria, Spain, and Switzerland. Schor, *L'opinion française et les étrangers*, 418.

48. Dr. Grégoire Ichok, "Les maladies professionnelles des immigrés et les traités internationaux de travail et d'assistance," *Revue d'hygiène* 48 (1926): 1105–10.

49. De Fontenay, "Rapport général au nom de la 5e Commission, sur le compte financier de 1937, les chapitres additionnels de 1938 et le projet de budget de 1939 de l'Assistance publique," Cons. mun., *Rap. et doc.*, no. 95 (16 December 1938), 106.

50. Ibid., 95–106.

51. De Fontenay, "Rapport général au nom de la 5e Commission, sur le compte financier de 1938, les chapitres additionnels de 1939 et le projet de budget de 1940 de l'Assistance publique," Cons. mun., *Rap. et doc.*, no. 40 (26 December 1939), 24.

commune of residence had to pay the medical bills of their indigent patients, poor suburban towns often faced daunting—many thought fraudulent— bills. Parisian councilors, on the other hand, feared pork-barrel management and countered that they had a proven track record of administering hospital affairs.[52]

In March 1929 the two camps put their bickering aside long enough to plan five new hospitals of four hundred beds each in Pantin-Aubervillers, Sceaux, Nanterre, Saint-Mandé, and Saint-Maur–Créteil. Six years later, Pantin and Aubervilliers still could not agree on a site, what size hospital to build, or how to organize its administration. The syndicate created to arrange construction in Sceaux disbanded in late August 1930. By that time, Nanterre had come up with detailed plans, but they had to be changed and the minister of public health was still perusing the revisions. Saint-Maur and Créteil were the only towns able to bring their project to term. It took them eight years, and they came in horribly over budget.[53] Despite a concerted effort and much agonizing, local authorities never did manage to push through a scheme to cope with the foreigners in Parisian hospitals.[54] For their North African subjects, however, they came up with an ingenious plan.

II

Godin rallied national and local politicians to the idea of building a special hospital for North Africans by trumpeting the power of colonial medicine. Dr. Marie of the Sainte-Anne Asylum and Godin told the Paris Municipal Council that "we have perhaps no greater propaganda tool in the world, in favor of Paris and France, than the Muslim patients we have cured."[55] As

52. "Programme de construction de nouveaux hôpitaux dans la banlieue de Paris," Cons. gén., *Proc.-ver.* (31 December 1928), 1593–96; "Approbation du programme de construction de nouveaux hôpitaux dans la banlieue de Paris," Cons. gén., *Proc.-ver.* (27 March 1929), 252–81; and "Création d'hôpitaux en banlieue," Cons. gén., *Proc.-ver.* (11 July 1930), 578–86.

53. De Fontenay, "Rapport général au nom de la 5e Commission, sur le compte financier de 1936, les chapitres additionnels de 1937 et le projet de budget de 1938 de l'Assistance publique," Cons. mun., *Rap. et doc.*, no. 113 (17 December 1937), 84–89.

54. For the hand-wringing, Joseph Denais, "Communication relative à . . . tendant à frapper d'une taxe tout ressortissant étranger occupant à Paris un local, meublé ou non pendant plus d'un mois," Cons. mun., *Proc.-ver.* (4 December 1925), 341. See also Ambroise Rendu, "Renvoi à la 5e Commission d'un projet de vœu . . . relatif au paiement des dépenses du traitement des étrangers dans les hôpitaux et hospices de l'Assistance publique," Cons. mun., *Proc.-ver.* (14 March 1927), 83–84; and Henri Torchausé, "Renvoi aux 4e et 5e Commissions et à la Commission du travail et du chômage d'un projet de vœu . . . tendant à la révision des conventions internationales de réciprocité en matière d'assistance, de chômage et d'enseignement," Cons. mun., *Proc.-ver.* (14 December 1937), 372–75.

55. Godin and Dr. Marie, "Proposition . . . concernant le problème de l'immigration et la mise à l'étude d'un programme de création d'hôpitaux spéciaux pour étrangers," Cons. mun., *Rap. et doc.*, no. 117 (15 December 1932), 4.

Godin put it elsewhere, "It must be agreed that we have never fully conquered them and shall never do so exclusively by means of force, or by ignoring our social obligations."[56] Every benefit granted to colonial subjects
in Paris, he argued, would only reinforce French authority overseas. Pointing to the recently completed Paris Mosque as an example, Godin claimed
that a new hospital could be presented overseas as an example of French
generosity: "Our undertakings in favor of our colonial subjects are not only
honest philanthropy. . . . They are also very good French policy, whose
echoes will spread far and wide, amplified not attenuated by distance."[57]
Godin insisted that the extreme poverty of North African migrants demanded a generous response, "fully to acquit ourselves of our civilizing
mission. The present condition of Muslims living in or passing through
France must be improved." Our country "cannot ignore its moral duty
under any pretext."[58] He went on to suggest that French generosity had en-
sured the colonies' loyalty during the Great War and lobbied for new measures to further strengthen the bond between empire and metropole.

In addition to imperial propaganda, Godin argued, a special hospital
would solve a fundamental social problem. As the poorest, least skilled, and
most exploited migrants, North Africans suffered disproportionately from
industrial accidents and work-related diseases. Mixing rubber involved op-
pressive high temperatures and dangerous fumes with high risks of lead
poisoning, as did mixing acids and making electric batteries. Sand-molders
and metal trimmers in foundries had to contend with fine particles that
caused silicosis after three or four years. Workers in chemical plants often
left with their hair red or green.[59] Living and working far from family and
friends in dangerous, difficult circumstances, young North African men appear to have suffered unusually high rates of tuberculosis, and most were
reluctant to take advantage of French medicine. Those who did go to hospitals were seriously ill, many of them more dead than alive. Over half of
the North African patients taken to Parisian hospitals in 1930 died that
year.[60]

56. Godin, "Hôpital franco-musulman—Création d'un cimetière annexe," Cons. mun.,
Proc.-ver. (1 April 1931), 246.
57. Godin, "Note . . . sur le fonctionnement des services de surveillance, protection et assistance des indigènes nord-africains résidant ou de passage à Paris et dans le département de
la Seine," in Cons. mun., Rap. et doc., no. 77 (1933), quote on 43. See also Norbert Gomar,
L'émigration nord-africaine en France (Paris: Presses modernes, 1931), 131–32; Octave Depont, Les berbères en France: L'hôpital franco-musulman de Paris et du département de la
Seine (Lille: Imprimerie Douriez-Bataille, 1937), 54, and Depont, L'Algérie du centenaire:
L'œuvre française de libération, de conquête morale et d'évolution sociale des indigènes; les
berbères en France; la représentation parlementaire des indigènes (Paris: Sirey, 1928), 137–38.
58. The undated flyer [c. 1926?] in MAE, K—Afrique 1918–1940, Affaires Musulmanes,
vol. 13.
59. MacMaster, Colonial Migrants and Racism, 78.
60. Émile Massard, "Rapport . . . sur le fonctionnement des services de la Préfecture de
Police," Cons. mun., Rap. et doc., no. 1 (1931), 162.

With the example of the Paris Mosque in mind, Godin hoped to obtain subsidies from parliament as well as from the three colonial governments that would never have been available for a "normal" city hospital.[61] The overwhelming majority of North Africans in local hospitals had lived in the city for at least a year by the mid-1920s. They had established residence, so the city was already paying for their care, and local authorities had failed to persuade colonial governments to offer any financial assistance. A subsidized facility for North Africans would thus have freed up three hundred desperately needed beds in existing institutions, essentially for free. Local authorities ultimately received little help. Algeria, Morocco, and Tunisia promised modest grants of a few thousand francs only after the hospital was up and running.[62] But the prospect of raising outside funding helped Godin build early support for his project, notably from public health authorities.[63]

In addition to whatever subsidies were raised, Godin argued, treating North Africans separately would be less expensive than keeping them in existing hospitals. A pamphlet issued by the city suggested that by relying on "Muslim custom, which is sober, the hospital will end up costing less" than European equivalents. In Algeria, the pamphlet noted, hospital days cost half as much as in "ordinary hospitals."[64] The author never explained what, exactly, about Muslim traditions would enable the city to save money on hospital costs or how expenses in Algeria corresponded to those in Paris. Other sources promised that a special hospital would be less expensive based on the experience of Sadiki Hospital in Tunis, but, again, without explaining why one would expect expenses in Paris to correspond with those in the colonies.[65] Authorities may have thought that they could feed colonial patients less-expensive food, and the prohibition of alcohol would have led to some savings. Building a hospital for North Africans would certainly enable existing hospitals to treat everyone more efficiently. Chronic tuberculosis patients could be treated much more economically in their own ward than in emergency rooms or intensive care units, which regularly had to admit them because of constant overcrowding in TB wards. North

61. The mosque was financed, in large part, from private contributions from North Africa and the Middle East. See MAE, K—Afrique 1918–1940, Affaires Musulmanes, vols. 11–14.

62. "Hôpital franco-musulman—Approbation des plans définitifs et de la solution financière," Cons. gén., Proc.-ver. (8 July 1931), 670–72; CAOM 9 H 113; and MAE, K—Afrique 1918–1940, Questions Générales, vol. 32.

63. Director of Assistance publique to Godin, 10 June 1927, cited by Dr. Josianne Chevillard-Vabre, "Histoire de l'hôpital Franco-Musulman" (thèse pour le doctorat en médecine, Diplôme d'État, Faculté de médecine Saint-Antoine, 1982), 63.

64. Préfecture de la Seine, L'hôpital franco-musulman de Paris et du département de la Seine (Paris: Diéval, 1935), 3, in APP D/a 768.

65. On the Sadiki Hospital, see Richard Keller, "Action Psychologique: French Psychiatry in Colonial North Africa, 1900-1962" (PhD diss., Rutgers University, 2001), 24–26, 32–36, 38, 40–41.

African immigrants were overwhelmingly working men, so they would not need pediatric or maternity services; patients who needed specialized care could receive it in other city hospitals.

The new hospital also promised to treat North Africans in more familiar surroundings. It could provide translators and treat patients in conditions that would be less disorienting than those presented by most European hospitals. A staff trained to understand North African languages and culture, the food, even the architecture would provide an environment that reminded patients of home. As the Socialist mayor of Suresnes, and future minister of public health, Henri Sellier, noted:

> M. Godin was right to emphasize that it is necessary, and in the interest of the natives themselves, that they be placed in a milieu corresponding to their habits and customs. If they shock and offend our fellow citizens, their customs are, for them, eminently respectable and preferable to our civilization. Because their ways may prove inconvenient for French patients, it is normal and legitimate that we treat natives in their own milieu.[66]

The standard of care would improve for all concerned, the argument went, and reduce the average cost per patient. North African Muslims would receive the care they so desperately needed. The city would save money at the same time by segregating Algerians, Moroccans, and Tunisians in a facility of their own. Although the director of Assistance publique tried, unsuccessfully, to gain control of a series of other hospital projects outside his jurisdiction, in the suburbs, he was happy to leave the care of North Africans to Godin. He went along with the conservative majority of the municipal council and supported a project that promised to save money, ease overcrowding in center-city hospitals, and make their administration easier.[67]

As this support suggests, respect for difference and a desire to provide colonial patients with care in familiar surroundings often merged with a biological racism that gained force in the 1920s. Responding to conservative questioning in the municipal council, Godin explained:

> Sent to their own special hospital, North African natives will free up 240 beds in our hospitals, thus benefiting the residents of the capital and the Department of the Seine.

66. Sellier, ". . . Création sur ces terrains d'un hôpital franco-musulman et désignation de conseillers municipaux et généraux pour faire partie de la Commission de surveillance dudit hôpital," Cons. gén., *Proc.-ver.* (9 July 1930), 511.
67. Director of Assistance publique to Godin, 10 June 1927, cited by Chevillard-Vabre, "Histoire de l'hôpital franco-musulman," 63. "Programme de construction de nouveaux hôpitaux dans la banlieue de Paris," Cons. gén., *Proc.-ver.* (31 December 1928), 1593–96; "Approbation du programme de construction de nouveaux hôpitaux dans la banlieue de Paris," Cons. gén., *Proc.-ver.* (27 March 1929), 252–81; and "Création d'hôpitaux en banlieue . . . ," Cons. gén., *Proc.-ver.* (11 July 1930), 578–86.

[We can provide an] addition, then, to our means for combating suffering in Paris and the Department of the Seine, without—if it even needs to be said—any consideration of race or religion. No one is disadvantaged. There are only winners.[68] .

Why, in this context, did Godin feel the need to distance himself from accusations of discrimination? The entire project depended upon a positive recognition of religious difference. North Africans could only be reminded of "home" if they were provided special treatment, kept apart from other patients and doctors ignorant of their ways. Godin ultimately championed the new programs as part of an effort to win over and help North Africans, but, as his defensiveness conceded, also as a means of protecting the metropolitan population from those migrants. Influenced by France's well-established Lamarckian tradition, Godin and his allies in the Radical Party hoped that North Africans could *eventually* be made fully French, but they agonized over potential problems in the short term.[69]

Many in France believed that virtually all North Africans were infected with congenital syphilis before they arrived on the mainland and predisposed to catch tuberculosis. An initial ambivalence toward North African workers had clearly been replaced with hostility by the 1920s, as they returned to the mainland in significant numbers. The fears they inspired were expressed increasingly in medical terms, especially as revolutionary movements developed overseas and social tensions grew at home. Godin told the municipal council, "By taking care of them, we are protecting ourselves and our fellow citizens." He went on:

Most of them brought syphilis with them from Africa. It is congenital in most natives. But, when they arrive in a different climate and have their customs entirely transformed, it reawakens with a vengeance and poses a threat not only to the natives themselves but to anything the contagion can reach. Any oriental immigration in France involves a new syphilitic invasion.[70]

Syphilis probably was endemic to North Africa, but then it was endemic in France, Russia, and elsewhere in Europe before the introduction of penicillin. Rates of venereal syphilis may well have been lower in the rural communities of the Maghreb than on the French mainland.[71] In Paris, however,

<hr/>

68. Godin, "Question de M. de Pressac à M. le Préfet de la Seine . . . ," Cons. gén., *Proc.-ver.* (9 July 1930), 497.
69. Clifford Rosenberg, "Albert Sarraut and Republican Racial Thought," *French Politics, Culture, and Society* 20, no. 3 (Fall 2002): esp. 104–5.
70. Godin, "Proposition . . . concernant les dispensaires spéciaux et les services médicaux réservés aux indigènes Nord-africains," Cons. mun., *Proc.-ver.* (5 December 1932), 169.
71. Laura Englestein, "Morality and the Wooden Spoon: Syphilis, Social Class, and Sexual Behavior," in her *The Keys to Happiness: Sex and the Search for Modernity in Fin-de-Siècle Russia* (Ithaca: Cornell University Press, 1992), chap. 5, esp. 168, 170–73, 177–85. See also Englestein, "Syphilis Historical and Actual: Cultural Geography of a Disease," *Reviews in In-*

French politicians and public alike saw an overwhelmingly young, male group loitering in red-light districts and coming down with feared diseases. If they were underrepresented in Parisian hospitals generally, colonial migrants made up a striking percentage in a handful of clinics.[72]

Popular writers added to the growing stereotypes. In his novel *Sidi de la banlieue* (1937), Jean Damase wrote:

> We're ruining ourselves. Do you realize what we paid in 1936? Five hundred thousand hospital days, in Paris alone. You heard me, five hundred thousand hospital days for foreign patients, costing us twenty million a year to import international diseases. Syphilis is awfully expensive!
>
> No, this is no longer assistance! It's a crusade, gentlemen—all the rot in the world arrives on our doorstep. All the world's plagues have set a rendez-vous chez nous . . . and Paris pays—twenty million for trachoma, leprosy, and the other beastliness.
>
> You want to see some specimens? At the moment, I have the most beautiful case of amoebic enteritis, amaurotic idiocy, and sclerotic bruises that used to be found only in Malaysia, Alexandria, or Baghdad.
>
> Ah yes, as an annex to the university, one can pursue studies on all the colonial rubbish. It's a museum.
>
> He added, laughing, that at least the young students can study sleeping sickness right here, leprosy (I have fourteen lepers), the Alep chancre, Maltese fever, trachoma, intestinal bilharzia, and other exotic poxes! They're always good for something.[73]

Instead of debunking this sort of fear-mongering, doctors contributed to it in a stream of learned articles and theses.[74] The initial ambivalence toward North African workers had clearly been replaced with hostility by the 1920s The fears they inspired were expressed increasingly in medical terms.

---

fectious Diseases 8 (November–December 1986): 1036–48; Alain Corbin, "Le péril vénérien au début du siècle: Prophylaxie sanitaire et prophylaxie morale," *L'haleine des faubourgs, Recherches* 29 (December 1977): 245–83; and, above all, Claude Quétel, *Le mal de Naples: Histoire de la syphilis* (Paris: Seghers, 1986).

72. See note 44.

73. Jean Damase, *Sidi de la banlieue* (Paris: Fasquelle, 1937), 107–8. My thanks to Mary Lewis for helping me with this translation.

74. In addition to the works cited above, and among many others, Dr. Lacapère, *La syphilis arabe* (Paris: Gaston Doin, 1923); A. Violette, *La race française en péril: Alcool, tuberculose, syphilis* (Saint-Brieuc: Imprimerie Moderne, 1920); Dr. Leger, "La syphilis des immigrants et travailleurs nord-africains pénétrant en France: Comment la combattre," *Archives de l'Institut prophylactique* 5 (1933): 152–66; J. Bercovici, *Contrôle sanitaire des immigrants en France* (Paris: Sagot, 1926); G. Dequidt and Dr. Forestier, "Les aspects sanitaires du problème de l'immigration en France," *Revue d'hygiène* 48 (1926): 999–1049; Dr. Even, "Protection de la santé publique et contrôle sanitaire des transmigrants," *Le mouvement sanitaire* 30 (April 1930): 208–34. For the United States, Alan M. Kraut, *Silent Travelers: Germs, Genes, and the "Immigrant Menace"* (New York: Basic Books, 1994).

Doctors regularly argued that colonial migrants presented problems that only they could solve. Germs and diseases foreign to the French climate and race demanded money and attention, in their view.[75] A specialized institution would allow doctors to keep North Africans away from other patients.

This was, of course, not the first time doctors and men of letters had taken up the pen against what they perceived as the health risk posed by new immigrants. In the mid-nineteenth century, Parent-Duchâtelet's obsession with syphilis and his regulation of prostitution is only the most striking example of doctors' efforts to control immigrant men. Nor were North Africans the only group to be viewed as a threat to the body politic between the wars.

Racial prejudice figured prominently in the mix of motivations behind the new hospital, but it does not explain why North Africans, alone, received separate medical facilities. Parisian politicians tried to segregate European migrants as well. In the early 1930s, Godin rehearsed the same arguments that he had used for North Africans in his bid to create a series of new hospitals, exclusively for Europeans. Those immigrants spoke foreign languages, and surely they would have appreciated the comforts of home as much as any colonial subject. Led by Godin, the councilors wanted to build European immigrants "hospitals where nurses who understand their language provide a familiar diet and special, sensitive care, and remind immigrants of their far away loved ones in the sad hours of their wandering lives."[76]

Godin repeated not only the paternal paeans to protecting French wards but portrayed Europeans, too, as dangerous, biological threats:

> Who knows what sort of swarming germs will emerge from areas overflowing with immigrants, where no public hygiene service can establish a cordon sanitaire? Has it not been proven, moreover, that since France has become a country of immigration, with Paris the principal center of the phenomenon, extremely serious diseases, some of them unknown, from faraway places have multiplied despite the desperate warnings and best efforts of doctors and hygienists?[77]

Europeans always fared better than colonials in the various ethnic surveys and studies carried out between the wars. Employers routinely found them more reliable and productive, and doctors found them healthier, with a greater affinity to the "French race."[78] Those endorsements, however, were

---

75. Depont presents a forceful version of these arguments in his campaign to restore research funding to the Franco-Muslim Hospital in *Les berbères en France: L'hôpital franco-musulman*, 70.

76. Godin and Dr. Marie, "Proposition," 1.

77. Ibid., 2.

78. See Gilbert Meynier, *L'Algérie révélée: La guerre de 1914–1918 et le premier quart du XXe siècle* (Geneva: Droz, 1981), 465, 478–80, for the unreliability of the surveys.

only relative. Special hospitals for Europeans, in addition to the one for North Africans, Godin argued, would guarantee the health of French citizens. They would become a "social filter" by teaching foreigners how to care for themselves. They would emerge "not only cleansed [*blanchis*], but, if I may say, no longer a threat to public health." The proposal for foreigners, like that for North Africans, was presented as a staunchly nationalist plan to defend the French taxpayer and hospital patient: "Now, if there are no special hospitals, the increasing number of immigrants will invade our hospitals. And it's happening already. . . . It is scandalous, and, moreover, a violent injustice! France and its assistance programs belong first and foremost to the French."[79]

Although the effort to segregate European migrants in hospitals of their own ultimately failed, Godin's use of the verb *blanchir*, meaning to bleach or whiten as well as to cleanse, underscores the anxieties European immigrants inspired well into the 1930s. The effort to segregate European immigrants from French patients did not fail for the moderation of its prejudice. It languished in committee because powerful patrons from the national government refused to support the cause. A special facility for foreigners would obviously not strengthen the bonds of Greater France; nor did foreign governments see the need to subsidize their citizens' care when a series of bilateral treaties guaranteed them the same health and social benefits as French citizens. Foreign governments increasingly took an interest in the fate of their citizens on French soil, and they did not hesitate to intervene through diplomatic channels when they suspected abuse. Ambassadors constantly reminded the French foreign minister of the host country's obligations, and they often intervened on behalf of individual citizens. Whatever misgivings they might have had about European migrants, French politicians worried about irate ambassadors protesting the segregation of their patients and setting off an international incident.[80]

III

The colonial consensus enabled Godin to achieve for North Africans what could not be accomplished for other immigrants. Godin created a special committee in 1926 to organize his bid to create a North African hospital. A veritable who's who of republican luminaries came aboard, including President Gaston Doumergue, Minister of the Interior Albert Sarraut, Radical leader Édouard Herriot, Senator Henri de Jouvenel, General Maxime Wey-

79. Godin and Dr. Marie, "Proposition," 2.

80. On the intervention of foreign governments, APP D/a 742, D/a 744, and B/a 278ᴾ; AN F⁷ 13,455, and esp. F⁷ 13,652; MAE Z—Europe, 1930–1940, vols. 206, 354, and 368; CAC 19940437, art. 234; CAC 19940457, art. 80; and CAC 19940500, art. 116; and ADY 1 W 1146 and 1147.

gand, and the scholars Louis Massignon and Louis Milliot, among others.[81] Their support enabled Godin to take over a private, philanthropic campaign to provide health care for Algerians, attach it to the new police brigade he had recently created, and to clear the innumerable administrative hurdles in its way. The special committee appears to have ceased functioning in 1930, when it was replaced by a special departmental commission, presided over once again by the ubiquitous Godin.[82]

He and his allies quickly chose two Prix de Rome architects, one of whom had just built the Paris Mosque. They agreed on the plans and organized financial backing with the help of Albert Sarraut, who pushed a tax plan through parliament. Sarraut had supported Godin's efforts for years and served on the initial committee to create the hospital.[83] He lobbied doggedly to assure colonial administrators would not stand in the way. Without his clout in parliament, the city never could have raised enough money to build a hospital, because new taxes, even local ones, had to be approved by national officials.[84] As Depont explained, the "effort would have failed without the effective intervention of a great imperialist, M. Albert Sarraut, then minister of the interior."[85] National officials granted a 2.5 million franc subsidy for the hospital in 1932 without which the project would have been scrapped.[86] The three colonial governments had promised subsidies of their own, but only after the new establishment opened, so the state's relatively modest contribution came at a crucial juncture. With their finances in order, supported mostly by local taxes, authorities settled on a plot of land in the Communist fiefdom of Jean-Marie Clamamus, Bobigny, in the heart of the suburban "red belt."[87]

Godin and his allies picked Bobigny in part because the department already owned the land, which it had purchased for next to nothing, but also to settle local political scores. Doing so allowed them to deprive the Communist municipality, a poor dormitory suburb whose residents worked in nearby industrial towns, of its prime industrial site. Bobigny was among the first towns of the emerging red belt of industrial suburbs to change its allegiance from the Socialist to the Communist Party, following its mayor, Cla-

81. Comité de Fondation de l'Hôpital Franco-Musulman de Paris to Monsieur le Ministre [des Affaires Étrangères], 6 August 1926, and a flyer listing the members in MAE, K—Afrique 1918–1940, sous-série Affaires Musulmanes, vol. 13.

82. Chevillard-Vabre, "Histoire de l'hôpital Franco-Musulman," 25–27; Godin, "Note sur le fonctionnement des Services de Surveillance, Protection et Assistance des indigènes Nord-Africains," 44; and Depont, Les berbères en France: L'hôpital franco-musulman, 62, 68.

83. Godin quotes a 27 October 1927 letter from Sarraut in his "Note sur le fonctionnement," 44.

84. Maurice Félix, Le régime administratif et financier du département de la Seine et de la ville de Paris, 2 vols. (Paris: Rousseau, 1946).

85. Depont, Les berbères en France: L'hôpital franco-Musulman, 62.

86. Note of 17 December 1932 by the minister of public health. See also "Hôpital Franco-Musulman—Approbation des plans définitifs et de la solution financière," Cons. gén., Proc.-ver., 8 July 1931, 670–72.

87. AP D12 N⁴ art. 7.

mamus, after the split at the Congress of Tours in 1920.[88] A prominent member of the PCF and one of the leading personalities in the working-class suburbs, Clamamus opened the country's first Leninist training school for party militants, whose short course contained a heavy dose of anticolonialism. As part of their course work, students traveled around the area haranguing workers as they left factories, lecturing them on the horrors of the Rif war and other supposed capitalist plots.[89] When the police raided the new school in late 1924, the government was aghast at the contents of student notebooks and accused the party of inciting treason in a series of acrimonious debates in parliament and press campaigns.[90] Octave Depont warned that "tomorrow, if we do not pay heed, ten thousand students from the Bobigny training school will be in contact with the Destour [nationalist polity party] in Tunisia and all the other nationalist groups."[91] The père Lhande, a Catholic priest who evangelized in the Paris suburbs, wrote in his *Le Christ dans la banlieue* (1927), "If there is one name that symbolizes the ultra-red Parisian suburbs to the general public, it is . . . Bobigny."[92]

Communist protests bothered all of the non-PCF members of the departmental council but stung Socialists in particular, and helped cement their participation in Godin's project. The chance to force their symbol of imperial largesse on a troublesome anticolonial enemy and deprive him of his only promising source of tax revenue clearly outweighed any apprehension about leaving colonial subjects in a hotbed of revolutionary activism.[93] It was also sufficient to override the recommendation of civil engineers at the Direction des ponts et chaussées, who found conditions at the site too unhealthy.[94]

Construction on the North African hospital began in Bobigny early in 1931. The new 25 million franc facility opened to great fanfare four years later. A troop of dignitaries and journalists trekked out to the suburbs to celebrate in front of the hospital's Moorish façade.[95]

88. Fourcaut, *Bobigny, banlieue rouge*.

89. Jean-Paul Depretto and Sylvie V. Schweitzer, *Le communisme à l'usine: Vie ouvrière et mouvement ouvrière chez Renault* (Roubaix: Edires, 1984).

90. Philippe Robrieux, *Histoire intérieure du parti communiste*, vol. 1, *1920–1945* (Paris: Fayard, 1980), 228; and Fourcaut, *Bobigny, banlieue rouge*, 147.

91. Depont, *L'Algérie du centenaire*, 144.

92. Lhande, *Le Christ dans la banlieue*, vol. 1, *Enquête sur la vie religieuse dans les milieux ouvriers de la banlieue de Paris* (Paris: Plon, 1927), 53.

93. For these fears, see "Question de M. de Pressac à M. le Préfet de la Seine sur les terrains de jeu aménagés à Bobigny par le Stade français—Création sur ces terrains d'un hôpital franco-musulman et désignation de conseillers municipaux et généraux pour faire partie de la Commission de surveillance dudit hôpital," Cons. gén., *Proc.-ver.* (9 July 1930), 492. Clamamus organized a petition campaign to counter the project. See the petition and other documents reproduced in Chevillard-Vabre, "Histoire de l'hôpital Franco-Musulman," 42–46.

94. "Rapport du subdivisionnaire," Direction des ponts et chaussées du département de la Seine, 8 September 1928, reproduced in Chevillard-Vabre, "Histoire de l'hôpital Franco-Musulman," 37.

95. AP D12 N⁴ art. 7; AP 10 W, art. 73; AP 106/56, arts. 21–29; AP 016/56/1; and AP 1027 W, art. 73. On the cost, see Depont, *Les berbères en France: L'hôpital Franco-Musulman*

The Franco-Muslim Hospital, soon after its opening in 1935. © Assistance-Publique Hôpitaux de Paris.

IV

By all accounts, the hospital provided perfectly good facilities. According to contemporaries, it was among the best-equipped hospitals in the country, and it served as a model for subsequent health-care facilities.[96] The new hospital was outfitted with X-ray machines, elevators, the latest surgical equipment, disinfecting ovens, and sulphuration rooms. More than one quarter of all hospital beds were located in a special, free-standing pavilion for tuberculosis patients, which also had a handful of isolation rooms.[97] In 1936, the hospital added a special laboratory of "colonial pathology," to conduct research in bacteriology, parasitology, histoparasitology, dermatology, serology, and venereology.[98] Henri Sellier, the minister of public health, opened the new lab along with the undersecretary of state for the

—but cf. the handwritten minutes of the Conférence de coordination de l'Afrique du Nord, 27 January 1938, MAE, K—Afrique, 1918–1940, sous-série Questions Générales, vol. 80, which reports a total expense of twenty-seven million.

96. Ministère des Affaires Étrangères, Circulaire no. 28 IP, 4 February 1948, AN F¹ᵃ 5060.

97. Dr. Ben Salem, *La tuberculose chez les ouvriers musulmans nord-africains en France (étude médico-sociale)* (Paris: M. Vigné, 1942), 43.

98. On the creation of the special lab, see René Fiquet, ". . . Achèvement et ameublement de l'hôpital et du laboratoire d'études et de recherches spéciales," Cons. mun., *Proc.-ver.* (30 December 1936), 1221–25.

protection of children, Suzanne Lacore, in December. It had room for consultations and a "center for specialized research on diseases particular to natives from North Africa."[99]

Some of the doctors were well-respected specialists and manifestly devoted to their patients. Dr. Ali Sakka, was a Chevalier de la Légion d'Honneur and a leader in tuberculosis research. He attracted a number of Muslim students, providing what remained a relatively rare access to first-rate medical training during the interwar years. At a time when French doctors blamed foreigners not only for threatening their jobs and for filling Parisian hospitals but also for threatening the national health, Sakka and his students took advantage of the resources available at the hospital to debunk some of the prejudices that had helped inspire its creation. In 1942, Mohamed Ben Salem defended a thesis under Sakka's direction on tuberculosis among North Africans in France, which showed that their plight was due to poor wages and living conditions and not any biological abnormality or ethnic predisposition.[100] North African migration, Ben Salem pointed out, played a more important role in spreading tuberculosis in the Maghreb—where it was virtually unknown before the arrival of Europeans—than it did in the metropole. According to another contemporary study, eight hundred tuberculosis patients died a year in Algeria before the Great War; eight hundred a year died in the city of Algiers alone during the interwar years.[101]

The most important research on the incidence of syphilis among colonial workers was also carried out under the auspices of the city's North African services. According to statistics kept at the hospital, 98 percent of all cases from 1936 to 1943 were contracted from prostitutes after the workers had arrived in France. The most thorough study of the subject, carried out in Parisian dispensaries in 1938, showed that of roughly twenty thousand North Africans examined, only 10 percent had venereal disease. They were no more likely than French citizens to be infected. Contrary to legend, "very few had tertiary or hereditary [congenital] syphilis."[102] In North Africa both tuberculosis and syphilis were known as *mardh el frandji*, "mal de France."[103]

Despite the presence of a handful of dedicated doctors, questions remain about the medical staff. In an effort to attract doctors with some familiarity

99. Prefect of the Seine to the Minister of Colonies, MAE, K—Afrique 1918–1940, Affaires Musulmanes, vol. 14, folio 136, and R. Fiquet, "Hôpital franco-musulman—fonctionnement en 1935 et budget de 1936," Cons. gén., *Proc.-ver.* (24 December 1935), 739–43.

100. Ben Salem, *La tuberculose chez les ouvriers musulmans*. See also Mohamed Habib Thamer, *La lutte antituberculeuse en Tunisie* (Paris: J. Haumont, 1938).

101. A. Lévi-Valensi, "La tuberculose pulmonaire chez l'indigène musulman algérien (adulte)," *L'Algérie médicale*, 4th ser., 37, no. 66 (June 1933): 347; and Dr. André Albou, *Etude sur la tuberculose des travailleurs indigènes algériens dans les grandes villes, France et Algérie: De son expansion des centres vers les campagnes* (Algiers: Imprimerie moderne, 1930).

102. Sanson quotes the two unpublished studies in "Les travailleurs nord-africains de la région parisienne," 183.

103. Depont, *Les berbères en France*, 57, for the quote.

with North African patients, the hospital's by-laws exempted from the otherwise required exam anyone with two years experience at one of the service's dispensaries. All but one of the doctors had some sort of connection to the Maghreb, which offered opportunities to Muslim medical students but also suggests that Assistance publique's standards were not applied.[104] The new hospital was not a prestigious post, and recruitment of both doctors and staff appears to have been difficult. After World War II, patients complained that they felt abandoned by doctors who kept positions at other hospitals. The prefect of police answered protests about the hospital staff by explaining that of seventy nurses in 1947, only twenty-eight were properly certified. Attracting qualified help was impossible, he said, because of the "eccentricity of the hospital's locale, insufficient salaries, and extremely vulgar patients."[105]

There can be no doubt about the nature of hospital conditions. Located near a barren working-class suburb, far from any form of public transportation, the Franco-Muslim Hospital was terribly isolated in a stinking field, right next to a waste treatment plant. Every day, the neighboring Société Moritz handled tons of fecal matter. A civil engineers' report objected:

> Until recently, this company poured tons of waste into ditches and left it in the open air until it dried completely, giving off nauseating odors that waft throughout the neighborhood. It may be that this method is no longer used (to be verified), but even if it is not, the handling of waste continues to give off the same odors.[106]

A plant processing animal remains in neighboring Aubervilliers and other factories gave off similar smells, and the prevailing breezes often blew from the north and west. Tuberculosis patients seeking a fresh-air cure on their elevated asphalt terrace had special awnings to protect them from the sun and rain,[107] but nothing could have masked the foul odor on a fine summer afternoon or the pounding noise that went on through the night.[108]

Most complaints focused not on the stench or the isolation of the new facility but on the police role of the administration. Messali Hadj complained that the hospital was segregated "as if we were of an inferior, plague-ridden race," which has "damaged our self-esteem."[109] Abderrahmane demanded

104. Ahmad Boukhelloua, *L'hôpital franco-musulman de Paris* (Algiers: S. Crescenzo, 1934), 91, and Chevillard-Vabre, "Histoire de l'hôpital franco-musulman," 83.

105. Prefect of police to the minister of the interior, 22 February 1947, ref. 240–I, AN F^{1a} 5060.

106. Lucien Douane's report of 9 August 1930 is reproduced by Chevillard-Vabre, "Histoire de l'hôpital Franco-Musulman," 43, 46.

107. Depont, *Les berbères en France: L'hôpital franco-musulman*, 66.

108. On the noise, see the initial report of the Direction des ponts et chaussées du département de la Seine, 8 September 1928, reproduced by Chevillard-Vabre, "Histoire de l'hôpital Franco-Musulman," 37.

109. Messali Hadj, quoted in Benjamin Stora, "Histoire politique de l'immigration algérienne en France, 1922–1962" (Thèse d'État, Université de Paris VII, 1991), 1:121.

the right for his compatriots to seek care at any of the city's hospitals, not only in Bobigny where "physical abuse and substandard care are character-istic."[110] A doctor, Ahmed Boukhelloua, took a more moderate, but no less damning, position:

> "While recognizing the [Franco-Muslim Hospital's] value for the police in gathering information," it is humiliating for Muslims to see an institution where the sick take refuge no longer remain neutral ground, "and it is regret-table that the only reason care is given by the hospital staff (doctors, surgeons, nurses) is to spy on the patients."[111]

The opinions of average workers are considerably harder to determine. They did not write for newspapers or speak up in party cell meetings. The same hard core of militants attended most of those meetings, which they consistently opened with denunciations of the North African Services. It seems unlikely they would have continued to do so if those protests failed to strike a nerve.

Most Muslims spoke volumes by their actions; they did everything in their power to avoid going to the new hospital. Only four to five patients a day from the neighborhood came for out-patient treatment, even though there was no other hospital in the area. The overwhelming majority of pa-tients arrived in police vans. Having sought care at one of the city's other hospitals or special dispensaries for North Africans, they were "invited"[112] to make the trek out to Bobigny under police escort. Not all North African patients were forcibly sent to the special hospital. Those with contagious diseases were usually treated at Claude Bernard Hospital, and psychiatric cases were handled at the Sainte-Anne Asylum or the Val de Grâce.[113] Au-thorities, however, soon grew concerned at the number of patients who asked to be transferred from Bobigny to other hospitals. As investigators from the Haut Comité Méditerranéen admitted, "Despite the excellence of the medical services we provide, at considerable expense to the state, some North Africans prefer to be treated in other hospitals." It was, in fact, quite a bit worse than that. The report recognized that segregating North Africans in their own hospital was "perhaps the principal factor inspiring

110. Abderrahmane, "Les travailleurs nord-africains en France," *El Ouma* 58 (December 1937), quote on p. 2. See also Georges Altman, "La Sombre vie des travailleurs racolés dans l'Afrique du Nord . . . Avec les 'sidis,' dans les baraques et les caves de Gennevilliers," *l'Hu-manité*, 29 August 1926, p. 1., and the numerous complaints at political gatherings and Com-munist cell meetings, from police reports in CAOM 9 H 35; APP B/a 56ᴾ; and AN F⁷ 13,131.

111. Boukhelloua, *L'hôpital franco-musulman*, 97, quoting René Fodère, "Médecine et police," *L'esprit médical* (May 1934).

112. De Fontenay, "Rapport . . . sur le compte financier . . . de l'Assistance publique," Cons. mun., *Rap. et doc.*, no. 95 (16 December 1938), 98.

113. Keller, "*Action Psychologique*," 150, 244–45, 268–69; and A. Fribourg-Blanc, "L'é-tat mental des indigènes de l'Afrique du nord et leurs réactions psychopathiques," *L'hygiène mentale* 22, no. 9 (November 1927): 135–44.

the resistance of Muslim workers, who are naturally hostile to any discriminatory measures."[114] For nearly every three patients admitted in 1937, one refused treatment.[115] Instead of a culturally sensitive environment, they saw a lazaret, segregating them from friends and loved ones as well as the rest of the population.

The surviving archival record does not permit an evaluation of specific complaints, but the general functioning of the Parisian services is abundantly clear. The surveillance and assistance efforts were supposed to be kept separate, but in practice the police controlled the entire operation. The prefect of the Seine confirmed as much in a letter to the foreign minister: "The two sections of this unit [surveillance and assistance] are both under the direction of its director, M. Gérolami, and work with the relevant services of the city and the department."[116] Before retiring from public life, Pierre Godin installed his son, André, as chief of the North African Brigade at the Prefecture of Police in 1932.[117] Instead of firing the former chief, Adolphe Gérolami, Godin transferred him to the new hospital—as its first director. Gérolami had no medical training and no experience in hospital work. Indeed, he had no other qualification than his experience overseas. He, like Godin senior, had spent years in rural Algeria, running roughshod over the local inhabitants before moving to Paris to run the North African Brigade. As hospital director, he reportedly interrogated patients before admitting them. Decades later, colleagues remembered him for his extreme "settler mentality."[118]

Like the Franco-Muslim Hospital, all of the city's social services provided information to the police, even as they offered assistance. Assistance programs enabled Godin's men to monitor North African immigrants much more intensely, with less violence, than any of their counterparts in the colonies. The prominent municipal councilor Émile Massard noted in 1931 that "at present, the natives are under the impression that this organization was created not so much to discipline them as to assist and protect them, which has contributed much more to its success than outright force could

---

114. Commission d'Études du HCM, "Rapport conforme aux propositions de la sous-commission des lois sociales et assistance," 17 June 1937, MAE, K—Afrique, 1918–1940, Questions Générales, vol. 75, pp. 2–3/fols. 25–26.

115. De Fontenay mentions 578 refusals in "Rapport général au nom de la 5e commission . . . ," Cons. mun., *Rap. et doc.*, no. 113 (17 December 1937), 49. The next year he reduced the number, slightly, to 564 refusals for 1,837 admissions: "Rapport général au nom de la 5e commission . . . ," in Cons. mun., *Rap. et doc.*, no. 95 (16 December 1938), 98.

116. Letter of 13 October 1926, MAE, K—Afrique 1918–1940, sous-série Questions Générales, vol. 32.

117. On the junior Godin, see Depont, *Les berbères en France*, 58–59.

118. Mlle. Rollen, a pharmacist at the hospital from 1935–1977, interviewed by Chevillard-Vabre, "Histoire de l'hôpital franco-musulman," quote on 89. See also the folder of complaints against Gérolami in AN F[1a] 5060.

have done." (The previous year, Massard had proudly explained that the city's approach actually "consists in protecting and assisting *in order* to discipline them more effectively.")[119] To find a job or a place to sleep, to receive food or medical assistance, to contact relatives back home or resolve a dispute in the metropole, even to take a language class, North Africans had to provide a range of personal information. Local authorities collected information from all of the assistance programs and forwarded it to the police. They created what later investigators called a "very complete [card] file" that served as the "nerve center [*cerveau*] of the ensemble of services . . . , which all the bureaus instinctively consult to find information on a North African."[120] The entire surveillance system sought constantly to control North African workers and to centralize all their vital information. Records of political activity, employment, and medical histories were all kept together. Massard claimed that "nothing concerning the natives remains unknown to us."[121] In 1937 his municipal council colleague Noël Pinelli wrote: "We have identified and arrested every North African perpetrator of a violent crime" reported this year; more generally, he boasted, the police knew the community so well that they could track down North African "delinquents" at will.[122]

The subsidized housing program provided little relief from the unprecedented housing shortage.[123] Wretched conditions and constant police surveillance anticipated by a generation the Sonacotra (Société nationale de construction pour les travailleurs) hostels established during the Algerian War in an effort to clear the bidonvilles and contain the influence of nationalist militants.[124] Three of the hostels closed almost at once, and a fourth closed shortly thereafter. By late 1936 all but one had failed because of financial mismanagement, wasting the substantial loans the city poured into

---

119. Massard, "Rapport . . . sur le fonctionnement des services de la PP . . . 1931," Cons. mun., *Rap. et doc.*, no. 1 (1932), 168; and Massard, "Rapport . . . sur le fonctionnement des services de la PP . . . 1930," Cons. mun., *Rap. et doc.*, no. 1 (1931), 160, my emphasis.

120. "Rapport de MM. Laroque et Ollive, auditeurs au Conseil d'État, sur la main d'œuvre nord-africaine," 3 vols., March 1938, CAOM 8 H 62, 3:291.

121. Massard, "Rapport . . . sur le fonctionnement des services de la PP . . . 1930," Cons. mun., *Rap. et doc.*, no. 1 (1931), 159. See also Godin, "Note . . . sur le fonctionnement," 9.

122. Noel Pinelli, "Rapport . . . sur le fonctionnement des services de la PP . . . 1937," Cons. mun., *Rap. et doc.*, no. 71 (1 October 1938), 349.

123. Susanna Magri, *Le mouvement des locataires à Paris et dans la banlieue parisienne, 1919–1925: Première approche* (Paris: Centre de sociologie urbaine, 1982).

124. Marc Bernardot, "Une politique de logement: La Sonacotra, 1956–1992" (thèse de sociologie, Université de Paris I, 1997); Amelia H. Lyons, "Invisible Immigrants: Algerian Families and the French Welfare State in the Era of Decolonization (1947–1974)" (PhD diss., University of California, Irvine, 2004), chaps. 3–4; Mireille Ginesy-Galano, *Les immigrés hors la cité: Le système d'encadrement dans les foyers, 1973–1982* (Paris: Harmattan, 1984); Gilles Kepel, *Les banlieues de l'Islam* (Paris: Seuil, 1991), chap. 3; and Vincent Viet, *La France immigrée: Construction d'une politique, 1914–1997* (Paris: Fayard, 1998), 204–20.

them and the high rates they charged: sixty francs per month, later raised to one hundred. The rates were no lower than in rooming houses,[125] and the police could search them at any time. When Pierre Laroque visited the Billancourt hostel in late 1937 or early 1938, he found 210 men living in squalor, with the plumbing out of order, an overpriced cafeteria, and signs of prostitution.[126] At least the hospital and dispensaries provided medical care. The housing and job placement services offered no meaningful assistance but helped authorities intimidate and keep tabs on colonial migrants.

The job placement office Henri Sellier defended with his own progressive bona fides blackballed North African nationalists and appears to have had ties to the right-wing leagues.[127] As minister of public health during Léon Blum's first Popular Front government, Sellier was no longer directly involved with the day-to-day business of local government in 1936, but he kept his seat in the municipal council and remained well informed. He retained enough interest in the North African Services after becoming minister of public health to inaugurate the special center for North African pathology at the Franco-Muslim Hospital. That same year, bands of Marcel Bucard's Francistes, led by a certain M. Laffite, visited North African neighborhoods to recruit new anti-Semitic shock troops. Laffite promised to share his contacts with employers and recommend any who joined his group. The Croix de Feu also sent teams to North African cafés in Paris early in 1936, especially the fifteenth arrondissement. After the messy split between Messali Hadj's Étoile nord africaine and the Communist Party, Croix de Feu members told the mostly Algerian patrons that their rightwing group was the "adversary of Jews and their Marxist allies" and that it would provide members with assistance.[128] In Parisian slang, François Coty's Solidarité Française was known as "Sidilarité Française."[129]

These rounds served not only to win over converts but also to scare colonial migrants away from radical political activity. Employers, and perhaps even the leagues themselves, regularly warned the police, who prevented the supposed troublemakers from receiving social benefits or finding work elsewhere.[130] Since North Africans tended to work for one of a handful of large

125. Jean Bastié, *La croissance de la banlieue parisienne* (Paris: Puf, 1964), 187, and Brunet, "Une banlieue ouvrière," 2:748–50.

126. Laroque report, 3:300–303, CAOM 8 H 62, and MacMaster, *Colonial Migrants and Racism*, 165.

127. Accusations of complicity with the leagues extended beyond the placement office, including the housing agency as well. "Conférence de coordination de l'Afrique du Nord," manuscript minutes, 27 January 1938, MAE, K—Afrique, 1918–1940, Questions Générales, vol. 80, fols. 184–85.

128. CAOM 9 H 35, police reports of 15 May 1936 and 28 February 1936.

129. "Sidi," Arabic for "sir," had by this time become a pejorative term for North Africans. I owe this anecdote to Robert O. Paxton.

130. "Question de MM. Léon Frot et Charles Rigaud à M. le Préfet de la Seine sur la politique préfectorale à l'égard des chômeurs . . ." Cons. mun., *Proc.-ver.* (12 July 1935), 805.

Funeral ceremony at the state-sponsored Paris Mosque for a North African killed in the street fighting of February 6, 1934. Notice the uniformed members of Solidarité Française flanking mosque director Si Kaddour Ben Ghabrit. © Keystone.

employers, running afoul of authorities could easily ruin a worker's prospects not only for holding on to his present job but of finding a new one as well.

In 1938 Laroque and Ollive condemned the job placement office as the least effective of the various services the city provided. Officials asked North Africans where they thought they might find work and then sent them there with a card that was no more than a letter of introduction. The bureau occasionally called around to companies known to hire colonial workers, but it never kept anything resembling systematic information on the condition of the labor market.[131] Jobs were scarce and bureaucracies often functioned badly for French citizens during the Depression, the report recognized, but this service made no credible effort to help people find work. Its main aim was to silence troublemakers.

Laroque, Ollive, and their team of investigators documented scores of abuses and recommended that surveillance and assistance be separated.[132] In one of the most revealing exchanges, the historian Charles-André Julien asked the director of the political branch at the Prefecture, Jacques Simon,

131. Laroque report, 3:295–96, CAOM 8 H 62.
132. CAOM 8 H 62.

why North Africans, who are born French, are tracked so mercilessly? Why, he went on, do foreigners receive no special assistance?

> Why have you not taken the trouble to create an organization that uses assistance to facilitate your police work? If you had Polish or Italian hospitals, those immigrants could be tracked more easily, no? International considerations may have prevented you from doing so, but you should know that North Africans find it bizarre that you have a special service for them and not the others.

In public meetings around Paris, Julien reported, North Africans repeatedly voiced their discontent:

> I can tell you that I have attended meetings with three thousand people where they spoke of [the colonial official Marcel] Peyrouton . . . , and howls went up. All you had to do was mention the rue Lecomte and a hundred people who all wanted to speak at the same time would start screaming.[133]

Simon replied coldly that there had been no meeting in the Paris region with that many people in attendance. He continued that the police needed contacts throughout the North African community; those contacts could only be maintained by combining surveillance and assistance. The effectiveness of the surveillance effort, he insisted, "depends in large measure on the fact that we have a comprehensive service, aware of every aspect of natives' everyday lives." Moreover, he went on, "I do not see how the separation [of assistance from surveillance] could be achieved, today, without compromising the police element." While conceding that mistakes had been made, he and Prefect of Police Roger Langeron insisted that assistance remain under police control. The investigative committee ultimately capitulated.[134] Despite the power of Julien's oratory, neither he nor any of his Socialist colleagues made any headway in their reform effort. By the time of the Popular Front, the North African Services were too well entrenched.

Although the minister of the interior named the prefect of the Seine and the prefect of police in Paris, local officials paid almost all of the North African Services' expenses. As a result, national leaders had little power to impose administrative changes, short of closing the services. Faced with the staunch defense of Simon and Langeron, and unwilling to abolish the services altogether, Blum and Minister of Colonies Marius Moutet settled for cosmetic reforms without making any substantive changes. Langeron simply placed Simon in charge of the North African Services, only to replace him soon thereafter with Jean François, a career policeman whom he would

---

133. This exchange did not make it into the final, mimeographed report. Commission d'Etudes du HCM, minutes of 5 July 1937 meeting, MAE, K—Afrique, 1918–1940, vol. 75.

134. Commission d'Etudes du HCM, minutes of 5 July 1937 meeting, MAE, K—Afrique, 1918–1940, vol. 75.

choose in 1940 to head the Prefecture's new Service juif. The North African Services were accused of forcing North Africans to collaborate with the Milice (Vichy's quasi-fascist parallel police force) during the occupation. The municipal council quietly, but unanimously, disbanded the operation in June 1945 and transferred its agents to other programs.[135]

V

In the midst of material hardship and isolation, a small handful of doctors quietly took advantage of the opportunities presented by the Franco-Muslim Hospital to advance science and challenge common prejudice. They looked out for their patients' interests and trained generations of North African students who went on to have long and productive careers, some of them at the Franco-Muslim Hospital itself. Over many years, those doctors and their students returned the hospital to the communities it was meant to serve: North African migrants and the population of the northeastern suburbs. According to Dr. Josianne Chevillard-Vabre, the hospital no longer played any police role by the time of the Algerian War. In 1962 it was placed under the direction of Assistance publique; it gradually began to offer the same services as comparable establishments and to accept patients from the neighborhood, regardless of origin. In 1978, its name was changed, to Avicenne Hospital, after the eleventh-century doctor Ibn Sina.[136]

During the interwar years, however, the hospital was an integral part of a surveillance effort that treated every North African as a potential threat, both physically and morally. What most distinguished the Franco-Muslim Hospital from other medical centers in Paris was not the stench or isolation, or the quality of the care, but the police role in the administration. The police monitored other groups on the mainland, of course, French and foreign alike, but they did not administer any other public health programs. They did not routinely drag other immigrants to hospitals and spy on them, or use the records of assistance programs in a systematic bid to achieve total control over any other marginal group. Inspired in part by noble sentiment, the new hospital was large enough to house all of the area's North African patients at a given time and to keep them a safe distance from the rest of the population. Run by a former policeman, it encouraged migrants to inform on one another. Many risked death rather than seek medical attention there.

Empire united local and national politicians more than any other issue. The colonial consensus enabled them to take advantage of resources that

135. On François, AN Z⁶ NL 12142; on the postwar accusations, M. Huet in the Cons. gén. meeting of 9 July 1947, minutes in APP D/a 768, and correspondence between Minister of the Interior Tixier and the prefect of police.
136. Chevillard-Vabre, "Histoire de l'hôpital Franco-Musulman."

were not available overseas. Politicians as far to the left as Marius Moutet and Henri Sellier worked with the likes of Pierre Godin, Émile Massard, and, by the late 1930s, Darquier de Pellepoix (who later served in the Vichy government as the director of the Commissariat général aux questions juives). The breadth of that support enabled Godin to avoid the administrative problems that plagued most other public health initiatives in the suburbs and enabled the police to watch North Africans much more closely than any other immigrants in the metropole. Given the relative size of the North African population and the resources brought to bear, the French may even have disciplined colonial subjects more completely in Paris than anywhere else in the empire.

Surveillance and assistance were supposed to be distinct. The prefect of Police ran the former, the prefect of the Seine the latter. In practice, the police oversaw the entire operation. The hospital, dispensaries, job placement service, subsidized housing, and even language classes all collected information to nourish extensive police dossiers. The social programs created for Algerians, Tunisians, and Moroccans were more intrusive and invasive than anything European migrants had to confront at the immigration service. They controlled people's bodies, taking advantage of them in their most vulnerable condition. Spies watched over residents of subsidized rooming houses. Employers used the job-placement service to blackball contentious workers and, it appears, force them to join extreme right-wing groups.

By treating North Africans so differently from other immigrants, by segregating them and subjecting them to an often brutal surveillance regime, republican authorities helped entrench what had been an unexceptional anti-"Arab" sentiment and reinforced a critical distinction between nationality and citizenship. In so doing, they also created a pattern of abuse and discrimination that continued well beyond the interwar years, at least until the end of the colonial period.

Epilogue

1942, 1961, and Beyond

World War I fundamentally altered world migration patterns. For a generation before the conflict, immigrants, especially from southern and eastern Europe, had sought a better life in the New World. But with the outbreak of war, and the decision of the United States in the early 1920s virtually to close its borders, the dispossessed began to seek refuge in France.[1] Within a few years, France became the leading country of immigration in the world, per capita. In some notable cases Poles and Italians made up more than 90 percent of the deep-pit miners in the eastern iron mines, and foreigners were vastly overrepresented in the crucial heavy industrial sector.[2] Although not a critical segment of the labor force before World War II, a significant number of North African workers came as well, allowed to enter the mainland as part of republican officials' efforts to combat anticolonial nationalism. France remained the world's leading immigrant-receiving nation throughout the 1930s, accepting a greater share of colonial workers and refugees than any other Western country.[3]

Dependent on immigrant labor to rebuild from the devastation of war, and committed to admitting colonial workers and refugees, French authorities feared the dangers, both real and imagined, those immigrants posed—

1. Dirk Hoerder, "Migration in the Atlantic Economies: Regional European Origins and Worldwide Expansion," in Hoerder and Leslie Page Moch, eds., *European Migrants: Global and Local Perspectives* (Boston: Northeastern University Press, 1996), 43–45.

2. Gérard Noiriel, *Longwy, immigrés et prolétaires, 1880–1980* (Paris: Puf, 1984); Janine Ponty, *Polonais méconnus: Histoire des travailleurs immigrés en France dans l'entre-deux-guerres* (Paris: Publications de la Sorbonne, 1988).

3. Michael R. Marrus, *The Unwanted: European Refugees in the Twentieth Century* (Oxford: Oxford University Press, 1985), and Neil MacMaster, *Colonial Migrants and Racism: Algerians in France, 1900–1962* (New York: St. Martin's, 1997).

political destabilization, violent crime, mongrelization. In response, they built on methods that had originally been used to monitor poor rural migrants from the French countryside. Although organized states have always had to mark boundaries, to decide whom to include and whom to exclude, the criteria used have changed dramatically over time. In a period of intense international rivalry, in the last quarter of the nineteenth century, central governments across Europe increasingly took an interest in the well-being of their citizens and invested in education and welfare programs. As they took over responsibility for these activities from local and religious communities, state membership, now called "nationality," took on a new importance.[4]

Distinguishing the native born from foreign nationals emerged as a particular problem in France. The France of the early Third Republic combined a precocious democratization and declining birthrate with a relatively backward heavy industrial sector, at least compared to Germany, England, and the United States. French peasants refused the demands of heavy industry much more successfully than their counterparts elsewhere. They compelled politicians and employers to recruit massive numbers of foreigners to perform the jobs French citizen-workers rejected. Ultimately, however, a great many French peasants, too, had to abandon the land and survive exclusively from factory work. As they did so, the nascent French labor movement won special concessions in the form of welfare benefits that were denied to foreigners. That combination, of welfare and massive foreign immigration, invested nationality with a material significance in turn-of-the-century France that it did not acquire elsewhere until after World War II.[5]

Although the presence of a significant immigrant population made it difficult to keep track of foreigners in the late nineteenth century, the experience of total war gave French politicians the idea that they could now do so much more effectively. The heightened social and political tensions of the interwar years gave a new urgency to the task. Fearing that Communist and colonial revolutionaries would enlist immigrants in their bid to destabilize

---

4. See, above all, Karl Polanyi, *The Great Transformation: The Political and Economic Origins of Our Time* (Boston: Beacon Press, 1944); and, for a broader perspective, Marc Raeff, *The Well-Ordered Police State: Social and Institutional Change through Law in the Germanies and Russia, 1600–1800* (New Haven: Yale University Press, 1983).

5. Gérard Noiriel, *Le creuset français: Histoire de l'immigration, XIXe–XXe siècles* (Paris: Seuil, 1988), esp. chaps. 2 and 6; Noiriel, *La tyrannie du national: Le droit d'asile en Europe, 1793–1993* (Paris: Calmann-Lévy, 1991), 83–100, 155–80; and Noiriel, *Les origines républicaines de Vichy* (Paris: Hachette, 1999), chap. 2. See also Alain Cottereau, "The Distinctiveness of Working-Class Cultures in France, 1848–1900," in *Working-Class Formation: Nineteenth-Century Patterns in Europe and the United States*, ed. Ira Katznelson and Aristide R. Zolberg (Princeton: Princeton University Press, 1986), 111–54; and Gary Cross, *Immigrant Workers in Industrial France: The Making of a New Laboring Class* (Philadelphia: Temple University Press, 1983).

the Republic and its empire, moderate national politicians forged a practical alliance with the right-wing leaders of the Paris Municipal Council to control a fast-growing immigrant population they could not do without. Together, they developed surveillance first and most fully in Paris, which had by far the country's largest police force as well as the most diverse immigrant community.

Before any other police force in the world, the Paris Prefecture of Police developed the ability to keep track of hundreds of thousands of people at a time by a variety of criteria. In an effort to protect the local labor market and prevent terrorist attacks, the police monitored the comings and goings of every legal immigrant in the capital—a half million of them—and sorted the information by nationality, citizenship status, profession, and residence. Setting down roots in France increasingly depended on government approval.

The inequalities created as well as the rights defended by these new police measures have been obscured by a particularly bitter debate over the Prefecture's card files. In 1991, as part of the fever that Henry Rousso famously diagnosed as the "Vichy syndrome,"[6] the historian and Nazi hunter Serge Klarsfeld claimed to have found the original *fichier juif*—the card file prepared by the Paris police that was used to draw up lists of Jews for deportation during the war—in the archives of the government's Office for Veteran's Affairs. He was wrong. He had stumbled across a derivative list, not the master file. But he drew a great deal of attention to the role the Paris police played in those deportations. Ever since, discussions of immigration control have been carried out under the shadow of Vichy.[7]

I

Historians were familiar with the broad outlines of the bureaucratic mechanisms used in the wartime deportations for at least a decade before the Klarsfeld controversy. When Prefect of Police Roger Langeron added

6. Rousso, *Le syndrome de Vichy: De 1944 à nos jours*, rev. ed. (1987; Paris: Seuil, 1990).

7. For Klarsfeld's "discovery," Annette Kahn, *Le fichier* (Paris: Robert Laffont, 1993). Jean-Marc Berlière was the first to make the connection between interwar police practice and the wartime deportation of Jews in "L'institution policière en France sous la IIIème République, 1870–1914" (Thèse d'État, Université de Bourgogne, 1991), 739. For the controversy, see Henry Rousso and Éric Conan, *Vichy: Un passé qui ne passe pas* (Paris: Fayard, 1994), chap. 2, and the official report, *Le "Fichier Juif": Rapport de la commission présidée par René Rémond au Premier ministre* (Paris: Plon, 1996). Gérard Noiriel set off a new round of polemics with *Les origines républicaines de Vichy*, followed by extreme versions of the same argument in Pierre-Jean Deschodt and François Huguenin, *La république xénophobe, 1917–1939* (Paris: JC Lattès, 2001), and Edwin Black, *IBM and the Holocaust: The Strategic Alliance between Nazi Germany and America's Most Powerful Corporation* (New York: Crown, 2001). See Robert O. Paxton, "Gérard Noiriel's Third Republic," *French Politics, Culture, and Society* 18, no. 2 (Summer 2000): 99–103.

"Jewish Affairs" to the responsibility of the sedentary branch of the immigration service in October 1940, he chose a trusted aide and able administrator, the director of his North African Services, Jean François.[8] To assist François, he turned to André Tulard, a man who had headed the unit since 1936. This office, the biggest at the Prefecture, was charged with carrying out the German ordinance of 27 September 1940, which called for a census of "Jews," as defined by Vichy, living in the Paris region. From that census, Tulard created a card file that was operational by the following March. Modeled on the card files of foreigners kept by the Prefecture, the new *fichier juif* was maintained by the same subaltern personnel, in the same room, and kept current by the same active service of the RG. Responding to German orders, the Paris police used those files to prepare lists of Jews for the dozen dragnets conducted in the city between May 1941 and February 1944.[9]

The origins of that file system stretch back farther than most specialists realize,[10] to the immediate aftermath of World War I. The so-called sedentary branch, the desk unit that drew up identity cards and expulsion orders and maintained the archives, fast became the busiest branch at the Prefecture of Police after its overhaul in late 1921. But it was not prestigious. Police units generally measure their relative prestige by the "clientele" they serve, and this was no exception. An examination of interwar personnel directories shows that promotions were rare; people spent years at the same rank and often their entire careers in the same office. If common surnames are any indication, the closed character of the unit and the unusually high percentage of women in an otherwise male-dominated police force allowed many to find their spouses at work.[11] The strong institutional culture that Alexis Spire has documented for the postwar period clearly stretches back at least to the 1930s, if not earlier.[12] The almost uniformly bitter memories migrants left of their encounters in the overcrowded offices on the boule-

8. AN Z⁶ NL 12142.

9. Serge Klarsfeld, *Vichy-Auschwitz: Le rôle de la France dans la solution finale de la question juive en France*, 2 vols. (Paris: Fayard, 1983–85); Klarsfeld, *Le calendrier de la persécution des Juifs en France* (Paris: Association les fils et filles des déportés juifs de France, 1993); Michael R. Marrus and Robert O. Paxton, *Vichy France and the Jews* (New York: Basic Books, 1981); and *Le "Fichier Juif": Rapport de la commission présidée par René Rémond au Premier ministre* (Paris: Plon, 1996).

10. Most still see the police concern with immigration as a response to the Depression and the refugee crisis of the 1930s. See, e.g., Jean-Marc Berlière and Laurant Chabrun, *Les policiers français sous l'Occupation: D'après les archives inédites de l'épuration* (Paris: Perrin, 2001), 223; Denis Peschanski, "Dans la tourmente," in *La police française, 1930–1950: Entre bouleversements et permanences*, ed. Jean-Marc Berlière and Peschanski (Paris: La documentation française, 2000), 65; and Marrus and Paxton, *Vichy France and the Jews*, 243.

11. *Annuaire-almanach du commerce* (Paris: Société Didot-Bottin, 1919–39). My thanks to Alexis Spire for pointing me toward this remarkable source.

12. Spire, *Étrangers à la carte: L'administration de l'immigration en France, 1945–1975* (Paris: Grasset, 2005), chap. 5.

vard du Palais suggest that agents were not only defined by their superiors but that they defined themselves against the immigrants they served.[13]

The recent opening of the police archives shows that the subaltern officers charged with carrying out Vichy's repressive measures saw little difference between their activity before and during the Occupation. Agents from the RG watched over immigrant neighborhoods, bridges and metro platforms, cafés and boulevards, around railroad stations; they took advantage of a chance arrest to discover an address, a name of someone they had been looking for on other grounds. They routinely stopped people on the street to check their papers, especially people who looked out of place or kept what they considered the wrong company. As before the war, they called upon their colleagues in the uniformed Municipal Police when they needed additional manpower for large-scale measures.[14] Although the numbers remain impossible to determine, their activity resulted in several thousands of arrests.[15] If the specific targets the police monitored were obviously different during the war, the methods they used were not. When questioned about a series of arrests at his purge trial, an officer replied:

They were illegal aliens, foreign women . . .
Q: Did you make arrests on your own initiative?
They were foreign women.

Pushed again, by the same magistrate, the officer exploded:

You have got to be kidding! If we can't stop foreigners on the street and ask for their papers, what are we supposed to do?[16]

Under questioning, agents from the RG pointed out that they were executing the orders of superiors, many of whom had been appointed under the Popular Front. The police had survived the constant ministerial instability of the interwar years by doing just that.

The question remains, however: What sort of causal link can be drawn between the Paris police's treatment of foreign immigrants during the Third Republic and France's role in the Final Solution? Most historians have re-

---

13. Julia Franke, *Paris—eine neue Heimat? Jüdisches Emigranten aus Deutschland, 1933–1939* (Berlin: Duncker and Humblot, 2000).

14. This point in particular has caused confusion. In his postwar purge proceedings— "Notes établies par Monsieur Émile Hennequin en complément de la note générale," 1945, AN Z⁶ 447, fols. 478–71 (in descending order in the carton)—the former director of the PM protested his own subordination to the RG during the war. As part of his defense, he exaggerated breaks with prewar routines when he suggested that agents from the RG had never checked identity papers before the war and that his own men had never helped out in such efforts.

15. Berlière and Chabrun, *Les policiers français sous l'Occupation*, 255.

16. Ibid., 277–78.

sisted drawing this sort of connection.[17] As we have seen, dealing with foreign immigrants did not necessarily lead to hostility toward them. If the
sedentary unit of the Paris immigration service earned a reputation for dismissive arrogance and condescension, the same cannot be said of border
guards,[18] the direction of the Sûreté nationale,[19] or the Parisian RG. The latter does not appear to have been a bastion of resistance during World War
II, but immigration services elsewhere in France, notably Nancy, used the
power of their office to fabricate false papers and hide refugees from the
Nazis at considerable risk to themselves.[20]

If dealing with immigrants did not necessarily provoke a nativist backlash from the police, neither did a lack of experience in tracking immigrants
between the wars prove a serious handicap for repression. In Bordeaux, for
example, Maurice Papon maintained registers of Jews and executed Nazi
orders to round up Jewish men, women, and children without apparent difficulty. As secretary-general of the Prefecture of the Gironde, one of the
areas of France least affected by immigration before the war, he oversaw
transport of 1,560 Jews to Drancy, a transit camp where they stayed before
being loaded onto trains for Auschwitz.[21] Elsewhere, in Holland, the Am-
sterdam police provided just as much assistance to the Nazis as their
Parisian counterparts, even though Holland did not experience significant
immigration between the wars and did not have a significant tradition of
xenophobia or anti-Semitism. There, a zealous administrator from the population registry office, the Rijksinspectie van de Bevolkingsregisters, Jakob
Lentz, took advantage of opportunities afforded him during the Occupation. In 1936, he had set out to create a complete registration system that
would include identity cards. Put off by Dutch authorities, Lentz found en-
thusiastic support from Nazi occupation officials a few years later. Using
watermarked paper and special inks, he created new identity cards that included personal details about the bearer in addition to photographs and fingerprints. According to Bob Moore, the Germans considered the cards
much better and more secure than their own *Kennkarte*, and the system
Lentz devised played a central role in the deportation of Dutch Jews.[22]

17. For a critical exception, Noiriel, *Les origines républicaines de Vichy.*
18. Vicki Caron, *Uneasy Asylum: France and the Jewish Refugee Crisis, 1933–1942* (Stanford: Stanford University Press, 1999), 209.
19. Patrick Weil, "Politiques d'immigration de la France et des États-Unis à la veille de la
Seconde Guerre mondiale," *Les cahiers de la Shoah*, special issue, ed. André Kaspi (1995): esp.
70–76; and Marc-Olivier Baruch, *Servir l'État français: L'administration en France de 1940 à
1944* (Paris: Fayard, 1997), 378 n.
20. Jean-Marie Muller, *Désobéir à Vichy: La résistance civile de fonctionnaires de police*
(Nancy: Presses universitaires de Nancy, 1994).
21. Paxton, "The Trial of Maurice Papon," *New York Review of Books* (16 December
1999), 32–38.
22. Bob Moore, *Victims and Survivors: The Nazi Persecution of the Jews in the Netherlands, 1940–1945* (London: Arnold, 1997), 196–99, and Gerhard Hirschfeld, *Nazi Rule and
Dutch Collaboration: The Netherlands under German Occupation, 1940–1945* (1984; Oxford: Berg, 1988).

Was there then no connection? Did the German use of local intermediaries to carry out the Final Solution in France have no tangible effect on its outcome? Comparisons of the various bureaucracies in occupied western Europe can only be advanced with extreme caution. As Michael Marrus and Robert Paxton have pointed out, generalizations break apart on the stubborn particularities of each country; many overlapping factors account for the incidence of genocide across western Europe.[23] But it is perhaps worth noting that in France, and especially Paris, where the card indexes of Jews were drawn up by men who had spent their careers tracking immigrants, foreign Jews suffered disproportionately. In the Netherlands, by contrast, where the wartime card files emerged out of a national system of population registers that recorded all residents, it was native-born Dutch Jews who suffered disproportionately.[24] While much more remains to be done to chart the precise nature of the influence, it seems that the bureaucratic forms collaborationist regimes mobilized influenced the wartime deportations in important ways.

Insisting on continuity between the Third Republic and Vichy is teleological; it assumes that events had to occur as they did and mistakes coincidence for cause. Insisting on a profound rupture between Republican practice and Vichy, as much of the literature continues to do, however, is no less problematic. The years from 1919 to 1939 constitute a historical period in its own right and cannot be understood exclusively by reading backward from their conclusion. Well-meaning government officials did not simply square off against an ill-informed public and an antirepublican opposition between the wars. The Vichy regime cannot be neatly distinguished from the French people.[25] As Philippe Burrin has written, "For any society, an occupation is a trial and, in a way, represents a moment of truth for it: all the tensions, frustrations and contradictions at work that undermine the social contract come to the surface."[26] This was no less true for the Paris police than for any other of the Republican administrations that embodied the divisions of the society they served.

If the controversy over the Jewish card files has understandably attracted a great deal of attention, it has done so at the expense of a fundamental shift in the relationship between immigrants and the state in France. The extension of nationality law to domains it had only imperfectly reached before the turn of the twentieth century leveled the playing field for all foreigners; it offered them important protections from abuse, and it structured the

23. Marrus and Paxton, "The Nazis and the Jews in Occupied Western Europe," *Journal of Modern History* 54, no. 4 (December 1982): 712–13.

24. Cf. Klarsfeld, *Le calendrier*, with Moore, *Victims and Survivors*, and Hirschfeld, *Nazi Rule and Dutch Collaboration*.

25. The distinction is drawn from the title of a landmark volume, *Le régime de Vichy et les français* (Paris: Fayard, 1992).

26. Burrin, preface to the English-language edition, *France under the Germans: Collaboration and Compromise*, trans. Janet Lloyd (1995; New York: New Press, 1996), viii.

terms of their incorporation into the host society. But if new police controls did not lead directly to Vichy, they nonetheless left foreigners vulnerable in ways that have not yet been fully appreciated.

II

The most dramatic inequality to emerge in interwar France was not between foreigners and French citizens, nor between immigrant workers and political refugees. Foreign nationals could turn to their embassies, so long as they remained in the good graces of their home countries. A wide range of independent committees and international agencies intervened on behalf or refugees. For all the inroads anti-Semitism made at the Prefecture of Police and throughout French society in the 1930s, it did not take institutional form before the war. No census form or police unit singled out Jews before Vichy.

The most striking inequality, rather, separated people who could lay claim to some form of political representation and those who could not—colonial subjects and protégés from Algeria, Morocco, and Tunisia. French governments took a unique interest in these Muslim migrants and subjected them to much greater disciplinary controls than any foreigners. The connection between the abuse endured by North African migrants between the wars and the violent repression of peaceful demonstrators on the notorious night of 17 October 1961 was both logical and direct.

Students of France's overseas empire frequently describe the colonies as a laboratory, a place where reforms were tested before being implemented in the metropole.[27] In the evolution of imperial surveillance efforts, however, serious "experiments" were conducted first on the mainland.[28] In the mid-1920s, a group of former colonial administrators whose careers brought them to Paris found themselves surrounded by a substantial colonial population. Unable to enforce the notorious "native codes," the arbitrary weapons of choice for coercion in the colonies, Pierre Godin and his associates took advantage of the greater financial and bureaucratic resources offered by the capital to control colonial migrants. They provided assistance

27. This image is pervasive in the colonial studies literature. See, e.g., Paul Rabinow, *French Modern: Norms and Forms of the Social Environment* (Cambridge: MIT Press, 1989), and Gwendolyn Wright, *The Politics of Design in French Colonial Urbanism* (Chicago: University of Chicago Press, 1991).

28. In 1917 Albert Sarraut overhauled the police in French Indochina to modernize law enforcement there, but limited manpower and financial resources restricted the scope of his enterprise. See Patrice Morlat, *La répression coloniale au Vietnam, 1908–1940* (Paris: Harmattan, 1990); Peter Zinoman, *The Colonial Bastille: A History of Imprisonment in Vietnam, 1862–1940* (Berkeley: University of California Press, 2001), and Mireille Favre, "Un milieu porteur de modernisation: Travailleurs et tirailleurs vietnamiens en France, pendant la première guerre mondiale"(thèse pour l'obtention du diplôme d'archiviste-paléographe, École nationale des chartes, 1986), 1:295–319.

in order to gain information about people, to keep track of them, and ulti-mately to control them.

For a brief moment, in the immediate aftermath of World War II, it seemed that a reaction against Vichy abuses would compel authorities to re-nounce the type of surveillance methods used by the rue Lecomte. After the Liberation, even the most hawkish, pro-Algérie française members of the municipal council admitted that the North African Brigade had been aber-rant, corrupt, and violent. A number of its agents were themselves petty thieves who had their own run-ins with the law. Some appear to have re-cruited North Africans to serve in Colonel François de La Rocque's Parti So-cial Français. Worst of all, during Vichy, officers from the brigade appear to have forced colonial subjects to collaborate with the Milice. The municipal council quietly, but unanimously, disbanded the operation in June 1945 and transferred its agents to other programs.[29] The postwar minister of the inte-rior, Adrien Tixier, dissolved his assistance programs so that the Ministry of Labor could "organize social assistance programs [*l'encadrement social*] for North African workers without any police considerations."[30] Two years later a fundamental constitutional reform granted Algerian Muslims on the main-land the same rights as French citizens—reinforcing their right to free move-ment and granting full political privileges as well.[31]

Almost immediately, however, the Prefecture began to reclaim its old turf, recruiting officers with experience overseas and offering assistance as a means of winning over immigrant populations. Administrators warned so-cial workers to be discreet, to avoid "giving ammunition to the separatists' arguments by reviving memories of the North African Brigade" at the Pre-fecture of Police.[32] In July 1953, the Prefecture created a new anticrime task force that singled out North Africans, re-creating the old brigade in every-thing but name.[33] As the Algerian War intensified, the confusion between surveillance and assistance grew on both sides of the Mediterranean. Au-

29. Accusations about coercing North Africans into serving the Milice were aired in the municipal council. See the minutes of those debates in APP D/a 768. On the abolition of the North African Brigade, see Emmanuel Blanchard, "La dissolution des brigades nord-africaines de la Préfecture de police: La fin d'une police d'exception pour les algériens de Paris, 1944–1953," *Bulletin de l'Ihtp*, no. 83 (1st Semester, 2004): 70–82, and Spire, *Étrangers à la carte*, 196–98.

30. Note pour le ministre du Travail, n.d., CAC 860271, art. 2, quoted by Vincent Viet, *La France immigrée: Construction d'une politique* (Paris: Fayard, 1998), 169.

31. Alexis Spire, "Semblables et pourtant différents: La citoyenneté paradoxale des Français musulmans d'Algérie en métropole," *Genèses: Histoire et sciences sociales*, no. 53 (December 2003): 48–68.

32. "Réunion sous la présidence du préfet Damelon des Inspecteurs général de l'adminis-tration en mission extraordinaire et des préfets des départements de la métropole . . . ," 24 May 1951, CAC 860271, art. 3, quoted by Viet, *La France immigrée*, 181. Curiously, Viet never discusses the SAINA (Service des affaires indigènes nord-africaines de Paris) or any other services at the Prefecture of Police.

33. Spire, *Étrangers à la carte*, 198.

thorities once again relied on circulars and administrative measures to circumvent the law.

In 1956 Maurice Papon was named High Commander (Inspecteur général de l'administration en mission extraordinaire) for the Constantine region in eastern Algeria, an area that saw some of the most brutal fighting of the war.[34] A special unit (Section administrative spécialisée or SAS) waged a pitiless campaign there, using a combination of assistance programs and physical torture to "pacify" the region.[35] Two years later, Papon brought their methods back to Paris when he became the prefect of police. Papon secretly flew in three army officers from the SAS to help undermine the National Liberation Front (Front de liberation nationale or FLN), which had brought the Algerian War to the capital, assassinating police officers as well as members of the rival National Algerian Movement (Mouvement National Algérien or MNA).[36] All three officers had trained as native administrators in the school for Native Affairs in Rabat, Morocco, and were familiar with the North African Services at the rue Lecomte.[37]

The next year, in November 1959, authorities created a new auxiliary force at the Prefecture of Police to penetrate the FLN, just as Godin's men had done to Messali Hadj's Étoile nord-africaine. Muslim Algerian volunteers (harkis) commanded by men with long experience in colonial wars resorted to brutality more readily than their predecessors in the North African Brigade during the interwar years.[38] As Jean-Paul Brunet has documented, the auxiliary police forces in Paris used torture in their bid to subdue Algerian revolutionaries.[39] That year, the Ministry of the Interior encouraged its agents to "control the state of mind of Algerian immigrants."[40]

Maurice Papon sounded some very familiar themes when he was called before the municipal council to account for his actions during the infamous night of 17 October 1961—the night the Parisian police beat hundreds of

34. On Papon's role in Algeria, Jean-Luc Einaudi, *La bataille de Paris: 17 Octobre 1961* (Paris: Seuil, 1991), 39–57.

35. Raphaëlle Branche, *La torture et l'armée pendant la guerre d'Algérie, 1954–1962* (Paris: Gallimard, 2001).

36. On the conflict between the FLN and the MNA, the older independence movement of Messali Hadj, see Benjamin Stora, "Histoire politique de l'immigration algérienne en France, 1922–1962" (Thèse d'État, Université de Paris VII, 1990). On the murders of 1961, see Jean-Paul Brunet, *Police contre FLN: Le drame d'octobre 1961* (Paris: Fayard, 1999).

37. MacMaster, *Colonial Migrants and Racism*, 196–97. On the recreation of the security services after the War, Peggy Derder, *L'immigration algérienne et les pouvoirs publics dans le département de la Seine, 1954–1962* (Paris: Harmattan, 2001).

38. Given the current state of documentation, it is impossible to determine whether the violence used by Godin's men approached that of their successors between 1958 and 1961, but it seems unlikely.

39. Brunet, *Police contre FLN*.

40. The original reads: "s'efforcer d'agir sur l'état d'esprit de la migration algérienne." Note de M. Blanchard à l'attention du directeur général de la Sûreté nationale, 16 April 1959, CAC 760133, art. 4, quoted by Viet, *La France immigrée*, 188.

peaceful demonstrators who sought Algerian independence, murdered at least thirty of them, and then dumped them into the Seine.[41] Echoing Pierre Godin, he told the councilors that necessity had imposed the coordination of surveillance and assistance efforts. The key had been to reach out to the Algerian community, to move in with them and ease their solitude. He then explained that we helped them find jobs, affordable housing, and looked after their health. In a word, he said, we had to assist them. Papon recognized that his approach was hardly original. All he did, he said, was "to bring together units that had been dispersed."[42] In brushing aside questions about police brutality, Papon placed his own efforts in the context of long-standing efforts to disarm any challenge to France's colonial authority.

III

Not long ago, historians and sociologists thought that the growth of industry and the modern state led to prosperity, stability, and social welfare. They embraced a broadly Hegelian vision of the modern state as emancipating subject populations. In the late 1940s T. H. Marshall famously argued that social welfare programs had finally enabled Western societies to realize their democratic promise, to provide the full benefits of citizenship to everyone. When they sought to explain episodes of violence along the path to modernity, scholars generally saw them as temporary deviations.[43] More recently, however, violence has moved center stage. Today's scholars increasingly emphasize the twentieth century's unprecedented levels of bloodshed. They have rediscovered the pessimistic side of Max Weber's work—

41. Under tremendous pressure during the Papon trial, French authorities opened their archives to three hand-picked scholars. The first book that uses police records significantly changes earlier accounts, notably by reducing the death toll: Brunet, *Police contre FLN*. The work of journalist Jean-Luc Einaudi, *La bataille de Paris*, remains valuable, though some of his wilder claims have been effectively challenged by Brunet. For a critique of both, see Joshua Cole, "Remembering the Battle of Paris, 17 October 1961, in French and Algerian Memory," *French Politics, Culture, and Society* 21, no. 3 (Fall 2003).

42. Papon, "Discussion relative aux incidents survenus au cours de la soirée du 17 et 18 octobre 1961," *Bulletin Municipal Officiel de la Ville de Paris* 81, no. 15 (8 November 1961), 656–64, quote on 657. Papon did not mention the affair in his autobiography, *Les chevaux du pouvoir: Le préfet de police du général de Gaulle ouvre ses dossiers, 1958–1967* (Paris: Plon, 1988). See also J. Massoue, "L'action sociale en faveur des français musulmans d'Algérie dans le Département de la Seine, 1960–61," in CAOM, 10 APOM 791.

43. G. W. F. Hegel, *Elements of the Philosophy of Right*, trans. H. B. Nisbet (Cambridge: Cambridge University Press, 1991), part 3, sec. 2C and sec. 3, §§ 230–360; and Marshall, "Citizenship and Social Class," in his *Citizenship and Social Class and Other Essays* (1949; Cambridge: Cambridge University Press, 1950), 1–85. Charles Tilly and Barrington Moore both emphasized the role of coercion and social conflict, but only as elements of a transition to the modern era: Tilly, "How Protest Modernized France, 1845–1855," in *The Dimensions of Quantitative Research in History*, ed. William Aydelotte (Princeton: Princeton University Press, 1972), 192–255; and Moore, *Social Origins of Dictatorship and Democracy: Lord and Peasant in the Making of the Modern World* (Boston: Beacon Press, 1966).

his portrayal of the impersonal, dehumanizing power of bureaucratic rationalization—and combined it with Michel Foucault's notion of "governmentality."[44] These efforts have gone too far. By linking a diffuse notion of modernity to the Holocaust and setting the Third Reich and Stalin's Soviet Union as standard bearers for the modern age, they mistake the most extreme forms of state violence for the logical outcome of the Enlightenment tradition.[45] They reduce all state practices to their repressive, all-controlling, panoptic, if not downright violent elements. A dark, postmodern reading of the modern state has been less influential in France than elsewhere, but there, too, polemics over Vichy and the Algerian War dominate the intellectual landscape. Historically rare, exceptional cases all too often set the standard against which immigration controls, assistance programs, and other social policies are judged.[46]

The emancipatory power of the welfare state cannot be disentangled from new forms of alienation and inequality that have been marginalized by the past century's spectacular crimes. Republican France's efforts to control immigration shaped Vichy's exclusionary measures and, more directly, the pervasive discrimination against North African Muslims. But these pivotal episodes must be set within a wider context that includes the new rights they afforded immigrants as well as the burdens they imposed.

The Paris immigration and North African Services gave abstract legal categories the force of law between the world wars. Card files of immigrants provided more than a map. Not simply descriptive, those files enabled the police to act, to identify foreigners and mark boundaries much more effectively than their predecessors. In the process, new documentary controls improved authorities' ability to regulate the labor market and to impose con-

44. Weber, *Economy and Society: An Outline of An Interpretive Sociology*, 2 vols. (1956; Berkeley: University of California Press, 1978), 2:956–1005, on bureaucracy; as well as Weber, *The Protestant Ethic and the Spirit of Capitalism*, trans. Talcott Parsons (New York: Scribner's, 1958), 181–83, for his image of the "stahlartes Gehäuse," rendered by Parsons as the "iron cage." Foucault's lectures on "governmentality" have been brought together in, *Sécurité, territoire, population: Cours au Collège de France, 1977–1978* (Paris: Seuil, 2004), and *Naissance de la biopolitique: Cours au Collège de France, 1978–1979* (Paris: Seuil, 2004).

45. See, e.g., Hannah Arendt, *The Origins of Totalitarianism* (New York: Harcourt Brace Jovanovich, 1951); J. L. Talmon, *The Origins of Totalitarian Democracy* (New York: Praeger, 1960); Max Horkheimer and Theodor Adorno, *Dialectic of Enlightenment*, trans. John Cumming (New York: Herder and Herder, 1972); Foucault, *Surveiller et punir: Naissance de la prison* (Paris: Gallimard, 1975); and, in their wake, among many others, Zygmunt Bauman, *Modernity and the Holocaust* (Ithaca: Cornell University Press, 1989); Detlev J. K. Peukert, "The Genesis of the 'Final Solution' from the Spirit of Science," in *Nazism and German Society, 1933–1945*, ed. David F. Crew (1989; New York: Routledge, 1994), 274–99; Anthony Giddens, *The Nation-State and Violence* (Berkeley: University of California Press, 1985); Noiriel, *Les origines républicaines de Vichy*; and Stephen Kotkin, *Magnetic Mountain: Stalinism as a Civilization* (Berkeley: University of California Press, 1995).

46. I owe the formulation of this paragraph to Mark Mazower, "Violence and the State in the Twentieth Century," *American Historical Review* 107, no. 4 (October 2002): 1158–1178, esp. 1158.

formity. Enforcing long-standing restrictions on residence and employment helped republican governments incorporate their own working-class population at the expense of foreign migrants and colonial subjects. If all policing is inherently political, the distinction between observation and action is especially hazy in this case. Driving on the wrong side of the road, failing to speak French, petty theft, or insubordination could now jeopardize one's legal status. The Republic policed its borders not only at the frontier but throughout the national territory, with a battery of administrative measures and documentary controls that structured immigrants' life chances and opportunities. Nationality and citizenship began to matter as they never had before when a massive police bureaucracy singled out the foreign-born for special attention. Those controls emerged in Paris in their modern form in the early 1920s, at the high point of what the German historian Detlev Peukert called "classical modernity," and not as an atavistic, xenophobic backlash during the Depression, in response to the Republic's enemies. They shared a similar ambition to harness a new instrumental rationality, honed during World War I, as contemporary police and welfare initiatives across the continent.[47]

At the same time, however, it is essential to bear in mind the defensive nature of the project from its inception. The history of immigration control in interwar Paris challenges a traditional distinction between liberal and authoritarian regimes, but it does not do away with it altogether. Implemented in a desperate attempt to hold on to some measure of the control afforded by the total mobilization of society during the Great War, the Paris surveillance effort was the product of compromise and not ideological zealotry. The more extreme elements in local Paris politics could not act without the support of more moderate ministers of the interior. The near monopoly of centrist Radicals over the Place Beauvau meant that overlapping jurisdictions and conflicts of interest—central to the spiral of police violence in Nazi Germany and the Soviet Union[48]—ultimately moderated the severity of enforcement in Paris. The political aspirations of republican leaders, moreover, differed fundamentally from those of the Gestapo or the NKVD. Officers from the political branch, the RG, paid particular attention to Communist hideouts and used their authority to cow foreign militants. But they also went out of their way to prevent Mussolini's henchmen from in-

47. Peukert, "The Genesis of the 'Final Solution' from the Spirit of Science"; and, more generally, Bauman, *Modernity and the Holocaust*; James C. Scott, *Seeing Like a State: How Certain Schemes to Improve the Human Condition Have Failed* (New Haven: Yale University Press, 1998); and Peter Holquist, " 'Information is the Alpha and Omega of Our Work': Bolshevik Surveillance in its Pan-European Perspective," *Journal of Modern History* 69, no. 3 (September 1997): 415–50.

48. Ernst Fraenkel, *The Dual State* (Oxford: Oxford University Press, 1941); Hans Mommsen, *From Weimar to Auschwitz*, trans. Philip O'Connor (Princeton: Princeton University Press, 1991); Kotkin, *Magnetic Mountain*, chap. 7; and Robert O. Paxton, *The Anatomy of Fascism* (New York: Knopf, 2004).

terfering with the assimilation of Italian workers in France. This was no muscle-bound purity campaign.

The repressive efforts of Paris's North African Services appear more closely to resemble the ideologically driven practices of the interwar dictatorships. They disciplined North Africans more intensely than any other immigrants. Agents sought to make reliable, docile workers out of their colonial subjects. They systematically stopped poor Muslims on the street and threatened them with deportation at the slightest pretext. Those migrants, in turn, did not enjoy any of the protections of citizenship and could expect no support from the international community. But for all the resources at their disposal, the North African services remained marginal within the Paris Prefecture. Leaders struggled to find qualified candidates for their dead-end jobs. If limited prospects for promotion reduced superiors' ability to control corruption and petty abuse, they also diminished excessive zeal. The young and ambitious sought out different avenues to make a name for themselves and rise quickly through the ranks. Here, too, oversight by progressive politicians and a free press helped contain police abuse.

At their most sinister, in the middle of the twentieth century, in the wake of a catastrophic depression and in the midst of a continent-wide civil war, identity controls marked out whole populations for physical destruction. They had already created a second-class status for colonial migrants in France that would endure at least until the end of the colonial period. Yet for all of the attention commanded by Vichy and now the Algeria syndrome, identity controls have most often been relatively harmless and indeed inseparable from the most ambitious redistributive social programs in human history. At a time when humanitarian intervention is being given a bad name and the idea of social assistance is under attack, it is perhaps worth recalling the power of welfare programs across Europe to integrate working-class populations and protect them. Even more than its genocidal counterparts—which routinely relied on such primitive forms of violence as starvation, forced marches, and open-air shootings—the twentieth-century welfare state could not exist without the bureaucratic means to distinguish those who belong to the nation from those who do not, the entitled from the unentitled. I have tried, in the preceding pages, to make sense out of these hugely contradictory state practices, which continue to regulate the admission and incorporation of newcomers in France and, since World War II, in all of the world's most prosperous countries.

Bibliography

Archival Series

Archives Départementales de l'Aude, Carcassonne (ADA)

12 J, Fonds Albert Sarraut

Archives Départementales de la Seine St. Denis, Bobigny (ADSSD).

Chevillard-Vabre, Dr. Josianne. "Histoire de l'hôpital Franco-Musulman." Thèse pour le doctorat en médecine, Diplôme d'État, Faculté de médecine Saint-Antoine, 1982.

Archives Départementales des Yvelines, Versaille (ADY)

5 M, Sûreté générale
16 M, Travail
1 W, Cabinet du Préfet, Sûreté générale

Archives Nationales, Paris (AN)

94 AP, Fonds Albert Thomas
AJ^{38}, Commissariat général aux questions juives
F^{1a}, Administration générale, ministère de l'Intérieur, objets généraux
F^{7}, Police générale
Z^{6}, Cour de Justice du département de la Seine

Archives Nationales, Centres d'Archives Contemporaines, Fontainebleau (CAC)

Pierre Laroque papers (uncatalogued)
Surveillance des étrangers, 19940493–19940497, 19940499–19940500, 19940505–19940506, 20010216

Dossiers personnels, 19940437, 19940451, 19940457, 19940462, 19940472, 19940474, 19940488

Archives de Paris, Paris (AP).

D2T¹, enseignement publique
AP DE¹, Bucaille papers
C, Conseil Municipal de Paris
1221/64/1 arts. 1–135, doubles de lettres envoyées par le président du Conseil Municipal (Pierre Godin) et son cabinet, 1926 à 1934. Villemoisson 1 B 294–295

Archives de la Préfecture de Police, Paris (APP)

B/a
D/b
D/a

Bibliothèque Administrative de la Ville de Paris, Paris (BAVP)

Con. mun. (Conseil Municipal de Paris)
Bulletin Municipal Officiel de la Ville de Paris
Proc.-ver. (Procès-verbaux)
Rap. et doc. (Rapports et documents)
Cons. gén. (Conseil Général de la Seine), *Proc.-ver.*

Bibliothèque Marxiste, Paris (BM)

Archives of the PCF, repatriated from l'Institut Marxiste-Léniniste, Moscow.

Centre d'Archives d'Outre-Mer, Aix-en-Provence (CAOM).

SLOTFOM (Service de Liaison entre les Originaires des Territoires d'Outre-Mer), Séries I–III, IX
AGENCE F.O.M. 254–255 (Sarraut)
AOM 9 PA (Sarraut)
3 CAB, cabinet Le Beau
8 H, Gouvernement Général d'Algérie, organisation administrative
9 H, Gouvernement Général d'Algérie, surveillance politique des indigènes
9 PA, Fonds Albert Sarraut
28 PA, Fonds Marius Moutet

Institut CGT de l'Histoire Social, Montreuil (CGT-IHS)

Local union congresses, press, and pamphlets

L'Institut Français d'Histoire Sociale, Paris (IFHS)

14 AS, Picart papers
C, union congresses

Ministère des Affaires Étrangères, Quai D'Orsay, Paris (MAE)

C.P.C.—Série C. Administrative, 1890–1940
Série K—Afrique, 1918–1940, Sous Série Questions Générales
La Série E—Asie, 1918–1929, Sous-Série Chine
Série Z—Europe, 1918–1940
  Italie
  Pologne

Office Universitaire de Recherches Socialistes, Paris (OURS)

Marcel Livian papers, 24 APO

Newspapers

L'araldo: Organo del Partito Comunista Francese (SFIC) in lingua italiana
L'aube
Bulletin du Ministère du Travail
Bulletin officiel de l'Union des Syndicats ouvriers du Département de la Seine (Unitaire).
  From 1925: *Bulletin officiel de l'Union des Syndicats Ouvriers de la Région Parisienne.*
  From 1927: *Bulletin officiel de la XXème Union régionale des Syndicats ouvriers.*
El Ouma: Organe national de défense des intérêts des Musulmans algériens, marocains et tunisiens
Le figaro
Fraternité: Organe de liaison entre les travailleurs français et immigrés
L'humanité
Le paria
Le petit journal
Le petit parisien
Le peuple
Le populaire de Paris
La riscossa
La semaine religieuse de Paris
Le temps
Le travailleur parisien: Bulletin de l'union des syndicats confédérés du département de la Seine
La vie catholique en France et à l'étranger
La vie syndicale
La voce degli italiani
La voix du Peuple de Paris: Bulletin officiel de l'Union des Syndicats Unitaires de la Région Parisienne

Other Printed Materials

About, Ilsen. "Les fondations d'un système national d'identification policière en France, 1893–1914." *Genèses: Sciences sociales et histoire*, no. 54 (March 2004): 28–52.
Adler, Jacques. *Face à la persécution: Les organisations juives à Paris de 1940 à 1944.* Paris: Calmann-Lévy, 1985.

Ageron, Charles-Robert. *Les algériens musulmans et la France, 1871–1919.* 2 vols. Paris: Puf, 1968.

——. "Du Mythe kabyle aux politiques berbères." *Mals de voir, Cahiers Jussieu* 2 (1976): 331–48.

——. "La France a-t-elle eu une politique Kabyle? *Revue historique* 223–24 (April–June 1960): 311–52.

——. *France coloniale ou parti colonial?* Paris: Puf, 1978.

——. *Histoire de l'Algérie contemporaine.* Vol. 2, *De l'insurrection de 1871 au déclenchement de la guerre de libération, 1954.* Paris: Puf, 1979.

Aïssa, Abdelmounim. "La Santé publique au Maroc à l'époque coloniale, 1907–1956." Thèse d'histoire, Université de Paris I, 1997.

Albou, André. *Étude sur la tuberculose des travailleurs indigènes algériens dans les grandes villes, France et Algérie: De son expansion des centres vers les campagnes.* Algiers: Imprimerie moderne, 1930.

Allard, Paul. "L'Afrique à Paris." *Le quotidien,* 25 October 1928.

——. *L'anarchie de la police.* Paris: Calmann-Lévy, 1934.

——. *Ce que le Front Populaire a donné aux immigrés.* Paris: Éditions de Fraternité, 1937.

Alexopoulos, Golfo. *Stalin's Outcasts: Aliens, Citizens, and the Soviet State, 1926–1936.* Ithaca: Cornell University Press, 2003.

Aly, Götz, and Karl Heinz Roth. *Die restlose Erfassung: Volkszählen, Identifizieren, Aussondern im Nationalsozialismus.* Rev. ed. 1984; Frankfurt am Mein: Fischer Taschenbuch, 2000.

Ameline, Léon. *Ce qu'il faut connaître de la police et ses mystères.* Paris: Boivin, 1926.

Ariès, Philippe. "La population parisienne." In his *Histoire des populations françaises et de leurs attitudes devant la vie depuis le XVIIIe siècle,* 119–98. 1948; Paris: Seuil, 1971.

Bade, Klaus. " 'Preußengänger' und 'Abwehrpolitik': Ausländerbeschäftigung, Ausländerpolitic und Ausländerkontrolle auf dem Arbeitsmarkt in Preußen vor dem Ersten Weltkrieg." *Archiv für Sozialgeschichte* 24 (1984): 91–162.

Baker, Donald N. "The Surveillance of Subversion in Interwar France: The Carnet B in the Seine, 1922–1940." *French Historical Studies* 10 (1978): 486–516.

Balensi, Jean. "Une administration que doit être pour ses administrés 'leur père et leur mère': Le 'Biro-Arrab.' " *Police parisienne,* no. 6 (May 1936): 5–13.

——. " 'Divisions Étrangères': Cinquante hommes qui en contrôlent cinq cent mille." *Police parisienne,* no. 12 (December 1937): 15–18.

Barrès, Maurice. *Contre les étrangers: Étude pour la protection des ouvriers français.* Paris: Grande Imprimerie Parisienne, 1893.

Barthelemy, Xavier. *Des infractions aux arrêtés d'expulsion et d'interdiction de séjour.* Paris: Éditions Domat-Montchrestien, 1936.

Baruch, Marc-Olivier. *Servir l'État français: L'administration en France de 1940 à 1944.* Paris: Fayard, 1997.

Bastié, Jean. *La croissance de la banlieue parisienne.* Paris: Puf, 1964.

Becker, Jean-Jacques. *Le carnet B.* Paris: Klincksieck, 1973.

Becker, Peter. *Verderbnis und Entartung: Eine Geschichte der Kriminologie des 19. Jahrhunderts als Diskurs und Praxis.* Göttingen: Vandenhoeck and Ruprecht, 2002.

——. "Vom 'Haltlosen' zur 'Bestie': Das polizeiliche Bild des 'Verbrechers' im 19. Jahrhundert." In Alf Lüdke, ed., *'Sicherheit' und 'Wohlfahrt',* 97–131.

Ben Fredj, Chokry. "Aux origines de l'émigration nord-africaine en France." Thèse d'histoire, nouveau régime. Université de Paris VII, 1990.

Ben Salem, Dr. *La tuberculose chez les ouvriers musulmans nord-africains en France (étude médico-sociale)*. Paris: M. Vigné, 1942.

Benoist, André. *Les mystères de la Police: Révélations par son ancien Directeur*. Paris: Nouvelles éditions latines, 1934.

Bercovici, J. *Contrôle sanitaire des immigrants en France*. Paris: Sagot, 1926.

Berlière, Jean-Marc. "L'épuration de la police parisienne en 1944–1945." *Vingtième siècle* 49 (January–March 1996): 63–81.

———. "La généalogie d'une double tradition policière." In *La France de l'affaire Dreyfus*, edited by Pierre Birnbaum, 191–225. Paris: Gallimard, 1994.

———. "L'institution policière en France sous la IIIème République, 1875–1914." Thèse d'État, Université de Bourgogne, 1991.

———. *Le monde des polices en France, XIXe–XXe siècles*. Brussels: Complexe, 1996.

———. "La naissance des Renseignements généraux." *Histoire* 585 (September 1995): 60–65.

———. "A Republican Political Police? Political Policing in France under the Third Republic." In Mark Mazower, ed., *Policing of Politics in the Twentieth Century*, 27–55.

Berlière, Jean-Marc, with Laurant Chabrun. *Les policiers français sous l'Occupation: D'après les archives inédites de l'épuration*. Paris: Perrin, 2001.

Berlière, Jean-Marc, and Franck Liaigre. *Le sang des communistes: Les bataillons de la jeunesse dans la lutte armée*. Paris: Fayard, 2004.

Berlière, Jean-Marc, and Denis Peschanski. "Police et policiers parisiens face à la lutte armée, 1941–1944." In *Pouvoirs et polices au XXe siècle: Europe, États-Unis, Japon*, ed. Berlière and Peschanski, 137–76. Brussels: Complexe, 1997.

Bernard, Augustin. *L'Afrique du nord pendant la guerre*. Paris: Puf, 1926.

Bernard, Léon. "Le problème sanitaire de l'immigration." *Revue d'Hygiène* 97 (September 1925).

———. "Rapport de la commission sur les malades étrangers dans les hôpitaux." *Bulletin de l'Académie de médecine* 45 (19 January 1926).

Berque, Jacques. *Le Maghreb entre les deux guerres*. Paris: Seuil, 1962.

Berstein, Serge. *Histoire du Parti Radical*. 2 vols. Paris: Presses de la Fondation nationale des sciences politiques, 1980–82.

———. *Le 6 février 1934*. Paris: Armand Colin, 1975.

Birnbaum, Pierre. "Paris leur appartient: La mobilisation électorale nationaliste en 1902." In *"La France aux français": Histoire des haines nationalistes*, edited by Birnbaum, 221–36. Paris: Seuil, 1993.

Blanc, Edouard. *La ceinture rouge: Enquête sur la situation politique, morale et sociale de la banlieue de Paris*. Paris: Spes, 1927.

Blanc-Chaléard, Marie-Claude. *Les italiens dans l'est parisien des années 1880 aux années 1960: Une histoire d'intégration*. Rome: École française de Rome, 2000.

Blanc-Chaléard, Marie-Claude, et al., eds. *Police et migrants: France, 1667–1939*. Rennes: Presses Universitaires de Rennes, 2001.

Bonnet, Jean-Charles. *Les pouvoirs publics français et l'immigration dans l'entre-deux-guerres*. Lyon: Centre d'histoire économique et sociale de la région lyonnaise, n.d. [1976].

Boukhelloua, Ahmad. *L'hôpital franco-musulman de Paris*. Algiers: S. Crescenzo, 1934.

Branche, Raphaëlle. *La torture et l'armée pendant la guerre d'Algérie, 1954–1962*. Paris: Gallimard, 2001.

Brasillach, Robert. *Notre avant-guerre*. Paris: Plon, 1941.

Brubaker, Rogers. *Citizenship and Nationhood in France and Germany*. Cambridge: Harvard University Press, 1992.

Brunet, Jean-Paul. "Une banlieue ouvrière: Saint-Denis, 1898–1939: Problèmes d'implantation du socialisme et du communisme." Thèse d'État. 3 vols. Lille: Service de reproduction des thèses, 1982.

———, ed. *Immigration, vie politique et populisme en banlieue parisienne, fin XIXe–XXe siècles.* Paris: Harmattan, 1995.

———. *Jacques Doriot: Du communisme au fascisme.* Paris: Balland, 1986.

———. *Police contre FLN: Le drame d'octobre 1961.* Paris: Flammarion, 1999.

———. *La police de l'ombre: Indicateurs et provocateurs dans la France contemporaine.* Paris: Seuil, 1990.

Buchet, Georges. "Gennevilliers: La cité arabe." *En Terre d'Islam* 4, no. 33 (December 1929).

Bunle, Henri. "L'agglomération parisienne et ses migrations alternantes en 1936." *Bulletin de la Statistique Générale de la France* 28 (October–December 1938).

———. "Le grand Paris de 1911 à 1931." *Bulletin de la Statistique Générale de la France* 24 (January–March 1935).

———. "Migrations alternantes dans la région parisienne: Déplacements journaliers de professionnels." *Bulletin de la Statistique Générale de la France* 21 (July–August 1932).

Burrin, Philippe. *France under the Germans: Collaboration and Compromise.* Translated by Janet Lloyd. New Press, 1996.

Camiscioli, Elisa. "Producing Citizens, Reproducing the 'French Race': Immigration, Demography, and Pronatalism in Early Twentieth-Century France." *Gender & History* 13, no. 3 (November 2001): 593–621.

Canali, Mauro. *Il delitto Matteotti: Affarismo e politica nel primo governo Mussolini.* Bologna: Il Mulino, 1997.

Caron, Vicki. "The Antisemitic Revival in France in the 1930s: The Socioeconomic Dimension Reconsidered." *Journal of Modern History* 70, no. 1 (March 1998): 24–73.

———. "Prelude to Vichy: France and the Jewish Refugees in the Era of Appeasement." *Journal of Contemporary History* 20, no. 1 (January 1985): 157–76.

———. *Uneasy Asylum: France and the Jewish Refugee Crisis, 1933–1942.* Stanford: Stanford University Press, 1999.

Castellani, Loris Orazio. "L'émigration communiste italienne en France, 1921–1928: Organisation et politique." Thèse de doctorat, nouveau régime. Institut d'Études Politiques, 1986.

Castels, Stephen. *Here for Good: Western Europe's New Ethnic Minorities.* London: Pluto, 1984.

Catalogne, Edouard. *La politique de l'immigration en France depuis la guerre de 1914.* Paris: A. Tournon, 1925.

Catrice, Abbé Paul. "Les étudiants orientaux dans l'enseignement secondaire et supérieur." *La documentation catholique* 27, no. 604 (13 March 1932): 749–63.

———. "Les étudiants orientaux en France." *La documentation Catholique* 26, no. 576 (15 August 1931): 239–49.

———. "Les musulmans en France: Enquête." *En terre d'Islam* 4, no. 33 (December 1929).

———. "Les travailleurs Nord-Africains en France." *En terre d'Islam* 6, no. 48 (June 1931): 226–29.

Cavanna, François. *Les ritals.* Paris: Belfond, 1978.

Céline, Louis-Ferdinand. *Voyage au bout de la nuit.* 1932; Paris: Gallimard, 1952.

Ceretti, Giulio. *A l'ombre des deux T: 40 ans avec Palmiro Togliatti et Maurice Thorez.* Paris: Julliard, 1973.

CGTU. *Contre la xénophobie: La main d'oeuvre étrangère sur le marché du travail français.* (Paris: CGTU, 1931).

——. *Main d'œuvre immigrée sur le marché du travail en France.* Paris: Maison des Syndicats, 1933.

Chapman, Herrick. *State Capitalism and Working-Class Radicalism in the French Aircraft Industry.* Berkeley: University of California Press, 1991.

Châtelain, Abel. "Les migrants temporaires en France de 1800 à 1914." Thèse d'État. Lille: Service de reproduction des thèses, 1977.

Chéronnet, Louis. *Extra-muros.* Paris: Au sans-pareil, 1929.

Chevalier, Louis. *Classes laborieuses et classes dangereuses à Paris pendant la première moitié du XIXe siècle.* Paris: Plon, 1958.

——. *La formation de la population parisienne au XIXe siècle.* Paris: Puf, 1950.

Chiappe, Jean. In Conseil Municipal de Paris, *Commémoration des vingt-cinq années de mandat de M. Émile Massard, Conseiller municipal.* Paris: Imprimerie Municipal, 1930.

Cohen, Lizabeth. *Making a New Deal: Industrial Workers in Chicago, 1919–1939.* New York: Cambridge University Press, 1990.

Cohen, William B. "The Colonial Policy of the Popular Front." *French Historical Studies* 7 (1972): 368–93.

——. *The French Encounter with Africans: White Response to Blacks, 1530–1880.* Bloomington: Indiana University Press, 1989.

Collot, Claude. *Les institutions de l'Algérie durant la période coloniale, 1830–1962.* Algiers: Éditions du Cnrs, 1987.

Combeau, Yvan. *Paris et les élections municipales sous la Troisième République: La scène capitale dans la vie politique française.* Paris: Harmattan, 1998.

Conklin, Alice L. "Colonialism and Human Rights, a Contradiction in Terms? The Case of France and West Africa, 1895–1914." *American Historical Review* 103, no. 2 (April 1998): 419–42.

——. *A Mission to Civilize: The Republican Idea of Empire in France and West Africa, 1895–1930.* Stanford: Stanford University Press, 1997.

Cooper, Frederick. "Conflict and Connection: Rethinking Colonial African History." *American Historical Review* 99, no. 5 (December 1994): 1516–45.

——. *Decolonization and African Society: The Labor Question in French and British Africa.* Cambridge: Cambridge University Press, 1996.

Corbin, Alain. *Les filles de noce: Misère sexuelle et prostitution, XIXe siècle.* Paris: Flammarion, 1982.

——. "Les paysans de Paris: Histoire des Limousins du bâtiment au XIXe siècle." *Ethnologie française* 10 (1980): 169–76.

Costa-Lascoux, Jacqueline, and Émile Temime. *Les algériens en France: Genèse et devenir d'une migration.* Paris: Publisud, 1985.

Cottereau, Alain. "The Distinctiveness of Working-Class Cultures in France, 1848–1900." In *Working-Class Formation: Nineteenth-Century Patterns in Western Europe and the United States,* edited by Ira Katznelson and Aristide R. Zolberg. Princeton: Princeton University Press, 1986.

——. "La tuberculose: Maladie urbaine ou maladie de l'usure au travail? Critique d'une épidémiologie officielle: Le cas de Paris." *Sociologie du travail* 20 (April–June 1978): 192–224.

Couder, Laurent. "Les immigrés italiens dans la région parisienne pendant les années 1920: Contribution à l'histoire du fait migratoire en France au XXe siècle." Thèse de doctorat, nouveau régime, Institut d'Études Politiques, 1987.

Couderc, Frédéric. *Les RG sous l'Occupation: Quand la police française traquait les résistants.* Paris: Olivier Orban, 1992.

Courtois, Stéphane, Denis Peschanski, and Adam Rayski. *Le sang de l'étranger: Les immigrés de la MOI dans la Résistance*. Rev. ed. Paris: Fayard, 1989.

Cross, Gary. *Immigrant Workers in Industrial France: The Making of a New Laboring Class*. Philadelphia: Temple University Press, 1983.

Dabit, Eugène. *Faubourgs de Paris*. Paris: Gallimard, 1933.

Dallier, Gaston. *La police des étrangers à Paris et dans le département de la Seine*. Paris: Arthur Rousseau, 1914.

Damase, Jean. *Sidi de la banlieue*. Paris: Fasquelle, 1937.

Delarue, Jacques. "La police." In *Le régime de Vichy et les français*, edited by Jean-Pierre Azéma and François Bédarida, 302–11. Paris: Fayard, 1992.

Delperrié de Bayac, Jacques. *Histoire de la Milice*. Paris: Fayard, 1969.

Demangeon, Albert. *Paris, la ville et sa banlieue*. Paris: Bourrelier, 1933.

Denys, Catherine. *Police et sécurité au XVIIIe siècle dans les villes de la frontière franco-belge*. Paris: Harmattan, 2002.

Depoid, Pierre. *Les naturalisations en France*, 1870–1940. Paris: Imprimerie Nationale, 1942.

Depont, Octave. *L'Algérie du centenaire: L'œuvre française de libération, de conquête morale et d'évolution sociale des indigènes; les Berbères en France; la représentation parlementaire des indigènes*. Paris: Sirey, 1928.

——. "Aperçu sur le recrutement de la main-d'œuvre indigène dans l'Afrique du Nord." *Bulletin de la Société d'Économie sociale* (September–October 1925).

——. "Les berbères en France." *Bulletin du Comité de l'Afrique française*, no. 9 bis (September 1925): 429–48.

——. *Les berbères en France: L'Hôpital franco-musulman de Paris et du département de la Seine*. Lille: Douriez-Bataille, 1937.

Depont, Octave, et al. *Les Kabyles en France: Rapport de la Commission chargée d'étudier les conditions du travail des indigènes algériens dans la métropole*. Baugency: Barillier, 1914.

Dequidt, G., and Dr. Forestier. "Les aspects sanitaires du problème de l'immigration en France." *Revue d'hygiène* 98 (1926): 999–1049.

Dermenghem, Émile. "Musulmans de Paris." *La grande revue* (December 1934): 15–21.

Deschodt, Pierre-Jean, and François Huguenin. *La république xénophobe, 1917–1939*. Paris: JC Lattès, 2001.

Dewitte, Philippe. *Les mouvements nègres en France, 1919–1939*. Paris: Harmattan, 1985.

Dornel, Laurent. "Les usages du racialisme: Le cas de la main-d'œuvre coloniale en France pendant la première guerre mondiale." *Genèses: Sciences sociales et histoire*, no. 20 (September 1995): 48–72.

Dreyfus, Michel. *Histoire de la CGT: Cent ans de syndicalisme en France*. Brussels: Complexe, 1995.

Dufourd, Pierre. *Un sillon dans la terre rouge: Monographie de la paroisse des Moulineaux, 1914–1929*. Paris: Spes, 1929.

Dumini, Amerigo. *Diciasette colpi*. Milan: Longanesi, 1958.

Duroselle, Jean-Baptiste. *Politique étrangère de la France: La décadence, 1932–1939*. Paris: Imprimerie nationale, 1979.

Einaudi, Jean-Luc. *Le bataille de Paris: 17 Octobre 1961*. Paris: Seuil, 1991.

El Ancari. "Le scandale continue." *El Ouma* 4, no. 28 (December 1934).

Even, Dr. "Protection de la santé publique et contrôle sanitaire des transmigrants." *Le mouvement sanitaire* 30 (April 1930): 208–34.

Fahrmeir, Andreas. *Citizens and Aliens: Foreigners and the Law in Britain and the German States, 1789–1870.* New York: Berghahn, 2000.

———. "Nineteenth-Century German Citizenships: A Reconsideration." *Historical Journal* 40 (1997): 721–52.

———. "Paßwesen und Staatsbildung im Deutschland des 19. Jahrhunderts." *Historische Zeitschrift* 271 (2000): 57–91.

Favre, Mireille. "Un milieu porteur de modernisation: Travailleurs et tirailleurs vietnamiens en France pendant la première guerre mondiale." Thèse pour l'obtention du diplôme d'archiviste-paléographe. 2 vols. École nationale des chartes, 1986.

Félix, Maurice. *Le régime administratif et financier du département de la Seine et de la Ville de Paris.* 2 vols. 3rd. ed. 1922; Paris: Rousseau, 1946.

Feraoun, Mouloud. *La terre et le sang.* Paris: Seuil, 1953.

Fosdick, Raymond B. *European Police Systems.* New York: Century Co., 1915.

Foucault, Michel. *Naissance de la biopolitique: Cours au Collège de France, 1978–1979.* Paris: Seuil, 2004.

———. "Omnis et Singulatim: Towards a Criticism of 'Political Reason.'" Tanner Lectures at Stanford University, 10 and 16 October 1979. In *The Tanner Lectures on Human Values*, vol. 2. Salt Lake City: University of Utah Press, 1981, 225–54.

———. *Sécurité, territoire, population: Cours au Collège de France, 1977–1978.* Paris: Seuil, 2004.

———. *Surveiller et punir: Naissance de la prison.* Paris: Gallimard, 1975.

Fourcaut, Annie. *Bobigny, banlieue rouge.* Paris: Presses de la Fondation nationale de sciences politiques, 1986.

Franke, Julia. *Paris—eine neue Heimat? Jüdische Emigranten aus Deutschland, 1933–1939.* Berlin: Duncker and Humblot, 2000.

Franzinelli, Mimmo. *I tentacoli dell'Ovra: Agenti, collaboratori e vittime della polizia politica fascista.* Turin: Bollati Boringhieri, 1999.

Fridenson, Patrick. *Histoire des usines Renault.* Vol. 1, *Naissance de la grande entreprise, 1898–1939.* Paris: Seuil, 1972.

Gaillard, Jeanne. *Paris, la ville, 1852–1870.* 1975; Paris: Harmattan, 1997.

Garosci, Aldo. *Storia dei fuorusciti.* Bari: G. Laterza, 1953.

Gellately, Robert. *The Gestapo and German Society: Enforcing Racial Policy, 1933–1945.* Oxford: Clarendon Press, 1990.

Gildea, Robert. *Marianne in Chains: In Search of the German Occupation, 1940–1945.* London: Macmillan, 2002.

Girardet, Raoul. *L'idée coloniale en France de 1871 à 1962.* Paris: La table ronde, 1972.

Glazer, Nathan, and Daniel P. Moynihan. *Beyond the Melting Pot: The Negroes, Puerto Ricans, Jews, Italians, and Irish of New York City.* 2nd. ed. 1963; Cambridge: MIT Press, 1970.

Godin, Pierre, and Dr. Auguste Marie. "Le Problème des malades musulmans à Paris." *L'hygiène mentale* (February 1934): 33–45.

Gomar, Norbert. *L'emigration nord-africaine en France.* Paris: Presses modernes, 1931.

Gosewinkel, Dieter. *Einbürgern und Ausschließen: Die Nationalisierung der Staatsangehörigkeit vom Deutschen Bund bis zur Budesrepublik Deutschland.* Göttingen: Vandenhoeck and Ruprecht, 2001.

Gousseff, Catherine. "Immigrés russes en France, 1900–1950: Contribution à l'histoire sociale et politique des réfugiés." Thèse, nouveau régime, École des Hautes Études en Sciences Sociales, 1996.

Gravier, Jean-François. *Paris et le désert français.* Paris: Le Portulan, 1947.

Green, Nancy L. *The Pletzl of Paris: Jewish Immigrant Workers in the Belle Epoque.* New York: Holmes and Meier, 1986.

———. *Ready-to-Wear and Ready-to-Work: A Century of Industry and Immigrants in Paris and New York.* Durham, N.C.: Duke University Press, 1997.

Green, Nancy L., et al. "Paris: City of Light and Shadow." In *Distant Magnets: Expectations and Realities in the Immigrant Experience, 1840–1930,* edited by Dirk Hoerder and Horst Rössler, 34–51. New York: Holmes and Meier, 1993.

Grenze und Staat: Paßwesen, Staatsbürgerschaft, Heimatrecht und Fremdengesetzgebung in der österreichischen Monarchie, 1750–1867. Edited by Waltraud Heindl and Edith Saurer. Vienna: Bölau, 2000.

Guillauté, Jacques-François. *Mémoire sur la réformation de la police de France . . . , illustré de vingt-huit dessins de Gabriel de Saint-Aubin.* 1749; Paris: Hermann, 1974.

Gutman, Herbert G. *Work, Culture, and Society in Industrializing America.* New York: Knopf, 1976.

Halévy, Daniel. *Pays parisiens.* Paris: Grasset, 1932.

Handlin, Oscar. *Boston's Immigrants, 1790–1865: A Study in Acculturation.* Cambridge: Harvard University Press, 1941.

Heilmann, Éric. "Des herbiers aux fichiers informatiques: L'évolution du traitement de l'information dans la police." Thèse de doctorat, Sciences de l'information et de la communication, Université de Strasbourg 2, 1991.

Herbert, Ulrich. *A History of Foreign Labor in Germany: Seasonal Workers/Forced Laborers/Guest Workers.* Translated by William Templer. 1986; Ann Arbor: University of Michigan Press, 1990.

Heuer, Jennifer. "Foreigners, Families, and Citizens: Contradictions of National Citizenship in France, 1789–1830." PhD diss., University of Chicago, 1998.

Higham, John. *Strangers in the Land: Patterns of American Nativism.* 2nd. ed. 1955; New Brunswick, N.J.: Rutgers University Press, 1988.

Holquist, Peter. " 'Information Is the Alpha and Omega of Our Work': Bolshevik Surveillance in Its Pan-European Context." *Journal of Modern History* 69, no. 3 (September 1997): 415–50.

Horne, John. "Immigrants in France during World War I." *French Historical Studies* 14, no. 1 (Spring 1985): 57–88.

Horowitz, Donald L., and Gérard Noiriel, eds. *Immigrants in Two Democracies: French and American Experience.* New York: New York University Press, 1992.

Ichok, Dr. Grégoire. "Les maladies professionnelles des immigrés et les traités internationaux de travail et d'assistance." *Revue d'hygiène* 98 (1926): 1105–10.

———. *La mortalité à Paris et dans le département de la Seine.* Paris: Marcel Rivière, 1937.

———. "La question de l'immigration." *Le progrès médical* (21 August 1926): 1284–88.

Ikor, Roger. *Les eaux mêlées.* 1955; Paris: Uge, 1963.

Jacquemet, Gérard. *Belleville au XIXe siècle: Du Faubourg à la ville.* Paris: Éditions de l'École des Hautes Études en Sciences Sociales, 1984.

Jankowski, Paul F. *Stavisky: A Confidence Man in the Republic of Virtue.* Ithaca: Cornell University Press, 2002.

Jeanselme, E., and Burnier. "La syphilis est-elle en décroissance dans la population ouvrière?" *Bulletin de l'Académie de médecine* 45 (9 March 1926): 214–36.

Jennings, Eric. "Last Exit from Vichy France: The Martinique Escapee Route and the Ambiguities of Emigration." *Journal of Modern History* 74, no. 2 (June 2002): 289–324.

Jérôme, Jean. *La part des hommes: Souvenirs d'un témoin.* Paris: Acropole, 1983.

Jessen, Ralph. "Polizei, Wohlfahrt und die Anfänge des modernen Sozialstaats in

Preußen während des Kaisserreichs." *Geschichte und Gesellschaft* 20, no. 2 (1994): 157–80.

Justinard, Lt.-Col. "Les Chleuhs dans la banlieue de Paris." *Revue des études islamiques* (1928).

Kahn, Annette. *Le fichier.* Paris: Robert Laffont, 1993.

Kaplan, Steven L. *La fin des corporations.* Translated by Béatrice Vierne. Paris: Fayard, 2001.

——. "Réflexions sur la police du monde du travail, 1700–1815." *Revue historique* 529 (January–March 1979): 17–77.

Kaspi, André, and Antoine Marès. *Le Paris des étrangers, 1919–1939.* Paris: Imprimerie nationale, 1992.

Kepel, Gilles. *Les banlieues de l'Islam: Naissance d'une religion en France.* Paris: Seuil, 1991.

Klarsfeld, Serge. *Vichy-Auschwitz: Le rôle de Vichy dans la solution finale de la question juive en France.* 2 vols. Paris: Fayard, 1983–85.

Kletch, Georges, *L'organisation syndicale des travailleurs étrangers en France.* Paris: Société d'études et d'informations économiques, 1937.

Kraut, Alan M. *Silent Travelers: Germs, Genes, and the "Immigrant Menace."* New York: Basic Books, 1994.

Kriegel, Annie. *Aux origines du communisme français, 1914–1920: Contribution à l'histoire du mouvement ouvrier français.* 2 vols. Paris: Mouton, 1964.

La Ligue des Droits de l'Homme. *Les étrangers en France.* Paris: Ligue des Droits de l'Homme, 1927.

"La main-d'œuvre étrangère en France." *Bulletin du Ministre du travail et du prévoyance sociale* 27, nos. 1–2 (January–February 1920): 19–25.

Lambert, Charles. *La France et les étrangers: Dépopulation, immigration, naturalisation.* Preface by Edouard Herriot. Paris: Delgrave, 1928.

Langeron, Roger. *Paris, juin 1940.* Paris: Flammarion, 1946.

——. *La politique d'abord . . . Souvenirs et anticipations.* Paris: Plon, 1943.

Lebovics, Herman. *Bringing the Empire Back Home: France in the Global Age.* Durham: Duke University Press, 2004.

——. *True France: The Wars over Cultural Identity, 1900–1945.* Ithaca: Cornell University Press, 1992.

Le Bras, Hervé. *Le démon des origines: Démographie et extrême droite.* La Tour d'Aigues: L'Aube, 1998.

Lefeuvre, Daniel. *Chère Algérie: Comptes et mécomptes de la tutelle coloniale, 1930–1962.* Saint-Denis: Société française d'histoire d'outre-mer, 1997.

Le "Fichier Juif": Rapport de la commission présidée par René Rémond au Premier ministre. Paris: Plon, 1996.

Lentacker, Firmin. *La frontière franco-belge: Étude géographique des effets d'une frontière internationale sur la vie des relations.* Lille: Université de Lille, 1974).

Lévy, Claude, and Paul Tillard. *La grande rafle du Vel d'Hiv, 16 juillet 1942.* Paris: Robert Laffont, 1967.

Lévy, Jean. *De la République à l'État français: Le chemin de Vichy, 1930–1940.* Paris: Harmattan, 1996.

Lewis, Mary Dewhurst. "The Company of Strangers: Immigration and Citizenship in Interwar Lyon and Marseille." PhD diss., New York University, 2000.

——. "The Strangeness of Foreigners: Policing Migration and Nation in Interwar Marseille." *French Politics, Culture, and Society* 20, no. 3 (Fall 2002): 65–96.

Lhande, Pierre. *Le Christ dans la banlieue.* 3 vols. Paris: Plon, 1927–31.

Livian, Marcel. *Le Parti Socialiste et l'immigration: Le gouvernement Léon Blum, la main-d'œuvre immigrée et les réfugiés politiques, 1920–1940*. Paris: Anthropos, 1982.

——. *Le régime juridique des étrangers en France: Recueil des lois, décrets et arrêtés en vigueur. Commentaires et renseignements pratiques, avec une introduction sur l'histoire des étrangers en France et une étude sur les différents aspects de la question des étrangers*. Paris: Librairie générale de droit et de jurisprudence, 1936.

Locard, Edmond. *La police, ce qu'elle est, ce qu'elle devrait être*. Paris: Grasset, 1919.

Lorcin, Patricia M. E. *Imperial Identities: Stereotyping, Prejudice and Race in Colonial Algeria*. London: I. B. Tauris, 1995.

Lucassen, Leo. "A Many-Headed Monster: The Evolution of Passport Systems in the Netherlands and Germany in the Long Nineteenth Century." In Torpey and Caplan, eds., *Documenting Individual Identity*, 54–55.

——. *Zigeuner: Die Geschichte eines polizeilichen Ordnungsbegriffes in Deutschland, 1700–1945*. Vienna: Böhlau, 1996.

Lüdke, Alf. *Police and State in Prussia*. Translated by Pete Burgess. 1982; Cambridge: Cambridge University Press, 1989.

——, ed. *'Sicherheit' und 'Wohlfahrt': Polizei, Gesellschaft und Herrschaft im 19. und 20. Jahrhundert*. Frankfurt am Main: Suhrkamp, 1992.

Lugand, Joseph. *L'immigration des ouvriers étrangers et les enseignements de la guerre*. Paris: Librairies-imprimeries réunies, 1919.

MacMaster, Neil. *Colonial Migrants and Racism: Algerians in France, 1900–1962*. New York: St. Martin's, 1997.

——. "The Rue Fondary Murders of 1923 and the Origins of Anti-Arab Racism." In *Violence and Conflict in the Politics and Society of Modern France*, edited by Jan Windebank and Renate Gunther, 149–60. Lewiston, N.Y.: Edwin Mellen Press, 1995.

Marcovich, Anne. "French Colonial Medicine and Colonial Rule: Algeria and Indochina." In *Disease, Medicine and Empire*, edited by Roy MacLeod and Milton Lewis, 103–17. London: Routledge, 1988.

Marneur, François. *L'indigénat en Algérie*. Paris: Sirey, 1914.

Marrus, Michael R. "The Strange Story of Herschel Grynszpan." *American Scholar* 57 (1987–88): 69–79.

——. *The Unwanted: European Refugees in the Twentieth Century*. New York: Oxford University Press, 1985.

——. "Vichy avant Vichy." *Histoire* 3 (November 1979): 77–92.

——. "Vichy before Vichy: Antisemitic Currents in France during the 1930s." *Wiener Library Bulletin*, n.s., 33, nos. 51–52 (1980): 13–19.

Marrus, Michael R., and Robert O. Paxton. *Vichy France and the Jews*. New York: Basic Books, 1981.

Martial, Dr. René. *Traité de l'immigration et de la greffe inter-raciale*. Paris: Larose, 1930.

Martial, Dr. René, and Dr. Laquieze. "Police sanitaire et immigration." *L'hygiène sociale* (10 December 1931): 1308–15.

Massard, Émile. *Les espionnes à Paris: La vérité sur Mata-Hari, Marguerite Francillard, La femme du cimetière, les marraines, une grande vedette parisienne, la mort de Marussia*. Paris: Albin Michel, 1922.

Massard-Guilbaud, Geneviève. *Des Algériens à Lyon: De la Grande Guerre au Front Populaire*. Paris: Harmattan, 1995.

Massignon, Louis. "Cartes de répartition des Kabyles dans la région parisienne." *Revue des Études islamiques* 2 (1930): 159–70.

Mauco, Georges. *L'assimilation des étrangers en France*. Paris: Institut international de coopération intellectuelle, 1937.

———. *Les étrangers en France: Leur rôle dans l'activité économique*. Paris: Armand Colin, 1932.

———. "L'immigration en France." *Cahiers du Musée Social*, nos. 2–3 (1947): 60–67.

———. "L'immigration étrangère en France. *Revue internationale du travail* (June 1933): 798–822.

———. "Le problème des étrangers en France." *Revue de Paris*, no. 18 (1935): 375–407.

Maunoury, Henry. *Police de guerre, 1914–1919*. Paris: Éditions de la nouvelle revue critique, 1937.

Mayer, Nonna, and Pascal Perrineau, eds. *Le front national à découvert*. Rev. ed. Paris: Presses de la Fondation nationale de science politique, 1996.

Mazower, Mark, ed., *The Policing of Politics in the Twentieth Century*. Providence, R.I.: Berghahn Books, 1997.

———. "Violence and the State in the Twentieth Century." *American Historical Review* 107, no. 4 (October 2002): 1158–78.

Merriman, John. *Police Stories: Building the French State*. Oxford: Oxford University Press, 2006.

Meynier, Gilbert. *L'Algérie révélée: La guerre de 1914–1918 et le premier quart du XXe siècle*. Geneva: Droz, 1981.

Millet, Raymond. *Trois millions d'étrangers en France, les indésirables, les bienvenus*. Paris: Médicis, 1938.

Milliot, Louis. "L'Exode des travailleurs algériens en France." *Afrique Française: Renseignements Coloniaux* (February 1925).

———. "Les Kabyles à Paris." *Revue des études islamiques* 6 (1932): 162–75.

Milza, Pierre. "Le fascisme italien à Paris." *Revue d'histoire moderne et contemporaine* 30 (July–September 1983): 420–52.

———, ed. *Les Italiens en France de 1914 à 1940*. Rome: École française de Rome, 1986.

———. *Voyage en Ritalie*. Paris: Plon, 1993.

Monnais-Rousselot, Laurance. *Médecine et colonisation: L'aventure indochinoise, 1860–1939*. Paris: Éditions du Cnrs, 1999.

Moore, Bob. *Victims and Survivors: The Nazi Persecution of the Jews in the Netherlands, 1940–1945*. London: Arnold, 1997.

Murard, Lion, and Patrick Zylberman. *L'hygiène dans la République: La santé publique en France, ou l'utopie contrariée, 1870–1918*. Paris: Fayard, 1996.

Murray, Robert K. *Red Scare: A Study in National Hysteria, 1919–1920*. Minneapolis: University of Minnesota Press, 1955.

Naudeau, Ludovic. *La France se regarde: La problème de la natalité*. Paris: Hachette, 1931.

Neuville, François. *Le statut juridique du travailleur étranger en France au regard des assurances sociales, de l'assistance et de prévoyance sociale*. Paris: Chauny et Quinsac, 1931.

Nobécourt, Jacques. *Le colonel de la Rocque, 1885–1946, ou les pièges du nationalisme chrétien*. Paris: Fayard, 1996.

Noël, Léon. "L'hospitalisation des étrangers en France." *Revue philanthropique* 97, no. 344 (15 April 1926): 225–40.

Nogaro, Bertrand. "L'introduction de la main-d'œuvre étrangère pendant la guerre." *Revue d'économie politique* 44 (December 1920): 718–33.

Nogaro, Bertrand, and Lucien Weil. *La main-d'œuvre étrangère et coloniale pendant la guerre*. Paris: Puf, 1926.

Noiriel, Gérard. *Le creuset français: Histoire de l'immigration, XIXe–XXe siècles*. Paris: Seuil, 1988.

——. *État, nation et immigration: Vers une histoire du pouvoir*. Paris: Belin, 2001.

——. *Longwy, immigrés et prolétaires*. Paris: Puf, 1984.

——. *Les origines républicaines de Vichy*. Paris: Hachette, 1999.

——. *La tyrannie du national: Le droit d'asile en Europe, 1793–1993*. Paris: Calmann-Lévy, 1991.

Nord, Philip G. *Paris Shopkeepers and the Politics of Resentment*. Princeton: Princeton University Press, 1986.

Nordman, Daniel. *Frontières de France: De l'espace au territoire, XVIe–XIXe siècles*. Paris: Gallimard, 1998.

——. "Sauf-conduits et passeports, en France, à la Renaissance." In *Voyager à la Renaissance*, edited by Jean Céard and Jean-Claude Margolin, 145–58. Paris: Maisonneuve et Larose, 1987.

Oualid, William. *L'aspect juridique de l'immigration ouvrière*. Paris: Alcan et Rivière, 1923.

——. "Les conditions actuelles de l'immigration en France et ses conséquences." *Le musée social* 3 (1930): 111–13.

——. "La France deviendra-t-elle un pays de minorités nationales?" *Le musée social* 5–6 (1927): 160–84.

——. "L'immigration ouvrière est-elle organisée en France?" *Le musée social* 5–6 (July 1927): 125–60.

——. "La protection de la main-d'œuvre nationale." *Revue de l'immigration* 47 (January–March 1933): 1–8.

Ourgault, Charles. *La surveillance des étrangers en France*. Toulouse: n.p., 1937.

Pairault, André. "Immigration et race." *Revue de l'immigration* 25 (1930): 1–4.

——. *L'immigration organisée et l'emploi de la main d'œuvre étrangère en France*. Paris: Puf, 1926.

Paon, Marcel. *L'immigration en France*. Paris: Payot, 1926.

Papon, Maurice. *Les chevaux du pouvoir: Le préfet de police du général de Gaulle ouvre ses dossiers, 1958–1967*. Paris: Plon, 1988.

Pascalis. "L'interdiction de séjour et le sursis." *Revue pénitentiaire* (1924).

Paxton, Robert O. *The Anatomy of Fascism*. New York: Knopf, 2004.

——. "Gérard Noiriel's Third Republic." *French Politics, Culture, and Society* 18, no. 2 (Summer 2000): 99–103.

——. "La spécificité de la persécution des juifs en France." *Annales, ESC* 3 (May–June 1993): 605–19.

——. "The Trial of Maurice Papon." *New York Review of Books*, 16 December 1999. 32–37.

——. *Vichy France: Old Guard and New Order, 1940–1944*. 1972; New York: Columbia University Press, 1982.

Paz, Magdeleine. "La situation des Nord-Africains en France et l'officine de la rue Lecomte jugées par une française." *El Ouma*, 22 April 1938.

PCF. *L'importance de la M.O.E. et les diverses immigrations*. Paris: Imprimerie Centrale, 1930.

——. *Rapport d'organisation pour la conférence de la région parisienne des 26, 27 et 28 février 1932*. Paris: PCF, 1932.

PCF, Région Parisienne. *Un an après Lille: Rapport moral et politique, 1926–1927*. Paris: La Cootypographie, n.d.

Pedersen, Susan. *Family, Dependence, and the Origins of the Welfare State: Britain and France, 1914–1945*. Cambridge: Cambridge University Press, 1993.

Perrot, Michèle. "Les rapports entre ouvriers français et étrangers, 1871–1893." *Bulletin de la Société d'histoire moderne*, 12th series, no. 1 (1960): 4–9.

Peschanski, Denis. "Dans la tourmente." In *La police française, 1930–1950: Entre bouleversements et permanences*, edited by Jean-Marc Berlière and Peschanski. Paris: La documentation française, 2000.

——. *La France des camps: L'internement, 1938–1946*. Paris: Gallimard, 2002.

——. *Vichy, 1940–1944, contrôle et exclusion*. Brussels: Complexe, 1997.

Peukert, Detlev J. K. "The Genesis of the 'Final Solution' from the Spirit of Science." In *Nazism and German Society, 1933–1945*, edited by David F. Crew, 274–99. 1989; New York: Routledge, 1994.

Piazza, Pierre. *Histoire de la carte nationale d'identité*. Paris: Odile Jacob, 2004.

Picard, Lucien. "Les étrangers à Paris." *Police parisienne*, no. 5 (29 February 1936): 19–27.

Poëte, Marcel, Henri Sellier, and A. Bruggeman. *Paris pendant la guerre*. Paris: Puf, 1926.

Ponty, Janine. *Polonais méconnus: Histoire des travailleurs immigrés en France dans l'entre-deux-guerres*. Paris: Publications de la Sorbonne, 1990.

Porter, Bernard. *The Origins of the Vigilant State: The London Metropolitan Police Special Branch before the First World War*. London: Weidenfeld and Nicolson, 1987.

Poznanski, Renée. "Avant les grand rafles: Les Juifs à Paris sous l'Occupation, juin 1940–avril 1941." *Cahiers de l'Institut d'histoire du temps présent* 22 (December 1992): 25–56.

——. *Les Juifs en France pendant la Seconde Guerre mondiale*. Rev. ed. 1994; Paris: Hachette, 1997.

Preston, William, Jr. *Aliens and Dissenters: Federal Suppression of Radicals, 1903–1933*. Cambridge: Harvard University Press, 1963.

Rabinow, Paul. *French Modern: Norms and Forms of the Social Environment*. Cambridge: MIT Press, 1989.

Rajsfus, Maurice. *La police de Vichy: Les forces de l'ordre françaises au service de la Gestapo, 1940–1944*. Paris: Cherche-Midi, 1995.

Ramette, Arthur. *A la porte les étrangers? Programme absurde, solution inhumaine*. Paris: PCF, 1934.

Ray, Joanny. *Les marocains en France*. Paris: Institut des hautes études islamiques, 1938.

——. "Le séjour des marocains en France." *L'Afrique française* (February 1937): 73–83.

Raynaud, Ernest. "La Préfecture de Police." *Mercure de France*, special issue (1 June 1918).

Raynaud, L., H. Soulié, and P. Picard. *Hygiène et pathologie nord-africaine: Assistance médicale*. 2 vols. Paris: n.p., 1932.

Remlinger, Dr. P. "Communication au sujet de l'hospitalisation des malades étrangers." *Bulletin de l'Académie de médecine* 89, no. 44 (15 December 1925).

Rémond, René. *Les droites en France*. Rev. ed. 1954; Paris: Aubier, 1982.

Riou, Noël. "Pouquoi avons-nous créé cette revue." *Police parisienne*, no. 1 (April 1935): 1–3.

Robert, Jean-Louis. "L'opposition générale à la main-d'œuvre immigrée." In *Prolétaires de tous les pays, unissez-vous? Les difficiles chemins de l'internationalisme, 1848–1956*, edited by Serge Wolikov and Michel Cordillot, 43–56. Dijon: Publications de l'Université de Bougogne, 1993.

——. "Ouvriers et mouvement ouvrier parisiens pendant la Grande Guerre et l'immédiat après-guerre: Histoire et anthropologie." Thèse d'État. Université de Paris I, 1989.

Published as *Les ouvriers, la patrie et la Révolution: Paris, 1914–1919* (Besançon: Annales littéraires de l'Université de Besançon, 1995).

Robrieux, Philippe. *Histoire intérieure du parti communiste.* Vol. 1, *1920–1945.* Paris: Fayard, 1980.

Roche, Daniel. *Humeurs vagabondes: De la circulation des hommes et de l'utilité des voyages.* Paris: Fayard, 2003.

———. *Le peuple de Paris: Essai sur la culture populaire au XVIIIe siècle.* 1981; Paris: Fayard, 1998.

———, ed. *La ville promise: Mobilité et accueil à Paris, fin XVIIe–début XIXe siècle.* Paris: Fayard, 2000.

Roscher, Gustav. *Großstadtpolizei: Eine praktisches Handbuch der deutschen Polizei.* Hamburg: O. Meissner, 1912.

Rosenberg, Clifford. "Albert Sarraut and Republican Racial Thought." *French Politics, Culture, and Society* 20, no. 3 (Fall 2002): 97–114.

Rousso, Henry. *The Vichy Syndrome: History and Memory in France since 1944.* Translated by Arthur Goldhammer. Cambridge: Harvard University Press, 1991.

Rygiel, Philippe, ed. *Le bon grain et l'ivraie: L'état-nation et les populations immigrées, fin XIXe–début XXe siècle. Sélection des migrants et régulation des stocks de populations étrangères.* Paris: Presses de L'École Normale Supérieure, 2004.

———. *Destins immigrés, Cher 1920–1980: Trajectoires d'immigrés d'Europe.* Besançon: Annales littéraires de l'université de Franche-Comté, 2001.

Saada, Emmanuelle. "La 'question métis' dans les colonies françaises: Socio-histoire d'une catégorie juridique, Indochine et autres territoires de l'Empire français; années 1890–années 1950." Thèse, sciences sociales, L'Ecole des Hautes Etudes en Sciences Sociales, 2001.

Sahlins, Peter. *Boundaries: The Making of France and Spain in the Pyrenees.* Berkeley: University of California Press, 1989.

———. *Unnaturally French: Foreign Citizens in the Old Regime and After.* Ithaca: Cornell University Press, 2004.

Sannié, Dr. Charles. "L'identification civile." *Police parisienne,* no. 3 (25 September 1935): 14–15.

Sanson, Robert. "Les travailleurs nord-africains de la région parisienne." In L'Institut national d'études démographiques, *Documents sur l'immigration,* travaux et documents 2 (1943; Paris: Puf, 1947).

Sarraut, Albert. *Grandeur et servitude coloniales.* Paris: Éditions du Sagittaire, 1931.

———. *La mise en valeur des colonies françaises.* Paris: Payot, 1923.

Sayad, Abdelmalek. "Les trois 'âges' de l'émigration algérienne." *Actes de la recherche en sciences sociales* 15 (June 1977): 59–79.

Schnapper, Dominique. *L'Europe des immigrés: Essai sur les politiques d'immigration.* Paris: François Bourin, 1992

Schneider, William H. *Quantity and Quality: The Quest for Biological Regeneration in Twentieth-Century France.* New York: Cambridge University Press, 1990.

Schor, Ralph. *L'antisémitisme en France pendant les années trente.* Brussels: Complexe, 1992.

———. *L'opinion française et les étrangers, 1919–1939.* Paris: Publications de la Sorbonne, 1985.

Scott, James C. *Seeing Like a State: How Certain Schemes to Improve the Human Condition Have Failed.* New Haven: Yale University Press, 1998.

Seine (Préfecture de la), Direction des Affaires Départementales, Service de l'Assistance

Départementale. *L'Hôpital franco-musulman de Paris et du département de la Seine.* Paris: Diéval, 1935.

Sellier, Henri. *Les banlieues urbaines et la réorganisation administrative du département de la Seine.* Paris: Marcel Rivière, 1920.

———. *La lutte contre la tuberculose dans la région parisienne, 1896–1927: Le rôle de l'Office public d'hygiène sociale.* 2 vols. Paris: Éditions de l'Ophs, 1928.

Sellier, Henri, et al. *La santé publique et la collectivité: Hygiène et service social.* Paris: A. Maratheux et L. Pactat, 1936.

Sellier, Henri, and Henri Rouselle. *L'Office public d'hygiène sociale du département de la Seine et la lutte contre la tuberculose dans l'agglomeration parisienne.* Paris: Ophs, n.d. [1920].

———. *L'Office public d'hygiène sociale du département de la Seine.* Paris: Ophs, 1922.

Shearer, David. "Elements Near and Alien: Passportization, Policing, and Identity in the Stalinist State, 1932–1952." *Journal of Modern History* 76, no. 4 (December 2004): 835–81.

Signoret, Simone. *Adieu Volodia.* Paris: Fayard, 1985.

Sirot, Stéphane. "Les conditions de travail et les grèves des ouvriers à Paris de 1919 à 1935." Thèse de doctorat, nouveau régime. Université de Paris VII, 1994.

Soysal, Yasemin Nuhoğlu. *Limits of Citizenship: Migrants and Postnational Membership in Europe.* Chicago: University of Chicago Press, 1994.

Spire, Alexis. *Étrangers à la carte: L'administration de l'immigration en France, 1945–1975.* Paris: Grasset, 2005.

Stein, Louis. *Beyond Death and Exile: The Spanish Republicans in France, 1939–1955.* Cambridge: Harvard University Press, 1979.

Sternhell, Zeev. *La droite révolutionnaire: Les origines françaises du fascisme.* Rev. ed. Paris: Seuil, 1984.

———. *Ni droite, ni gauche: L'idéologie fasciste en France.* Paris: Seuil, 1983.

Stone, Judith. *The Search for Social Peace: Reform Legislation in France, 1880–1914.* Albany: State University of New York Press, 1985.

Stora, Benjamin. "Histoire politique de l'immigration algérienne en France, 1922–1962." Thèse d'État. Université de Paris VII, 1990.

Stovall, Tyler. "Color-Blind France? Colonial Workers during the First World War." *Race & Class* 35, no. 2 (1993): 35–55.

———. "The Color Line behind the Lines: Racial Violence in France during the Great War." *American Historical Review* 103, no. 3 (June 1998): 737–69.

———. "National Identity and Shifting Imperial Frontiers: Whiteness and the Exclusion of Colonial Labor after World War I." *Representations* 84, no. 1 (November 2003): 52–72.

Stroh, Louis. *L'étranger et les assurances sociales.* Paris: Sirey, 1929.

Taguieff, Pierre-André. *Face au racism.* 2 vols. Paris: La Découverte, 1991.

Thistlethwaite, Frank. "Migrations from Europe Overseas in the Nineteenth and Twentieth Centuries." In *A Century of European Migrations, 1830–1930,* edited by Rudolph J. Vecoli and Suzanne M. Sinke, 17–49. Urbana: University of Illinois Press, 1991.

Thomas, Martin. "Albert Sarraut, French Colonial Development, and the Communist Threat, 1919–1930." *Journal of Modern History* 77, no. 4 (December 2005): 917–55.

Thu, Trang-Gaspard. *Ho Chi Minh à Paris, 1917–1923.* Paris: Harmattan, 1992.

Tombaccini, Simonetta. *Storia dei fuorusciti in Francia.* Milan: Mursia, 1988.

Torpey, John. *The Invention of the Passport: Surveillance, Citizenship, and the State.* Cambridge: Cambridge University Press, 2000.

Torpey, John, and Jane Caplan, eds. *Documenting Individual Identity: The Development of State Practices in the Modern World*. Princeton: Princeton University Press, 2001.

Trepper, Léopold. *Le grand jeu: Mémoires du chef de l'Orchestre Rouge*. Paris: Albin Michel, 1975.

Tribalat, Michèle, with Patrick Simon and Benoît Riandey. *De l'immigration à l'assimilation: Enquêtes sur les populations d'origine étrangère en France*. Paris: La Découverte/Ined, 1996.

Tripier, Maryse. *L'immigration dans la classe ouvrière en France*. Paris: Harmattan, 1990.

Valdour, Jacques [Dr. Louis Martin]. *Ateliers et taudis de la banlieue parisienne, observations vécues*. Paris: Spes, 1923.

——. *De la Popinq 'à Ménilmuch' . . . observations vécues*. Paris: Spes, 1924.

——. *"Le Faubourg." Observations vécues*. Paris: Spes, 1925.

——. *Ouvriers parisiens d'après-guerre: Observations vécues*. Paris: Arthur Rousseau; Lille: René Giard, 1921.

——. *Les puissances de désordre vers la révolution. Ouvriers de la Plaine Saint-Denis et d'Aubervilliers, Paris-Belleville*. Paris: Nouvelles éditions latines, 1935.

——. *Sous la griffe de Moscou; ouvriers de Paris (La Chapelle), de Billancourt et d'Issy*. Paris: Flammarion, 1929.

Vec, Miklos. *Die Spur des Täters: Methoden der Identifikation in der Kriminalistik, 1879–1933*. Baden-Baden: Nomos, 2002.

Vieillard, Madame R. "Chez les étrangers à Paris." *Police parisienne*, no. 12 (December 1937): 19–53.

Viet, Vincent. *La France immigrée: Construction d'une politique, 1914–1997*. Paris: Fayard, 1998.

Viollet, Jean. *Un Essai d'apostolat populaire dans la banlieue rouge*. Paris: n.p., 1932.

Watson, D. R. "The Nationalist Movement in Paris, 1900–1906." In *The Right in France, 1890–1919: Three Studies*, edited by David Shapiro, 49–84. *St. Antony's Papers* No. 13. London: Chatto and Windus, 1962.

Weber, Eugen. *The Hollow Years: France in the 1930s*. New York: W. W. Norton, 1994.

——. *Peasants into Frenchmen: The Modernization of Rural France, 1870–1914*. Stanford: Stanford University Press, 1976.

Weber, Max. *Economy and Society: An Outline of Interpretive Sociology*. 2 vols. Berkeley: University of California Press, 1978.

——. *The Protestant Ethic and the Spirit of Capitalism*, trans. Talcott Parsons. New York: Scribner, 1958.

Weil, Patrick. *La France et ses étrangers: L'aventure d'une politique de l'immigration, 1938–1991*. Paris: Calmann-Lévy, 1991.

——. "Politiques d'immigration de la France et des États-Unis à la veille de la Seconde Guerre mondiale." *Les cahiers de la Shoah*, special issue, edited by André Kaspi (1995): 55–84.

——. *Qu'est-ce qu'un français? Histoire de la nationalité française depuis la Révolution*. Paris: Grasset, 2002.

——. "Racisme et discrimination dans la politique française de l'immigration, 1938–1945/1974–1995." *Vingtième siècle* 47 (July–September 1995): 77–103.

Weinberg, David. *The Jews of Paris in the 1930s*. Chicago: University of Chicago Press, 1977.

Wietog, Jutta. *Volkszählungen unter dem Nationalsozialismus: Eine Dokumentation zur Bevölkerungsstatistik im Dritten Reich*. Berlin: Duncker and Humblot, 2001.

Wurtz, Pierre. *La question de l'immigration aux Etats-Unis*. Paris: Dreux et Schneider, 1925.

Zimmer, Lucien. *Un septennat policier: Dessous et secrets de la police républicaine.* Paris: Fayard, 1967.

Zincone, Giovanna. *Da sudditi a cittadini: Le vie dello stato e le vie della società civile.* Bologna: Il Mulino, 1992

Zinoman, Peter. *The Colonial Bastille: A History of Imprisonment in Vietnam, 1862–1940.* Berkeley: University of California Press, 2001.

Zolberg, Aristide R. "International Migration Policies in a Changing World System." In *Human Migration: Patterns and Policies,* edited by William H. McNeill and Ruth S. Adams, 241–86. Bloomington: Indiana University Press, 1978.

———. "International Migrations in Political Perspective." In *Global Trends in Migration: Theory and Research on International Population Movements,* edited by Mary M. Kritz et al., 3–27. Staten Island, N.Y.: Center for Migration Studies, 1983.

Index

Page numbers with an *f* indicate figures; those with a *t* indicate tables.